T

Daniel Pick is Professor of History at Birkbeck College, ⌐ ____ of London. He is also a practising psychoanalyst and a fellow of t⌐. tish Psychoanalytical Society. His books on European cultural history ⌐—ide *Faces of Degeneration* (1989), *Svengali's Web* (2000) and, most recently, *Rome or Death: The Obsessions of General Garibaldi* (2005). He is an editor of *History Workshop Journal* and is currently completing *Psychoanalysis: A Very Short Introduction* for Oxford University Press.

By the same author:

Faces of Degeneration: A European Disorder, c. 1848–c. 1918

War Machine: The Rationalisation of Slaughter in the Modern Age

Svengali's Web: The Alien Enchanter in Modern Culture

Rome or Death: The Obsessions of General Garibaldi

As co-editor, with Lyndal Roper, *Dreams and History: The Interpretation of Dreams from Ancient Greece to Modern Psychoanalysis*

As editor, *Trilby* by George Du Maurier, Penguin Classics, with an introduction and notes

THE PURSUIT
OF THE NAZI
MIND

HITLER, HESS, AND THE ANALYSTS

DANIEL PICK

OXFORD
UNIVERSITY PRESS

OXFORD

UNIVERSITY PRESS

Great Clarendon Street, Oxford, OX2 6DP,
United Kingdom

Oxford University Press is a department of the University of Oxford.
It furthers the University's objective of excellence in research, scholarship,
and education by publishing worldwide. Oxford is a registered trade mark of
Oxford University Press in the UK and in certain other countries

© Daniel Pick 2012

The moral rights of the author have been asserted

First Edition published in 2012
First published in paperback 2014

Impression: 1

Published in the United States of America by Oxford University Press
198 Madison Avenue, New York, NY 10016, United States of America

British Library Cataloguing in Publication Data
Data available

Library of Congress Control Number: 2012931194

ISBN 978–0–19–954168–3 (Hbk.)
ISBN 978–0–19–967851-8 (Pbk.)

Printed in Great Britain by Clays Ltd, St Ives plc

'so plainly mad...'
(Rebecca West, *A Train of Powder*)

Praise for this book

The Pursuit of the Nazi Mind …'the most important study of the reception of psychoanalysis as part of the American war effort during WWII and after, a tale rarely told in such depth and insight. This solid and useful reminder that truth lies in the details, makes exploring the history of psychoanalysis both exciting and a real part of general intellectual, medical and cultural history …'

Sander L. Gilman, *International Journal of Psychoanalysis*

'A superb new book…Pick, a distinguished historian of admirable breadth as well as a psychoanalyst, is the ideal author of such a study. His treatment of psychoanalysis is both historically framed and theoretically nuanced.'

Paul Lerner, *Times Literary Supplement*

'This is a terrific book…soberly and clearly written…profoundly illuminating.'

Eli Zaretsky, *Jewish Quarterly*

'This is a fascinating field of enquiry, the gate of which this book has opened or in some cases, reopened …'

Contemporary Review

'This is a meticulous work of history and an impressive achievement.'

New Statesman

'fascinating…meticulously researched'

Jewish Ideas Daily

'Unlike many spurious and sensationalist efforts on this subject, *The Pursuit the Nazi Mind* successfully shows how analysts at the time set out to make sense of the Nazi leadership's motives and actions, and crucially reveals how complex and puzzling their findings were to interpret.'

Times Higher Education Supplement

'Remarkable, richly informative, and profound. This thought-provoking work marks a major contribution to understanding this very complex period. Highly recommended.'

CHOICE

Contents

List of Plates	xi
1. Introduction	1
2. Characters and Causes	24
3. 'The Deputy Madman'	44
4. Getting Through to Hess	65
5. Madness and Politics	86
6. The OSS	108
7. Hitler's Mind	128
8. So Plainly Mad?	153
9. Nuremberg: Conspiracy and Confession	166
10. Sane Futures?	182
11. Legacies	216
12. Afterword	259
Appendices	271
Notes	286
Further Reading	338
Acknowledgements	345
Index	347

List of Plates

1. Into exile ... 1938. Sigmund and Anna Freud on
their journey from Vienna to London after the Anschluss (© Hulton-
Deutsch Collection/Corbis)

2. Picture of Hess and his sister Margarete, as children.
This image was reproduced in *The Case of
Rudolf Hess* (1947)

3–5. The Führer as a baby, alongside his parents, Klara Poelzl
and Alois Hitler, recycled in Walter Langer's *The Mind of
Adolf Hitler* (1972) (© Bettman/Corbis; Interfoto/
akg-images; akg-images)

6. Hitler's messianic performances (© International
News Photo)

7–9. From a postcard series in the 1920s, 'Adolf Hitler
Speaks, 6 Photographic Moments' (© akg-images)

10–12. Stills from Leni Riefenstahl's *Triumph of the Will* (1935)

13. A Nuremberg rally, 1934 (© Bettmann/Corbis)

14. Hitler addresses the SA, Dortmund, 1933 (© 2004 TopFoto/
ImageWorks)

15. Walter Langer (Courtesy of The Boston Psychoanalytic
Society and Institute)

16. Henry Dicks (Courtesy of Adrian Dicks)

17. 'Wild Bill' Donovan (Courtesy of the Library of Congress)

18. Rebecca West (Cecil Beaton/Vogue, © Condé Nast
Publications Ltd.)

19–21. Scenes from Fritz Lang's *The Testament of Dr Mabuse* (1933)
(Nero-Film AG)

22–3. The hero of Fritz Lang's *Ministry of Fear* (1944) discovers
the mysterious Dr Forrester's tome, *The Psychoanalysis of
Nazidom* (© 2011 NBCUniversal, Inc., all rights reserved)

24. Hess at the International Military Tribunal, interviewed
by Col. Amen and other officials, 1945 (© akg-images)

25. Hess, Göring, and Ribbentrop in the dock (© De Agostini
    Picture Library/akg-images)

26. Hess in old age, imprisoned at Spandau (© ullstein
    bild/akg-images)

27. The site of Spandau prison, after the building was razed
    to the ground following Hess's death in 1987
    (© Jason McAlister)

I

Introduction

It was in May 1941 that Henry Dicks, a dapper, German-speaking British army officer, physician, and psychiatrist, was summoned by his superiors and assigned to work on a secret and highly sensitive mission.[1] In civilian life Major Dicks was a practising psychotherapist and the deputy medical director of the Tavistock Clinic in London, but his task that wartime summer was to take care of Rudolf Hess (the Führer's deputy within the hierarchy of the Nazi Party) who had, most unexpectedly, and to the consternation of the German government, flown to Scotland.

When this Nazi official first came into custody he brought various diplomatic proposals; he sought a swift end to Germany's conflict with Britain, so that the real battle (as he saw it) between Nazism and Bolshevism could proceed unimpeded. But for reasons described in this book, his status shifted from that of self-styled political intermediary to world-famous psychiatric case. It was not at all beside the point, as things turned out, that Hess arrived on British shores armed with an outlandishly large supply of medicines and alternative health remedies for maladies that appeared at times to have little organic basis. It was as though he was determined from the start to ward off all prospective illness, whilst practically announcing himself (so at least his doctors later came to believe) as a mental patient in the making.

This is a study of the wartime encounters between Hess and his psychiatrists, and of a host of other British and American inquiries into the psychic life of the Nazis. The story of how such work was commissioned and disseminated is intriguing and revealing in its own right, but it also has broader implications. Occasionally, the investigations of army psychiatrists and psychoanalysts were placed in the political limelight; more often, however, inquiries were conducted behind the scenes. Much of the wartime literature on this subject remains unexamined. Drawing upon a variety of archives on both sides of the Atlantic, this history asks what such investigations set out to do and shows how the 'talking cure' (to borrow the term that had been coined by a patient of a colleague of Sigmund Freud, to describe the nature of this new method of treatment) was harnessed to the particular needs of military intelligence and post-war reconstruction. Claims were made about the unconscious motivations of Hitler, Hess, and other particular leading individuals in the regime. But these cases were soon matched and eventually eclipsed by quite different kinds of argument regarding the implications of Nazism for group psychology and human relations at large.

Some influential commentators in the past believed that knowledge of the unconscious could contribute to making a better, more democratic world after 1945. Such endeavours to consider Nazism from a Freudian point of view or to draw upon psychoanalysis in policy-making for post-war international recovery had mixed outcomes in practice. Curiously, however, the nature of the wartime and post-war clinical and 'applied' psychoanalytical work has rarely been assessed by historians; as a consequence the roles played by psychoanalysts and psychiatrists in the war effort remain mostly overlooked. Perhaps it is because, for so many historians, the question of psychoanalysis is now linked to debates about good and bad methodology in the investigation of the past that the annals of the Freudian movement are also now often regarded as obsolete. Psychoanalytic investigations of the Third Reich have been criticized, but only rarely have they been historicized.[2]

Recent studies, films, and novels tell us more about psychoanalysis in *fin-de-siècle* Vienna and the place of Freud's ideas in the treatment of 'shellshock' in the First World War than about the visions of mind that prevailed in and followed the Second World War. Despite some important scholarly work covering the history of psychoanalysis during the middle decades of the twentieth century, the significance of the Second World War for psychoanalysis is still generally less well known than the implications of earlier periods for the development of the Freudian tradition.[3] When it is discussed, it is often in shrill partisan terms 'for' or 'against'. Moreover, along with psychoanalysis, the larger field of psychological discourse on Nazism has also largely fallen out of favour in the modern historical profession. Indeed the term 'psychologism' is often now used routinely (and pejoratively) by historians and social theorists to suggest an incapacity or unwillingness to think in properly historical terms; for instance, it might indicate a failure to recognize that the forces we easily take for granted as natural or as universal constants (such as 'self', 'sex', or 'life') may in fact be infused with the values of our culture, even indeed be in crucial respects time-bound concepts. 'The problem of any psychologism', argued the editor of *New Left Review*, Perry Anderson, in an influential article in 1968, 'is to account for historical change, since the initial assumption is a self-contained, universal psyche.'[4] Much of the wartime clinical literature on Nazism exemplified such suspect 'psychologism', assuming the universality of certain key models in psychoanalysis such as the Oedipus complex or the death drive. But whatever the value of such concepts in themselves, neither the clinical material that emerged nor the wartime attempts to understand it should be treated as mere ephemera, irrelevant to that past or our present. Whether psychoanalysis is now admired or reviled, it is evident that historically it has mattered: the encounters between clinicians and prisoners of war, for example, and ensuing interpretations of their meaning had significant impact on the human sciences. Psychoanalysis of fascism and Nazism also produced substantial echoes in political thought in the decades after 1945.

Dicks and his fellow clinicians took their place alongside other human scientists (notably anthropologists) in these endeavours to analyse the fantasies exploited in Nazi ideology, and to map the minds of leaders and followers.[5] On occasion, analysts focused upon the psychopathology of particular individuals; at others, upon the mentality that was said to be typical in particular organizations (such as the SS), or even upon the entirety of those who became enthralled by Hitler. It would be tedious to place the phrase 'Nazi mind' in scare quotes each time it is used in this book; it is intended as a shorthand to indicate the notion that such an (elusive) psychological object existed and could be recovered in some shape or form. This expression is one way to convey the psycho-political quarry that so many researchers keenly pursued during and after the war. Not only were countless hypotheses made about Hitler's unconscious, the desires and feelings of his coterie, or the wider fantasies and identifications of the electorate, but terms such as 'Nuremberg mind' or 'Nazi mind' became commonplace concepts, captions, and titles. For example, in a study of Hitler for the American wartime intelligence agency and forerunner of the CIA, the Office of Strategic Services (OSS), the psychoanalyst and Harvard psychologist Henry Murray declared that the proper interpretation of this one personality would be an important step 'to understand the psychology of the typical Nazi mind'.[6]

During the war some prominent officials in the armies and intelligence services of the Allies came to believe that a psychoanalytic or psychiatric

body of knowledge could provide a deeper understanding of the attractions
of authoritarianism and of the subterranean forces that drove the policies of
the Nazi leader, bound his supporters in unquestioning declarations of love,
and inspired the 'masses' to vote for him in their millions. During the conflict and in the aftermath of victory, such ideas were brought to bear in
British and American propaganda operations and in considering the problem of German recovery.

———•———

Hitler, Hess, and their 'analysts', Walter Langer (1899–1981) and Henry Dicks
(1900–77), make up the central quartet of characters in the first part of this
book. Langer—an American follower of Freud—wrote a secret report on
Hitler's mind at the behest of US intelligence in 1943. Even as the British
faced the conundrum of Hess, Langer was embroiled in interpreting Hitler's
florid speeches. Together with several East Coast psychoanalytic colleagues,
he laboured to understand the sources of the Nazi leader's outlook on life.
Langer received his instructions to use psychoanalysis to profile Hitler
from the director of the OSS. This commission, to investigate from afar
the Führer's dreads and desires, contrasts with the immediate 'live' clinical
experience of those who attended to Hess.

Like so many other physicians, psychiatrists, and therapists of their generation, Langer and Dicks argued that Nazism arose in particular historical circumstances, although it spoke from and to the unconscious. What occurs *within*
the mind, they argued, was relevant to understanding the cult of the Führer
and the popularity of the 'strong man'. Power was secured through whips,
clubs, knives, guns, tanks, and planes, but also through the psycho-political
manipulations of love and desire, hatred, envy, and anxiety. The sources of those
feelings and passions, it was said, lay not only in culture, politics, and society, nor
even in innate personal endowments, but in the unconscious meanings associated with the experiences of infancy, the nature of parent–child relations, and
the complex milieu of the family. Each infant, in short, was a political subject
in the making.

The rise of participatory democracy made mass psychology an especially
salient political issue. Towards the end of the nineteenth century, a number
of European writers offered influential funeral orations on the passing of
the old 'elites'. These authorities spoke with foreboding of the 'age of the
crowd'. They insisted that a new science (combining evolutionary biology,
the close observation of animal behaviour, psychology, psychiatry, and criminology) was required to study the human aggregate. The minds of the so-

called mass or masses mattered as never before; the formation, development, and external manipulation of those minds were widely debated. The Great War that was unleashed in 1914 demonstrated not only the reality of vast industrialized slaughter, but also the power of populist propaganda. Various social psychologists as well as some psychiatrists and psychoanalysts turned their attention to such unstable modern political phenomena. People, it was said, lost their individuality in crowds; worse still, even when each of us is alone a crowd mentality or 'herd instinct' all too easily pervades individual thought and mutates doubt into blind certainty.

Wilfred Trotter (a British surgeon with close links to a number of the early psychoanalysts) pulled together many of these perturbing ideas about the limits of reason and of individualism in his influential book *Instincts of the Herd in Peace and War* (1916). The morale, beliefs, and identifications of populations were seen to derive from sources of which they were not consciously aware. Instinctual propensities, it was said, led people to flock together in body and in mind. Such tendencies were not thought to be new, but they were perceived to have become more important; indeed, they might ultimately determine the social and political outcomes of nations. In 1921, Freud placed his own very particular stamp on this field, publishing *Group Psychology and the Analysis of the Ego*. Although steeped in the crowd literature that had flourished at the *fin de siècle*, it considered the problem of mass enthusiasms from the point of view of ordinary, unconscious fears, longings, and narcissistic needs, rather than in terms of some residual herd instinct or primordial remnant of 'the beast in man'.[7]

Much has been written about Freud and the vicissitudes of his psychoanalytical movement during his lifetime. Nonetheless, a full account remains to be written of how, under the shadow of Nazism, problems of authority, power, and obedience came to be addressed and reconceptualized by psychoanalysis. *The Pursuit of the Nazi Mind* (which might be seen as an introduction to such a large-scale history) argues that Allied investigations of the enemy's psychology drew significantly upon psychoanalytic ideas and in turn played a part in reshaping Western understanding of how minds work and groups operate. This book also asks how Freudian inquiries into such problems connected to other scientific accounts, cultural representations, or political theories of the time. Neither a general history of twentieth-century psychology, psychiatry, or psychoanalysis nor, still less, a reappraisal of the origins, development, and downfall of the Third Reich (numerous works exist on such matters), it traces instead particular confrontations between clinicians and Nazis during the direst decade of the twentieth century and considers their legacies.[8] Psychoanalysis is singled out for especially close scrutiny here, but evidently it was part of a spectrum of approaches to the investigation of Nazi mentalities during the war and in its aftermath.[9] Post-war visions of human nature, not just historical accounts of German society and history, were significantly affected by revelations of the barbarism of the Third Reich *and* by the several distinct diagnostic discourses that first surrounded it. These modes of thought derived from various sources, but in substantial part from Freud, as did theories about the neurotic traits that were thought prevalent in particular national cultures. Concepts that were crucial to the psychoanalytic account of the self, for instance regarding narcissism, sadism, identification, idealization, or the superego, were also to be deployed, in diverse combinations, in the political analysis of fascism.

Despite offering cautionary notes against the risks of conducting 'wild analysis' (that is, speculating about the unconscious minds of people who were not psychoanalytic patients), Freud made plenty of exploratory historical and cultural interpretations of his own. Analysts of the Third Reich followed in these tracks, endeavouring to delineate particular Nazi characters (Hess and, of course, Hitler among them), asking whether these could be seen as 'types', and speculating about what went on 'deep down'.

Much applied psychoanalytical work was undertaken around the fringes of intelligence operations during the war and in its immediate wake, but the bulk of the material was never published, or only in abbreviated form many years later. In the 1960s and 1970s, while a new generation of German students and intellectuals demanded a far more substantial reckoning with the Nazi past, a number of clinical practitioners, who had lived through the 1930s and 1940s, published new and controversial work in this field that sought to lift the lid on human destructiveness. Such work was often well attuned to a more angry and interrogative mood in the counter-culture. There was indeed growing suspicion in many young people of a previous generation's silences and evasions, and protest against cases of social conformism with grotesque 'norms'.

Nearly three decades after the Second World War Erich Fromm published *The Anatomy of Human Destructiveness* (1973). Fromm had trained as a psychoanalyst in the 1920s and devoted much of his energy to investigating different forms of Nazi psychopathology and then drawing larger conclusions. His work was originally produced under the auspices of what came to be known as the 'Frankfurt School'; this was the name for a group of remarkable intellectuals who had worked closely together at the Institute for Social Research, which was first created in Frankfurt in 1923. Fromm, however, parted company with the group in the 1940s, after years of collaboration. This 'School' was to move its base to the United States after Hitler came to power. Led by the philosopher Max Horkheimer, it attempted, among other things, to combine elements of Marxism and Freudianism. On occasion members of the group also strove to apply their theories to evidence that could be derived from modern social-science sampling techniques. One aim was to combine theory and empirical material in order to understand more deeply the power of Nazism to co-opt swathes of the German working classes (but of course not only them) during the 1920s and 1930s.

After 1945 the nature of Nazi ideology continued to preoccupy many of the left-wing intellectuals who had worked at the Institute for Social Research. Traditionally, Marxist theorists had understood the crisis brought about by fascism in inter-war Europe as the consequence of structural 'irrationality'; this was understood as a particular feature of capitalism as a mode of production. This irrationality, it was often assumed, was merely temporary: it would be swept away by a deeper rationality that governed history itself: out of class struggle would come the 'finally revolutionary epiphany heralded by the crisis'.[10] Non-Marxist historians also tended to focus upon the lack of reason that governed the behaviour of the 'masses', but suggested (after 1945 at least) that good sense, order, and a spirit of enlightenment could be firmly re-established once the madness of inter-war politics had been overcome. The Frankfurt School tended to assume the Marxist analysis of 'crisis' but at the same time to express grave doubts about the belief (be it liberal or socialist) that the return of peace would do away with the fascist darkness that lay 'within'. Increasingly, they turned to the relationship of fascism and Nazism to the psychic interior. In *The Anatomy* Fromm extended this argument and laid the greatest possible emphasis on Nazism's perverse desire to destroy and to kill, as though death itself was the aim, rather than the by-product, of the system. As in previous publications, the author described the sado-masochism that he felt was central to this German ideology, but here he placed the most emphasis on Hitler and on Nazism's 'necrophiliac' fascination with realizing its own ending, manufacturing corpses and exulting in death and murder.[11] Moreover, Fromm sought to use the example of Nazism to describe a much wider human propensity, a constant potential for death and destructiveness that lurked in the psyche and the modern social order.[12]

Around the same time that *The Anatomy* appeared Dicks and Langer published rather different works, respectively, on a group of Nazi mass murderers who had been interviewed in German prisons, and on the mind of Hitler. These contributions in the 1970s were part of a spate of books that revived interest in the psychoanalytical investigation of Nazism. Among other notable publications of this period was *Male Fantasies*, a memorable study of fascist and Nazi desire by the German writer Klaus Theweleit.[13] This extraordinary and controversial work began with the private diaries and letters of proto-Nazi men of the *Freikorps*, those organized paramilitary gangs that contributed so much of the political violence that bedevilled German society in the aftermath of the First World War. Reprising ideas that Wilhelm Reich had pioneered in his seminal work *The Mass Psychology of Fascism* (1933), Theweleit quoted extensively from his sources and speculated about the sadistic, misogynistic fantasies that shaped these political bonds; whatever the wider implications may be of his study, he showed how political and sexual hatreds were profoundly confused in the outpourings of these foot-soldiers of the far Right.

Langer's and Dicks's studies emerged from a quite different context. The provenance of these American and English books lay in the authors' own wartime service. They were not supposed to be mainstream works of history at all. Such texts, however, were sometimes treated as though intended to replace rather than complement more conventional narratives of the Third Reich. Langer's wartime study of the German Chancellor was, admittedly, especially vulnerable to the charge of reductionism. Dicks was more inclined to refer to the *limits* of psychoanalytical understanding, although even Langer included no small number of caveats. Nonetheless, Langer was to be heavily criticized by historians for the shortcomings of his book on Hitler. By this time the kinds of assumptions that this American analyst and many of his colleagues had made about mind, normality and pathology, sexuality, selfhood and identity were all dated, to say the least. But these writers, and the stories behind their enterprises, were more deeply embedded in the history of the war than their later detractors may have realized.

In the 1940s such Freudian applications had a particular Anglo-American stamp. Many of the European analysts who had worked on such problems during the inter-war years had fled to the English-speaking world by the time the war broke out; they contributed their ideas to the Allied endeavour to defeat the Third Reich and to proposals for 'denazification' and 're-education'. Psychoanalysis was, by this period, anathema in the Soviet Union; France, under occupation, did not produce substantial equivalents of the type described in these pages, and anyway, French psychoanalysts tended to be more circumspect about, or even outrightly critical of, the 'applied' forays into Nazi psychobiography and mass psychology of the kind at issue here.[14]

It was commonplace in the 1930s and 1940s to argue that Nazism not only grossly amplified but also perversely twisted widely held European ideas derived from social Darwinism, racial theory, imperialism, and nationalism. But conscious political belief was only part of the story; many people were infatuated with the leader and the Nazi cause, as though the two were one and the same. It was noted by a number of commentators that the personality of Hitler, his style of performance, and the panoply of rituals that surrounded him and his henchmen inflamed his followers far more deeply than they knew. There was, it appeared, an erotic and destructive enjoyment at stake in politics. Hitler was perceived to be a megalomaniac, a man who craved absolute power and was thrilled by his own exorbitant impact. He exploited and drew sustenance from emotions in others, and his allure, it was understood, had less to do with any particular policy objectives than with more elemental feelings of devotion and of dread.

The wartime prisoner/patient Hess became a much-studied exemplar of the Nazi fanatic. Yet the case of Hess also suggested how much could go awry in the minds of the Führer's faithful servants. The connections between psychic life, social relationships, and political outcomes in Nazi Germany were to be studied again and again in the middle decades of the twentieth century through particular biographies and general social surveys. Interviewers were soon encouraged to widen their quest from German prisoners of war to political subjects in post-war democracies and to try to uncover the sinister political beliefs that interviewees were fearful of recounting, increasingly embarrassed to acknowledge, or not even consciously aware they held.

After Hitler's suicide in 1945, and then during the Cold War, influential works of political thought about liberty and tyranny bore direct traces of psychoanalytical views about the obstacles to freedom that existed inside the mind.[15] These views had already been expounded in 1941, in Fromm's influential book *Escape from Freedom*. Liberal accounts of political pathology that followed sought to make some psychological sense of the German people's enduring loyalty to Hitler. Some would never relinquish him; but very many others remained convinced of his invincibility until very late in the war. Well before Hitler was defeated, a variety of analysts who worked for the Allies, or at least on behalf of Allied victory, explored why internal resistance proved so ineffectual in the German case after 1933.

For example, some analysts zeroed in upon Hitler's subliminal impact on others and the significance not only of his passionate words but the rhythm of his speech and the use of his whole body in the performance. To be sure, there were myriad political reasons why people identified with the Nazi cause during the 1920s and 1930s, including a powerful sense of grievance and injustice regarding the peace settlement at the end of the First World War, but the unconscious, charismatic effect of the Führer was widely recognized to be of central importance. The combination of the Führer's language, intonation, contorted face, and convulsed limbs did indeed have an electrifying effect upon many of his audiences. The mass enthusiasm for his person that was epitomized by those notorious scenes of the Nuremberg rallies of the 1930s remained an enduring cultural image. Beyond the many thousands who attended in person were many more who shared the same sentiments, and who hung on Hitler's every word on the radio. This was a 'virtual' community of millions. In the face of these ecstatic crowds, audiences and readerships, cheering for the man who would lead them to untold horrors and disasters, psychoanalysis was, in some eyes at least, an obvious and necessary resource.

These days the field of psychoanalysis has less political purchase—at least in Britain and America—than sixty or seventy years ago; it may also now seem more remote from the conduct and understanding of world affairs. The prominence of certain behaviourist systems of thought that clash with and rival the Freudian account of the self has, no doubt, contributed to the current low ebb of psychoanalysis, but many factors can be identified in explaining the difficulties of and challenges for the discipline and why the larger hopes of social and political transformation *through* psychoanalysis are harder to detect than in previous periods. Freudian practitioners have perhaps become appropriately more wary of 'wild analysis' than the rather gung-ho pioneers were, but they have also sometimes lost touch with the radical political ambitions and social aspirations of many of the key writers of the past. Nowhere is this clearer than with regard to the Allied struggle against Nazi Germany. The investigation of complicity, collusion, and authoritarianism within the structure of the mind was perceived to be important for understanding how and why the Führer and the German people responded to each other so fervently.

A distinction needs to be made between the situation of psychoanalysis before and after Hitler's rise to power. In 1920s and early 1930s Germany a number of analysts did directly write about and protest against Nazism. Between 1933 and 1939, however, many of Freud's followers fled from central Europe. Increasingly, the psychoanalytical investigation of, and campaign against, Hitler and his cause emanated from Britain and America, and from the émigrés who had settled there.

How far did psychoanalysts actively engage with the political crises of the 1930s and the catastrophes of the 1940s? The answer is, extensively. It is true that internal theoretical and technical disputes consumed much time; during the war, for example, crucial 'Controversial Discussions' occurred in the British Psychoanalytical Society.[16] Nonetheless the myriad political, civic, and military engagements of psychoanalysts in the struggle against Nazism bear close examination. For example, psychoanalysts (or sometimes officials without formal psychoanalytical training but with Freudian leanings) interviewed and assessed prisoners of war. Anna Freud and her close colleagues set up the remarkable Hampstead War Nurseries in London. Established in 1941 and funded by the British War Relief Society and the American Foster Parents' Plan for War Children, it offered a place of safety for children and families who had become refugees or who had in other ways become homeless in the war. Significant research was conducted in the War Nurseries. Psychoanalysts were also closely involved in work with survivors of air-raids and the rehabilitation of men who had spent years in prisoner-of-war camps in Germany or Japan.

Psychoanalysts did not only argue among themselves. In Britain, for instance, they were often at loggerheads with psychiatrists over methodology. Psychoanalysts were often first of all psychiatrists themselves; but they tended to be clinicians who had been disappointed by the medical approach to mental health, or at least who felt acutely aware of its limitations; they searched for and found in Freud what they took to be a more profound account of the nature of mental illness, and sought through the talking cure to relieve and even remove human neuroses and to enlarge patients' insights into themselves. In some cases, especially after 1945, they also sought to make sense of and treat the psychoses through Freud's interpretative science. The psychoanalytical account was controversial and the efficacy of its treatment was often placed in doubt. If some doctors in Britain embraced a Freudian approach enthusiastically, others frowned upon it and regarded its truth-claims as entirely bogus. Thus, although the psychoanalytically ori- entated Tavistock Clinic and psychiatrically dominated Maudsley Hospital both provided mental-health services for Londoners, they regarded each other with suspicion and at times worse. Neither the psychoanalysts nor the organic psychiatrists who treated military and civilian casualties in the 1940s, however, were insouciant about the catastrophic and terrifying cir- cumstances of the war.[17]

Innovations in the treatment of some (but by no means the majority) of psychiatric casualties bore traces of Freudian theory or technique.[18] New methods of officer selection pioneered by a plethora of Tavistock staff and members of the British Psychoanalytical Society were of substantial sig- nificance.[19] Some analysts were called upon by the intelligence services to weed out closet authoritarians in post-war Germany; others undertook a related task in seeking to denazify practitioners within the psychoanalytic and psychiatric professions. Among those to engage in this work was John Rickman, who wrote reports for the International Psychoanalytical Association and the British Psychoanalytical Society about the erstwhile colleagues who had remained in Germany through the war; following per- sonal interviews he graded them, according to their capacities to face the past openly, to think critically, and to deal with the interviewer honestly, as 'black', 'grey', or 'white'.[20]

It would be a mistake, of course, to credit psychoanalysis as the only discipline that sought to engage with Nazi psychopathology. Just as Freud had deliberately blurred the lines between the study of the psychology of the individual and of the wider social group, and alluded freely to classi- cal literature, history, and anthropology, others, caught up in the wartime struggle, blurred the lines between Freudian psychoanalysis, general psy- chiatry, medicine, and various brands of modern psychology derived from sources quite distinct from Freud. Indeed, the 'psychoanalysis' at issue in many of these wartime and post-war discussions also needs to be taken as a loose term. Much of the documentation on which this book draws—a miscellany of letters, reports, surveys, articles, and logs from the war and its aftermath—took note of psychoanalysis. But on closer inspec- tion, the literature in question here adopted a miscellany of theories— behaviourist tracts, psychiatric diagnoses, and experimental psychology—as well as Freud.

This eclectic approach can be seen in an American textbook on military intelligence by Paul Linebarger that was published in 1948. It placed Ivan Pavlov and Freud comfortably side by side. The Russian scientist Pavlov, who won the Nobel Prize for medicine in 1904, had managed a large team of empirical researchers in a laboratory setting. He made his mark above all thanks to his experiments with dogs, in which he studied the nature of their responses to set stimuli.[21] The most famous concept that came to be associated with Pavlov was 'conditioned reflexes'. Freud had, admittedly, begun his career in neurology, but by the 1940s he and Pavlov made a puzzling pairing. Yet the text did not draw out the differences; rather, it implied that these authorities were both indispensable resources for the canny political speechmaker who wanted to captivate an audience.[22]

In the applied clinical work that emerged during and after the Nazi period Freudian thought was often combined with other seemingly disparate techniques or models. Hess, for instance, was interpreted in several distinct ways: his 'degenerate' family tree was considered, he was subjected to shock tactics (to jog his memory), and on occasion invited out for bracing country walks and light picnics as though his case was a throwback to Victorian times, or at least to some sanatorium ministering to nervous members of the gentry. To some extent this jumble reflected the doctors' assortment of old and new ideas, perhaps culled over a lifetime of training or from a combination of textbooks written in different decades. Whilst it is true that some Victorian psychiatrists had indeed been interested in recovering and interpreting the experiences and circumstances of individual patients (even in crowded public asylums), it was often apparent that such cases had been treated without much regard for first-person accounts of disorders and developments at all. Indeed, 'introspection' had often seemed beside the point, or even a symptom of pathology in the patient. Psychoanalysis, however, was always concerned to focus upon patients' words and stories, and the versions of personal history and relationships presented to the therapist. Increasingly, psychoanalysis had also come to explore how important aspects of the unconscious world of the patient were made manifest 'here and now', in the larger atmosphere and in the tiniest details of the relationship that emerges in the consulting-room.

———•———

Before embarking on this history of the wartime clinicians who delved into the Nazi mind, a sketch of psychoanalysis between the wars is required. Even the briefest snapshot of the field in Britain or America after the rise of

Hitler reveals how far things had come since Freud's small 'Wednesday meetings' in Vienna, and how profoundly its history was marked by the triumph of Nazism. From a group of devoted followers (few enough to fit around a table) soon after the turn of the century, by the 1920s and 1930s Freud's movement had expanded to become a multifaceted and fissiparous organization with affiliates in many countries. In 1924, when a head-count was taken, analysts were still primarily based in northern and central Europe, and America, but had also established centres in India and (for a short-lived period) in Russia; confirmed worldwide numbers of practitioners were in the low hundreds; later they would run into thousands, with burgeoning numbers of adherents and practitioners spread far beyond the original locations of Freudianism.[23] This was very notably the case post-war, for example, in the development of the movement in Latin America.[24]

Many of the original enthusiasts—and certainly most of those who were based in Austria and Germany—were Jews, with backgrounds broadly related to Freud's own. This was less true in inter-war Britain and some of the other emerging societies in the first part of the century. One of the very early followers, the gifted psychiatrist from Switzerland Carl Jung, initially had the particular advantage (in Freud's eyes) of being a gentile, and thus in a good position to ensure that psychoanalysis was not dismissed as the 'Jewish science'. Under the Nazis it was in fact cast as exactly that. Freud's work was consigned to a bonfire of books in Berlin, not long after Hitler took power.

As many of the analysts fled, Freud's movement fell into ruin in Nazi Germany, to be replaced by a mode of psychotherapy more congenial to the regime. The most notorious embodiment of this transformation was the now well-studied phenomenon of the Göring Institute in Berlin, run by the neurologist cousin of the eponymous Reichsmarschall.[25] A number of Freud's erstwhile followers accommodated themselves to a purged and so-called racially purified version of psychotherapy. Freud himself continued, mistakenly, to hope (long into the 1930s) that the rump organization could somehow be salvaged—keeping the psychoanalytic flame alive—as though any remnant of his work was to be preferred to none. The disaster of the Nazi period for German psychoanalysis had consequences that continued to shadow the field decades after the war.[26]

The therapeutic organization led by Matthias Heinrich Göring was established in 1936. The director of the Göring Institute, as it came to be known, insisted that Hitler's thought was in no way incompatible with therapeutic work. Racial health and 'mental hygiene' were to be the aims of the new institute that had eclipsed the Berlin Psychoanalytical Society. Mental hygiene had many incarnations in the Western world during the first half of the twentieth century, but the Göring Institute gave it a new twist.[27] Traditional psychoanalysis, meanwhile, was branded a harmful Jewish practice.

Thus Göring, and numerous other German doctors and psychiatrists, viewed Hitler and his cause not only as tolerable but even as an inspiration for clinical endeavour. All German mental-health organizations were brought into line with the Nazi state. The German Society for Psychotherapy was reconstituted as the more accommodating International General Medical Society for Psychotherapy; the German Society for Psychology was quickly reconfigured. Hitler was extolled as a 'great psychologist' and, in the keynote speech of the 1933 meeting of the German Society for Psychology, was championed as a bold and emotionally deep leader who set an example to others.[28] The fate of psychoanalysis in Germany thus reflected a wider reorganization of mental health, as also of the medical profession. Jewish practitioners were persecuted and it became impossible for them to carry on their work. A few psychoanalysts were killed, others imprisoned. Many lost their property.[29] Those with the means and foresight left; Max Eitingon, who had led the German psychoanalytic movement, went into exile in Palestine in 1933 and was succeeded by the gentile Felix Boehm.

Jung and Freud had acrimoniously parted company before the First World War. Jung went on to found the tradition known as 'analytical psychology' in distinction to psychoanalysis. His association with the ideas of the Nazi regime in the 1930s was an embarrassment to many of his followers then and since. Indeed, it proved hard even decades later for Jungians fully to acknowledge their founding father's intellectual collusion with Aryan ideology. Similarly, it took considerable courage and a work of mourning on the part of certain younger German psychoanalysts to expose the degree of complicity of various 'elders' of the movement during the Third Reich.[30]

Other schisms had also occurred; erstwhile followers, such as Alfred Adler, developed their own ideas beyond the psychoanalytic movement. The growing chill between Freud and his once very close associate, the Hungarian Sándor Ferenczi (who died in 1933), resulted in part from disagreement about how clinical technique should be applied most usefully in order to help patients who had suffered from early infantile traumas. The rupture over these personal and technical disagreements was itself traumatic, espe-cially for Ferenczi. Some differences of approach and theory between the founder of the discipline and other key psychoanalysts who took up his ideas were contained within the movement. These led to new directions in psychoanalytic thought and prompted Freud himself to extend his own work; other disputes led to splits and the eventual departures of disillusioned and/or disgruntled former colleagues.

But what features essentially characterized psychoanalysis? And what particular concepts did the wartime interpreters of fascism and Nazism apply?[31] The most crucial touchstone for Freud and his followers remained belief in the existence of the unconscious, as the realm into which thoughts were actively repressed, only to return, in various guises, despite our defences against knowing. It was often conceptualized as though an actual place or space, although this was not to be taken too literally. Civilized sexual moral-ity, Freud posited, was radically at odds with the drives of our own natures; unlike some of his more utopian followers, he believed that the mind would always be split within itself, even in a less hypocritical and repressive social order. In his pioneering early work Freud had shown how dreams, jokes, and slips of the tongue revealed evidence of other scenes inside the mind, condensed and distorted. Underlying wishes and anxieties could be discov-ered via the patient's free associations, revealing 'latent thoughts', sometimes provocatively, even obscenely, at odds with social convention. What was revealed most importantly in Freud's work on dreams was the dream work itself: that is to say, the constant, unconscious activity of the mind as it trans-muted and rearranged, condensed and distorted the original thoughts.

For Freud, illness was often the price of the impossible conflict between unconscious desire and social constraint. Moreover, increasingly Freud had emphasized the complexity of the conflicts within the mind and had stressed the defensive forces that existed and that enabled the subject to shy away from painful, uncomfortable, and/or obscenely exciting thoughts. There were, he suggested, multiple conflicts and divides 'within'. Neurosis (but not necessarily psychosis) constituted for Freud a shared human fate. Freud sug-gested that infants and children have powerful and confused sexual feelings (of which adults especially prefer not to speak), linked to their own oral, anal, and genital development. Many of these ideas were already in place in the first decade of the twentieth century, but it was during and immediately after the First World War that psychoanalysis came to be written anew: the accent was then increasingly placed upon psychic repetition; the difficulty of mourning what is lost and irretrievable; the patient's resistance to 'cure'; the struggle of the life and death drives; and the various dynamics that surround cruel, aggressive, hateful, loving, guilty, or other (often unmanageable) feelings inside ourselves.

Many of the new ideas resonated with fears of socio-political degeneration and a wider sense of cultural malaise, even as they addressed clinical questions and difficulties internal to the discipline.[32] Freud's *Beyond the Pleasure Principle* (1920), *Group Psychology and the Analysis of the Ego* (1921), and *The Ego and the Id* (1923) seemed of more than passing relevance to the tumultuous historical events that were contemporaneous with their first appearance in print. Indeed, in *The Ego and the Id*, Freud (drawing inspiration from several other writers) reformulated his basic mental model; the mind could be conceptualized, he now proposed, in terms of the ego, id, and superego. The last was the critical (sometimes hypercritical and sadistic) and also idealizing agency that watches over and makes demands of the ego. Freud had already intimated something of this kind, although in more fleeting fashion. For instance, in a paper in 1907 he had commented on the self-reproaches of the obsessional neurotic: 'the sufferer from compulsions and prohibitions behaves as if he were dominated by a sense of guilt, of which, however, he knows nothing, so that we must call it an unconscious sense of guilt, in spite of the apparent contradiction in terms.'[33]

In the 1920s the superego was installed within psychoanalytic thought as a major, structuring feature of the mind.[34] The superego is at work largely unbeknownst to the subject. Its lacerating criticisms or impossibly inflated demands lead the ego to accommodate as best it can to the relentless authority that judges it. A number of the interpreters of politics who are discussed in this book also came to see Nazism though this lens. The ego struggles to deal with and accept external reality and to cope with the superego. It is also confronted and disturbed by 'das Es' (originally translated into English as 'the id'), the unconscious, seething cauldron of our most basic 'excitations'. Even a part of the ego is unconscious, repressing unwelcome thoughts, for instance, but at times leaving us none the wiser that it has done so.

Freud's account revealed how ferocious social morality could be; it also suggested how punishments and judgements taking place from inside us may be still more terrible than the prohibitions and demands that come from outside. This aspect was taken up and developed by various followers during the 1920s. Apropos of this new work, Ernest Jones (the most influential early follower and promoter of psychoanalysis in England) declared admiringly to Freud in July 1923: 'You take us into deep waters.'[35]

Analysts became especially interested in the *excessive* aspect of the superego. If we enquire into the actual composition of the superego, mused Jones in 1926, 'the most obvious constituent to be perceived is sadism, usually desexualized'. In a footnote he added: 'The finding is not surprising when one reflects how sadistic and persecutory even ordinary (outwardly directed) morality often is; in the formation of the super-ego we have an example of the "turning round upon the subject", which Freud described in connection with sadism as one of the vicissitudes of instincts.'[36]

The Ego and the Id (1923) appeared in the year after Mussolini's March on Rome and a few months before the 'Beer-Hall Putsch' in Munich in which Hitler, Hess, and their cronies sought to seize power in the city, only to be defeated and brought to trial. Many analysts of the 1920s and 1930s found the superego a useful concept in applying clinical knowledge to modern social and political problems. Under-achievers, over-achievers, criminals, religious devotees, obsessive hand-washers, manic partygoers or depressed recluses, tyrants, gang leaders, 'slavishly' acquiescent fascist followers, and any number of other people could be thought about in relation to the strength, weakness, and particular timbre of the superego. It might be expected that the person with the weakest superego should be the most delinquent in character, but this was not necessarily so, at least according to the authors of various influential inter-war psychoanalytic papers on criminality: some people, for instance, might commit crimes in order to seek punishment from the community, as though to make their social fate consonant with their guilty or masochistic states of mind.

An embryonic psychoanalytical organization had first been created in Britain before 1914. It was constituted on a firmer footing, or at least on a more consistently Freudian (rather than Jungian) basis, after the First World War. During the 1920s and 1930s its development was enriched and complicated, first by the contribution of Melanie Klein, one of Freud's more challenging and innovative followers, and second by the arrival of Freud and his family, together with other refugees from Vienna and associated central European psychoanalytical centres, in the mid- and late 1930s.

The British tradition was also notably affected by the presence of Freud's daughter Anna, who could, of course, claim a special contact with the founder (whose affection she had always enjoyed). Her book *The Ego and the Mechanisms of Defence*, first published in German in 1936, was translated into English in 1937. It included an extended discussion of a concept—identification with the aggressor—that was soon taken up in interpretations of the psychology of Nazism and even sometimes of concentration-camp inmates. In this situation, it was surmised, subjects become unconsciously identified with the aggressive and perhaps actively sadistic figures who dominate them, whilst someone else (in reality or at least in the person's fantasy) would take on the role of the victim. Anna Freud became the custodian of her father's work before and, all the more, after his death in 1939, yet, as critics were quick to point out, her thinking was far less capacious than his. The mantle of Freud's true heir was also sought and claimed by others. Sharp differences of technique and belief had opened up, most notably between Anna Freud and Klein. Their ensuing arguments were at once personal, theoretical, and technical.

From the 1920s onwards Klein's close interest in, and speculation about, the earliest thoughts and feelings of babies and very young children marked her out as a radical thinker. Claiming always to be a faithful Freudian (true, above all, to Freud's most disturbing insights), Klein described the terrible feelings of destructiveness that raged inside the mind. Love, and the wish to make reparation for harm done, were far from ignored, but fury, envy, and the wish to 'scoop out', devour, or in other ways ravage the object (above all, the mother's body and mind) were named openly and clearly in her writings and in her utterances to her patients. Klein focused closely on the infant's relationship to the mother's breast, an object that cannot in fact be omnipresent and all-satisfying, that nourishes but also disappears, that is needed, loved, and hated by turns. An ever-present inner world of fantasies, she believed, exists beneath the surface of children's lives. The same is true in adults, albeit more decorously disguised. She concentrated upon the most primitive features of psychic life and the nature of the most basic defences against raw feelings and helpless dependency. Thus, she described omnipotent states, total denial of painful knowledge, and the propensity to 'split' confusing thoughts and feelings into discrete and opposite entities containing either total goodness or absolute badness. The tendency to project substantial parts of ourselves into the minds of others, she argued, stemmed from the wish to be rid of, indeed sometimes entirely to disown, the awareness of the disturbances that plague us within.

Klein placed the formation of the Oedipus complex much earlier in life than had Freud, and she also undertook treatment of the very young. Her technique was adapted somewhat from the classical approach; thus, having furnished her small patients with various simple toys—for example, 'little wooden men and women, carts, carriages, motor-cars, trains, animals, bricks and houses, as well as paper, scissors and pencils'[37]—she studied the communications they made through their drawings, games, and activities, and endeavoured to discover and to name the child's conflicting feelings and beliefs. She did not shy away from their darkest thoughts and most troubling wishes, even when they were directed violently against her.

One of Klein's most remarkable and detailed accounts, only published in full much later, concerned her work with a 10-year-old child, known as Richard.[38] This treatment occurred in Scotland during 1941; Klein and the family of her young patient had moved north to escape the Blitz. Klein could point out, in justifying her analysis of children, that Freud had advised such bold methods in his own treatment of adults, or even in his own somewhat more indirect analysis of a young boy—'Little Hans'. The detailed analysis of Richard was not in the public domain at the time, but plenty of other work by and about Klein and her followers was publicly available in the 1940s and found some reflection in political assessments and social diagnoses of the period. This work also revealed how politics and war became intricately entwined with her patients' own particular fantasies, dreams, and terrors. The clinical case study about Rudolf Hess that was published in 1947, containing the work of Henry Dicks and others, had several passages that draw upon Freud, and also show some affinities with Klein's ideas and technique.[39]

Given the diversity of Freud's ideas and writings, many developments inside the psychoanalytical movement were possible without the kind of overt apostasy that had driven away the likes of Jung, Adler, and Reich. Some sought to push Klein out of the British Psychoanalytical Society, but did not succeed; she remained a central figure. In American psychoanalysis the ideas of Anna Freud (relayed from London) were influential in and after the war. So too were the views of a number of analysts who had escaped fascism in Europe and crossed the Atlantic.[40] Heinz Hartmann, Erik Erikson, Karen Horney, Helene Deutsch, Franz Alexander, Ernst Kris, Rudolph Loewenstein, Erich Fromm, and several other notable interpreters, custodians, and/or discontented challengers of Freudian thought shaped the discipline. None ever stopped reading, or quoting from, Freud, even if some baulked at his rigidities and prejudices. It was indeed to America that the majority of central European Freudians fled in the 1930s. There they were assimilated, not without serious difficulty, into the existing psychoanalytic societies.[41] They were in one sense following in Freud's footsteps. Yet the culture of the American continent and the direction of psychoanalysis in the New World aroused Freud's mistrust. His one visit across the Atlantic had been to give lectures at Clark University in 1909. The New York Psychoanalytic Society opened for business two years later, founded by, among others, the devoted disciple and early translator of Freud, Abraham Brill. His renditions of the master were later much criticized, but his *Fundamental Conceptions of Psychoanalysis* (1921) and *Basic Writings of Sigmund Freud* (1938) defined the field for countless Americans.

In New York and the other major psychoanalytical centres which developed, with swelling numbers of recruits, in the great cities of the United States during the first half of the twentieth century, psychoanalysis was no more a monolith than it was in Britain, but its history was certainly different. A variety of intrigued English and American people had travelled to Vienna after the First World War in order to undergo psychoanalysis with Freud or his associates. Their guineas and dollars were to be crucial to the fortunes of the Freud family in those straitened times. Some of these returned to their homelands as practitioners and enthusiasts. But to a still greater degree than in Britain, the course of the movement was affected not by these voluntary travellers overseas, but by the European refugees. Some critics have complained that leftist politics and other firebrand ideas previously developed by psychoanalysts (such as Otto Fenichel) were toned down as soon as the voyagers' ships had reached American shores. The same criticism has been made of the Frankfurt School intellectuals such as Max Horkheimer and Theodor Adorno, who were at pains to ensure they did not cause undue political offence to the American authorities because of their residual Marxist beliefs. Some of the psychoanalysts and the Frankfurt School writers also gave consideration, however, to the unconscious lures of American capitalism: for it was perhaps otherwise all too easy for interpreters of European fascism to treat the liberal, capitalist political system within which they then functioned as the unproblematic 'norm' and to concentrate all of their fire on the psycho-political pathologies to be witnessed abroad.

By comparison with her impact in Britain, Klein had, initially at least, very little resonance in the United States, but this was not to say that American-based analysts only conserved old verities from the founder of the field. Klein's merits were never entirely ignored, although her work was frequently criticized by the dominant authorities on the subject.[42] The most

influential development in the United States built upon the idea that psychoanalysis should strengthen the patient's ego and help it to adapt to external reality. This might easily imply that health and conformity were one and
the same thing. This concern with ego adaptation to 'reality' was associated
particularly with three of the émigrés who settled in New York, Hartmann,
Kris, and Loewenstein. Health and illness, normality and pathology, loomed
large in their accounts of the ego. Such concerns were also evident in Freud's
own work, but often, as Hartmann acknowledged, Freud undercut the distinction between the normal and the pathological, and offered a wry critique of that external reality.

In a paper in 1939, 'Psychoanalysis and the Concept of Health',
Hartmann sought to define the healthy mind psychoanalytically and came
up with a view that emphasized (among other things) the importance of
self-accommodation to the environment. He felt that clarifying the nature
of normal psychic processes was crucial, although he did note, perhaps
with a laconic awareness of where his own thoughts might be leading, that
an excessive interest in health might itself be regarded as a symptom of
neurosis.[43] Although he did not refer directly in this article to the European
tyranny from which he had recently escaped, he did place the capacity to
enjoy freedom from overwhelming anxiety and other crippling states of
mind, and thus to be at liberty to perform a chosen task or aim, at the
centre of his notion of mental health.

Since the 1910s and 1920s American psychoanalysis had also come into
contact with a range of other ideas drawn from psychiatry as well as broader
visions of social and mental hygiene. In the United States, medicine and
psychoanalysis did indeed become for a time comfortable bedfellows, and
increasingly the American psychoanalytical societies required that analysts
had medical training first. Thus did American psychoanalysis declare a
degree of independence from the International Psychoanalytical Association:
the latter had not stipulated this prior qualification. American candidates for
psychoanalytical training would for the most part be confined to physicians,
although a number of European émigrés who were already members of the
International Psychoanalytical Association were exempted from the restric-
tion. Freud had cast his lot against the prohibition of 'lay analysis' (as it was
known), but to no avail. The medical appropriation of Freudian theory and
technique in the United States is a complicated story in its own right.[44]

Psychoanalysis had always been affected by surrounding politics.
Throughout its history it has also been seen by its devotees as highly rele-

vant to the understanding of politics. This association became much more explicit and elaborate after 1918 and, all the more so, after 1933. Important consequences flowed from the conviction that new forms of psychobiography and group analysis might be deployed as an arm of political thought, social policy, and intelligence-gathering. Indeed, the intellectual impact of psychoanalysis on modern thought about authority, freedom, and democracy should not be underestimated; nor the clinical and theoretical fallout for psychoanalysis itself of its painful encounters with Nazism.

2

Characters and Causes

After the Nazis came to power in 1933 speculation about Hitler's mental state and the psychopathology of his acolytes proliferated. In the second half of the 1930s key diplomats, politicians, and writers on both sides of the Atlantic wondered if the Chancellor was out of his wits, the German leadership in the grip of a collective delusion, and the whole field of international politics beset by this madness. Some suggested that vast numbers of the population were functioning as robots or hypnotized subjects. It was in this context that British doctors and psychiatrists gained their wartime assignments to treat Rudolf Hess, and that a group of American analysts set to work upon an investigation of Hitler's mind. Before turning to their findings, several key characters (and the causes that they espoused) require introduction.

Dr Henry Dicks (Hess's British army psychiatrist by the summer of 1941) was widely respected by his colleagues and became a key figure at the Tavistock Clinic. In the 1930s this institution began to consolidate and widen its international reputation. By the post-war period it had become Britain's pre-eminent centre for psychotherapy for both children and adults, and attracted growing numbers of clinicians and researchers from home and abroad. It was founded in 1920 by the psychiatrist and neurologist Dr Hugh Crichton-Miller, who had developed a close professional interest in the problem of shell-shock in the First World War and who also sought to promote new forms of treatment to address the mental-health problems of ordinary civilians. The Tavistock's original base was in Bloomsbury in central London. It began work on a small scale, reliant on various private grants and donations, but by the 1930s had become a well-known centre for training, treatment, and conferences on adult mental health and child guidance. By the war years the Tavistock had been re-housed in Hampstead in north-west London, temporarily occupying premises belonging to Westfield

Women's College, which was part of London University. Here at the Tavistock Dicks found his niche.

Courteous and cultured, personable and astute, Dicks appeared the quintessential upper middle-class professional; he became an august figure not only at the Tavistock Clinic but also within the officialdom of British psychiatry and psychology. He worked in the field of public health but also in private practice, seeing patients in consulting-rooms at an elegant address near Harley Street, bastion of the medical elite.[1] Later in life Dicks would suggest to young hopefuls that the best place to train as a clinician was the British Psychoanalytical Society; yet he had not undertaken psychoanalytical training himself. What personal experience of analysis he may have obtained during the interwar period is unknown.[2]

Dicks may have appeared a stalwart English member of the psychiatric establishment, but he had an unusually cosmopolitan upbringing. He had in fact only come to reside in England as a young adult. Born in 1900, when Queen Victoria was still on the throne, Dicks grew up in the town of Pernau in Estonia. He had three older brothers and two older sisters. Their father, Julius, was probably London-born and of Jewish background, although Henry, it seems, did not know this for sure, or at least conveyed some uncertainty about this point when recounting the family history to his children, perhaps just as his father had done with him.[3] Dicks (senior) had left London in the late nineteenth century, traded in timber, made his fortune as a merchant, and became the honorary vice-consul in Estonia. Henry's mother, Wilhelmina (known as Wilma), was from a German family that had long lived in Estonia. A number of her relations were Protestant clergymen. Henry, like his mother, was brought up as a Lutheran, and he was bilingual in English and German. Wilma strongly influenced him and oversaw his education. She arranged for him to travel to school in St Petersburg (he attended a German Gymnasium there that was also frequented by children of the Russian elite) and later encouraged him to study at Cambridge. Henry acquired excellent Russian and remained deeply interested in the country.[4] In his later years he became an energetic campaigner against the abuses of psychiatry in the Soviet Union.[5] Russia as well as Germany, Stalin as well as Hitler, loomed large in his political imagination. Dicks's children recall stories of the time of the Russian Revolution and how their father had been in St Petersburg, not very far away from the riotous crowds, at the time the Winter Palace was stormed in 1917.[6] Henry and his three brothers found themselves in danger and were forced to flee: they escaped across the ice to Finland, where they had to avoid further skirmishes between 'red' and 'white' Finns before reaching Norway and finally England.

In 1918 Dicks joined a volunteer regiment of the British army, the Artists' Rifles. Before long his linguistic skills were recognized and he worked as an interpreter for Military Intelligence. He was not demobbed at the end of the war, but served with British forces in north Russia, 1918–19, and in south Russia and the Caucasus, 1919–20, fighting against the Red Army after the Revolution. Subsequently Dicks went up to Cambridge; there he was a foundation scholar at St John's College and excelled in examinations in natural sciences.[7] As was not unusual at this time, he did not remain to take the second part of the degree, but left in 1923 in order to pursue his medical studies at St Bartholomew's (known as 'Bart's', one of the great London teaching hospitals); apparently rumour spread among his peers there that he had once been a colonel in the Cossacks.[8] Everything suggested he was destined for a glittering career in medicine: Henry even won a medical prize at Bart's. He was expected to become a consultant but decided to change direction and specialise in psychiatry.

Dicks's stint as a junior doctor at Bart's was followed by an appointment to the Bethlem Royal Hospital (the famous mental asylum, heir to the old 'Bedlam'), where he worked in 1927 and 1928. This experience deepened the young man's interest in the psychological aspects of medicine. Like many other people who had lived through the First World War, he was also drawn to certain esoteric beliefs that challenged the Victorian natural sciences; in the inter-war period he developed, alongside his explorations of Freud and Jung, an interest in the mystical claims of theosophy, the movement that had been founded by Madame Blavatsky and other intriguing free spirits and entrepreneurs of the 1870s. Dicks also apparently became a freemason, although the nature of his involvement remains somewhat obscure.[9] If Dicks had a powerful wish to belong to the establishment, he was also clearly attracted by an assortment of controversial ideas and investigative practices.[10]

Perhaps Dicks's fascination with the doctoring of minds rather than the care of bodies was first stimulated during his undergraduate years in Cambridge. It was a time, after all, when Freud drew the attention and the enthusiastic engagement of a number of eminent scientists, mathematicians, and philosophers in the university, including the illustrious botanist and founder of ecology Arthur Tansley.[11] In Cambridge Dicks would have encountered the ideas of one of the most influential early commentators on

Freud and the unconscious, the polymath W. H. R. Rivers, who was a fellow in his own college. Rivers (who died in 1922) was, among other things, a path-breaking experimental psychologist, neurophysiologist, ethnologist, and a pioneer of new therapeutic treatment methods (including a somewhat bowdlerized version of Freud's) for the psychiatric casualties of the Great War.

From Bethlem Royal, Dicks found his way, in 1929, to the Tavistock Clinic. This was a few years after its foundation. Enthusiasm for mental health and the ambience of the Tavistock set the seal on his decision to abandon his earlier ambitions in general medicine. In 1939 the first of his several books appeared: *Clinical Studies in Psychopathology*.

The Tavistock, created after the First World War, came of age during the Second. In the 1920s the clinic had an eclectic theoretical orientation: Jung and Freud had both been influential at the outset. Increasingly, however, Freudian psychoanalysis, albeit adapted into a new, less intensive form, became the key discipline. Tensions between the official organization of the Freudian movement, the British Psychoanalytical Society, and the Tavistock Clinic complicated collaboration. One issue of dispute was technique: some felt that the so-called pure gold of the classical Freudian psychoanalytic approach should not be debased by the admixture of other theoretical traditions or the pursuit of immediate mental-health 'goals' that tended to be required in running a public service, then as now. Indeed, senior members of the BPS, such as Ernest Jones and Edward Glover, made it clear that any candidate for analytic training who was working at the Tavistock Clinic must choose between the institutions. In 1938 Dr Wilfred Bion became the first candidate accepted at the BPS who refused to submit to this requirement.[12]

The Tavistock was to prove an oasis for those such as Dicks with a close interest in mental health, social reform, and the public provision of new therapeutic methods, above all the talking cure. Increasingly, its staff would also branch out into 'applied' questions, relating to problems of war, peace, and industry. The mental health of individuals was seen to be closely linked to the larger well-being and productivity of society. Such mid-twentieth-century debates perhaps harked back to late nineteenth-century languages of national efficiency, but they also made reference to the unconscious. As a psychiatrist Dicks had spent the early years of the Second World War assessing the mental health of British soldiers at facilities in and around London, before he was assigned other duties, including the care of Rudolf Hess.[13]

Although late in his life Dicks publicly acknowledged his irritation with the institutional politics of the psychoanalytical organization, he also made clear his sympathy with the psychoanalytical approach.[14] He was never a doctrinaire follower of one line, but was happy to gather those clinical ideas he found useful, regardless of provenance. Dicks had several close personal and professional links with British psychoanalysts. For many years he lived and worked in Hampstead, thus in close proximity to a number of the British and émigré Freudians who established the psychoanalytical movement in London. Numerous followers of Freud and Melanie Klein lived there or in surrounding neighbourhoods. It was but a short walk from Frognal Lane in Hampstead (where Dicks lived after the war) to the house in which Freud had passed his final year (on the eve of the hostilities) and Anna Freud continued to live: 20 Maresfield Gardens.

Dicks had married in 1927; he and his wife became generous and lively hosts, with a wide social network. They entertained many English and foreign academic friends, clinical colleagues, and other guests in the years before and after the war. Henry's children recall his friendship with a keen amateur anthropologist who wrote copiously on 'national character', Geoffrey Gorer. Dicks was well acquainted with Gorer's friend, the anthropologist Margaret Mead. He also had a close association with the psychoanalyst Tom Main (a fellow army doctor and, after the war, the director of the Cassell Hospital in London) as well as with several of the pioneers of applied analysis and the study of 'human relations' at the Tavistock, such as 'Tommy' Wilson and Eric Trist.[15] The American sociologists Talcott Parsons and Edward Shils were among Dicks's good friends.[16] They had much in common with Dicks, not least the fact that all of them laboured to identify the causes of German popular enthusiasm for Hitler and then put forward ideas on denazification at various Allied intelligence organizations during the war.

As Dicks puzzled over Hess in 1941, Walter Langer's career in American intelligence was about to get under way. He had been a restless figure before he settled down as a clinician. During the Second World War Langer became, in his own words, 'a freelance psychoanalytic consultant'.[17] He was one of four children of émigré Germans (his father from Silesia, his mother from Bavaria) who had met on board the ship that took them to the United States in 1888. The Langers settled in South Boston, where Walter and his brothers, William and Randolph, were born during the 1890s.[18] An older sister died of diphtheria at the age of 2. Their mother fell on hard times after

Langer (senior) died in 1899 (the year of Walter's birth), but she managed
to ensure the successful education of her sons. Walter gained a place at the
Massachusetts Institute of Technology in 1917, but chose to join the Signal
Corps and spent two years in France. He suffered badly in a gas attack and
lived thereafter with weakened lungs and sporadic health problems.

On his return from France Walter decided to study psychology, following
his brothers to Harvard. All went on to combine academic research (Walter
in psychology, William in history, and Rudolph in mathematics) with applied
work, directly or indirectly, for the US army or intelligence services. The
eldest of the three, Rudolph, worked on probability theory and its practical
applications. William, a major presence at the OSS in the war, was also a
highly regarded diplomatic historian. He was to become president of the
American Historical Association in 1957. Walter became a psychologist and
later trained as a practitioner of Freudian analysis. After the completion of
his undergraduate education, in which he had been inspired by courses in
psychology by Morton Prince and William McDougall, Langer gained more
practical experience of clinical disorders at the Boston Psychopathic
Hospital. It was advice from its director, Dr C. Macfie Campbell, and sessions with the Boston psychoanalyst Dr Martin Peck that consolidated his
ambitions to become a clinician.

In 1925 Langer seized the opportunity to look after a troubled adolescent
boy in New Mexico, and within a year had established a larger enterprise
that could house eight children at a ranch in Silver City. It would enable
him, as he put it later, 'to apply what psychoanalytic knowledge I had
acquired'.[19] For a period the school thrived, and Langer, previously in debt,
became solvent again. Known as the Old Bear Mountain Range School,
this residential home aimed to provide a supportive environment, in the
words of the publicity brochure Langer produced (entitled 'Mental Hygiene
School for Boys'), for those suffering a 'malignant emotional or mental disorder'. Walter's nephew, Leonard Langer, later recalled that it was designed
as a haven for 'disturbed boys from wealthy families'.[20] The school, however,
ran into difficulties.

Not much is known about the workings of the school, although some
information can be gleaned both from Langer's papers and from interviews
that were conducted with him much later by Dr Sanford Gifford, a
psychoanalyst and archivist in Boston. Judging by these interviews and by
Langer's files (lodged at the Boston Psychoanalytic Society), the ranch provided a dramatic setting for camping and other energetic outdoor pursuits

for the young people. Walter's ex-wife, Juanita Franks, who also spoke to Gifford, would recall very late in her long life (she lived to be 100) the good times that she and Langer enjoyed at the school, and how the venture foundered in the financial crash of 1929.[21]

In the face of the economic crisis demand for places at the school declined. Langer moved the enterprise to Massachusetts (in Gifford's words, 'to a Moorish palazzo on the Charles River'), but it came to an abrupt and disastrous end when a fire destroyed the school building in 1931.[22] His marriage broke up around the same period, his wife moved to Arizona, and he faced the risk of bankruptcy, for the business had not been properly insured.[23]

With financial support and encouragement from his brother William, Walter became a researcher in experimental psychology at Harvard. Working at the university's psychology clinic he closely observed how people accomplished various sensorimotor tasks, and investigated the effectiveness of the tremograph machine. This, as the name suggests, was an apparatus designed to gauge the patterns of the body's involuntary shaking and trembling. Langer's interest and approach at this stage was that of an empiricist, and his work was based in a laboratory.[24] Thanks, in part, to the labours of Henry Murray, with whom Langer became well acquainted, this discipline developed strongly at the university during these years. Displaying his growing curiosity about Freudian approaches to the field, and offered firm advice about where best to train by the psychoanalysts Hanns Sachs and Erik Erikson, Walter travelled back to Europe, nearly twenty years after he had seen active service in the war. By this stage armed with a doctorate in psychology (awarded in 1935), a background as an educationalist/therapist, the German language he had acquired from his mother, and something of the buccaneering spirit, Langer landed on Anna Freud's couch in Vienna in 1936 and entered into analytic supervision with Edward Bibring.

As he learned about the Freudian method at first hand, Langer also witnessed the spiralling political catastrophe in Austria and across Europe. When Hitler annexed and invaded Austria, to much popular approbation, in 1938, the American visitor played a role alongside others in helping Freud and his family to leave their old flat at Berggasse 19, Vienna, and escape abroad. All of this occurred after escalating tension for Freud and his followers. One day, as is well known, Anna was summoned to an uncomfortable, extended meeting with the Gestapo. Langer recalled this tumultuous episode in an interview many years later: 'My personal analysis with Anna Freud went on as best it could', amidst the wider political crisis. On one occasion the Freud family's maid, Paula, told him that his analyst had been taken by the Gestapo for questioning, but the analysis resumed the next day, 'as if nothing had happened'.[25]

Langer, along with a number of other foreigners who were staying in Vienna at the time, was drawn into assisting fugitives and anti-Nazi activists, above all in helping them to flee. He returned briefly to New York and Boston in 1938 to garner support (and affidavits) that could prove useful in arranging exit visas. Anna's disturbing encounter with the Nazis, along with other threats, intrusions, and indignities, finally persuaded her aged, ill father (so long reluctant to leave his home) that it was essential to go. His four sisters remained in Vienna; they were trapped, later to die in the camps— three at Treblinka, one at Theresienstadt. Their brother never knew of their fate; he died in London in 1939, about a year after his flight from Hitler's Austria.[26]

Langer was apparently discreetly seated in another carriage of the train that took Freud and his immediate family to the Austrian border in 1938, the first leg of their journey to Paris and then London, the culmination of weeks and months of tense negotiation and string-pulling by influential people in Britain, France, and the United States.[27] The American had gained more than enough of a glimpse of Hitler's triumph in Europe. He was exposed on the old continent to what William Langer would later call history's 'irrational and demonic forces'.[28] Meanwhile, he had become well acquainted with the Freud family.

After Vienna, Walter Langer spent some time in England, where he briefly continued his analysis with Anna Freud and attended some meetings of the British Psychoanalytical Society. Here he also learned about the controversies surrounding Klein.[29] By the end of 1938 he was back in the United States, having earned not only the gratitude of the Freuds for his role in their escape but also, it would seem, the affection of Anna's companion and colleague Dorothy Burlingham. Langer's analysis was evidently not very 'boundaried' (in modern parlance), as he clearly had some social contact with Anna Freud's immediate family and loved ones. (These days more effort is generally taken to try to ensure discretion.)[30] It was a confusion of the personal and the professional that occurred in the practice of many analysts at the time, including Sigmund Freud himself—who, it is now known, had analysed and written about his daughter, albeit with some attempted disguise—and Melanie Klein. Anna warned Dorothy against any liaison with Walter, pointing to her patient's 'unreliability'; by this she meant, it seems, his tendency to blow hot and cold with women.[31] Whether Langer was relieved to extricate himself from this tricky triangle and head home is not clear; he remained, as far as can be gathered, entirely silent about the matter.

Walter Langer settled back on the East Coast. No doubt he discussed the increasingly dire news from Europe with William, whose academic interest in diplomatic and political affairs was by then taking second place to his practical, hands-on engagement. Indeed by 1941, even before America found itself at war, William was spending an increasing proportion of his time in Washington rather than in his office at Harvard.[32] Walter, meanwhile, began to build his own practice while also working as a researcher. In recognition of his analysis in Vienna and subsequent work and training, he became in due course a member of the Boston Psychoanalytic Society, despite his lack of medical qualifications.[33]

In the early 1940s Walter (with his brother's help) applied for funds from Washington intelligence chiefs for the pursuit of his Freudian approach to the analysis of the German crisis. He had read about the creation of a new department that would coordinate war information. It was to be led by a certain Colonel (soon after promoted to General) William Joseph Donovan.[34] Langer first encountered news of this while recovering from a double hernia operation in 1941. To his surprise (and that of his brother) he received an immediate reply to his approach, and an invitation to breakfast with the intelligence maestro, known as 'Wild Bill', at his house in the capital.[35] Here Langer found he was preaching to the converted, for despite Donovan's intolerance of what he considered academic fence-sitting and jargon, he was apparently well versed in psychoanalytic theory.[36] Langer's approach was not always greeted so enthusiastically: sometimes he had to deal with social scientists—and accountants—who were more than sceptical about the value for money of such an endeavour. He was nothing if not tenacious.

Walter Langer saw his work on morale for the Department of Information and then on Hitler and propaganda for the OSS as a patriotic duty. It was also a useful source of additional income. Some commentators have suggested that the organization got nothing much in return for the expenditure. The historian Bradley Smith notes that Langer's 'spiced-up' report on the unconscious phantasmagoria in Hitler's mind cost the organization $2,500 in fees; he dismisses it as of little consequence, one of many 'wild schemes'

dreamed up by the Morale Operations specialists of the OSS.[37] Much of
the paper trail about Langer in the OSS files at the National Archives in
Maryland concerns funding and payments.[38] (Even in retirement, much
later, Walter had a taste for business; he took a close interest in his beloved
nephew Leonard's banking career and kept a lookout for real-estate opportunities.) His OSS report would finally see the light of day after decades as
a secret document: *The Mind of Adolf Hitler* became a surprise best-seller in
the early 1970s.

———•———

To complete these preliminary sketches, it is worth looking briefly at Rudolf
Hess's upbringing, war service, and emerging political attitudes. Whatever
the differences between Hess and Hitler's childhood circumstances, the two
men's experiences, or at least the political conclusions that they derived
from those experiences, began to converge in the trenches during the Great
War.[39] Hess was born in Alexandria, Egypt, in 1894, the eldest of four children.[40] His father, Fritz Hess, of Lutheran background, made his living
importing and exporting goods; his mother, Klara, was from Hof in Bavaria.
Biographers generally refer to Hess's father as punctilious, formal, domineering, and frightening to his children. In Egypt, Fritz Hess apparently
restricted himself to a narrowly German circle of acquaintances.[41] Rudolf
Hess's mother would be pictured later on by her son in dreamy, idealized
language: 'One's whole youth is incorporated in one's mother', the 30-year-
old declared to his future wife Ilse. 'She is part of one's being, one's own
original essence—even today...without her one would have become
someone else.'[42]

The family returned from Alexandria to Germany in 1908 and Hess was
subsequently enrolled at boarding school. His father convinced him, against
his initial inclination, to engage in commercial matters with a view to entering the family business. To this end the young man spent time studying in
Hamburg and Switzerland. On 3 August 1914 Hess wrote to his parents
about his desire to enlist in the army and to play a part in giving Germany's
'barbarous' enemies 'the thrashing they deserve'.[43] Soon after he joined a
Bavarian field artillery regiment and saw service at Ypres the following year.
During the conflict, in which he received the Iron Cross (second class), he
was twice wounded. On the second occasion, in 1917, he suffered gunshot
wounds to the chest which damaged a lung and could easily have been fatal.
On recovery he lobbied to become a fighter pilot, was transferred to the Air
Corps, and reached the rank of lieutenant, although the war ended before

his flying skills were tested. After the Great War his martial interests continued and his political commitment to the far Right deepened: influenced by
ultra-nationalist and anti-Semitic political sentiments, he became active in
militias, and was again wounded, this time in the leg, during skirmishes with
Social Democrats in May 1919.[44]

Hess's accounts of his experiences on the battlefield were laced with
references to death, camaraderie, and the conviction that political betrayal
had undermined Germany. His tale of wartime action, grievance, and
increasing militancy was not dissimilar to the more famous story of Hitler's
contempt for the rulers of the Hapsburg Empire and his bitter disillusionment with Germany's leaders, nor to the sagas of many others who ended up
in the far-Right militias known as the *Freikorps* after 1918 or who, through
other routes, rallied to the Nazi cause in the 1920s. The Great War was cast
as the decisive political education of their lifetime. The Nazi Party was in
fact to gain support from a plethora of constituencies, from men and women
in varied circumstances and walks of life, not just from the ranks of disgruntled, scarred ex-soldiers. Nonetheless, Hess became a mythic embodiment:
the prototypical loyalist, depicted as such in both Nazi and anti-Nazi
literature.

Looking back on the war, in a letter to a cousin in 1927, Hess recalled
the military struggle in which he had participated 'for the honour of our
flag'. He referred to the hell of Verdun, Artois, and other sites of war, and
described the heavy bombardments, mud and dirt, hunger and pain, as well
as the constant proximity of death. For example, he remembered how he
had slept in a dugout beside the dismembered and decayed corpse of a
Frenchman. With defeat came immense despondency. Hess, like so many
others, perceived the armistice conditions as monstrous; he wondered what
purpose so much death had served and saw Germany as betrayed by its
elders. The defeat was experienced as an intense form of shame, a bitter
humiliation. Moreover, Hess believed that his life after 1918 could only ever
be meaningful again if the sacrifice of so many soldiers' lives could be shown
ultimately to have produced victory. Without that, he apparently confessed
in the 1920s, 'I would today regret that I did not put a bullet through my
brain'—'I did not do it at the time solely in the hope that in one way or
another I might still be able to do something to reverse fate'.[45]

After the war Hess enrolled at Munich University, studying history, economics, and geopolitics, but did not go on to graduate. He befriended a
former high-ranking soldier, military expert, and university teacher, Karl

Haushofer. The latter sympathized with the Thule Society, a virulently anti-Semitic organization whose political dreams of Aryan supremacy were suffused with a variety of occult beliefs. Hess 'fell under his spell'.[46] He lapped up his mentor's account of Germany's natural need for *Lebensraum* ('living-space'). Dicks noted in 1941 how some of those who had encountered Hess, twenty years earlier, as a student in Munich recalled him as a 'pathetic lonely queer, but striking figure dogging Professor Haushofer's footsteps'.[47]

Hess's infatuation with Hitler began at the very moment of hearing him speak for the first time in a Munich beer-cellar in 1920. Hess saw Hitler as decent, kind-hearted, and self-sacrificing as well as charismatic and far-seeing.[48] Hitler's smitten follower could easily rationalize his crush: total devotion to a sacred leader was precisely the medicine that Germany supposedly needed. Indeed, Hess wrote an essay at the university in 1921 that addressed the question: 'How Must the Man be Constituted who Will Lead Germany Back to her Old Heights?' This piece sketched his vision of the nation's likely future saviour. Such a leading man, Hess wrote, must not shun using the weapons of his enemy (that is, the communists): demagogy, slogans, street parades, and so on. 'Where all authority has vanished, only a man of the people can establish authority.' Yet the leader was not made of the same stuff as the average, nondescript person: 'like every great man, he is all personality.' Hess spoke of how parliaments may go on 'babbling' but the powerful man *acts*. He also 'knows how to keep silent', and, in order to achieve his purpose, 'is prepared to trample on his closest friends'. He may even be required, in pursuit of his great goal, to 'appear a traitor against the nation in the eyes of the majority'. As the need arises, 'he can trample [the people] with the boots of a grenadier, or with cautious and sensitive fingers spin threads reaching as far as the Pacific Ocean'.[49]

The words seem especially striking in view of Hess's later actions: perhaps he did indeed see the temporary appearance of treachery, be it by Hitler or himself, as justified if it served the ultimate aim of Nazi victory. The great man is not squeamish about taking harsh measures, Hess argued; he may need to spin subtle webs of influence, but must have no compunction about stamping on friends and foes alike if so required.

Hess also liked to emphasize the probity of the leader and the cause. On questions of violence he sometimes clashed with more overtly thuggish Nazis. After the Beer-Hall Putsch of 1923 Hess escaped to Austria, but on reading of Hitler's light sentence gave himself up and returned, whereupon he received eighteen months imprisonment, of which he served six.[50] In

prison with Hitler, Hess became an assistant—perhaps more—in the creation of *Mein Kampf*.[51] Haushofer too was a regular visitor. Following his role
as amanuensis, Hess was installed as a kind of political secretary to Hitler
and, in the view of one observer, 'something like the maternal head of a
family consisting of Hitler's most intimate followers'.[52]

In the 1920s and 1930s Hess apparently valued the Nazi new order above
all else, and insisted on the importance of allegiance and obedience to Hitler
at all costs. This made the way he seemed to fall apart all the more compelling and disturbing for his peers and for his wartime analysts. He accepted
the need for ruthlessness (and was evidently capable of thuggish and violent
behaviour himself); he was a militant anti-Semite, but he resented disorgan-
ized 'Jew-baiting' as at odds with the spirit of the Party. Nazism was to
involve violence, yes; but it was, according to Hess, necessarily to be disci-
plined by the Führer throughout.[53] Certainly, Hess was not squeamish. He
had made this clear in practice, as well as in principle. In 1925 Hess wrote to
his parents of his special bond with Hitler and of the bridging role that he
believed he provided for the Führer and the Party between the mass movement and educated opinion. 'On the other hand,' he added, 'I am far too
convinced of the necessity of the often unpleasant methods and nature of
the struggle in terms of mass psychology to allow this to frighten me away
from participation in this Movement, as are so many other members of the
intelligentsia. I am convinced that by exerting influence in many directions
I can do some good in *that* respect.'[54] Nor, he claimed to his parents, was he
bound thereby forever to Hitler.

Developments in Hess's personal life, however, were a good measure of
Hitler's influence over him, and indeed of the Führer's ability to meddle in
the affairs of his followers at will. In 1927, with strong interference and
encouragement from Hitler, Hess married Ilse Pröhl. They had a son in
1937, Wolf Rüdiger ('Wolf', in part, as homage to Hitler, who liked to use
it as a code-name).[55] As Walter Langer remarked in his 1943 report, the
Führer believed he had licence to prognosticate on everything from foreign
affairs to education, propaganda to movies, music to marital advice, women's
dress style to architecture.[56] Langer did not deny that many areas of government decision-making entirely eluded Hitler during the 1930s. Swathes of
policy were taken up and then abandoned when his attention shifted
elsewhere, or were left for others to interpret according to their idea of
what he would want of them. But when it mattered to Hitler, or caprice
took him, he could have the final word in any detail, as he clearly did in

some of the intimacies of Hess's private life. In Langer's briefing notes there was a comment about Hess, in the presence of the Führer, describing his ideas about a beautiful house to which he would like to withdraw. He envisaged it as lying between fields and forests, and said that it was the retreat where he would prefer to end his life. Hitler apparently told him not to talk in this fashion, and Hess at once slavishly agreed.[57]

Yet it was sometimes said that Hess was the only man who felt free to speak openly and frankly to Hitler. He was also viewed as the underling most trusted to speak for him. Historians nowadays do not tend to regard either claim as entirely accurate; it was not uncommon, however, to believe as much at the time. The Irish translator James Murphy, who lived in Berlin in the 1930s, suggested that when the leader was absent Hess was entrusted with complete plenipotentiary authority. Perhaps he sought to present the two men as utterly kindred spirits. Murphy was hardly a dispassionate witness, and no doubt wanted to believe in the deep bonds of mutual affection between the leader and his closest lieutenants. The Irishman had become a convinced Nazi, worked for Goebbels, and translated *Mein Kampf* into English in 1939. Moreover, his translation, critics pointed out, was anything but scrupulous: it played down Hitler's aggression and frequently bowdlerized the text.[58] Murphy certainly suggested that a special tie held Hitler and his old companion Hess together. 'This means', so he claimed, 'that when [Hess] speaks officially he is *ipso facto* speaking for Hitler.'[59] Karl Haushofer, interviewed by the OSS in September 1945, also conveyed not only Hess's allegiance to Hitler but his very special place in the mind of the leader; he recalled his first impression of Hitler in 1924 as 'an angry man with excited eyes whom only Hess could calm'.[60] Others made similar observations as well, not only regarding the Deputy's precise duties but also regarding the supposedly unique *mutual* emotional reliance of the two men.

In April 1933 Hess became the most senior official responsible for Party affairs and acquired an important role gathering intelligence about other Nazi Party members.[61] He became Reich Minister without Portfolio, a member of the Ministerial Council for the Defence of the Reich, and was included in the secret Cabinet Council of Germany. One of Hess's particular tasks was the reorganization of the agency that dealt with Germans abroad; his responsibilities included the encouragement of pro-Nazi sympathizers outside German-controlled territories, not least in America.[62] In theory at least, Hess had certain rights of veto over draft legislation emanating from government ministers and, from 1935, a significant say in the appointment of senior civil servants.[63]

Whatever his precise place in the Nazi pecking-order, Hess became an emblematic figure of the regime and admiring onlookers cast him as the ideal Party official and a perfect specimen of manhood. Thus, the well-connected Nazi supporter Kurt Ludecke dubbed him 'masculinity personi-fied', remarked upon his greyish-green eyes under thick, bushy eyebrows, and praised his 'square, determined chin'. Yet even Ludecke was perturbed by Hess and discomforted by his eyes, which, he felt, had 'an expression of suppressed fanaticism'. 'Not once', he noted, did Hess 'look straight into my eyes.'[64] Hess was renowned for his personal probity—a model family man. He was proud to serve his master, but was also thought to be humble, knowing that the cause was much bigger than him. It was thus fitting that Hess's speeches would sometimes end in a kind of spasm of obeisance, with the speaker, by then intensely excited, pouring out the words, several times in a row, 'Heil Hitler'.

This can be seen, for example, in actor/director Leni Riefenstahl's *The Triumph of the Will* (1935). The film—influential in Germany and notorious abroad—presented the week-long Nuremberg rally of 1934 and brought Hess and Hitler together in a telling scene.[65] Nowhere was Hess's role as sidekick and cheerleader more clearly displayed than in this pseudo-documentary. A close-up showed him, in uniform, approaching the speaker's podium in a large, packed hall. The audience appeared keenly expectant as it attended to Hitler's staunch ally, while he prepared in turn to introduce the Führer.

In this speech Hess did not begin with Hitler. Instead he recalled the recently dead war-hero and president Hindenburg who, after being installed to oversee the Weimar Republic in 1925, had evidently done the decent thing, in Hess's eyes, by failing effectively to counter Hitler's growing provocations and gathering political triumphs.[66] Hess followed his evocation of Hindenburg with a reference to fallen comrades of the Great War, the dead brothers whose sacrifice must never be forgotten—indeed, whose supposed betrayal Hitler was intent on avenging at all costs.

Hindenburg's image was left floating whilst Hess moved toward his inevitable paean to the Führer who sat behind him on the podium. The film is edited in order to juxtapose close-ups of Hess with images of Hitler and other top brass, as well as with the faces of German men, women, and a child, closely and attentively *listening*. The viewer is invited to join Hess and his audience in homage not only to the warriors of the Great War but also in excited observance and endorsement of the nation's present saviour. Shots of the 'esteemed representatives' from Imperial Japan, Fascist Italy, and Spain, as well as the sight of contented German well-wishers hanging on these words signal approbation, buttressing the ideological message: namely, that Hess and the Party merit the cinema viewer's respectful silence and trust.

In this scene from Riefenstahl's film the true charismatic object is, of course, Hitler himself. Perhaps in the fantasy conjured up by Hess, in his chilling speech, the dead soldiers (Hindenburg and the 'fallen' combatants of the Great War) are meant to anoint the triumphant Nazi Party, replete with its images of burning fire and searching light. Hess and the other avatars of Nazism are cast as a cleansing force, the very antithesis of obscenity, dirtiness, or impurity. The film seeks to represent a great morally redeeming crusade, to capture its aura of sobriety and seriousness, even whilst revealing, and revelling in, its jubilant festivals of power.

An onlooker at the time, the American journalist and broadcaster William Shirer, was fascinated and repulsed by what he called the 'plunge madly down the road to Armageddon'. He had attended the 1934 rally and provided cameo descriptions to an audience back home of the faces and gestures he saw there. Shirer did much to entrench the view that Germany had gone mad, writing diagnostic accounts of Hitler and his immediate disciples, and of the many thousands of 'hysterics' who, he declared, even besieged the street in front of the Führer's hotel, as though they were before the Messiah.[67] Shirer painted a picture of a nation in the grip of mass hysteria, enchanted by 'magical spells'. If Nazism disclosed, for this observer, something insane at its core, it was nonetheless characterized, Shirer thought, by the brutal, cynical nature—even the evil genius—of the leader. Despite the passionate nature of Hitler's public performances and the insanity of his message, Shirer suggested that the Nazi leader possessed a frightening clarity of mind and relentless determination.[68] Madness and reason appear not as opposites but as bound together, like those reversible perspectives where you see now, perhaps, two faces in profile, then, even as they disappear, the unmistakable shape of a vase.

For Hess, Hitler, and countless others, the rallies symbolized the Party's promise of cultural redemption, racial regeneration, and national rebirth. The future, so they proclaimed, would be the very reverse of the dog-days of depression, grievance, and despair that had marked the lives of Germans since the war. The Führer, as envisioned by Hess in that Nuremberg speech, epitomized love and peace. This was the case, apparently, even as he directed the murder of opponents and those erstwhile colleagues who had become unreliable. The necessity of such murders was the lesson immediately drawn from the 'Night of the Long Knives' in 1934 (another off-screen backdrop to Riefenstahl's film).[69]

After Hess's flight and arrest some wartime Allied clinicians would work over the story of the murder of Hitler's former ally Ernst Röhm and many other members of the SA. They speculated about the sexual undercurrents of the killing and the psychic, rather than overtly political, motives for the decision. Some placed Hess and Hitler in an active homosexual relationship; there was, in fact, no evidence of this, whatever the homoerotic aura of Hess's infatuation or the well-known mutterings about his sexual identity in the 1930s. Others suggested that Hess's hatred for the homosexual Röhm might have owed something to his own repressed tendencies.[70] When these analysts conjured up the specifics of Hess's sexual activities, for instance regarding a supposed homosexual relationship with Hitler (or others), they were misguided: there were no sure facts to support conclusions about such supposed trysts or even intentions on the part of Hess, even if he had indeed acquired a sexually ambiguous *reputation* and was nicknamed 'Fraulein Anna' by some of his Nazi colleagues. When focusing upon what they had gleaned from their own direct encounters, though, their words carry more conviction. For example, they sometimes drew attention to the strong impression they gained in talking with the prisoner of Hess's unconscious, erotized infatuation with Hitler; they also identified the grandiose, hysterical, and hypochondriacal qualities of his self-presentation in meetings, described his increasingly confused and precarious sense of self, and even noted his disturbing and bewildering impact upon his interlocutors.

In *The Triumph of the Will* Hess had declared, under the eye of the camera as well as of Göring, Bormann, Goebbels, and the rest, his blind love for the Führer. To the sound of public applause, and amidst shots of Nazi flags, he promised that only when their cloth had decayed would 'humanity', looking back, be able finally to comprehend what Hitler truly meant to Germany. Addressing Hitler, he added: 'You are Germany, when you act, the nation acts, when you judge, the people judge!' Through thick and thin, good times and bad times—'come whatever may!'—Hitler must be honoured and the Nazi homeland secured. Before the scene faded out Hess was to be seen working himself up into a further frenzy of salutes to his leader.[71]

This sequence works effectively as propaganda, and must have fostered in many German cinema viewers of the 1930s the very fervour that the film records in the live Nuremberg crowds. Hess, for the most part, preserves a solemn expression, but for a second he almost smiles or smirks, as though revealing a trace of his pleasure in the audience's adulation. He is unable entirely to hold back the signs of his enjoyment of the role, basking in the effect on the multitude of *his* voice, *his* phallic stance. He can be observed in this sequence all puffed up in the limelight, evidently admired by Hitler and the crowd before them. Perhaps, in his own mind, Hess became the star attraction, before reverting, almost instantly, to his traditional position as the adoring subordinate. The expression of vain gratification is fleeting, the cover-up so nearly instant that it is easy to miss.

A contemporary journalist and (by the 1930s) exile from Germany, Konrad Heiden, referred to Hess as Hitler's 'alter ego'.[72] Heiden's account of Hitler's mind, written in the United States during the war, was influential and widely admired.[73] It presented Hitler as a 'depersonalised soul' in a 'depersonalised world'. Rather than a 'purposive mind' in possession of the masses, Hitler, according to Heiden, was 'a personality without centre, a restless pulsating force'. He was a 'torn' figure, driven to rebel, and carried along 'with the people'; in turn Hitler, it was said, became convinced of 'the absolute necessity of trampling, coercing, and shaking the master's fist'.[74] Inside the mind of Hitler, Hess (so Heiden intimated, albeit relying here on the opinions of others) acquired a Svengali-like role:

> Suddenly, in the midst of a conversation, Hitler's face grows tense as with inner vision; these are the moments in which the humanly repulsive falls away from him and the unfathomable is intensified until it becomes terrible. His eyes peer into the distance, as though he were reading or gazing at something which no one sees; and if the observer follows the direction of his gaze, some- times it has been claimed, Rudolf Hess can be seen in the far corner with his eyes glued to his Führer, apparently speaking to him with closed lips.[75]

Hess was presented at different times as the Führer's stooge, interlocutor, and deepest influence. The image of some uniquely intimate relationship between the two men stuck. Writing shortly after Hess's flight, Heiden called him Hitler's 'better half' and declared that the pair had been 'conjoined to a degree that is possible only in abnormal personalities'. Indeed, he added, they had 'grown into one personality consisting of two men'. Without Hess, Heiden surmised, Hitler would go to pieces.[76] He described Hitler batten- ing upon Hess as a 'necessary complement to his own personality; as a stage director or spiritual ballet master who helped him shape his own powerful but formless and uncertain nature into whatever image he momentarily wanted'.[77] Hess was a 'human tuning-fork', supremely sensitive to his master; his admiration for Hitler 'filled his whole person'.[78] Similarly, a much-cited book that appeared soon after the start of the war was to characterize the German nation itself as a combination of Jekyll and Hyde.[79] Heiden's picture of Hess and Hitler as bound so closely together was overblown (Hitler had other close allies; Hess was in fact politically a marginalized, second-order figure in the later 1930s), but it was a pervasive perception.[80]

A report on Hess, probably written by Dr Charles Irving Dwork (later an OSS officer) some time before America entered the war, underlined the fact that this militant figure was utterly devoted to his boss. Undated, but probably based on notes taken in the later 1930s (before the OSS was constituted), this account presented Hess as one of the real 'wolves', the inner guard, and suggested that he might even be 'the real author of the Nazi Evangelion [*Mein Kampf*]'. If Hess was quiet, this did not mean he was mild, the intelligence report declared; quite the contrary. In comparison with other 'Nazi bonzes', Hess 'spoke and wrote but little.' But when he dealt with matters of race, 'he excited the broad masses against Jewry' and linked the Chosen People constantly to Bolshevism.[81] Transcripts of several of Hess's rabid speeches were attached to the file to drive home the point.

That report was soon out of date. While the anti-Semitism remained intact, much else changed in Hess's circumstances, pronouncements, and public image after 1940: his flight made him an international talking-point, a source of countless conspiracy theories. In the United Kingdom he would become the particular object of medical and psychological scrutiny. Here his reception perhaps felt to him as puzzling as his own messages seemed to his captors. Hess may well have been bewildered by the British response to his flight: at one moment he found himself interviewed by high-ranking government officials and obscure intelligence agents; at another, in colloquy with doctors, psychiatrists, and medical orderlies.

Army doctors were soon heavily engaged in the study of Hess's mysterious psychological condition and extensive psychosomatic complaints; before long they found in his every gesture, retort, or expression rich material for their analyses. Even on first arrival, as the medical case report would tartly observe, Hess's pockets were stuffed full of pills and potions, including a curious elixir that had been given to him by the Swedish explorer Sven Hedin, who had in turn received it from a Tibetan lamasery.[82] When the dust settled in 1941 the British discovered that they had been presented with a problem that could not be solved by conventional diplomatic or military means, and before long Hess was handed over to the care of the doctors. As the conflict raged, Henry Dicks and his medical colleagues grappled ever harder with the symptom-ridden German patient and pondered the larger question of the Nazi mind. A keen student of national character and an intelligence adviser on psychology and morale, Dicks availed himself of the chance to study as well as treat this high-ranking official. But the psychiatrist found himself embroiled in controversy and difficulty. Before long, the enigmatic prisoner of war was observing his observers just as keenly as they watched him. Hess lodged complaints about his treatment by his captors with the Swiss authorities (who oversaw the welfare of German prisoners). He was to become convinced that certain members of the medical team were engaged in a monstrous conspiracy to destroy him.

3

'The Deputy Madman'

How was Hess's psychiatric case assembled and where did it lead? This Nazi official's strange personal story was to form the basis for numerous secret reports and an extensive published dossier. Before turning to the clinical material and psychiatric interpretations that were made during the war, it is important to note how the question of madness informed public discussion of the affair within days of Hess's enigmatic departure from Germany.

On 4 May 1941 Hess was at work as expected; he was witnessed standing close to Hitler at the Reichstag.[1] Over the next few days he continued with his duties. Few, if any, knew of his plan to depart. Hess was 'weak and ineffectual', perhaps, but there seemed no reason to doubt he would remain a staunch loyalist.[2] Yet the astonishing flight that brought Hess to Britain on 10 May led to him sitting out the remainder of the hostilities in a succession of closely guarded facilities.

During what Churchill called his 'sojourn in our midst', Hess came to be regarded as a suitable case for treatment and his communications were interpreted by a variety of clinicians.[3] Indeed, it is clear that in the early weeks of his captivity Hess's role as emissary or intelligence source was to be complemented and eventually eclipsed by his status as patient. Medical doctors as well as interrogators were to be involved in the Hess affair from the start. Moreover, within a month of his arrival (as one of those physicians later recalled) Hess's 'grandiosity' and 'flimsy, woolly substance' offered compelling grounds for shifting the focus from Hess's injured body to the state of his mind, and thus it was found necessary to call in the psychiatrists.[4]

A vast speculative literature has grown up around Hess's flight, and certain more dubious 'histories' have edged ever closer towards fiction. Some have suggested that Hess's journey to Britain was not only manipulated by but also coordinated with rogue elements in British Intelligence or dissident circles within, or close to, the court and the government. Much heat was also generated some years ago by the theory, since widely challenged and discredited, that 'Hess' was actually a double. Hess's personal odyssey, it has also been said, could have dramatically changed the entire course of the military conflict, and some have bemoaned his wartime mistreatment.[5] Others, such as the British wartime intelligence officer and historian Hugh Trevor-Roper, make lesser claims, but still describe the Hess affair as the most bizarre set of events to have occurred during the larger world-changing conflagration.[6]

The prisoner was certainly hard to read. But so, he must have thought, were his British hosts/jailors. It was not always clear if he was being interrogated or psychoanalysed, debriefed or diagnosed, in the years that followed. The messages sent to the outside world in the days after Hess's arrival were also opaque, leading Roosevelt and Stalin alike to doubt the official story.[7] There was considerable debate in the British government not only about why he had come but also about how best to secure a propaganda advantage from this remarkable turn of events.[8] The German leadership, smarting at Hess's dismaying disappearance, remained puzzled by why the British did not do more to press home this propaganda coup. Some days later Goebbels observed that there was talk within the British Cabinet of Hess as a murderer and a madman, 'to whom they have nothing to say'. Goebbels added, with palpable relief: 'That is, of course, precisely what we wanted to hear. Eden [the British Foreign Secretary] has put in a word too. I think we have the worst behind us.'[9]

First, the famous headline story of the flight: Hess said goodbye to his wife Ilse and his young son Wolf on the afternoon of 10 May, announcing that he would be gone for the weekend, and drove by Mercedes to the Messerschmitt works in Augsburg. He changed into the uniform of a flight-lieutenant from the Luftwaffe and took command of a plane. The weather was clear and bright as Hess set off. Rumour that he was accompanied some of the way by other aircraft has never been confirmed; he piloted the plane alone and completed the journey without escort. He probably circled for some time over the sea, waiting for dark before he could proceed to his destination in Scotland.[10] Nearing the shore, Hess brought the plane in low, presumably attempting to go undetected by radar. Around 11 p.m., over the Lowlands, he managed to bail out, not without difficulty as the wind kept blowing him back into his cockpit. Despite previous flying experience this was apparently his first parachute jump and he sustained minor leg injuries, including a sprained ankle, in the process.

A local farmhand called David McLean found Hess still struggling to extricate himself from his harness. Meanwhile, some distance away, his crashed plane had burst into flames. Hess supplied the name Hauptmann Alfred Horn, an invention but not, it seems, without connotations: the initials chosen, 'AH', were those of the Führer and Albrecht Haushofer, the son of Hess's old mentor. Hess said that he had an important message for the Duke of Hamilton. The location that Hess may well have been aiming for was one of Hamilton's properties—the Duke's hunting lodge at Dungavel in South Lanarckshire, Scotland. Hess probably viewed the Duke (then a wing commander in the RAF) as a rebellious and influential advocate for peace. Hamilton had been a leading figure in an Anglo-German friendship society, but Hess evidently overestimated his influence and perhaps also mistook his views. If there had been prior communication and planning, something went amiss. Representatives of the local Home Guard, who soon arrived on the scene (brandishing an old gun) to relieve McLean, placed Hess under arrest.[11]

Hess's arrival occurred at a critical moment in the war: the survival of Britain as an independent power lay in the balance. British and Imperial troops had been mobilized around the globe, but in May 1941 the British army was still reeling from the evacuation at Dunkirk, under desperate circumstances, a year earlier; much valuable heavy equipment had been abandoned in France. Hitler held much of Europe in thrall. Rommel was in a dominant position in North Africa. Plans for the invasion of Russia—Operation Barbarossa—had reached an advanced stage of preparation. They would in fact be implemented the following month, leading of course, in the end, to disaster for the German army, as though Hitler was fated to emulate first the stunning territorial domination and then the ultimate strategic miscalculation of Napoleon Bonaparte.[12] On the night that Hess bailed out of his plane the British capital was suffering its latest horrors. The air-raids that afflicted London and other cities caused significant casualties, massive disruption and material damage, and huge fires that often raged out of control.[13]

The capture of the 'Deputy Führer' (as he was often, if not entirely accurately, described) became a major talking-point in wartime Britain.[14] For many, although not for Hess himself, the week of his arrival remained thereafter an indelible memory. One example can be found in the recollections of Norman Cohn. A British army officer at the time, Cohn was to become an important scholar of the medieval period, author of several extraordinary studies, including *The Pursuit of the Millennium* and *Europe's Inner Demons*; in the 1960s he was the director of a large-scale collaborative investigation into the history, culture, and psychology of anti-Semitism, Aryan mythology, racism, and genocide, under the auspices of the Columbus Trust, funded by the editor of the *Observer* newspaper David Astor. Cohn recalled the immediate aftermath of Hess's arrival in Britain and the strong personal impression that it made on him:

> If I were to write an autobiography that story would figure, because that's one of the most notable things that's ever happened to me. One often wonders, one must wonder, how this country, at a time when the whole of Europe was dominated...from Calais to Vladivostok...by two raving lunatics...and there was this little impoverished and ruined island...why we didn't capitulate...I was in Hull at the time as an infantry officer, and Hull was badly blitzed. My job with my platoon was to clear one road of the bricks [that] had fallen from an egg store....So I was stood there heroically saying 'men, do this and do that'. My sergeant arrived at the bottom and says "Ess is 'ere, Sir', as people did in those days. So I didn't understand this, "Ess is 'ere, Sir'. And eventually I did manage to find out that Hess had arrived and so I said, 'Well Sergeant, what do you make of that?'
>
> This was at a moment when...this country stood alone [and] when the shipping that brought food was being sunk at an enormous rate. Bletchley hadn't yet got on top of the U-boats, and it was one of the blackest periods of the war. So he said "e sees which way it's going, Sir'. If you want an encapsulated account of why we didn't capitulate or lose the war, there...that spirit...because people were really like that, whatever they might have thought higher up in the political scheme.[15]

The circumstances of Hess's departure were astonishing. Some, it is true, had already imagined an airborne visit from the Nazi leadership, but nobody could have foreseen that it would be Hess or how he would subsequently behave. Peter Fleming's fanciful tale *The Flying Visit* (1940) sought to provide light relief as Britain awaited possible invasion. Fleming presented an absurd Hitler who pilots a small plane across the sea from Germany, hoping to survey the land he will conquer; his plane is shot down, but just in time the Führer parachutes to safety, tramps the back-roads of Oxfordshire, hides out in the woods, and spies on the locals. He decides to present his unexpected arrival as part of a secret peace mission and makes contact with an

English aristocrat with whom he is already acquainted. Hitler eventually gives himself up to the British government, but the Cabinet are, in the end, so reluctant to hold him here as prisoner that they decide to dispatch him back to Germany, where he faces an uncertain fate.[16] Other aspects of the Hess story were also redolent of fiction: Charlie Chaplin, for example, had included the plot-line of a soldier whose memory is wiped out after the crash of his plane in his 1940 production *The Great Dictator*. The pilot finds himself hospitalized for years. But here the amnesiac is a Jewish soldier in the Great War, not the fugitive and—as it turned out—forgetful colleague of Adolf Hitler (or 'Adenoid Hynkel', as Chaplin renamed the German Chancellor). The patient in Chaplin's film wakes up, after years spent in a daze, to the horror of the Third Reich.

The saga of Hitler's notorious associate took a very different course from any previous make-believe, and led to a storm of conflicting interpretations. Historians have long debated Hess's motives for leaving Germany. They ask, for instance, how far his marginalization by Hitler may have affected him and to what extent he may have wished to restore his position by pulling off some unexpected diplomatic coup. Official secrecy and the mixed messages Hess subsequently gave enabled speculation to run riot.[17] Some have suggested that he had fallen out completely with the leader or, conversely, that he had tacit instructions to negotiate. No such evidence has come to light and this can now be regarded as a red herring.[18] The British authorities quickly reached the almost certainly correct conclusion that Hitler had been left in the dark.[19] Probably Hess had no authorization from any senior colleague (even if he did accurately reflect Hitler's desire to reach a settlement with Britain and concentrate his forces on the assault against the Soviet Union). Thus, if he was thinking it through he should perhaps have known that he risked becoming an outcast. That would assume his relative sanity before his flight and his ability to calculate such odds for himself. Alternatively, he may have been let down by intermediaries, inveigled by agents, or led to believe that he could broker a deal single-handed and return in triumph.

The phrases 'escape from freedom' or 'fear of freedom' (to cite again Fromm's seminal book of 1941, which appeared under those different titles, respectively in America and England) were ideally suited to describe the mentality of Hess during the inter-war years. He seemed to have surrendered all psychic autonomy to the external authority *par excellence*, Hitler. That is, he did so until his unlikely departure. But even then his blind allegiance to the German leader was not necessarily broken. Fromm warned that it was easy to underestimate people's unconscious craving for the extremes of masochistic submission to a tyrant—inside or outside the self. The willingness gladly to submit to the supreme authority was, arguably, hitherto Hess's most notable feature.

Hamilton was soon informed about 'Horn' and went to meet him. When they were brought together the prisoner acknowledged that he was Hess. Hamilton phoned London to alert the Prime Minister and Foreign Secretary. Some have read into Churchill's private secretary's response, 'Has somebody arrived?', the possibility that it was no surprise and the 'somebody' was code for Hess, but this appears a still more doubtful surmise than some of the other conspiracy theories.[20]

At subsequent meetings with British intelligence officers, government ministers, and diplomats Hess reviewed the history of Anglo-German relations and explained his wish to secure peace. The deal he vaguely proffered involved a free hand for the Nazi state in continental Europe, with Britain allowed to keep its Empire. He was intent on avoiding compromising Hitler's war aims against the Soviet Union. For Hess (and, so he argued, for Hitler) war with Britain was an unwarranted and depleting distraction when the real—shared—enemy was the Soviet Union. Hess alluded to Hitler's desire for friendly relations with Britain. Seen in that light, Hess was perhaps, even in his self-imposed exile, 'working toward the Führer' (to quote the phrase that, according to Ian Kershaw, became for so many Germans the required purpose of every public action).[21] Others have surmised that he may, wittingly or unwittingly, have been working away from the Führer, disenchanted, doubtful, disillusioned, lost. It has even been mooted that he may have vaguely hoped to return to Germany and resume his career.[22] In second-guessing Hess's precise thoughts and covert alliances, historical analysis largely cedes its place to guesswork and even make-believe. These were soon woven into the story. But as a guide to 'what really happened', the conspiracy literature regarding Hess's flight in 1941 can be given a wide berth. Moreover, it is of only peripheral significance for the present history: it was Hess's own accounts of British 'conspiracies', and the manner in which they were diagnosed, that will be the key considerations here.

Whatever Hess may have intended, the question of his underlying mental state was soon unavoidable. In any case, a diagnostic political language about Nazism was already in circulation; during the previous decade many observers had underscored the combined insanity *and* criminality of the Third Reich and, above all, of its presiding figure.[23] Hess (the oddest of emissaries) was seen by many to be Hitler's alter ego, and he was also a symbol of the rise and fall of the Nazi cause. Ironically, he too floated the idea that a pathological diagnosis of his actions might prove desirable. In a parting letter to Hitler he pointed out that, if so required (should his mission fail), he might be declared mad.[24] The initial reports that came in from German wireless (admitting Hess was missing) were vague, but they included the explanation that his action was indeed the result of his illness; mental disorder was given regularly by the Nazi state thereafter as the reason for Hess's flight.[25]

Between the night of the secret journey and the first official announcements a flurry of political and diplomatic activity had taken place in Germany and in Britain. It is said that Hitler first heard about the departure on 11 May, the morning after. It was Karl-Heinz Pintsch, one of Hess's adjutants, who brought these bad tidings to the Berghof. Hitler discovered the details when he opened the sealed letter that, shortly before flying off, Hess had handed to Pintsch with the express order that it be consigned personally to the leader. Hitler's furious response to Hess's flight has often been described: when he read the letter he went pale, before frantically shouting for Martin Bormann to attend him immediately. Bormann, Hess's private secretary, was already an important Party official and increasingly powerful figure behind the scenes; he would emerge as one of the beneficiaries of this crisis, garnering a number of new roles, including a position as Hitler's private secretary that would give him significant control over access to the leader. Pintsch, together with another adjutant, Alfred Leitgen, was placed in custody.[26]

Karl Haushofer, Willi Messerschmitt (the aircraft manufacturer and an associate of Hess, who, perhaps entirely unwittingly, provided the plane and facilities for the mission), and Frau Hess emerged relatively unscathed, but Haushofer's son Albrecht was detained for three months and Pintsch himself for three years, after which he served on the Eastern Front, only to become a prisoner of war in Russia.[27] A significant number of alternative healers, fortune-tellers, anthroposophists, Christian Scientists, clairvoyants, and graphologists—people that Goebbels referred to scathingly as 'Hess's darlings'—were rounded up and imprisoned soon afterwards.[28] This clampdown on such fringe practices seems to have had various causes, although at least in some part it was linked to the (not entirely implausible) view that occult ideas had influenced Hess's decision to leave.

Hess's political duties were swiftly reallocated, mostly to Bormann. The Foreign Minister, Ribbentrop, was dispatched to Rome to reassure Mussolini that there was no secret peace-deal under negotiation.[29] Hess was disowned by the German leadership, although later Hitler intimated how much he had felt the loss of this singular companion 'who has flown away from me'.[30] At other times he talked of having him shot. In 1944 Hitler ruminated that he had no appropriate successor, for the potential candidates had gone mad (Hess), thrown away the attachment of the people (Göring), or suffered from a lack of personal 'artistry' and party support (Himmler).[31] Nonetheless Hitler identified Hess, alongside the engineer Fritz Todt (who was the supervisor, among other things, of the Autobahn building programme of the 1930s, and who died under mysterious circumstances in an air-crash in February 1942), as someone that he particularly missed.[32]

The initial delay in German radio broadcasts reflected confusion about Hess's motives and how to limit the public-relations damage, and even uncertainty as to whether he had survived. When the disappearance was eventually announced, on 13 May, mention was made of a letter that had disclosed 'in its confusion unfortunately the traces of mental derangement'.[33] This version of the story was picked up in the House of Commons. Hansard reported an ironic question from the MP John 'Jack' Lawson (Labour) to the PM that same day: 'In view of the German propaganda statement over the wireless that this gentleman was suffering from mental instability, has the Prime Minister any information to give us on this matter, or is that particular disease limited to the Chief of the German propagandists?' To which Churchill simply replied that he would be making a statement later.[34] In private, politicians and diplomats were speculating feverishly about the visit. 'Immense excitement' over Hess's arrival, noted the British diplomat and secret agent Sir Robert Bruce Lockhart in his diary that same day, as he tried to guess whether the German had come to escape the wrath of the Gestapo or to sue for peace.[35]

Although not the first to be consulted, Goebbels had soon been summoned by Hitler. Reflecting on the unexpected development, he confided to his diary that the Führer was 'shattered'. Goebbels was horrified that Hess's madness should be paraded before the public: 'What a sight for the world's eyes: the Führer's deputy a mentally disturbed man. Dreadful and unthinkable.' Goebbels immediately had shots of Hess removed from the latest newsreels. By 14 May he was describing the case as 'tragi-comedy'; for 'one doesn't know whether to laugh or cry'. It was impossible, he declared,

to have anticipated such an affair: 'One can never be prepared for the aber-
rations of a lunatic.'[36] Hess's failure to anticipate that Churchill might have
him arrested struck Goebbels as the most absurd schoolboy idiocy, and he
decried the Deputy as a 'shambles'.[37]

The German propaganda chief feared that damage to the nation's morale
would ensue, and during the following days endeavoured to monitor closely the
impact of the news on the population. A stream of rumours and complaints, in the
wake of the flight, did indeed bring questions of high-level corruption and eva-
sion of responsibility back to the fore. 'It's like an awful dream,' wrote Goebbels:
'The Party will have to chew on it for a long time.' He reassured himself with the
thought that nobody can really see into the depths of another soul and predict
human behaviour.[38] In fact, before long Goebbels was noting his relief that public
interest in the affair appeared to be dwindling, and marvelled that the British did
not make more of the propaganda opportunity.[39] Hitler and the Party's preliminary response to the crisis struck him as unfortunate: he would have preferred
official pronouncements to have emphasized his errant colleague's weakness and
loss of nerve; to admit that an idiot or madman had remained so high and mighty
in the regime might well, he suspected, prove harmful to the cause.[40]

On the other hand, tales of Hess's insanity could be linked to earlier
known stories of his eccentricities, introspection, and general restless penchant for each new passing health-fad: he was renowned for his consultations
with astrologers, herbal specialists, dietitians, chiropractors, and irido–diagnosticians. It was easy enough to assemble evidence of his hypochondria.
Such preferences hardly marked Hess out, given all the other unorthodox
health predilections of the Nazi elite (starting with Hitler and Himmler).
However, a picture of this man's anxiety, obsessionality, and even psychosis
was to be drawn by the Party in terms that might help explain his recent,
monstrous abberation.

Hess may well have been encouraged in his mission by Karl Haushofer
and his son Albrecht, who was later executed on account of his connections
with the plot against Hitler of 20 July 1944. That Haushofer (junior) was a
direct intermediary in the Deputy's flight is indeed quite possible; he had
already sought to make contact with Hamilton before the Hess affair, but
apparently had not received replies to his letters.[41] The Haushofers had presumably believed they were furthering the interests of the German state in
endeavouring to ensure there would be peace with Great Britain whilst the
real ideological battle with Bolshevism was pursued.[42]

———•———

On 11 May 1941, the day after his arrival, Hess was admitted to the Drymen Military Hospital at Buchanan Castle in Stirlingshire; for the duration of the war, the Castle had been requisitioned on behalf of this medical facility. The next day an army doctor, Lt.-Col. J. Gibson Graham, visited Hess. The medical staff dealt with the immediate injuries that were incurred when the pilot had baled out of his plane. It was confirmed that he had a chip fracture of his back and an ankle injury. Hess was required to produce samples of urine; blood was taken, and X-rays and other tests arranged. That same day the Duke of Hamilton flew south to meet the Prime Minister at Ditchley Park, the stately home in Oxfordshire where Churchill was spending the weekend. It is said that the Duke arrived to find him engaged in a dinner party at which the hosts had arranged for a recently released film, *The Marx Brothers Go West*, to be screened. As Hamilton came into the dining-room Churchill is supposed to have exclaimed: 'Now, come and tell us this funny story of yours.' The PM insisted, however, that a full verbal report be postponed until after midnight. For 'Hess or no Hess,' Churchill apparently announced, 'I am going to see the Marx Brothers'.[43] Churchill's own version was slightly different, however, and certainly less serene. The PM described leaving the film twice to enquire about bomb damage that evening in London (he had heard it was bad). He welcomed the diversion of the film, but learning, on the Duke's arrival, the identity of the German prisoner, Churchill declared: 'Hess in Scotland!' He added: 'I thought this was fantastic. The report however was true.'[44] Establishing its truth, however, took some time. The British had to identify their man, find out why he had come, who he intended to meet, whether he was under orders or had seized the initiative alone, and finally whether he had indeed gone mad.

The British PM played no direct part in the interviews with the prisoner. Nonetheless, in one joke that apparently did the rounds in Germany, Churchill was said to have asked Hess directly: 'So you're the madman are you?' 'Oh no,' Hess replied, 'only his Deputy.'[45] An air of surreal comedy and quips about madness also peppered British responses. Black humour perhaps relieved tension; the surrounding military circumstances, with London and other cities pounded by the Blitz, and German power across Europe at its zenith, were grim.

By 12 May arrangements were in place for a German-speaking diplomat, Ivone Kirkpatrick, then based in London, to investigate what he believed, on first hearing, to be the 'cock and bull' story that a prominent colleague of the Führer had arrived in Scotland.[46] Kirkpatrick was an obvious choice, having seen Hess at close quarters in the not too distant past, although one colleague at least felt him the wrong man for the job, because 'he has no knowledge or understanding of psychology.'[47] This suggests how the question of Hess's mental state and its deciphering preoccupied some British officials from the start. In his memoirs, written years later, Kirkpatrick presented the story with his own psychological observations on the case; he referred to Hess's 'monomania' in seeking peace, as well as his strong streak of fanaticism and propensity to grievance and sulking.[48] Whatever his psychological acumen in 1941, Kirkpatrick had the necessary diplomatic background, language skills and extensive knowledge of the Nazi leadership, derived from a long stint at the British Embassy in Berlin during the 1930s.

Kirkpatrick went north, accompanied by the Duke. They were required to meet the prisoner and Kirkpatrick was also asked to submit a report on the matter to key members of the Cabinet, first of all in order to settle the question as to whether the captured pilot might be a German plant or (alternatively) a crank and impostor. A night flight from Hendon Aerodrome brought the men within reach of Buchanan Castle, near Loch Lomond, sometime after midnight. There they encountered the detained man, dressed in grey flannel pyjamas, temporarily placed in the servants' quarters, and, at this time, fast asleep on an iron bedstead covered with a brown army blanket. Newspaper was wrapped around the white enamel shade of the ceiling bulb in order to reduce the unpleasant glare.[49] Kirkpatrick soon confirmed that the visitor was Hess. His report, according to Churchill's biographer Martin Gilbert, was sent only to the Prime Minister, Attlee, Eden, and Beaverbrook, although doubtless the head of MI6, colloquially known as 'C', had it too.[50] Churchill declared in the House of Commons on 13 May that the episode was 'one of these cases where imagination is sometimes baffled by the facts as they presented themselves'.[51]

Among the several baffling aspects of the affair was why Hess had chosen Hamilton. One school of thought suggests that Hess believed, or was perhaps induced by secret-service machinations to imagine, that the Duke was ready to lead a plot against Churchill; elements within the British secret services may have played him along, or, as is often said, intercepted and manipulated various letters between the two.[52] The role of the Scottish aristocrat appeared murky, with speculation that he may have been a double or triple agent a continuing feature of discussion. Rumours of Hamilton's complicity were circulated—and scotched—within days of Hess's capture. John Colville,

Churchill's private secretary, recorded in his diary on 13 May 1941: 'The poor Duke of Hamilton feels acutely the slur of being taken for a potential Quisling—which he certainly is not.'[53] The Duke, who had travelled back to Scotland with Kirkpatrick, appeared to become increasingly riled by talk of his supposed collusion with the Nazi visitor.

One thing Hess and Hamilton did have in common was a passion for aviation. After Eton and Oxford, Hamilton had become a flying-ace and was renowned for his participation in a British team's successful first flight over Everest in 1933. Hess too was a keen pilot and admired such exploits. Further afield, the achievement of Charles Lindbergh—charismatic pioneer of trans-Atlantic flight and a noted sympathizer with the cause of European fascism—spurred Hess to envisage undertaking the same journey, but in the opposite direction. It is said that he sought funding for the attempt from Henry Ford—another fascist sympathizer—after Lindbergh's flight in 1927, but was turned down.[54]

When Hess was brought south from Scotland it was not for an audience at the Palace or discreet discussions with dissident grandees perhaps capable of unseating Churchill. Rather, the disconsolate Hess was taken by train to London on 16 May 1941, then bundled unceremoniously into an unmarked ambulance under heavy guard and moved to the Tower of London, where he was incarcerated for a few days before being relocated, again via an ambulance, through South London to Mytchett Place, a Victorian country house in Surrey. 'C' orchestrated these various arrangements in the strictest secrecy. Hess's prison residence was to be referred to by the code-name 'Camp Z'. Even within the confines of the house and grounds Hess was 'J', 'Jay', or 'Jonathan'. His interrogators were also referred to in code; Kirkpatrick, for instance, was 'Dr Mackenzie'.[55]

Specially arranged earthworks, gun emplacements, barbed wire, and floodlighting were designed to deter intruders. Soldiers patrolled the grounds; regular drills were arranged, sometimes to the sound (vexatious to Hess) of bagpipes and drums.[56] Intelligence personnel supervised Hess's day-to-day care and meetings. These officers included Colonel Thomas Kendrick (listed, apparently, as Colonel Wallace in records), an unidentified officer with the cover-name of Captain Barnes, and Major Frank Foley.[57] For a time Hess clearly was regarded as a useful source of military information. Enough was gleaned for Churchill to be able to suggest, on 5 July 1941, that intelligence estimates of German submarine building 'tallies with Hess's talk'.[58]

Was Mytchett Place secretly wired for sound? Although many of the original papers and presumably transcripts associated with the Hess affair have yet to be released into the public domain or perhaps were destroyed, it does seem that Hess was 'bugged', judging, for example, by one account of a meeting in 1943 between a high-level Soviet delegation and two members of the British Cabinet, Anthony Eden and Herbert Morrison. The Russians asked to see transcripts of conversations with Hess from 1941; Eden agreed on the condition that these were not published, since Hess must not get wind of the fact that he was being monitored.[59]

There has been considerable recent discussion of these hitherto elusive Hess transcripts, and ingenious sleuthing has been undertaken to discover at least some of the details from ancillary sources.[60] In the case of some other German prisoners secret recordings undoubtedly were made. The most famous instance occurred after the capture of a group of eminent German scientists, including Otto Hahn and Werner Heisenberg. They were confined in a house in Cambridgeshire, and both the property and the surrounding grounds were planted with hidden microphones.[61] German generals were also extensively monitored.[62] It is entirely probable, therefore, that the main interviews with Hess were indeed systematically recorded and then secretly preserved, and that his views were closely analysed at the time for clues as to Nazi intentions, at least in the early months of his captivity, even if, increasingly, it was the German's inadvertent, or unconscious, communications that preoccupied the medical staff.

Various secret meetings were arranged at which high-ranking government officials sought to assess Hess for themselves. Thus, a month after his arrival in Britain he met with the veteran politician Viscount Simon. John Allsebrook Simon, who had become a Liberal MP in 1906, was later offered a peerage and served in several important roles in British governments of the 1930s. He became prominently associated with Chamberlain's 'appeasement' policy, and partly as a consequence was not asked to serve in Churchill's war Cabinet, even though he held the senior government position of Lord Chancellor. Accompanied by Ivone Kirkpatrick, Simon met the prisoner. Hess had asked for a German witness to attend as well, so he was flanked by a somewhat bemused former consular official who had been brought to the meeting from a British internment camp.[63] Presented as negotiators, Simon and Kirkpatrick actually sought to gather as much information about German military and political plans as they could, whilst making no concessions to the prisoner. Hess stressed his humanitarian motives in flying out of Germany in the first place and declared himself pained by all the unnecessary suffering caused by the continuing hostilities. He also let it be known that he and his Nazi colleagues regarded the British position as hopeless.[64] It has been suggested that Hess may have sought to compare his mission to Chamberlain's flight to Munich in 1938, or Göring's proposal to fly to London in 1939.[65] Simon had introduced himself as an intermediary and stressed that he was there to listen: 'Herr Hess will, of course, understand that if I do not contradict or challenge what he says about the war it is not because I agree, but because the real purpose why I have come is to hear from him about his mission.'[66] The listener was not there to bargain, even if Hess may have imagined he was. As Sir Robert Bruce Lockhart declared of the Lord Chancellor's role: 'We are to have a pseudo-negotiator, Lord Simon.' When the idea of sending Viscount Simon was mooted, he added mysteriously, 'Winston roared with laughter—"the very man".'[67] Presumably Churchill referred here wryly to the Lord Chancellor's previously emollient attitude towards Germany's 'case', and thus thought his presence might add to the illusion of negotia-tion. On 14 June 1941 Churchill referred in parliament to Lord Simon's conversation with Hess, but instantly dismissed the offers made by the German as the outpourings of a disordered mind.

When the PM had first informed Roosevelt about Hess's arrival, how-ever, he did not suggest that the German was suffering from a psychiatric disorder. He took the opportunity instead to let the President know that Hess had made 'disparaging remarks about your country'.[68] The story of what happened, and who said what to whom in these early weeks and months, is rather murky and confusing; many mixed signals were given out, whether by design or otherwise. Initial British ambiguity about what they were doing with Hess was explained to Roosevelt as an attempt to keep the enemy guessing. By holding Hess in the shadows, perhaps the intention was indeed to maintain uncertainty among German or Italian officials regarding British thinking; but the paucity and blur of information in the early days also owed as much, if not more, to uncertainty and debate, as to some instantly conceived master plan by the British government designed to sow maximum confusion.[69] Whatever British deliberations may have been regarding the exploitation of the Hess story in propaganda operations against the Axis powers, in America Churchill's key task was to scotch the idea that a peace deal was actually being struck secretly with Germany. The British Consul-General in New York, Gerald Campbell, reported that the most serious consequence of the affair thus far was the 'introduction into the minds of some industrialists [in the United States] of doubts as to the advisability of vast plant expansion lest this rumoured peace negotiation should prove a reality'.[70] Meanwhile Stalin remained acutely suspicious of Britain's covert intentions.[71] In other words, Churchill played a complicated hand in the first couple of months of Hess's stay. Despite increased cooperation between the OSS and British intelligence, the White House apparently remained unconvinced that it was being given the full story.

Although Mytchett Place was, according to some, a 'dingy mansion', efforts were made to ensure conditions of 'dignified comfort'.[72] This was as much, if not more (it was claimed later), for the benefit of the officers who were to spend their existence here as for the prisoner.[73] The material conditions were, by all reports (save those of Hess himself), quite soft. Sofas, a few antique pieces, and paintings drawn from Ministry of Works stores were even brought in to decorate Mytchett Place.[74] Hess was well fed and was allowed to receive some books, including works by Goethe and other German writers. When a consignment including Schiller and Schopenhauer failed to materialize, however, Hess apparently thought that the sender had been put into some kind of 'abnormal' state in order to prevent him from delivering the material.[75] The relatively comfortable conditions were intended to ensure that no propaganda ammunition be given to the enemy regarding British maltreatment of the prisoner; it was also feared that any act of self-harm or suicide by Hess would lead to a publicity field-day in Germany.

Notwithstanding such efforts, the prison remained a creepy and forbidding location; security was paramount, with measures frequently reviewed to ensure no attempt would succeed should a German plot be hatched to capture the prisoner, enable his escape, or assassinate him. Hess's subsequent removal to a hospital in Wales may have reflected further security fears, although cost and convenience are more probable explanations. The aim throughout the war years was to keep Hess out of harm's way, preventing escape, murder, or simply prying eyes.[76] One doctor wondered how far the dismal, if gilded, setting at Mytchett Place contributed to Hess's paranoid reactions.[77] His guards were instructed not to speak about the inmate outside the prison, although some sporadic news reports did filter through.

———•———

In the opening remarks of the *The Case of Rudolf Hess*, the book by his physicians that was published in 1947, the prisoner/patient is described as 'an interesting diagnostic problem'. This study suggested that the analysis of an individual could pay dividends in understanding Nazi fanaticism at large.[78] The idea that this prisoner constituted a particular psychiatric puzzle was signalled in the subtitle: *A Problem in Diagnosis and Forensic Psychiatry*. This publication contained reports from the various Allied physicians who treated Hess between 1941 and 1946. It combined much medical and psychiatric language, and juxtaposed measurements of the body, medical and family history, reference to hereditary taints, degeneration, and so forth with the findings of contemporary psychological testing (IQ, for instance) and a more probing quasi-psychoanalytic interest in the prisoner's internal world.

Apparently of his own will, Hess wrote a supportive preface to this psychiatric account that covered his treatment in Britain and later at the Nuremberg trial, as though again inviting an assessment of his delusions, or at least, as he implied, an analysis of the hypnotic suggestibility of men such as himself.[79] Edited by Brigadier John Rawlings Rees, *The Case of Rudolf Hess* was a compilation of the treatments of, theories about, and close observations of the prisoner since his arrival. Rees, a colleague and friend of Dicks since the 1930s, was the medical director of the Tavistock Clinic. After the war he became president of the World Federation for Mental Health. As the most senior psychiatrist in the British army, he played a role in overseeing Hess's case and reported clinical developments to higher authorities.[80]

Earlier in his life Hess had been caught up (as *The Case* put it) in 'the swirling political currents of his country'; with his cramped, tormented body, dread of mesmerism, and interminable suspicion of poisoning, he was battling, it was claimed, with a host of persecutory figures. Hess feared both that he himself might be subliminally or medically manipulated, and that those who cared for him might fall into strange states of automatism. Such fears were evidence, the doctors argued, of Hess's paranoia. But no discrete diagnostic view of Hess lasted for long without some amendment. He was conceptualized variously, or in combination, as obsessional, hysterical, paranoid, and schizoid; a malingerer, manipulator, and fantasist; highly neurotic; dissociated and confused; perverse and phobic.[81] Terms such as 'inferiority complex' (associated with Freud's one-time follower and later critic Alfred Adler) and 'neurotic alibi' were used. The latter phrase implied that Hess made unconscious use of his own illness as a kind of smokescreen to evade insight; there were advantages to his befuddled state, and the escape into make-believe explanations of the situation in which he found himself was one way, so it was thought, to avoid awareness of shame and/or guilt. The report suggested how Hess's agitated and restless behaviour enabled him to 'resist' any suggested remedy to his troubles: the symptoms protected him, in short, from painful truths about himself and his cause.[82] The report also insisted, more prosaically, that he showed childish pique and was selfish, aggressive, lifeless, and empty. Was he a law unto himself? Some said yes and declared him a most idiosyncratic case. Others disagreed and considered him an emblematic psychopathic personality type.[83]

Signs of mental disturbance in his family were noted in the clinical reports: one of Hess's mother's brothers had committed suicide, and a paternal aunt had apparently lived and died in an asylum. Hess seemed to take the view that alcoholism had contributed to his aunt's unhappiness and decline.[84] The British doctors tabulated known medical facts about the patient, including gall-bladder and renal problems, colitis, and heart pains. He was tested (negative) for syphilis.[85] The minutiae of his fads and feelings were listed. Although he accepted wine on occasion, he generally drank little and did not smoke. The prisoner, it was shown, increasingly dreaded infiltration by toxins, disapproved of unhealthy ingredients or stimulants, and watched his diet carefully. He avoided eggs and caffeine whenever possible. This may have been part of Hess's own private system of belief, but it also needs to be understood in the context of the alternative health fads, anti-smoking and anti-pesticide campaigns, vegetarianism, and other particular dietary habits to promote health and fitness that were commonplace in Nazi Germany. These came in turn to be linked to medical and scientific beliefs about resistance to cancer in individuals, and the dream of a purified body politic, an Aryan 'racial utopia' free of all taint.[86]

After landing in Scotland Hess was found to be carrying a mini-pharmacy of medicines and alternative remedies, including that curious Tibetan elixir, homeopathic and nature-cure treatments, vitamins, glucose, and sedatives.[87] During his imprisonment Hess complained regularly that he was racked by aches, pains, and assorted discontents from which he could get no relief and for which there was no demonstrable organic cause. Many other people used such treatments or complained of similar ailments, but this evidence became part of the wartime scientific discussion of Hess and his particular psychosomatic symptoms. The medical orderlies rarely made an entry in the case notes that did not contain further disclosures about his cramps, upset stomachs, constipation, headaches, or insomnia.[88] Hess's endeavours to self-medicate also featured in such bulletins. Some of the doctors concluded that Freud's account of hysteria was rather more relevant to the case than medical treatment of the body.

Psychoanalytic theory suggested that in hysteria the body spoke what the mind unconsciously thought. Thus, one could see how forbidden desires, linked to an underlying bisexuality for example, might be repressed and yet be represented through discernible 'symptomatic' actions. Through the analysis of gestures, jokes, slips of the tongue, and dreams (or rather, in the course of treatment, the free associations that emanated from subjects' responses to their dreams) some trace of the contents and process of the unconscious could be inferred. In this way the observer could gain some inkling of that other space of the mind. Unwitting bodily actions and pre-occupations also offered clues. Freud described, for example, a hysterical woman patient whose physical gestures dramatized an unconsciously imagined sexual scene. Her hands were constantly busy with her garment; this appeared to him to gesture at a 'primal scene' (the fantasized intercourse of the parents) about which, consciously, she knew nothing. The one hand, he thought, signified the woman in the scene (holding her clothes on) while the other hand (representing the man) was busy tugging the clothes away. The patient was in both places at once, playing the different parts in her identification. Freud argued that her body was used to enact the fantasy of the man and woman in a sexual relationship; in the unconscious this patient was flooded with thoughts of that scene, whilst at the same time consciously she remained ignorant of the thoughts and oblivious of the possible significance of her gestured actions.[89]

Hess's presumed masculine and feminine identifications, or more particularly his putative homosexual preoccupation with Hitler, were seen as the actively repressed desires that lodged in his unconscious. His diverse identifications were said to be glimpsed, for instance, in his masquerade of super-manliness. Here in temporary lodgings in England, as later at the Nuremberg trial, observers complained of how he adopted a flamboyant goose-stepping gait when permitted to exercise.[90] Yet it also appeared that he was in a state of confusion—unsure of who he was and how he wanted to relate to others—although he remained, somehow, passionate in associating himself with Hitler's troops. It was noted that he was capable of being kind to subordinates before his flight, but had also demonstrated often enough his ruthlessness. Perhaps, for example, he was loyal to Hitler even as he abandoned him, both a true Nazi and a treacherous subordinate.[91] The unconscious was capable of housing such contradictions.

Some of those who scrutinized and wrote of Hess seemed as much concerned with the prisoner's perceptions of his history as with the past itself, as interested in what he made of his confinement, here and now, as they were curious about his family, schooling, and war record. Doctors took notes of how their patient treated people around him, and what kind of attitudes he developed, unconsciously, toward his carers and the group at large. It was remarked that on some occasions Hess embodied a martyr-like posture, luxuriating in a state of masochistic surrender to his fate. This appeared to satisfy some internal need. Moreover, Hess's behaviour could provoke frustration or perplexity in the guards and doctors. It was thought that Hess might have gained some secret gratification from such reactions. His moods and attitudes were not stable, and the doctors were often kept guessing (in some instances to Hess's evident amusement) as to what kind of patient they might find before them.

The Case of Rudolf Hess was cleared surprisingly swiftly by the Foreign Office for public release. The work was designed to show, as the introduction put it, how men such as Hess and Hitler, when joined in a cabal, could unleash catastrophic consequences. It was intended to provide a clinical account that might also serve as a political warning for the future in the light of what was perceived as the still very present threat of Nazi resurgence. It was not simply published as data for the annals of psychiatry. As we have seen, Hess added his own prefatory letter justifying the publication on the grounds that it showed the role of fascination and hypnosis (this document is reproduced as Appendix 3 below). His letter refers to his loss of capacity, even the elimination of his will.[92]

In the course of the early months of Hess's confinement diplomatic and intelligence concerns blurred with, or sometimes entirely gave way to, medical and psychiatric investigation. Psychiatric discourse also sometimes shaded into a psychoanalytic mode of inquiry. Rather than being merely eccentric, repugnant, and/or evil, the psychiatrists showed the myriad ways in which Hess might be termed *ill*. His marked suspiciousness, for instance, was said to have tipped over into paranoid delusions. On various occasions he was seen putting together mysterious sheaves of papers and assorted packages, sometimes wrapped elaborately in tissue-paper, scribbling notes densely across the page in every direction, and hiding odd pieces of paper around his room and under a couch.[93]

That these gestures were signs of the subject's mental disturbance, or indeed deterioration, is certainly plausible. Perhaps his flight was an indication of his developing madness. Others would see his fanatical love for Hitler as the real mental illness. Some accounts of his furtive actions have referred rather to his not unreasonable expectation of being bugged, if not drugged, in Britain, and have noted his grounds for dismay as his 'negotiations' were rebuffed. The different possibilities, of course, are not necessarily mutually exclusive. Hess's sense of disgruntlement in the early period of his exile was no doubt exacerbated by the authorities' frustrating refusal to sanction further private meetings with the Duke of Hamilton.[94]

A commentary produced for the Medical Research Council at the end of May 1941 suggested that Hess's medicine cabinet might have a quasi-magical status, designed to ward off 'all assault of the devil as far as his flesh was concerned',[95] and this reflected an interest in the unconscious symbolic dimension of Hess's thought and behaviour that only grew as contact with him increased. It dawned soon enough on his doctors that his anxieties could never be assuaged by realistic reassurance, and for every 'good' physician or benign guard there were always others that he considered hell-bent on his destruction. Taking tea outdoors on one of the excursions that were arranged for him during the later years of his captivity in Britain, Hess was observed diligently rescuing some wasps trapped in a honey-jar then putting them in the sun to dry out their wings. Such an incident was felt to be interesting as a marker of unconscious attitudes; the implication was presumably that Hess had projected something of himself into the wasps (the vulnerable state and the capacity to sting, the predicament of creatures stuck in the jar, perhaps). It was as though they symbolized his own plight.

The Deputy Führer's reactions to the conduct of the war were also recorded. Hearing on 28 May 1941 of the sinking of the battleship *Bismarck* the day before, he apparently looked anxious and sick, and requested to be allowed to dine with his captors that night. After dinner (surprisingly, given his usual habits) he asked for a whisky.[96] Apart from such anxieties, Hess continued to grumble about the way he was treated, detailing the cruel way in which his rest was interrupted by the din of clicking heels on uncarpeted stairs, motorcycle engines, buzzing planes, drilling soldiers, or the inconsiderately loud opening and shutting of doors.[97] Much of the noise was clearly real, but the doctors regarded Hess's beliefs about the malicious motivations of those who produced the noise as symptoms of his agitated and deteriorating condition.

In one sense, of course, the mystery of Hess's identity had been quickly cleared up. Nobody was in much doubt after Kirkpatrick's first visit that the man who had presented himself as 'Alfred Horn' in May 1941 was Hess, the genuine article. In another sense, however, the enigma only deepened. The psychiatrists sought to make meanings out of his muddled gestures, confused signals, and obsessive preoccupations with his health. In the last week of May 1941, with the medical and psychiatric aspects of the matter ever more to the fore, Brigadier Rees and his colleagues agreed that Major Dicks should take on the treatment of Hess at Mytchett Place.

4

Getting Through to Hess

In his history of the Tavistock Clinic, Henry Dicks makes only passing reference to the 'extraordinary and secret duty' he performed in the war: the care of Rudolf Hess.[1] As a member of the German prisoner's medical team, Dicks would become, as he also put it, 'a participant in the inner history of world events'.[2] What kind of participant was he? What did he actually make of Hess, and what did the patient make of him? It was perhaps increasingly plain within weeks of the Nazi's arrival in 1941 that his plans for negotiation with the British had gone up in flames. Hess was finished as any kind of political force. Yet, as his diplomatic significance waned his psychological significance increased. His conduct interested and sometimes confounded his doctors; none more so than Dicks, who met the prisoner regularly at Mytchett Place and later, during inspection visits to Hess's second prison, at Maindiff Court in Wales.

Dicks's clinical records, which he retained and left upon his death with his family, offer intriguing glimpses of his contacts with Hess.[3] Indeed, between 1941 and 1944 this army doctor emerged as a central psychiatric figure in the care of the patient/prisoner. Dicks was an assiduous interpreter of German psycho-political attitudes, and it was he who (for reasons described below) would eventually oversee Hess's treatment with 'truth drugs'. The relationship of the two men is intriguing and merits scrutiny here. Moreover, the records of their encounters reveal a number of competing theories about the Nazi's mind that circulated at the time.

There had in fact been an indirect connection between the families of Dicks and Hess long before their meeting. Charles Dicks (one of Henry's older brothers) had married Alice Evald, a French Catholic, whose family had been based in Lausanne. She grew up, however, in Alexandria, where her father was the head of a French school and where Fritz and Klara Hess were near neighbours; Alice became acquainted in this way with their son Rudolf and his siblings. Henry Dicks was no doubt aware of his sister-in-law's slight association with the increasingly high-profile Nazi official during Charles and his wife's visits to London in the 1920s and 1930s.[4]

There is no evidence that Hess himself was informed about this coincidence or any other details of Dicks's family and background, although of course he knew that the English doctor spoke fluent German.[5] Hess expressed suspicions about his doctors in more general terms; he let it be known, for example, that he believed 'the Jews' had infiltrated some of his British captors' minds (including, notably, that of Dicks). He also believed that the Jews had contaminated the minds of some Nazis. Dicks' psychoanalytical interpretation of Hess's defensive manoeuvres did not convince his patient any more than the Nazi persuaded the doctor that Jewish mesmerism was to blame. 'Dr Dix' (*sic*), Hess complained, 'told me that my mental fixations were a consequence of bad conscience about the treatment of Jews, for which I was responsible—I replied that it had not been one of my duties to decide the treatment of Jews. However, if this had been the case, I would have done everything to protect my people from these criminals and I wouldn't have had a bad conscience about it.'[6]

Dicks offered certain interpretations to Hess about his guilt and the defences he employed against any feeling of responsibility. He also sought to probe the nature and meaning of the prisoner's anti-Semitism. But Hess insisted that the fate of the Jews was brought upon them by their own malign qualities. He appears to have believed that where harm was actually done to the Jews, this could be explained by the fact that they had hypnotized gentile Germans into maltreating them. Even when confronted with direct information about the Nazi concentration camps, Hess claimed that the guards must have been subliminally influenced in order for them to act so inhumanely. Dicks suggested to Hess that his theories of nefarious Jewish influence were an effort at rationalizing and thus avoiding the guilt he felt. Hess denied this, maintaining that if the Nazis had done terrible things, it was the Jews who were to blame.[7] There was no clearer example than this of the clashing explanatory systems through which the doctor and his recalcitrant patient tried to make sense of contemporary history and of the immediate discussions taking place between them.

At one stage Hess came to the view that the secret poisoning he was suffering in Britain might be orchestrated by a German Jewish immigrant acting for international Jewry.[8] If in this way he exonerated some of the British (such as the Duke of Hamilton) for his suffering, he was also said to have wondered if the Jews had driven the gaolers to the point of insanity.[9] Judging by the clinical records, Hess had his own very particular ideas about the nature of his captivity. It was a theory of unconscious influence of sorts, but conceived in terms of nefarious hypnotic rapport, or even perhaps by the lights of that earlier Viennese healer (a full century before Freud), the 'animal magnetist' Franz-Anton Mesmer.[10]

Where Nazism had always been, for Hess as for his political superior, a living demonstration of the power of the will, he came to insist to his doctors that he personally had no volition of his own; it had been eliminated without his being conscious of it by the dark arts of others. So subtle and pervasive was the poisoning and magnetizing effect of the Jews, Hess maintained, that it actually might explain not just his pains but also his occasional (false) sense of well-being.[11] Bursts of energy after eating, followed by 'sudden subjective exhaustion', only showed that the poison and influences he was imbibing were devilish in their subtlety. One of those poisoners, in Hess's eyes, was Dicks.

Dicks and some of the other army doctors took careful note of this 'paranoid' tendency in the patient. The study of anti-Jewish hatred and fear was nothing new, of course, and even a cursory glance at the subject catalogue of the British Library or the Library of Congress reveals the steady stream of new English-language publications on this issue in the 1930s and 1940s; some were sponsored by the American Jewish Committee, and explored the insidious emotional appeal of anti-Semitism in the modern age and in earlier periods of history.[12]

A number of the key doctors and psychologists who worked on the question of the Nazi mind and who contributed to the task of 'denazification' in the 1940s were in fact Jewish. How far this had an impact on their work, or at least their experience of their work, is generally not stated in the memoirs of these medical men and 'psy' experts; whether their interviewees guessed or were sometimes informed that they were Jewish is also mostly unclear. Gustave Gilbert, the Jewish American army psychologist who interviewed prisoners of war at the Nuremberg trial provides a case in point. When he appeared as a witness at the trial of Adolf Eichmann in 1961, Gilbert was asked about the significance of this factor in his interviews with Nazis at the International Military Tribunal at Nuremberg in 1945–6. Had the war criminals known that he was Jewish? He replied that at first they had not, but that he had sought eventually to enlighten them. He said that he had wanted to see whether they could tell he was Jewish, for 'according to the Nazi ideology ... you could always tell "these despicable Jews". Not a single one could.' One of the accused men, Julius Streicher (whose infamous past included his position for some years as Gauleiter of Franconia and his creation and editorship of the vicious anti-Semitic paper *Der Stürmer*) revealed to Gilbert that he believed (erroneously) that some of the judges were Jews. Gilbert then 'let it be known that I was Jewish and they, in turn, did not seem to react to this, beyond making it clear that they never had anything against Jews personally, that this was all silly ideological nonsense, and that some of their best friends had been Jews'. When questioned as to whether this revelation of his Jewish identity had any effect on his subsequent talks with the prisoners, Gilbert replied:

> There was not really much, except in the case of Streicher and Rosenberg [one of the key Nazi ideologues], who seemed to be a little nervous about it, but they reacted in rather strange way: Streicher, for instance, decided that, since the Jews were fighting courageously to make a homeland in Palestine, he wanted to 'lead' them, because he admired their courage. Outside of such nonsense, there was really no appreciable effect. I behaved absolutely correctly—they appreciated it, and the study went on in a perfectly dignified professional manner.[13]

Through his sudden changes of mood, insouciant manner, clamorous complaints, and fears Hess kept his wartime guards and doctors guessing as to his next move. He might insist on dining alone when invited to join the officers, then urgently request company when he felt isolated. If he feared that a 'clique of war-mongers' (who had hidden him in his present surroundings) was trying to drive him to suicide, he also seemed on occasion to will his own death, perhaps even attempting to kill himself in the second month of his custody, not long after Dicks had taken on the case. The episode occurred in the middle of the night, when the doctor was called to Hess's rooms to provide the insomniac patient with a sleeping draught. In Dicks's report of 15 June 1941 the sequence of events was described as follows. A guard had stood back outside Hess's bedroom door to let Dicks enter, when Hess emerged suddenly from the shadows, in his full air-force uniform and flying boots, and dashed towards them. Dicks noticed a ghastly expression on his face, which he took to be a look of despair; he was struck by the man's general dishevelment. Fearing that Hess was about to attack and possibly murder him, Dick was preparing to tackle him when the prisoner unexpectedly took a flying leap over the banisters, only to collapse on the floor of the hall beneath, making agonized groaning noises.[14]

The report, prepared by Dicks, of this serious incident was delivered with a hint of dry humour. As the drama unfolded in what Dicks called 'this house of mystery', a second soldier had been in the process of bringing Hess's guard a cup of tea.[15] In the mayhem the tea fell to the floor, the guard drew a revolver, and Dicks had to call out to him not to fire. Hess, by then writhing on the floor, demanded morphine to relieve the pain. Examined afterwards, the prisoner was found to have fractured his femur, but was otherwise mostly unscathed. It being Britain, he was soon brought a cup of tea. He was examined by doctors and was seen, not long after, by a surgical specialist. The staff seemed unsure how far to regard Hess's action as a studied decision to die, evidence of his general confusion, or a mere histrionic performance. Could it be, the report asked, that he was no longer able to project 'the evil' out of himself into the enemy, notably the Jews, and felt himself so bad within that he could not go on? Did he feel his mission had failed, and he had thus become a liability to his own side? Was it perhaps a sign of the collapse of his unconscious identification with Hitler, fear that all was lost, a lacerating self-attack in the face of the mismatch between his grandiose peacemaking plan and his resulting humiliating imprisonment?

As to Hess's motives for wearing his air-force uniform while taking this last flying leap, who knows whether this bore some trace of his earlier plunge into the dark, the parachute jump that had spelt his political suicide in May of that year. Summarizing his impression of Hess at the time of what Dicks called his 'complexly motivated' suicidal action, the doctor believed that the prisoner was obsessed with the wish to 'save his own mental integrity only by some dramatic act of redemption'.[16] Hess, he believed, had come to idealize the Duke of Hamilton and King George VI (as he had previously idealized Hitler), and had dreamed of meeting them in order to end the slaughter between countries he regarded as potential allies. As his scheme collapsed and he was faced by a 'hostile prison regime', Dicks went on, Hess may have felt overwhelmed by feelings of persecution, a wish to atone for his failure, as well as by masochism and hunger for revenge against his British captors, which he may have sought to achieve by revealing their impotence and landing them in trouble for having failed to keep him safe.

What is certain is that Hess's unexpected action led to a tightening of security: his waking and sleeping hours were monitored still more carefully. Nursing orderlies were constantly attached to him, working in teams of two for eight-hour shifts and expected to record their impressions without fail.[17] After the episode it was observed that Hess behaved curiously, combining a 'schoolboy' interest in the technical aspects of his medical treatment with apparent annoyance at having failed to kill himself. The management of the patient was easier for a time: he became calm and even docile in manner, as though all tension had drained away. Moreover, the doctors now felt on firmer ground in treating him psychiatrically and had official support for so doing: it had become 'an overt case of mental illness recognised as such by the politicians and [we] were able to enforce a proper psychiatric regime' and gain 'complete clinical control over him'.[18] On some occasions Hess was able to talk openly about the suicide bid 'in semi-rational terms'.[19] On others, he made no reference to what Dicks called this 'kind of hara-kiri on the enemy's doorstep'.[20] Hess sought to advise the doctors and orderlies on how they should proceed. Required to be X-rayed after his fall, Hess complained that the procedure might render him sterile; hence 'he carefully used the lid of the sterilizer to cover his genitalia during exposure'.[21]

On the afternoon of the next day, following radiography, Hess was given for purposes of anaesthesia a medication called Evipan (the drug that was later also used by Dicks for a very different task). The fragments of bone were aligned, the limb put in extension, and a proper fracture bed was set up. Expert nursing orderlies were summoned, according to the report. The provenance of this account of the attempted suicide and subsequent treatment needs to be emphasized, since evidently one of the aims was to make clear no blame could be attached to either the doctors or guards. However, the language used also suggests the real curiosity of Dicks and others regarding Hess's mental state. They believed there was much to be gleaned about his, and perhaps other Nazis', character structure from such minute observation of his behaviour and communications.

After his fall the patient showed signs of urinary retention and was given a catheter. When Hess discovered that an anaesthetist was not available for this procedure—or perhaps he suspected one was intentionally not to be made available—he screamed for help.[22] Later, convalescing from his injuries, Hess complained that he was being tortured with powders that made the broken leg itch and that contributed to his 'heart poison'.[23]

———•———

Hess evidently had several strategies for avoiding a 'bad conscience'. One approach was to imply a moral equivalence between his own country's behaviour and that of Germany's enemies. This form of comparison for purposes of exculpation was standard fare among the Nazi elite; many of Hess's colleagues made similar comments that cast doubt on the moral scruples expressed by outsiders at Hitler's domestic and foreign policies, by likening them to the measures other European powers had taken to ensure internal security or expand territorial domination. When asked about the function of concentration camps in Germany and its conquered territories, for example, Hess nonchalantly declared: 'You should know, you invented them'[24]—thus equating the Nazi camps with the notorious British policy of internment during the Boer War.[25] He took refuge in similar comparisons when countering remarks about acts of barbarism by the soldiers of the Third Reich. Even if rumours of harsh measures employed against Germany's enemies turned out to be true, he shrugged, what about the atrocities orchestrated by the communist leader, Béla Kun, in Hungary?[26]

On 22 June 1941 Hess was told that the Nazi invasion of Russia had begun. He betrayed a smile and said coolly: 'So they have started after all.' When, a few months later, it was put to him that American involvement in the war might prove fatal to Germany, he said, equally casually: 'All discounted.'[27] At times Hess willingly engaged in such political and historical conversations with his captors, but at others he would sit tight, fearful of his own safety and alert to any hint of psychological or physical 'infiltration'.

Hess also complained of pain in his eyes and acute headaches. How far his physical state in the early months of imprisonment in 1941 (and thereafter) may have been affected by secretly administered drugs is unclear. Beaverbrook, who as a government representative saw Hess in September 1941, wondered if he might have been drugged at the behest of the secret services.[28]

Given continuing official secrecy on this matter, many details of policy and practice remain undisclosed; the treatment that Hess received might be seen as benign, brutal, or perhaps an oscillation between the two, depending on the viewpoint of the observer. Dicks suggested there was a masochistic component to Hess's presentation of himself and his predicament. The relatively calm phase that followed his attempted suicide did not last long. By 19 July Dicks reported that the patient was becoming agitated again, displaying delusions of persecution and complaining of a plot against his life and sanity.[29] Hess, however, was apparently as interested in remarking upon the malign motives and cruelty of some of the officers in charge of him as he was in indulging himself in, or posturing about, his own suffering.[30] He believed he was being deliberately maltreated and that the British orderlies, doctors, and guards who now controlled him, or at least the Jews who supposedly manipulated them, were deriving some pleasure from this. Yet what may equally be inferred is that those who organized Hess's care were concerned to stop any realistic complaint about maltreatment being made public, for fear that this would be exploited in German propaganda.

————•————

Dicks, Rees, and their colleagues were more interested in drawing psychological than pharmacological lessons from their patient's cryptic behaviour, which in their eyes mixed sentimentalism and dog-like devotion with much harsher, sadistic propensities, which they considered to be typical of a certain kind of German attitude. Hess's strange character, after all, had been formed much earlier than 1941, whatever misgivings Beaverbrook or anyone else had about the use of mind-altering drugs. Furthermore, theories about Germany's (or sometimes more specifically Prussia's) tendency to produce psychopathological 'types' and to foster a brutal 'national character' had proliferated in the human sciences between 1870 and 1933.[31] The triumph of National Socialism had led to a vast elaboration of such ethnographies and psychologies on both sides of the Atlantic. According to some of these theories, both the culture at large and the milieu of certain families privileged soldierly manly bearing and extolled the virtues of ruthless determination and success at all costs. A kind of hyper-masculinity, based on a cult of violence and contempt for weakness or even tenderness, was commonplace; meanwhile women (except in kitsch and unreal, idealized representations) were denigrated. A marked propensity to sadism laced with pseudo-sentimentalism, it was sometimes said, characterized many men of the German far right; they had learned from their earliest years to distance themselves from genuine maternal goodness, kindness, and softness, and to identify with the cruel paternal aggressor. Yet deep down, it was argued, they were profoundly confused by their conflicting attachments and identifications, and driven, more and more, to insist on their hyper-masculine identities in order to retain their equilibrium.

As a line of psycho-social and ideological inquiry—a starting-point for exploration rather than a settled conclusion—this was, no doubt, suggestive and significant; but as a bald characterization of what so-called 'German domestic culture' necessarily favoured or what the majority of 'the German people' necessarily suffered from or wanted it ran towards the loosest form of speculation, even into absurdity, and need not be taken seriously now as either history or sociology. The so-called quintessential German 'type' (like other national caricatures) tends to fall apart on closer inspection. Sometimes the vision of 'the German' in this period was simply an expansion of older, highly stylized collective portraits of the Prussian *Junker* officer caste. Gender, regional identities, religious affiliations, class, age, and several other obvious variables would need to be taken into account, even in a preliminary sketch of what constituted Germanness. Perhaps the theories of 'typical' German character and personality that were presented in *The Case of Rudolf Hess* could serve as pointers to particular values, images, or traits. But to suppose that the analyst can know how a national culture affects the unconscious desires of millions of people who have never been near a psychoanalytic couch is quite another matter.

Modern sociologists and historians have done a great deal to identify the many varieties of belief, upbringing, social outlook, and personal circumstance that prevailed in early twentieth-century Germany. Even cursory examination of such literature shows how inadequate any diagnostic-style headline about the overarching psychology of 'the Germans' must be. To locate shared myths and dominant stories, to gather personal case studies and memoirs, or to note certain striking trends, tendencies, and fantasized scenarios that prevail in a given milieu is a far cry from claiming to have identified the entire German field. Historians in recent years have suggested the existence of certain patterns of belief—for instance, regarding war and death—but are rightly wary of reproducing stereotypes about national character or collective psychology.[32] Psychoanalysts and psychiatrists could only invite retrospective derision when they veered towards such stereotypes. *The Case of Rudolf Hess* was double-edged in this regard. At points in the text the commentaries seem attentive to the risks of such generalizations; at others, though, they lapse into precisely such very broad claims about Germany.

In fact, various empirical surveys (to whose design Dicks contributed) sought to test more carefully the stark and potentially misleading propositions about the beliefs of German POWs and (later on) the civilian population. The wartime and post-war endeavour to trace what people consciously and unconsciously believed built on a number of social-scientific and commercial survey methods, ranging from the pioneering endeavours of 'Mass Observation' in Britain to 'Gallup' polling in the United States. Whether designed for overt military, academic, political, or business purposes, such projects had often aimed precisely to get behind clichés about what certain other people, or classes of people, are assumed to think. None of this guardedness was very much in evidence, however, when Rees *et al.* baldly generalized as follows:

Many psychological observers are agreed that the German domestic culture favours this sado-masochistic, dominant–submissive cleavage or duality. The inability successfully to resist the father's power, and the feeling of weakness or inferiority so created, are apt to result in a persistence of adolescent hero-fantasies. At the core of such romanticism lies the primary need to overcome the father and deliver one's mother—a theme upon which countless myths and fairy tales of monsters slain and damsels rescued are founded.[33]

————•————

Hess for one had indeed seemed to worship Hitler as though he were a heroic slayer of monsters. But the Führer's stalwart follower now saw himself equally as the victim of a nefarious British plot to lock him up for no good reason. He regarded Dicks with grave misgiving, suspecting that he might be a party to a plot to poison him.[34] Dicks offered Hess criticisms and psychological explanations, but on other occasions he deliberately eschewed such moralism, either in dealing with the patient or in conceptualizing the nature of his mind: he sought rather to understand Hess in relation to the unconscious drives and the defences that fend off guilt. For instance, after the suicide attempt, as Hess was resisting the attempt to introduce a catheter, Dicks (exhausted after having worked some twenty hours at a stretch) lost for a moment all semblance of medical distance or psychoanalytical curiosity and snapped at the patient: 'Aren't you ashamed of yourself? You, the second man in the German Reich, causing us all this trouble and then bellowing like a baby; I shall do nothing further to relieve your bladder.'[35] Hess apparently became silent, glanced balefully at Dicks, and in due course emptied his bladder naturally.

During his captivity the patient was also prescribed a host of other treatments of questionable efficacy, including rest, tonics, and massage—interventions about which he remained no less suspicious.[36] Hess's view was that the regime was becoming harsher and more devious over time; the doctors believed, rather, that his mind was deteriorating. Hess's odd habit of turning his head and eyes toward some corner of the ceiling and looking intently at a particular spot was interpreted as a sign of hallucination.[37] Dicks reported at one stage that Hess asked an orderly to take charge of certain secret pieces of paper on which he had written notes, as he feared they were being read while he was asleep. Hess put them in a large envelope, sealed it with candle-wax, and used the orderly's signet ring to stamp it.[38]

The suicide bid marked one major turn of events in the case; a drama of a different kind occurred a few months later. On 4 December 1941, around half a year into his captivity, Hess announced that his memory had vanished. A couple of months earlier Hess's father had died in Germany, but there is no certainty as to his deeper feelings about this bereavement or indeed precisely when he first learned of it. (His mother would not die until 1951.) Hess's loss of memory was noted briefly by another army doctor, Captain M. K. Johnston, who had taken charge of the patient late in July 1941, and who provided a record of this period of treatment in the published casebook.[39] Dicks meanwhile had been assigned some other work, but returned later on to the case. Johnston merely noted at this stage that the patient complained of his loss of memory and how it 'could never return', before reverting to discussion of Hess's continuing fear of poisoning.[40] The memory-loss problem would be briefly taken up again in January 1942, when Johnston concluded that it was quite genuine and wondered if it was caused by depression.[41] The question of Hess's amnesia (real or faked) was to feature more prominently in the later years of his captivity in Britain and at the Nuremberg trial.[42] Of course it was noted soon enough that Hess had something to gain from his new, 'convenient' condition—blotting out the past might be in his own interest, from the medico-legal point of view, if ever his case came to trial; it also eased the pain, Dicks and others clearly believed, of any fleeting feeling of guilt.

In the weeks before Christmas 1941 Hess had referred yet again to the feeling that his body was being infiltrated, and requested the chemical analysis of a bottle of wine to see if any toxins were present. On 13 January 1942 he asked for containers for his faeces and urine so that laboratory tests could be conducted on them, through an intermediary acting for the Swiss government, the protecting power in the case.[43]

Dicks's clinical log offers some further illumination of his own attitudes to Hess's mental state and his attempts to breach the patient's defences. Dicks expressed uncertainty about Hess's motives for coming to Scotland in the first place, and surmised that perhaps the German was 'ambivalently in love with us'. Did Hess view this country that Hitler was erroneously fighting, Dicks mused, as the 'superior race'? Dicks kept careful notes of the treatment and made passing references to the role of the intelligence officers, such as Major Foley, and their 'educative talks' with the prisoner: those talks, Dicks believed, helped to reduce Hess's delusions.

It had been a wise decision to give the prisoner access to English newspapers, so Dicks confided to his log, in order to encourage Hess's unconscious admiration of England. Part of the task, he proposed, was to get Hess to accept that the source of his fears lay in his own fantasy. The doctor apparently hoped to effect a change in Hess's political outlook by reducing his paranoid delusions—how far this was with a therapeutic intent and how far with the aim of gleaning useful intelligence remains unclear.[44] Dicks wanted Hess to become aware of the benign nature of England and the conspiratorial and evil character of the Third Reich, although he went on to acknowledge that there was no evidence that the patient had changed his position.

During 1941 Dicks still hoped that Hess might achieve insight—be treated, as it were, for the sickness and blindness within. Later on that therapeutic aspiration becomes less apparent; Hess was presumably regarded as incorrigible, and thus placed in a different category to the kind of people that Dicks and his colleagues hoped to denazify and re-educate in the new Germany post-1945.

In June 1942 Hess was moved to Maindiff Court, a secure hospital in Abergavenny, South Wales, which had previously been an admissions facility for psychiatric patients in the county of Monmouthshire. During the war, however, it had become a general hospital for the Ministry of Health, taking injured men from the British armed services who were in need of treatment or convalescence. One wing was specially adapted for Hess.[45] He had the use of a bedroom, sitting-room, and veranda (with high railings) leading onto a courtyard.

Here he was put under the care of two psychiatrists, Major Ellis Jones and Nathaniel Richard Phillips, the medical superintendent of the mental hospital. Information about the prisoner leaked out only occasionally to the press and public. Hess appeared briefly to recover some of his faculties, and even described some of his previous convictions as possible delusions.[46] Yet soon he resumed his complaints about his captivity and was inclined again to interpret friendly gestures by any of his captors as subterfuge. Thus, according to one report, he suspected that the provision of flowers in his room was really designed to make him look bad in the face of general British austerity. He made the same complaint when hot baths were drawn for him.[47] Enquiries as to the health of his family, he insisted, were designed to upset him; chemicals were administered in order to cause him toothache; 'poisons' to irritate his bowels and nose.

With the prisoner securely lodged in Wales, Dicks was no longer a central participant in the case and was assigned a series of specialized military intelligence tasks elsewhere.[48] Dicks interviewed and assessed many German

POWs and wrote secret papers that focused, for example, on attitudes within the German army, the Wehrmacht.[49] He also produced a War Office report in 1943 on the situation likely to face the Allies after Hitler's defeat, entitled 'An Appreciation of Some Psychological and Medical Aspects of Post-Invasion Duties'.[50]

Dicks, however, occasionally returned to see Hess and to report to the army authorities on the nature of his care and condition. He recalled a picnic arranged for the prisoner one summer in Wales: the German made an impression on him by the way he 'devoured' the sandwiches provided.[51] Country walks and rambles were occasional features of his treatment; when news of this leaked out it led to some critical rumblings in the press.[52]

On discovering evidence of a 'nocturnal emission' in the prisoner's quarters at Maindiff, the doctors returned to their hypotheses about Hess's sexual life and repressed feelings. It was observed that he attributed the emission to an egg he had eaten the day before; no doubt more could have been made of the blame that Hess attached to the egg, but the clinicians did not speculate further (at least not in writing). Hess, at any rate, immediately vowed to abstain from such food.[53] Efforts to probe the nature of Hess's attitude to masturbation (which, in the formal account given, was termed 'adolescent auto-erotic sexual practices') did not get far. None of this was of interest to the patient, who saw his plight and apparently even the 'emission' in terms of contamination that came ultimately from sources outside of himself.[54]

Dicks's papers contain copies of the once-secret reports that he submitted to his army superiors covering his visits to Wales, notably in February and March 1944 and again in February 1945. For instance, between 26 and 29 February 1944 he had various meetings with Hess and with the attending doctors. He discussed the management of the case and the question of how the German might react if administered 'truth drugs' such as sodium pentothal. There was continuing discussion of Hess's status (as POW) and the lingering possibility of his repatriation. On this occasion Dicks described the patient as a cold, huddled creature, with simian features and vacant eyes. Hess was said to display a curiously affectless attitude toward his own amnesia; he was observed closely as he met particular individuals that he knew. It was said that he showed no sign of recognition, save for a few occasions when his eyes flickered, for instance, when a doctor referred to some previous insult that Hess believed to have been directed at him.[55]

Dicks noted that the patient betrayed no response when others mentioned his wife's or son's name. Hess described to him how anything but the immediate present and past would slip away into the mists. In further entries Dicks referred to Hess's eating habits as 'still peculiar' (driven, he suggested, by a mixture of greed and guilt). He included a few words about a medical discussion that had taken place as to whether Hess's amnesia may have been due to concussion, and also mentioned his chronic spasms and enduring suspicions of his doctors and guards. Scraps of dialogue between patient and doctor were also reproduced. Dicks quoted Hess's view, for example, that if he managed to get back to Germany he might be able to get some treatment, but in the meantime he preferred the amnesia: 'If I got my memory back I may suffer more' (underline in the original). 'My present state is good enough for my purposes here', Hess declared.

A day later, on 29 February 1944, Dicks observed his subject in an aggressive and critical mood: Hess was petulant and presented an array of accusations. After Dicks (together with an escort officer) accompanied the prisoner on an afternoon excursion, he jotted down in his log: 'I was conscious of an "atmosphere", and he walked less than usual.' In the evening, when the doctor came to say goodbye, Hess professed to be sorry that he was leaving, as he was a German-speaker. But Dicks was in fact still in Wales in the first week of March, conferring with colleagues about the possibility of administering Hess a drug. It was decided to give him 5.5 c.c. of Evipan in an endeavour to produce total anaesthesia and muscle relaxation, thereby enabling the prisoner to remember and to talk.[56] According to the casebook, Dicks, in the presence of doctors Ellis Jones, Phillips, and others, administered the substance at 9 p.m. on 10 May 1944.[57]

The use of such preparations in the hope of inducing true confessions in prisoners had been a development of the 1920s.[58] Ink-blot tests (usually known as 'Rorschach' tests, after their Swiss inventor), to which Hess was also subjected later, had emerged as a new technique in the same decade. Both methods had aroused considerable enthusiasm and excitement, particularly in the United States.[59] The Rorschach test was used at Nuremberg, in pursuit of Hess's (and other prisoners') underlying fantasies, whereas the barbiturate was intended to have a direct effect upon his brain. Such chemicals, it was hoped, could bring Hess out of what the doctors called his 'hysterical situation' and lead to a clearer picture of his past.

This type of experiment needs to be set in context: throughout this period Allied intelligence services were busy developing chemical products for use in war. The OSS even established a 'truth drugs' committee in 1943 to see how such measures might be of service in loosening the tongues of prisoners of war or other potential intelligence sources.[60] Although some believe Hess was 'medicated' many times, it appears that the British authorities did not dare to administer these drugs without the prisoner's consent, for fear that they might deliver a propaganda victory to the other side.

After much vacillating Hess had agreed in the spring of 1944, for reasons never fathomed, to be injected with Evipan, a barbiturate known to have hypnotic and sedative effects.[61] Even under the influence of this preparation, however, his vague and evasive communications nonplussed his interrogators. Dicks's transcript, recorded first in a pencilled note in the original German in his private log then in English translation in the published casebook, gives the gist of Hess's response:

[*Dicks*] What troubles you?
[*Hess*] Pains! In my belly! (*Severe groan.*) Oh if only I were well. Bellyache (*groans*). Water! Water! Thirst!
[*D*] You will soon have water. Tell us now what you have forgotten.
[*H*] Oh, I don't know. Pain! Thirst!
[*D*] You will tell us now what you have forgotten.
[*H*] Water! Pain in my body! A fog...[62]

After the session Dicks saw Hess again. The patient was fairly bright and apparently relieved. Dr Jones told him that his memory had been found to be intact underneath, an assertion based on no particular evidence judging by the verbatim report of the session. There is a reference in Dicks's notebook to a further meeting with Hess soon after, in which he expressed reluctance to go through the process again unless it was deemed medically essential. Given Hess's suspicion that he was being poisoned, it was remarkable that he had agreed to the procedure even once. That evening Dicks had a further long chat with Hess, in which he tried to flatter the patient by saying it was a pity that such a 'rich mind' was being 'needlessly starved'. Hess was unmoved, responding that whilst alone in Britain it was better for him to have no memory and thereby to suffer less boredom and torment. He was reported to have said that he knew he would recover at some date in the future.[63]

Hess continued to refuse additional treatment of this kind. In February 1945 a further stage of psychological withdrawal was noted: Hess (who was being watched carefully by an orderly) appeared lost in a world all of his own, but the conviction that he was being gradually corrupted and destroyed by secretly administered toxins remained alive in his mind. He became so desperate about the acid that he thought laced his cakes and bread that he scratched lime from the walls in the hope of counteracting it.[64] He feared there were drugs in his cocoa, and that beans and peas (thought to be as hard as stones) were given to him with the intent of ruining his digestion, weighing him down, and causing cramps. He required above all willpower, he believed, in order to resist this slow poisoning, but willpower was precisely what he went on to confess that he lacked.

Poison appeared everywhere: the cook assigned to him was felt to be at work contaminating his bladder, kidneys, and guts, and curry powder was supposedly used in order to irritate his bowels.[65] He talked too of obscure heart poisons. When given apples, he suspected they had been injected with a deadly substance.[66] Hess apparently resented the way fires were lit, with the intention to put smoke into his eyes, and believed that the air smelled of corpses; food, he claimed, carried some faint smell of pigs' glands, or indeed camels' glands (possibly—one might surmise—some confused shards of memory from his childhood in Egypt, although this was unremarked at the time).[67] A sense of decay and of persecuting signals afflicted him day and night, judging by the clinical accounts provided by the doctors. He complained of screeching whistles emanating from the trains at Abergavenny, chemicals that induced toothache, and poisons that irritated his mucous membranes.[68]

The state of amnesia continued. In one letter (quoted in Rees's report) Hess addressed his wife Ilse in capital letters as 'DEAR LITTLE MUMMY' and alluded to his raddled mind, in which 'the past fades away as behind a grey fog'.[69] Occasional dramas in the prison punctuated days and months of monotony. Another quasi-suicidal incident occurred on 4 February 1945, when once again Hess changed into his air-force uniform and stabbed himself in the lower chest with a bread-knife.[70] It led to a relatively superficial wound, requiring two stitches. He had been tempted, he revealed, to commit suicide by the Jews, as he was the only person who knew of their secret powers of hypnosis.[71] After this latest failed action Hess refused to be shaved, turned down food, and announced that he planned to starve himself to death.[72] He got as far as requesting that his body be sent back to Germany, where tests could be conducted. He was sure that traces of toxins would be found. The doctors speculated as to whether the hunger-strike was a way of avoiding feared poisons or unconsciously signifying a death wish.

Hess's doctors noted his endless somatic preoccupations and the way he drew the team into complex and confusing transactions; he would withhold information from one and give it to another, make paranoid accusations, endeavour to arouse uneasy feelings in his guards. Dicks gave some sense of what it was like for the officers who were obliged to spend time with the prisoner. Some complained, he noted, of Hess's dullness, others of his worthlessness, lack of manners, surliness, hysterical childish attitudes, and so forth.[73] Dicks seemed intuitively to grasp how the feelings and attitudes of the captors (even when unmeasured, overheated, rude, or expressed—as he put it—in 'unparliamentary language') might be revealing of something about Hess himself, or at least about what it was like to be with him.[74]

This might suggest (at least from a later theoretical vantage-point in psychoanalysis) how Hess disavowed certain feelings and projected them into others, thereby giving clues to his own underlying state. Perhaps he unconsciously nudged others at times to feel contemptuous of and superior to him, or alternatively required on occasion that his carers should suffer what he secretly suffered—for instance, tormenting doubts, feelings of helplessness, depression, or clumsiness—while all the time he claimed to know nothing about what was going on. The casebook furnished raw material that indicated how such processes might be in play, although the authors did not elaborate this point.

Nonetheless, Dicks and some of the other psychiatrists involved in the case were clearly intrigued by the psychic meanings of Hess's delusional system, the symbolic nature of his eating or fasting, cramps and pains, self-medicating and careful camouflaging, friendly alliances and hostile rejections. On an inspection visit on 12 and 13 February 1945 Dicks talked with the medical staff in Wales and found nothing untoward in the nature of the treatment regime. He described Hess as alert and rather grandiose, but suffering a 'partial dissociation of the personality'.[75] This suggested that parts of his thinking and mental apparatus were so far broken apart from others that they were no longer recognized as his own. It was a 'partial' process, in the sense that Hess had not disintegrated and fragmented altogether: there was still a singular person of sorts available to talk with.

What is interesting is the varying frames of reference that were used in the medical records, as the doctors drew freely upon their general knowledge of Germany and Nazism whilst interspersing medical, psychiatric, and psychoanalytical ideas. Sometimes their language seemed sharply at odds with itself. Dicks, for example, evoked images from the criminal anthropology that had been both fashionable and highly controversial in the late nineteenth century. Passages of his report echo, in fact, the ideas of a generation of doctors and psychiatrists who had described the so-called stigmata of 'degeneracy'. Felons had once been described as 'atavists', throwbacks to the past. Degeneration was a key word of the Victorian and Edwardian period, and it connoted a condition of hereditary deterioration (revealed, generally speaking, in criminals and the insane, but sometimes too in the 'effete' upper classes). Degeneration was perceived by various influential commentators to be widespread in modern societies; it appeared to represent an alarming reversal of the politically desirable and advantageous evolution that had been celebrated, for example, by the philosopher and social commentator Herbert Spencer, inspired by Darwin's far more meticulous research.[76]

In an idiom reminiscent of the nineteenth-century Italian criminal anthropologist Cesare Lombroso, Dicks described Hess's 'full face [that] produced an impression of baleful strength'. His profile 'disclosed a receding forehead, exaggerated supra-orbital ridges covered with thick bushy eyebrows, deeply sunken eyes, irregular teeth which tended to be permanently bared over the lower lip in the manner of "buck" teeth, a very weak chin and receding lower jaw'. His ears were 'misshapen and placed too low in relation to the height of the eyes'. His palate was said to be 'narrow and arched'. To sum up: 'The whole man produced the impression of a caged great ape, and "oozed" hostility and suspicion.'[77] Such observations made in the patient's wartime notes would have sat comfortably alongside a plethora of earlier investigations of madness, criminality, and perversion. At this point in the clinical report, however, the commentator unexpectedly turned towards the description of feelings rather than supposed bodily anomalies, picking up perhaps the nature of the hostility and suspicion of the patient, and even the emotions evoked in the doctors by being with him. This occurred, for instance, when the colleague who had affected the first introduction between Hess and Dicks withdrew: Hess at this point produced what was described as 'an awkward tense feeling'. Here, in other words, the discussion was framed in a language that was attentive to inter-personal dynamics.

The case notes registered at many points the feelings of the patient and his effect upon others, evoking his moods of pathos and his melancholy bearing. Dicks also considered the emotional dimension of Hess's tiniest gestures and the meaningful nature of his every response—and at times of his extended silences. Perhaps these references owed something to the psychoanalyst John Rickman, who was one of several people to receive the manuscript before publication and who apparently 'spent much time and thought in help[ing] to improve the book'.[78]

Dicks and his colleagues studied Hess's physical activities and behaviour as well as his mode of speech; perhaps there were echoes here of Melanie Klein's clinical work with young children, in which play was taken as representing aspects of unconscious fantasy. For example, the report gives a detailed description of the imaginary objects Hess constructed during his hours of leisure. When he produced architectural plans for an ideal house of the future, it was implied that this was some kind of unconscious attempt to rebuild the world he had destroyed; Hitler's own intense preoccupation with the post-war rebuilding of German cities lent itself to similar interpretations.[79]

Hess was found to be 'something of a gadgeteer, who would delight in fantasies of hidden knobs working concealed wirelesses, sliding doors and tricks of illumination'. Dicks was interested in the meanings of this 'play' and suggested that these would 'not elude the psychopathologist'. 'This fantasy of his own inviolable home in which he could entertain and shape life exactly as he wanted it was perhaps his best moral support during this phase of his captivity.' Hess created, through his drawings, a kind of 'dream house'. This was 'a very egocentric project in which his study and the public reception rooms played a much greater part than his wife's bedroom or his son's nursery. He gave the impression constantly that, though a model family man, he was not in fact greatly interested in his wife as a sexual partner or a love object.'[80]

Bits of Victorian criminological theory were interspersed in the reports with the latest psychological experimental approaches and elements of contemporary psychoanalytical thought. Dicks observed the patient's medical symptoms, but also his fixed division of the environment into evil persecuting forces on one side and healthy 'good' agencies on the other. His 'little rituals and fads at meal-times' were noted down keenly, as were his various projections.[81] Crucially, behind much of the interest in the background of Hitler and Hess was the inkling that these (and many other Nazi) men's experience of and identification with cruel and frightening fathers was complicated by their preoccupation with subdued, subordinated, 'soiled' mothers. The vicissitudes of infancy, compounded by later cultural and social influences, it was felt, entrenched the ferocious superego of these proto-Nazi subjects, and eventually contributed to a sado-masochistic form of politics that was consonant with their inner worlds; the 'Jews' served, moreover, to carry a myriad of unwanted and despised parts of the self.

Was Hess an example of what Anna Freud and others had called the identification with the aggressor? Or was he masochistically caught up in a role as lackey to the master? Hess, it was said, had sought out, in his political orientation, new authoritarian surrogates for an original more intimate constellation of relationships: he wanted to find a father/leader to whom he could fully submit, who would structure his life and in whom he could place absolute trust.[82]

Hitler too, Walter Langer suggested in 1943, was the child of a savagely punitive, petty-minded, domineering, and fickle man and became, in turn, a monstrous and absolute authority with power that his father, old Alois, could never have dreamed of.[83] The finding about Hess was not dissimilar, although in this case he was the abject follower of the tyrant (albeit with very considerable powers of his own). There were several parallels between the two investigations: in both cases the nature of the subject's supposed unconscious identifications with parental figures and Oedipal struggles were brought into view. And behind even this, clinicians sometimes envisaged a more inchoate and primitive ferment of feelings. Certainly the subject's psychosomatic symptoms and perverse solutions to psychic uncertainty and turmoil were closely considered.

To leaf through the many entries that were kept in those logs of Hess's treatment in England and Wales is to encounter a world of much administrative tedium, steady medical routines, and surrounding bewilderment about what to do with the difficult patient. If there were occasional outbursts of anger, impatience, and sarcasm on the part of the doctors, the records on the whole suggest their attempt to maintain their clinical *sang froid*, to interest themselves in the 'case', and even on occasion to display a certain empathy with the prisoner, whose flight from Germany and subsequent collapse was seen by some as a morally mitigating factor to set against the many evils and disorders of his character.[84] It is puzzling that the British authorities did not take more obvious propaganda advantage and exploit rumours of Hess's defection; several theories have been given for this official reticence, none of which entirely make sense. One could imagine how (had the occasion arisen) Hitler and Goebbels might have dealt with the news that a senior British cabinet minister had taken it into his head to land in Germany unannounced and without authorization. Hess never claimed, of course, that he was seeking asylum when he flew to Britain, any more than that he sought British psychiatric treatment. The doctors' notes record the sharp upswings and downswings of his mood, the signs of resignation and perhaps (beneath the often seeming deadness of affect) the intermittent state of panic and despair; periods of rage and bitter accusation were juxtaposed with the flatness of ritual behaviour.

Hess remained with his doctors and guards in Britain for just over four years before Major Ellis Jones accompanied him, on 8 October 1945, to the airstrip at Madley, near Hereford, where a flight took them to Brussels. From there the prisoner was transported overland and consigned to the care of Major Douglas Kelley, a psychiatrist with the US army. Having previously served as an officer at a holding camp for senior Nazi prisoners at Mondorf-les-Bains in Luxembourg, Kelley was one of a number of doctors who monitored Rudolf Hess and the other war criminals at Nuremberg. Their ambition was to derive insights from such individual cases that might inform the investigation of the psychopathological field of Nazism at large.[85]

5

Madness and Politics

In considering the importance that was once ascribed to the interpretation of the interior life of the Nazi leadership and the desires of the 'masses', it is useful to turn back at this point to note shifts in political thought during the 1920s and 1930s. Well before the Allied intelligence profiling that characterized the 1940s there had been widespread intellectual interest in investigating the destructive, even deadly, emotions stirred up by Nazi orators, and growing attention was paid in the 1930s to the particular psychological dynamics that were in operation between the leaders and the led on the far right in general. Fascist Italy and Nazi Germany, if not the entire modern world, were cast in this period as suitable cases for treatment; critical observers of the German political scene painfully concluded that negotiation with Hitler would not work to maintain world peace and that the Chancellor and his cause were mad.

How far was this attention to the role played by psychopathology in politics new? And what did such research owe to psychoanalysis? Certainly the recognition that subliminal or instinctual factors shaped political allegiances had already been widely explored in various domains of the human sciences in the nineteenth century. But psychoanalysis created a new resource for the consideration of this problem in political thought after 1900. Moreover, the Great War and the political convulsions that occurred in its aftermath led many to stress, with renewed urgency, the limits of reason. Leaders and governments, not just mobs and crowds, it was argued, easily succumbed to passions of which they were consciously unaware. Britain and America faced major upheaval in the 1920s and growing dread that Soviet-style communism would spread. The year 1926 saw the General Strike in Britain, and many liberals and conservatives, as well as some Labour party politicians, feared that the country was breaking into warring sides and wondered if the state would be plunged into total anarchy. The turmoil of social and economic life in much of continental Europe, most crucially in Germany, was of course more extreme; it created a context in which any new political ideology could gain considerable traction by guaranteeing that it could clean up the 'mess' of democracy, restore order, and rebuild national strength. Fascism and Nazism promised to end contemporary 'chaos'; the Party would gather the people into a unity; all difficulties would be resolved under the supreme will of the leader. In practice fascist parties were, of course, characterized by jockeying power-brokers and shot through with competing interests, but their ideological promise was of unity, singularity, and resolute direction: only through total allegiance to the masterful leader (possessed of a clear sense of destiny), it was said, could the hopeless confusion of modern life be ended.

Psychoanalysis was harnessed to several distinct kinds of explanations of the attractions of the far right. Some suggested that Hitler had merely exposed, rather than created, the pathological desires and craven will to obedience that lurk in 'the Germans'; others, however, took the view that the same propensities to extreme and irrational political fantasy lie dormant in all of us. It was also sometimes implied that Hitler had tuned in to widespread terrors about 'ego disintegration' in the face of modern rootlessness and loss; alternatively, he was cast more like the 'imp of the perverse', adept at exploiting anxieties and dreams, but also excitedly leading his followers to transgress—knowingly and ultimately self-destructively— the very boundaries of accepted humanity and civilization. Certain commentators saw the Nazi leader as closer to an empty vessel, filled with the most destructive and perverse unconscious thoughts of others. Hitler was cast as both subject and object, creator and recipient of ideological messages; it was equally possible, in other words, to cast the Führer as cause or effect of this psycho-political instability.

Psychoanalysis was well placed to enter into such debate. It intersected with modern art, political thought, and medicine, and lent itself to explanations of the desperate state of the contemporary human condition: some saw it as a timeless theory of the psyche, others as a diagnosis of the particular travails of modern Western men and women. In the 1920s, on both sides of the Atlantic, psychoanalysis was redolent of 'the modern': it was entwined, after all, with modernism in the arts: a number of key experimental figures in painting, literature, poetry, cinema, and philosophy dallied with Freud and the unconscious. Increasingly, however, especially in America, Freudianism was thought to be naturally allied to—even to have coalesced with—medicine and psychiatry. There were indications of this development in the inter-war period, but above all in the United States after 1945 medical ideas of 'social hygiene', political ideas of international health, and psychoanalytical accounts of the self converged.

Many argued that a new science was required after 1918 to identify and explain the direction of modern history, and psychoanalysis offered itself precisely as such a resource. Unlike the crowd theorists of the late nineteenth century, the psychoanalysts did not generally exempt themselves from the categories they studied; this created if not an egalitarian spirit then at least a sense of inclusivity; this was particularly important perhaps in America, where the kind of '*de haut en bas*' accounts by well-heeled commentators of the irrationality of the crowd or the mental frailty of the 'common man' easily sounded like old European snobbery, or merely self-deceiving elitism. Psychoanalysis was nothing if not a theory of everyman and everywoman.[1] If it was criticized for anything it was for its universalizing claims: it did not exempt the petit-bourgeois, tycoon, professional politician, or aristocrat from its analyses of human neurosis (or worse).

It was the possibility of mass *enjoyment* of submission to fascist authority and the nature of unconscious identification with the tyrannical leader that cried out for a new explanation. Landmark dystopian works of fiction not only showed how oppressive political systems could crush all opposition (defining the entire horizon of what it was permissible for the individual to think) but suggested how such regimes might also be capable of instigating, or at least exploiting, a certain kind of pleasure in this 'robotic' form of takeover. It was the vision of people in synthetic states of 'bliss', drugged and numbed, but luxuriating in this bovine non-thinking life that was the hallmark of the 'brave new world' set out in Aldous Huxley's classic tale of 1932.

For anxious liberals and conservatives, the 'Red scare' of the 1920s was soon matched, even eclipsed, by horror at the violent fervour and obscene excesses of the Brown Shirts and Black Shirts. For some English-speaking writers, sneaking or open admiration for Mussolini in the 1920s began to pall thereafter, even if it was argued that liberal democracy must somehow 'learn the lesson' of common enterprise that characterized the emergent fascist and Bolshevik powers. Between 1933 and 1939 leading politicians on both sides of the Atlantic became ever more doubtful that compromise and negotiation would suffice to resolve the crisis with Germany and its political allies, despite the intense wish of most of them to avoid the renewal of war at all costs. In that decade a psychological and political tipping-point occurred for the British and American leaderships: for both Roosevelt and, eventually, for Chamberlain, all vestiges of hope that a 'reasonable' deal could be struck with the German Chancellor dwindled and then disappeared.

Admittedly there was a gulf between the general sense that Hitler was a fanatic and a madman, and some of the more arcane Freudian accounts that were elaborated in these years. But the point here is that psycho-analysis increasingly resonated with commonplace mainstream views of the irrational features that bedevilled political life, and of the uncon-scious wishes and hopes that led to the rise of fascism. The direct psycho-analytical inquiry into fascist thought in the 1930s was often to be led by left-wing Freudians—or, to put it the other way around, psychoana-lytically informed Marxists and socialists. For instance, in an anguished article on National Socialism and public health (1932) the German Jewish doctor and psychoanalyst Ernst Simmel exhorted people to awake from their dreams of Hitler and turn to socialism, although the pessimistic tone of his essay suggested he was far from confident that this appeal would be heeded. Nazism, he warned, was akin to a drug for those who seek freedom from anxiety and conflict within. Simmel urged the people to abandon this delusion, which 'estranges you from reality and leads you to the abyss!' For Simmel, Nazism had emerged in the 'hellfire of collaps-ing capitalism'; Hitler was the stooge of rapacious industrialists and fin-anciers, who cynically used the Nazi cause to 'mislead the masses' and entrench their power. Simmel wrote self-consciously as a socialist *and* a clinician, declaring at one point that 'We psychotherapists and psychia-trists know . . . '. What did they know? Apparently, according to Simmel, that the evidence showed it to be hard, or in some cases impossible, for many of his contemporaries to divert their aggressive drives towards more creative, socially useful (or at least harmless) wishes. Paradoxically, war made many people feel better: violence and hate created some psycho-logical problems, but also solved others; it brought life into harmony with what Simmel called the 'murderous drives'.[2]

In 1933, just as Hitler came to power, the Austrian psychoanalyst Wilhelm Reich published his political and psychoanalytic account of this modern disorder: *The Mass Psychology of Fascism*. Reich was one of several key left-wing analysts of the 1920s and 1930s who sought to combine the insights of Freud and Marx. He was drawn to, but not uncritical of, Soviet commu-nism.[3] There was a utopian dimension to his thought that was (advisedly) missing in Freud. For this reason among others, tensions soon emerged between the two men. Reich left the psychoanalytic movement under a cloud in 1933, but he remains significant for the present discussion as a pioneer of the application of psychoanalysis to political thought on fascism; he stimulated others, including the luminaries of the Frankfurt School, to pursue such research more rigorously.

Reich tended to emphasize particular *phases* of human history and their role in producing neurosis; he believed that stultifying social and economic conditions cramped the expressive and free dimension of human nature. Freud agreed that modern nervous illness was intimately connected to the demands of 'civilization', but by contrast with Reich he seemed to view a certain degree of neurosis as more or less ubiquitous and inevitable. For example, no amount of social freedom, he implied, could spare people the task of negotiating the Oedipus complex. Since, for Reich, psychic conflict was contingent on particular political arrangements, a more equitable social order would enable people to repress far less and to be more 'whole'. He also took an altogether rosier view of the potential creativity and progressive force of crowds. Freud regarded 'the mass' as an invitation to the individual to regress towards primitive functioning.[4] He viewed such aggregates almost entirely negatively and sceptically. Although, according to Freud, the union of people in the streets unleashes the most primitive anxieties and precipitates blind capitulation of the subject to the ego of the charismatic leader, Reich believed that mass action could equally well be the catalyst for justice.[5]

Perhaps there was some glimmer of this more benign picture of the defensive rather than aggressive and destructive purpose of the group in Freud's anthropological fable of the alliance of brothers in *Totem and Taboo*, which had appeared before the First World War. The group here was envisioned as a 'horde', in which individuals join forces to defend themselves against, and ultimately overthrow, the absolute authority of the omnipotent father. But there was not much solace in this, for the resulting solution was always potentially unstable. 'Sexual desires', Freud declared, 'do not unite men but divide them.' Though the brothers had grouped together to kill their father, they were also rivals with regard to the women and held back uneasily by the taboo on incest; at the same time, Freud added (perhaps also paving the way for later psychoanalytical speculations about the homoerotic dimensions of fascism and Nazism) that the band of brothers might really be bound together by latent homosexual ties.[6] For Freud also conveyed the primordial violence that remains as a residue of this cooperative effort: the group that once took on and killed the violent, primal paternal chief was haunted thereafter by the guilt of its own murderous act. It was as though the original moment of parricide, repressed from social knowledge, nonetheless always informed the 'community'. Moreover, that deep ferocity of purpose was never really banished in the polity: Freud was fond of pointing out that the state never abolishes violence; rather, it seeks to monopolize it.

———•———

Before the Great War a number of commentators on both sides of the Atlantic had argued that instinctual forces shaped or even governed social interactions far more than was generally imagined. Better scientific knowledge of this process, it was said, must become the basis for a new kind of political analysis. Among others, Graham Wallas took this view. He was an English socialist and social psychologist, who lectured at the London School of Economics in the Edwardian period. Wallas's *Human Nature in Politics* appeared in 1908 and attempted to draw together several intellectual trends of recent years in a more realistic assessment of the large role of instinct and passion in human affairs. Wallas still hoped that the benign impact of education, better nurture, and a spirit of international fraternity could counter the rising threat of war that was always a lurking human propensity.

If the emerging science of psychology was sometimes deployed by advocates of nationalism and theorists of national character in the second half of the nineteenth century, it also contributed to a new set of diagnostic approaches to the study of militarism, and other volatile modern political phenomena.[7] Some influential Victorian writers presented revolutionary political groups and mass movements of protest as being akin to degenerate patients or atavistic criminals.[8] Crowd psychology, as pioneered by Gustave Le Bon and others, may have lacked academic *gravitas* in some eyes, but still proved influential. Images of deranged throngs of urban-dwellers fed into wider cultural discussion of a modern 'crisis of reason'.[9] Around the beginning of the twentieth century, commentators such as Boris Sidis, a Russian-born émigré and one-time student of the philosopher William James at Harvard, and J. A. Hobson, a wide-ranging 'new liberal' writer and critic in England, drew on this language. They described in quasi-clinical fashion the ease with which reason was overthrown, especially when people operated en masse. Vignettes of panicky financial markets, disgruntled, seething strikers, fanatical anarchist bombers, or for that matter jingoistic demonstrators for the British Empire seasoned such accounts of collective psychological disorders.

It was, according to Le Bon, the era of crowds. But none of these *fin-de-siècle* theorists of mad mobs, fascinating demagogues, and rattled elites foresaw the precise terminus of Hitler and Nazism. The pathologies of the Third Reich lay beyond the expectations of such earlier writers. The key works of the pioneer of sociology Max Weber (who died in 1920), the theorist of elites Vilfredo Pareto (d. 1923), and the crowd psychologist Le Bon (d. 1931) not only preceded the existence of Nazi Germany but also spoke to the tribulations of a different age, although Weber's account of charismatic forms of authority has always remained an important starting-point for discussion of the special rapport between Hitler and his supporters. Weber died, as it happened, in the very year that the Nazi Party began its formal institutional life. Social psychologies of various forms tried to keep pace with the rise of fascism in the 1920s and 1930s, but many critics claimed that neither these nor any other political theories or scientific models were able to explain the psycho-political insanity besetting one of the most advanced nations of Europe.

Soon after the end of hostilities in 1918, but before he became world-famous as an economist with a remedy for slumps and depressions, John Maynard Keynes took up the diagnostic approach to nationalism and politics in a similar but more pessimistic vein to Graham Wallas in 1908. *The Economic Consequences of the Peace* (1919) was based on Keynes's first-hand knowledge of the international negotiations that followed the Great War. It reflected his immense disappointment with the French and British leaders, and above all with the American president, Woodrow Wilson. The latter, Keynes felt, had promised so much with his talk of new dawns and delivered so little. He had caved in to the demands for major financial reparations from Germany made by the French statesman Clemenceau, egged on by many others. Between them the former Allies had produced a settlement that would not only cripple the vanquished power economically, he argued, but would also have disastrous knock-on consequences for the rest of Europe. Keynes identified not only diplomatic illusions but also something bordering on delusional thought amongst the victors.

Keynes made a remarkable intervention here with regard to the group-psychological interactions at Versailles, and railed against the self-defeatingly punitive 'logic' of the negotiators. He anticipated not only the dangers of German resentment in face of the harsh terms of the war settlement, but also the psycho–political form of analysis that accompanied Germany's resurgence in the 1930s. Deep human passions, he suggested, were no less significant factors to reckon with than conscious calculations of advantage and interest. In fact, he came to argue that inchoate emotional feelings, including one person's intuitive sense (or lack) of trust in others, brought moods of optimism or pessimism to the fore in economic affairs. In *The General Theory of Employment, Interest and Money* (1936), Keynes famously referred to people's 'animal spirits' and the importance of considering them in understanding the conduct of markets. Earlier, in *The Economic Consequences of the Peace*, Keynes had also intimated the importance of those spirits when he expressed his fears of renewed hatred and bitterness in the defeated population, which, he anticipated, would result in further violence and conflict. He spoke here of how madness was overwhelming reason, and decried the myopic and vainglorious attitudes of leaders. He believed that the prospect of crippling the defeated power, to nullify its threat permanently, was akin to a dream. In Keynes's account, the machinations of the parties to the talks sound more like infantile narcissism, or perhaps the gestures of somnambulists, than the *Realpolitik* of statesmen.

The economist became a keen reader of Freud; indeed, he viewed the founder of psychoanalysis as a genius, albeit one prone to produce theories that were seriously short on empirical evidence.[10] Perhaps echoing both Nietzsche and Freud, he alluded to subterranean depths, fearful convulsions, voiceless tremors, and submerged resentments in his *Economic Consequences of the Peace*. Keynes stressed the importance of understanding historically and psychologically the significance of communal hatred, the simmering role of envy and bitterness, and the perverse pursuit of politically destructive policies. The German people before 1914, he wrote, had been '[m]oved by insane delusion and reckless self-regard'; this madness led them to overturn 'the foundations on which we all lived and built'. But the spokesmen of the French and British people after 1918 'have run the risk of completing the ruin, which Germany began, by a Peace which, if it is carried into effect, must impair yet further what it might have restored, the delicate, complicated organisation, already shaken and broken by war, through which alone the European peoples can employ themselves and live'.[11]

The First World War led many intellectuals to question the wisdom and good faith of their political leaders and the values of Western civilization. It was the evidence of enthusiasm for war in 1914, not the disillusionment that set in thereafter, that led some retrospectively to harbour doubts about

the instinct for survival in the human aggregate. Notions of gradually unfold-
ing moral improvement or evolutionary advance had often been assumed in
narratives of history in the previous century. Not everybody had believed in
these ideas before 1914, of course; nor did everybody agree after 1918 that
the Great War had put paid to such assumptions. There was no consensus on
either side that the four years of fighting had been for a futile and disgrace-
ful, let alone insane, cause.

However, many prominent writers and artists did profess exactly that.[12]
They cast the First World War as the end of innocence, arguing that it
revealed in retrospect the myopia of nineteenth-century dreams of historical progress, peace, and advancing civilization. It was common for writers
and poets to describe feelings of disillusionment and profound historical
disorientation; it was often said that previously cherished cultural, moral, or
political ideals were now tarnished or even absurd. Excitement gave way to
despondency and despair. Even Freud, who was not prone to nationalist
mania, confessed ruefully that he had temporarily given his 'libido' to
Austro-Hungary in 1914.[13] The rise of nationalism in conjunction with
militarism was seen to have led to pointless destruction of vast proportions.
Much of this 'crisis of reason' had been presaged before the war, but the
knowledge of millions of avoidable deaths between 1914 and 1918 prompted
numerous participants and onlookers to describe the implosion of faith in
the human mind and the social bond.[14]

The possibility that civilization was on the wane or that 'progress' lay in
ruins was a frequent matter of debate; some saw degeneration as terminal,
others talked of collective 'regeneration'. Many, for instance, pinned their
faith in the 1920s on the powers of socialism and communism to transform
collective life for the better. Minds, bodies, and the entire world order, it was
said, could be radically transfigured, or, as some argued in a more medical
and psychiatric idiom, 'sanitized'. Various commentators dusted off nineteenth-century arguments about the role of science as guarantor of future
progress, hoping that a new caste of disinterested doctors and engineers
could transcend politics and steer the ships of state. One example of the
belief that science held the key to moral regeneration and material advance
was the international lobbying movement that came to prominence in
America and elsewhere, led by doctors, psychiatrists, social workers, and
researchers, to argue that shared mental health was the key factor to consider in interpreting and surpassing political enmities. Proponents of such a
view often took 'extremism' to be the symptom of mental illness, and thus

came to advocate moderation in politics as the solution that was best in harmony with human nature. But some advocates of mental hygiene were also impressed by socialism or fascism; in addressing social problems laissez-faire would no longer do.

Contributors to the American mental-hygiene movement in the 1920s hoped to achieve widespread social enlightenment by placing psychiatric and biological knowledge at the core of public policy. Major think-tanks and funding organizations recognized a new social role for psychiatry and elevated its significance in public-health campaigns. The Rockefeller Foundation argued that as bodily disease was tamed through advances in medical knowledge, the treatment of both individual and collective disorders of the mind would become a vital new frontier of science.[15]

It was commonplace in the English-speaking world to link the improvement of mental health with the case for eugenics. This tendency waned somewhat once Nazism established itself in Germany and eugenics came to be indelibly associated with its racist obsessions, but arguably only lost its respectability in mainstream Western opinion after 1945. The individualism that featured strongly as an ideal in the American tradition of mental hygiene in the inter-war years contrasted with the dominant German emphasis on the integrity and solidarity of the national or racial group.[16] In the 1930s Hitler's increasingly aggressive behaviour on the world stage led to growing confusion and dissent within the international mental-hygiene movement. Those campaigners who had assumed, along with Woodrow Wilson, that a better and more pacific world could be achieved through entrenching powers of national self-determination had to rethink their positions, first in response to the First World War and the massive social disruption and violence that also followed in its wake, and now in view of the rapidly deteriorating prospects for European cooperation and peaceful coexistence during the 1930s.[17]

—————•—————

Interpretations of the European dictatorships in Western liberal thought changed dramatically during the inter-war period.[18] Whatever enthusiasm overseas industrialists, mainstream politicians, fund managers, or foreign correspondents (from the United States and elsewhere) had shown for the idea of the strong man in the 1920s—when Mussolini was often portrayed as an admirable and dynamic figure putting an end to chaos and taming the 'mob'—the coming of the Third Reich led many of these erstwhile admirers to express deep fears for the future. As Harold Lasswell, Professor of Political Science at Chicago, warned in an article in the *Political Quarterly* in

1933, 'Hitlerism' signified a vastly important modern psychological development. The German people, he argued, had become receptive to the violent creed of National Socialism in the context of various factors, including political outrage (stemming from Versailles), adroitly orchestrated political messages that played upon the unconscious mind amidst the 'slow tortures of economic adversity'. Chastened liberals, such as Lasswell, recognized that democracy needed powerful new safeguards in order to survive in an age of profound economic insecurity *and* insidious modern propaganda.[19] Whatever the precise cause, 'the German mentality', he warned, 'has been ripening for an upsurge of the masses'.[20] The language of psychoanalysis became an important ingredient of Lasswell's substantial wartime work on the nature of Nazi political communication. The title of his book *Psychopathology and Politics* (1930), and the frequent citation of Freud in its pages, already indicated the direction his thinking would take.

Increasingly, liberal American commentators on international politics began to adopt a quasi-Freudian language of suspicion when describing the mass appeal of leaders, and to ask what unconscious function omnipotent dictators fulfilled in the psychic lives of their followers. Interpretation was required not just to reach the covert 'known' meaning (the disguised intent), but also the terrors and longings of which the subjects in question were perhaps largely unaware. Walter Langer caught this mood in 1943, when he made use of Hitler's earlier comparison of his own self-assurance to the 'precision and security of a sleepwalker', to suggest that the Nazi leader might indeed be akin to a somnambulist on the road to Armageddon.[21]

As the dominant face of dictatorship in the 1930s Hitler was especially closely scrutinized from the clinical point of view, and it was often asked whether the German pathology would spread through Europe, the United States, and beyond. For the American journalist and broadcaster Dorothy Thompson, for example, the German dictator was a megalomaniac whose grandiose style masked the 'little man' within, a hidden figure who was, in reality, both terrified and sick. Thompson observed the transformation in Germany at first hand. In a book published in 1932, *I Saw Hitler!*, she zeroed in upon the diseased mind and malignant psychological effects of the Nazi leader.[22] Thompson had already repudiated Soviet communism as a form of mind-numbing in *The New Russia* (1928), describing a trip to the Soviet Union in which she witnessed the dismaying effects of Soviet re-education on children.[23] A chapter of the book was entitled 'Making a New Mental Type'. Comparing Russia to Germany after Bismarck, she believed that social indoctrination had been taken to its extreme by the Soviet leadership; but her position soon changed, and by 1932 she made it clear that Germany terrified her the most.

Anxious discussions of the mental disease of Nazism proliferated amongst both military 'hawks' and pacifist 'doves'. This concern can be found in *Headway*, the journal of the League of Nations Union that promoted British support for disarmament and internationalism. In 1933 and 1934 it included leader pieces and articles exonerating Hitler personally from responsibility for the 'Jew-baiting' that National Socialism had unleashed.[24] Contributors cautioned against pursuing belligerent action against Germany and acknowledged her 'reasonable' claims for equality of treatment.[25] But at the same time a string of articles and letters in the same issues remarked upon Hitler's irrational failure to moderate his diplomatic positions, identified the driven nature of his inflammatory rhetoric, and bemoaned his instinctual skill in exploiting popular resentments in order to arouse violent responses. Articles on 'mass psychology' warned that reason had very little to do with Germany's aims. One article quoted Bertrand Russell's observation that leaders who absorbed the lessons of modern psychology could sweep their countries with them and lead the people to perdition.[26]

In 1933 the British Conservative Prime Minister Stanley Baldwin came to a similar view, declaring that he was living in a madhouse. He diagnosed Hitler and Mussolini as lunatics, and hoped that the disease was not catching.[27] Endeavours by governments in London, Paris, Washington, and elsewhere to reason with Hitler continued, of course, throughout the decade. The question of whether it was better to mollify or confront the Nazi tyrant divided public and parliamentary opinion in European capitals and in Washington. The case for coming to an accommodation with Hitler—thus accepting as legitimate, or at least unavoidable, some of the regime's territorial and military 'aspirations'—was evidently the more popular view in Britain and, for different historical reasons, in the United States. This was so despite powerful protests and warnings that any accommodation with Hitler would prove fatal. The merits and risks of 'appeasement' were debated again and again in parliament and the press. In this context the word meant policies of 'pacification by concession to an enemy'; but as the *Oxford English Dictionary* also notes, by 1938 appeasement had come to imply disparagement of attempts at conciliation made by Neville Chamberlain, the British Prime Minister of the time. During the 1930s Churchill offered countless warnings from the political 'wilderness' as to the gravity of the Nazi threat and the vital need for British rearmament. Military hawks such as the British diplomat Robert Vansittart also provided a running commentary on the lethal nature of the German pathology. A consistent opponent of appeasement through the 1930s, Vansittart summarized his views that Germans past and present were innately and dangerously aggressive in *Black Record* (1941).

Despite the attempts of various commentators to alert opinion to the threatening nature of Hitler's intentions (already so clearly spelled out in *Mein Kampf*), it is well known that majority British sentiment in the 1930s was anything but bellicose. Concessions, negotiations, and the maintenance of peace at all costs remained the favoured options. Neither the governments led by Ramsay Macdonald, Stanley Baldwin, nor, of course, Neville Chamberlain (from 1937) sought renewed military confrontation with Germany. Even the unmistakable imperialism of Hitler's move from the Sudetenland into the rest of Czechoslovakia in 1938 did not lead Chamberlain to give up hope that all-out war was avoidable; only with the invasion of Poland did he fully despair of the prospects for 'peace in our time'.

Some argued that appeasement of the Third Reich was itself a symptom of neurosis and required psychological explanation. The 'pusillanimous' British and French failure to act in the 1930s, and the supine response of the League of Nations to the aggressive acts of the Italians and Germans long before the war broke out, could be understood in terms of a defensive avoidance of 'reality'. In 1940 the psychoanalyst Joan Riviere wrote to her colleague Melanie Klein about the 'Munich complex', in reference to the Munich conference of 1938 and Chamberlain's illusions about the possibility of peace with Hitler.[28]

Even as President Roosevelt made his final appeals to 'Herr' Hitler's power of judgement, he had actually concluded that the Chancellor was 'a nut'.[29] A spate of new published diagnoses of Hitler by several individuals who had fled Germany, despite their early enthusiasm for Nazism, were to be relayed to the White House, confirming the President's view that he was dealing with a deranged enemy leader. Disillusioned fugitives and émigrés contributed a plethora of 'insider' accounts that gained public attention in America during the later 1930s and early 1940s. Among them was Hermann Rauschning, who had left Germany well before the war and settled in America in 1941. Claiming to have enjoyed numerous intimate conversations with Hitler, his stream of translated publications such as *Germany's Revolution of Destruction, Hitler Speaks* (both 1939), *Hitler Wants the World, The Beast from the Abyss* (both 1941), and *Time of Delirium* (1946) significantly affected American views of the Nazi pathology. Roosevelt too, though he may have addressed Hitler as a calculating and thoughtful politician in diplomatic cables in the late 1930s, spoke privately to colleagues of the Führer as a 'wild man', beyond all reasoning. He remarked to a group of senators in January 1939 that Hitler was paranoid and had a 'Joan of Arc complex', by which he presumably referred to his unshakeable belief in divine inspiration and implacable sense of mission, replete with hallucinated visions and the willingness to face whatever immolation would ensue.[30]

At least one of Roosevelt's most important ambassadors in Europe contributed to such diagnoses. William C. Bullitt was a senior diplomat during the 1930s, first in Moscow and then in Paris, who had also been a patient of Freud's and remained an admirer of psychoanalysis. Bullitt was keen on the application of the talking cure to politics, and authored, in collaboration with Freud, a highly speculative psychobiography of Woodrow Wilson (to be slated by historians when it finally appeared, several decades after it was written, in 1967) which sought to pay close attention to the unconscious determinants of the former US President's politics and style of leadership.[31]

FDR and Bullitt eventually fell out after the defeat of France in 1940.[32] During the 1930s, however, Bullitt had sent the President regular dispatches by letter and telephone from Europe, warning him in 1935, for example, that Europe's statesmen and diplomats 'without exception seem to be neurasthenic'. This had to be taken into account, for 'in such a neurotic state of mind... anything is possible'. Two years later he characterized the 'gangster' tyrants in Italy and Germany as akin to rampaging animals that 'bray' and 'bark'.[33] Bullitt passed on the fruits of his conversations with the garrulous and, in his words, 'irrational' 'Putzi' Hanfstaengl (part of Hitler's social circle and later to be an important OSS informant), whom he met in Berlin in 1934.[34] Bullitt had swiftly concluded, on the basis of his own observations and conversations with others, that Hitler would stop at nothing to achieve his aims; for instance, he warned Washington in 1937 (in terms similar to those that Walter Langer and Henry Murray would use in 1943) that Hitler was committed to either total victory or, far more probably, to total defeat, as though national annihilation was the necessary consequence of any failure to achieve the complete triumph of the will.

In a published report to the American people in 1940 Bullitt declared that war was coming to the United States, regardless of whether it wanted to fight. Hitler, he cautioned, always counted on the division and tardiness of the democracies in order to get his way. There would never be an end to his aggression without decisive confrontation. There would be no compromise, ever, from Hitler's Germany.[35] In November 1937 Bullitt had sent Roosevelt an account of a conversation he had with the Duke and Duchess of Windsor, the former Edward VIII and his American wife Wallis Simpson; they were acquainted with—and, notoriously, expressed some sympathy for—the German 'case'. Meeting them in his ambassadorial capacity, Bullitt gave FDR their description of an encounter with Hitler:

> The most interesting thing last evening was when the Duchess remarked, in describing Hitler's intense interest in architecture, that the Führer had said to her: 'Our buildings will make more magnificent ruins than the Greeks'. That seemed to me about as revealing psychologically as anything I have heard. The curse of the Germans is that they have swallowed the *Nibelungenlied* and do not recoil even before the Götterdämmerung.[36]

It is true that some other American ambassadors and intelligence advisers took a more emollient view of the German situation, at least until the late 1930s, and provided the President with different, and certainly less combative, advice than that which was offered by Bullitt. Nonetheless a sense of impending calamity was widely shared.[37] Even as Roosevelt dispatched his last, urgent diplomatic appeals to Hitler in a bid to avert war, a perturbing variety of diplomatic materials were piling up at the White House: so many tales of Hitler's murderous perversions, rages, and delusions.

Our knowledge of the resolute nature of Allied leadership in an all-out war against the Third Reich should not mask the fact that, at an earlier stage, many senior British and American politicians (including FDR himself) underestimated Hitler's nefarious intent. Moreover, a number of high-ranking fellow-travellers and cheerleaders for Italian Fascism and German Nazism had emerged during the 1920s and 1930s. It was not only the British Union of Fascists, led by Oswald Mosley, that openly admired the Duce and the Führer: the former British Liberal Prime Minister, David Lloyd George, to take but one particularly dismaying example, argued for the Nazi leader's good faith, even as Germany's aggressive intentions were plain to many of his colleagues.[38] At the same time, however, growing numbers of senior ministers and intelligence mandarins were coming to think of Hitler not only as evil and dangerous, but also as mentally ill. This was not merely standard political mudslinging or moral distaste: rather, it bore comparison with, and sometimes echoed, the diagnostic language of psychiatrists and psychoanalysts. The head of MI6, Hugh Sinclair, was slow to shift his attention from the perceived Bolshevik danger to the threat of Hitler (astonishingly slow, to judge by the conclusions of the organization's official historian Keith Jeffery); nonetheless he reported by 1938 that a fatally aggressive and mentally unstable figure was in charge of Germany. In a paper prepared for the Foreign Office, Sinclair stressed Hitler's speed of decision-making, incalculable nature, fanaticism, mysticism, ruthlessness, cunning, vanity, mood swings from exaltation to deep depression, fits of bitter and self-righteous resentment, 'and what can only be termed *a streak of madness*, but with it all there is great tenacity of purpose'.[39]

In this way, despite the tardy nature of such responses to the German menace, and the continuing noises off arguing for more time for international negotiation, political and clinical accounts of Hitler's folly converged in the 1930s. Hitler's circle was subjected to similar forensic forms of analysis. Gossip about the morphine-addicted Hermann Göring, who had spent time in a lunatic asylum in Sweden in 1925, is an obvious example. Certified as a drug addict and known to be prone to outbursts of violence, he spent time in a closed ward before managing to secure his release, albeit initially only into the care of a notionally supervising psychiatrist.[40] This troubled past did not inhibit Göring from turning the tables, when in 1939 he declared the American President to be the victim of a 'mental disorder'.[41]

George Orwell, who held no particular candle for psychiatry or psychoanalysis, warmed to this diagnostic approach to political leadership, and in a telling intervention argued that it was important for commentators to look inside themselves before laying claim to have the faintest grasp of Nazism. This analysis was written in the year of Hess's arrival on British shores (although Orwell said little about that particular matter, other than to express his puzzlement).[42]

The point here was not simply the madness of Hitler (something which Orwell assumed), but the fact that he had impelled vast numbers to follow in his tracks. Orwell complained about what he took to be H. G. Wells's facile attempt to ridicule the Nazi leader in his own writings. Wells had assumed that modern reason would triumph over old superstitions and archaic beliefs. But it was a grave mistake, Orwell warned, to judge the Führer as some pre-modern remnant or absurd 'witch-doctor', or to assume that victory over Germany was guaranteed in advance, as though civilization was bound to supersede barbarism. Hitler, he grimly reminded Wells, is 'a criminal lunatic' who commands 'an army of millions of men'. To deride him as a pathetic, even comic tyrant ('the screaming little defective in Berlin') was to fail to grasp the true menace: the combination of his popular success, founded on modern techniques of persuasion and immense military power. It was clear from Orwell's essay that he believed Wells to have drastically misjudged not only Hitler's nature, but also his political significance for the future of humanity, when he reassured his audience that the threat of such brutality and carnage was ultimately doomed to disappear in the face of science, reason, and light. Instead, the lesson was that science and a kind of twisted rationalism served the monster across the North Sea all too well. Irrationalism had co-opted rationalism.

Orwell argued that any serious interpreter of the problem must endeavour to get right inside Nazism: it required, he insisted, either suffering under Nazism or discovering a touch of the 'fascist streak' in oneself in order to understand what is at stake.[43] Whether he may have had in mind his own anti-Semitic sentiments here is not apparent. Although characterizing such racial animosity elsewhere as a 'neurosis', he suggested that '[w]hat vitiates nearly all that is written about antisemitism is the assumption in the writer's mind that *he himself* is immune to it'.[44] Germany was a sophisticated, scientific nation, and yet, Orwell pointed out, vast numbers of the electorate had sided with the Nazi cause. He was in no doubt that Hitler would have to be 'eliminated' and his armies crushed before Wells or anyone else could plausibly talk of peace, let alone world reconstruction. Much of the modernization that Wells had extolled and dreamed about, Orwell tartly observed, was made manifest in the Third Reich. The bleak conclusion: 'Wells is *too sane* to understand the modern world.'

———•———

By the 1950s the diagnostic account of Nazism frequently shaded into the discussion of totalitarianism; the latter concept was not new, and it derived ultimately not from the literature of those who sought to diagnose it but from celebratory descriptions of Italian Fascism's totalizing ambitions produced by Mussolini and others in the 1920s. The concept was revived, however, and its significance greatly extended around the middle of the twentieth century in a number of landmark publications, especially in the United States, that were as much reflections of as commentaries upon the Cold War.[45] Dicks, for example, was keen to demonstrate affinities between the Soviet and Nazi worlds of thought. He considered that the Soviet Union (based, he believed, on 'fanatical rationalism') and Nazi Germany (founded on anti-rational and anti-scientific thought) were much more similar to each other than to any democratic polity. Dicks pointed to hidden but unmistakable borrowings in both directions, suggesting, for instance, that the Gestapo found inspiration in the Russian secret police, whilst Lenin and Stalin had long admired German method and efficiency more than they ever acknowledged.[46] In his later years Dicks joined other doctors in protesting against the abuses of psychiatry in the repression of political dissidents in the Soviet Union. A letter that he and others signed in *The Times* on this subject in 1972 found its way into the proceedings of a US Senate Committee into such Soviet abuses. The protest appeared alongside a statement by Alexander Solzhenitsyn that read: 'Like the gas chambers, these crimes will never be forgotten, and all those involved in them will be condemned for all time, during their life and after death.'[47] But this is to move too far ahead: in the 1930s it was Hitler's pathology and the phenomenon of what Dorothy Thompson called Germany's 'robots' that constituted—increasingly—*the* overriding question for liberal commentators on both sides of the Atlantic.

Human nature *could* be changed for the worse, Thompson warned. Hitler was the voice of 'unreason', screaming 'to the accompaniment of a tom-tom of mechanized howls from a drilled mob—howls that seemed to come from the throats of ten thousand robots'.[48] Thompson declared Hitler a psychopath, who used the threat of his own, future complete psychosis as a means of ensuring international compliance: infuriate him and he would go still crazier. Thompson warned of Hitler's cynical calculations, as well as his 'Napoleonic obsessions', anti-Semitic ravings, and sadism. Nazism relied on, or in many cases engineered, the pathology of captive minds. Göring's helpless addiction and crazy bombast, Röhm's depravity, and Goebbels' paranoia were all frequently cited in diagnostic assessment of Nazism during the 1930s.[49] These qualities not only marked them as deficient people, but also found expression, so it was argued, in their warped political thought.[50]

Such references by statesmen and journalists on both sides of the Atlantic to the gathering Nazi madness were, in effect, endorsed by the German émigré and doyen of management theory in the United States, Peter Drucker. His notable book *The End of Economic Man: The Origins of Totalitarianism* (1939) argued that all existing mainstream approaches, including Marxism, failed to get to the core of this modern political sickness. He included the Soviet Union under the heading of totalitarianism, but above all conjured up the image of the Nazis and lurking behind them, of Mussolini and his Black Shirts.

It was an illusion, Drucker warned, to see such political phenomena as just a passing phase of modern history or to deny their mass appeal. Fascism, he argued, represented a wholesale assault on all other political philosophies. It was truly radical in its negativity and in its utter repudiation of conventions; moreover, psychically *it worked*. Even so, according to Drucker, its ultimate meaning remained unknown. He added: '[It] is not in spite of but because of its contradictions and its impossibility that the masses turn to fascism.'[51] It was no use basing a study of such a phenomenon upon premises about the necessary human pursuit of self-interest or even of collective interest, nor upon notions of consciousness alone. Drucker expressed his belief that there had been a failure to conceptualize human nature with sufficient complexity, in light of the emergence of the modern dictators. It might appear that we have never stopped asking, since those days, how and why the attractions of a Hitler arose. How had this cause achieved mass support? How was it sustained? The terms of that discussion, however, have changed markedly over time.

During the war some commentators treated the German 'problem' as akin to the case of a mental patient whose condition appeared to be beyond all help. Thus it was also asked, in all seriousness—in fact with the greatest sense of urgency—*Is Germany Incurable?* This was the title of the New York psychiatrist Richard Brickner's book, published in 1943, which exemplified the merger of moral, psychological, and medical categories in the discussion of the Nazi catastrophe. The question for Brickner was not simply whether the war could be won and Germany defeated, but whether the Nazi-supporting population, heir to earlier forms of militarism and authoritarianism, could ever be cured of this pathology.

Brickner did not focus primarily upon the so-called degeneracy of the Germans, as previous human scientists in France and elsewhere had been prone to do during the Great War, or still earlier, after the Prussian army had rapidly defeated the French in 1870. Rather, he suggested there were deep-seated cultural and familial propensities to paranoid thinking that affected the German people's unconscious mode of relating to others. Brickner convened a major conference in New York in 1944 whose aims included the study of the psychodynamics of Nazism and the possibility of denazification: psychoanalysts, including Franz Alexander, compared notes here with luminaries such as the anthropologist Margaret Mead and the sociologist Talcott Parsons.[52] Parsons was both interested in and wary of psychiatric and psychoanalytic approaches, frequently pointing to their risk of reductionism.[53] Few of those who attended such conferences on denazification doubted that applied psychiatry, if not psychoanalysis, was crucial in political analysis, although delegates clearly differed on the precise weight that should be given to features of mind or processes of group psychology, as opposed to contingent social or economic conditions.

Three years before Brickner's conference a work was published in New York that purported to be based on the case notes of Hitler's personal analyst. Kurt Krueger's *Inside Hitler* illustrates the cultural wave of interest in the importance of the Führer's deep-rooted psychiatric disorders and the attractions of the authoritarian 'solution' to life.[54] Endorsements from enthusiastic fellow-writers and experts added to its lustre of seriousness and authenticity. The text shows how psychoanalysis pervaded discussion of the time and how prevalent were ideas of Hitler's insanity; or, to put it the other way around, it reveals how satirical jibes against Hitler drew upon medical, psychiatric and overtly psychoanalytical imagery. *Inside Hitler* described the paranoid delusions and intimate fantasies of a leader enslaved by a madly demanding superego. 'I will obey you', Hitler was said to have declared at a first meeting with his supposed Freudian therapist, Dr Krueger. The doctor claimed that Hitler had walked into his office in August 1919 in the 'unhappy knowledge' that he was deeply maimed, 'to plead with me to help restore him to normalcy'. The doctor bent forward gravely and asked his potential patient if he knew anything about psychoanalysis, in response to which AH, folding his shabby hat as if he were about to run out of the office declared, 'Enough to mistrust it'.[55]

The character that emerges from Krueger's account is a 'fascinating species of madman'.[56] Obscene and murderous fantasies set the context for a particularly lurid dream, featuring Hitler's dead 23-year-old niece, Geli Raubal, with whom he had been infatuated and of whose other relationships he had been pathologically jealous and who had shot herself in Hitler's flat in 1931. She reappears, decapitated, in a pool of blood, to haunt her tormentor. Hitler says: 'Sometimes I see a mammoth shark opening its jaws to devour me, and howling with terror I swim into the darkness.'[57]

Interestingly, in some first-hand accounts from the 1940s, it was noted how Hitler played with the idea of his own madness; according to one recollection, he was said to have retorted to his doctor in 1945 (whom he accused of drugging him) with words that were perhaps more self-revealing than he intended: 'Do you take me for a madman?'[58] In sensational sections of his report, Krueger provided a long list of Hitler's pathologies, including masochism, bestialism, a castration complex, fetishism, and so on.[59]

In an appendix to *The Psychopathic God*, one of the major psycho-bio-
graphical accounts of Hitler produced in the 1970s, Robert Waite dismissed
Krueger's account briskly enough as a hoax. The text was but one of many
tongue-in-cheek portraits of Hitler that promised some insight into the
secrets of his mind and had clearly succeeded in deceiving many people.
Although some astute readers at the time were puzzled by the various
American mannerisms that appeared to mark the Führer's style of speech,
after the book was repackaged under a new title—*I was Hitler's Doctor*—in
1943, it went on to sell, according to one estimate, 250,000 copies.[60] In fact
Inside Hitler was not written by 'Kurt Krueger' at all but by 'Samuel Roth',
and this in turn was the invented identity of a Galician Jew whose original
name was apparently Meshullum.[61] Roth was a notable chancer in the
'underworld of publishing' even before he penned his popular (fictional)
analysis of Hitler.[62]

—— • ——

Written accounts of Hitler that stressed his uncanny power to influence his
followers, through his siren words, compelling eyes, and mesmerizing gestures, presented a figure which bore more than a passing resemblance to
some of the darker products of Weimar-era literature and cinema. The first
of director Fritz Lang's 'Dr Mabuse' films, for example, *Dr Mabuse, the
Gambler* (1922), had accompanied the rise of Nazism; his second film dealing with the omnipotent criminal leader, *The Testament of Dr Mabuse* from
eleven years later, marked the coming of the Third Reich; and both can be
seen as providing an oblique running commentary upon politics.[63] For
much of the second film Mabuse is invisible, but his voice floats freely—the
disembodied sound of the mesmerizing master villain that hovers over the
action, suggestive perhaps of Hitler's own weird ventriloquizing power.
Here it is as though the controlling voice has become autonomous, a force
in and of itself. Confined to an asylum at the end of the first film, in *The
Testament* Mabuse carries on his criminal outrages from his insane cell
through exercising hypnotic powers on outside agents. Mabuse—or at least
his voice—remains an eerie, unseen presence in the story. He is lodged in
an asylum at the end of both of Lang's films; but in *The Testament* the
criminally insane genius, even after death, is far too strong a figure to remain
confined, precisely because he has possessed the very people who are
meant to contain him: indeed Mabuse fascinates the psychiatrist professor
who treats him. The ghostly criminal genius is omnipotent: the undead madman escapes and (close to the end of the film) is seen opening the doors of the

asylum. This was the year that Hitler outflanked the politicians who believed they could confine and moderate him, inside that first coalition cabinet of 1933. Lang himself referred to the connection between Mabuse and Hitler: *The Testament*, he declared, substituted the promised thousand-year Reich with Mabuse's thousand-year regime of crime.[64]

Lang's picture of society in the grip of an insane criminal mastermind, then, can be seen as a reflection of the terrifying vision of Germany helpless in the hands of a lunatic fanatic, backed up by a gang of pathologically violent thugs, with whom there could be no conventional reckoning. American intervention was sometimes described as an attempt to save good Germans from servitude to the bad and mad, but this view was under pressure, as the nation at large was increasingly perceived to have fallen prey to delusion.

6

The OSS

Psychoanalysis and psychiatry had percolated through the political language of the 1930s; during the war they were applied still more directly, featuring, for example, in several branches of Allied intelligence. Clinicians and academic psychologists were also to participate in intelligence work in order to complement the activities of military strategists, political propagandists, spies, and saboteurs.

This is well illustrated by Walter Langer's studies of propaganda and of Hitler's mind, projects that were developed under the auspices of American intelligence organizations, most notably the Office of Strategic Services (OSS). It was thought essential to understand Hitler's character and ideas from within; to this end, diverse strategies and models were proposed. Although there was nothing new about the desire to glean the plans and purposes of the leadership of an enemy power, the deployment of clinical professionals for such tasks was carried further during the 1940s than in any previous period. This can be seen most clearly in the activities that were undertaken at the OSS. Psychoanalytic contributions to intelligence were part of the wider belief at this time that all intellectual resources, and certainly all of the human sciences, should be mobilized in order to defeat the Third Reich.

There is no shortage of academic specialists in the universities on either side of the Atlantic today who are requisitioned for government duties, shadowy or otherwise; some are also well remunerated by commercial organizations for their consultancy. But it it hard to exaggerate the pressing urgency and sheer extent of the mobilization by the American and British governments of leading figures from the natural and social sciences, and from the humanities, that took place in the 1940s. Numerous multidisciplinary teams of researchers were brought together in the Allied struggle against the Axis powers.

Enormous efforts were made on both sides of the Atlantic to translate the latest scientific knowledge and academic expertise into useful instruments of war. Recall, first of all, some of the large-scale projects that were undertaken to pool intellectual assets in order to help defeat the Third Reich: for instance the code-breaking work that played so important a role in wartime intelligence; or, on a still larger scale, the human and material resources that were needed in order to produce new and extraordinary weapons of war, most notably nuclear bomb technology. The extensive collaborative work conducted by the teams at Bletchley Park in Britain made use of academic talents from across the disciplines;[1] the US Army Signals Intelligence Service ran parallel operations, and the combined efforts of all of the code-breakers shortened the war.[2] Meanwhile, vast numbers of skilled personnel were assembled as part of the 'Manhattan Project' to develop the first atomic weapon.[3]

The human scientists who worked at the OSS and other intelligence organizations sought to unravel something rather more amorphous than the codes that concerned the Bletchley teams. And evidently the pursuit of the Nazi mind was of less immediate urgency for the Allies than the work of either the code-breakers or the physical scientists. But this is not to say the wartime research of psychologists, psychiatrists, and psychoanalysts was historically or culturally inconsequential.

—•—

Some months before the United States entered the war plans for reform of intelligence-gathering in Washington were already afoot. Roosevelt had been persuaded that new streamlined organizations were required to combat the Third Reich and its allies. One outcome of these developments was the creation of the Office of the Coordinator of Information in July 1941, with the aim of pulling together propaganda and intelligence that had hitherto been produced by a plethora of different American agencies. In 1942 (by which time America was at war) the President split its functions into two, and the OSS and the Office of War Information emerged as separate entities. Walter Langer worked for both; he produced research for the Office of the Coordinator of Information in 1941, and in the following years wrote various reports for the OSS.

The OSS had no precise equivalent in pre-war America, nor did it approximate closely to intelligence agencies in wartime Britain. It is instructive to compare the rather cosmopolitan and open-minded climate of opinion at the OSS with the narrower and starkly chauvinist outlook that had predominated at the Military Intelligence Division (MID), created in 1885.

The MID dominated the field of intelligence in the United States until the 1930s. Conservative-minded army officers had run the organization and viewed independent intellectuals (especially of the Jewish émigré variety) with grave suspicion. Although the MID had employed specialist advisers to investigate so-called German national character in the First World War and, increasingly, had taken note of developments in anthropology and psychology, the characterizations of the enemy psyche that were commissioned here tended to be broad-brush, and often crude and stereotypical.[4] Moreover, the primary political focus of official intelligence in the 1920s was communism (as it would be once again in the 1950s).[5] Some MID staff had very close links with right-wing politicians in Washington. They also maintained regular contact with J. Edgar Hoover at the FBI (then still called the Bureau of Investigation). A number of MID officers participated in eugenic organizations, extolled the virtues of the 'Nordic race', and dreaded the consequences of admitting rising numbers of politically suspect immigrants into the New World.[6] After the Russian Revolution in 1917, and throughout the 1920s, the MID was greatly exercised by the menace of Bolshevik and anarchist troublemakers and spies, as well as the dangers of American reliance upon 'Jewish' finance.

By the 1940s, however, US intelligence had not only benefited from a major expansion of financial and logistical resources, but also incorporated large numbers of civilian personnel, many of whom were just the kind of people the MID had dreaded.[7] Like its successor the CIA (created in 1947), the OSS sustained close relationships with experts from the universities, involving large number of professors from the arts, literature, and human sciences in its burgeoning organization. Among its several purposes was the task of deciphering the state of mind of foreign leaders and gauging the morale of overseas populations.

The OSS merits consideration here in its own right; for nowhere else was the problem of Nazi psychology more vigorously and closely studied. The papers of the OSS director General 'Wild Bill' Donovan, in the US national archives (covering his directorship of the OSS) and the Cornell Law Library (focusing on his role in assisting the preparation of the prosecution case at the Nuremberg trial), provide ample indication of his concern with the *psychological* dimensions of Nazism.

Although the organizational contexts of Langer's and Dicks's work on the Nazis were very different, nonetheless there were affinities between their research questions and recourse to psychoanalysis. As we have seen,

Dicks tried to understand Hess and other senior officers, sought to identify the nature of the emotional attachment to Nazism and the Reich prevalent in POWs from the Wehrmacht and the SS in the later years of the war, and endeavoured to track the real, often unspoken, and perhaps unconscious beliefs of German civilians. Langer and his colleagues at the OSS would explore related questions.

In his history of the Tavistock Clinic, Dicks revealed how many of his immediate associates in the field of mental health moved seamlessly from army service to high positions in post-war organizations in Britain, the United States, and elsewhere, served on the advisory boards of commercial corporations, or gained university posts in business studies, industrial psychology, and human relations. So many of the men and women who made up the staff of the Tavistock Clinic were linked to the military services in the fight against Hitler that an entire section of Dicks's history is entitled 'The Tavistock at War.'[8]

Walter Langer and Henry Dicks probably never met, despite their criss-crossing paths—the American had a spell in Hampstead; the Englishman at Harvard—and shared concerns.[9] And while the head of the OSS, General Donovan, developed close links with the director of MI6 during the war, it is unlikely they would have discussed the inquiries of relatively low-profile contributors to army intelligence such as Langer or Dicks. Nor is it clear that any specific recommendations by the far more senior intelligence mandarin, Walter's brother William, regarding the relevance of psychoanalysis generated any particular heat at the highest levels of government or the army. What is more apparent is that the broad findings of clinicians regarding Hitler's psychopathology were congruent with the assumptions of senior American officialdom anyway. Whether or not direct government ministerial discussion of the clinical reports that were produced by intelligence officers ever took place, it is clear that testimony by some Nazi fugitives regarding the psychology of the German leadership was taken seriously at high levels, at least in Washington. Be that as it may, the head of MI6, 'C', realized that Wild Bill was a key figure to cultivate, even before the American's prominent stewardship of the OSS: he urged Churchill to meet Donovan personally, and they duly lunched together on 16 December 1940.[10]

Before undertaking his study of the Führer, Walter Langer offered Donovan several possible applications of clinical knowledge to wartime propaganda and intelligence activities. They discussed whether insights drawn from the psychoanalytical literature on neurosis could be used to make more general assumptions about anxious and conflicted American attitudes towards Germany and the fight against fascism. Langer suggested that the theory of neurosis provided a 'magnified picture' of the 'average person' and urged that domestic and foreign propaganda messages should be crafted with more attention to their emotional and subliminal impact, and with greater sensitivity to the cultural context in which such communications were received.[11] He also advised that propaganda at home was likely to be ineffective where it insulted the recipient's intelligence or too obviously manipulated facts.

A number of other psychoanalysts undertook studies of German propaganda in these years and played a similar role in wartime intelligence. A case in point was the émigré Austrian psychoanalyst and art historian Ernst Kris, who compiled reports on German radio propaganda for the BBC and collaborated (after his move to New York) on Langer's OSS Hitler study.[12] Leonard Langer (Walter's nephew) later recalled how his father, William (who was installed as head of the OSS research and analysis branch not long after the organization's foundation in 1942), was convinced of the utility of psychoanalysis, and made the case to Donovan for a Freudian approach to propaganda.[13] William Langer wrote to the Director to state: 'I am personally convinced that psychological warfare operations can be strengthened by bringing in people in the psychoanalytic field.'[14]

William Langer also made the case more specifically for the employment of his brother at the OSS. In fact, the two Langers were knocking on a semi-open door in suggesting that the intelligence agency might fruitfully attend to the unconscious minds of Germans and Americans, since Donovan had reached a similar view. Evidently the ghastly presiding figure in Nazi Germany merited especially careful appraisal. So although from the vantage-point of today it seems surprising that such constituencies for the application of Freudian thought existed at all within these agencies of the state, in sanctioning a psychoanalytically sensitive exploration of Hitler's mind Donovan was expressing the commonplace cultural view that Hitler was a leader whose policies and actions were driven, to an accentuated degree, by unconscious factors, and that these could be decoded by the shrewd interpreter.

Walter Langer feared that too much was hoped of him, and he seemed to play down expectations at the start of his research by pointing to the limitations entailed in writing psychoanalytically of a figure who was never a patient. Despite those misgivings, Langer was keen to secure a professional connection with the OSS, and he was pleased to obtain freelance assignments, including the preparation of reports on German morale and the deciphering of the underlying meanings and emotional effects of the Nazi leader's speeches, before finally, in 1943, taking on the task of producing a full-blown 'psychoanalytical' study of Hitler. Even so, he found himself vexed by organizational constraints on his freedom of manoeuvre at the OSS, and fretted over the limited resources afforded to him.[15]

Langer's institutional significance at the OSS should not be overstated. The organization was involved in investigating an enormous range of issues: for example, relationships and tensions within Germany's bureaucracy; the distribution of power across its state organizations; the location and preparedness of German troops; the effects of bombing; the impact of propaganda messages; details of Nazi policies and practices in occupied territories; assessments of broader socio-political attitudes; and more. Langer had his brother's active support, but probably only Donovan's sporadic personal attention.

His was one of a number of ventures into Nazi psychology that were supported around the same time by the OSS leadership. Another commission to study Hitler was undertaken by the OSS officer and psychologist Henry Murray, while other public organizations on both sides of the Atlantic also solicited reports of German character and morale that drew on psychoanalysts and psychiatrists, and, directly or obliquely, assumed the significance of unconscious attitudes to political authority in the conduct of the war and the creation of a post-war settlement. In short, Langer's psychoanalytic interventions were far from isolated ventures. A range of other work was produced, varying from studies of the psychological impact of German radio propaganda to analyses of the mentality of German soldiers, workers, or concentration-camp guards, and proposals for the effective re-education of adults and children in post-war Germany.[16]

The problem with which Walter Langer began his intelligence career in 1941—how to strengthen American motivation to fight in the war—was soon eclipsed by that of de-motivating the nation's enemies. As William Langer recalled: the attack on Pearl Harbor in December 1941 marked the shift from one enterprise to the other. Plenty of Americans were keen thereafter to support the war and the aim of total victory: they flocked to enlist or to contribute in other ways once Hitler decided to follow up on the Japanese attack by his declaration of war on the United States.[17] Even so, a sizeable minority of Americans believed that a negotiated peace, rather than absolute victory, would suffice.[18]

———•———

That Donovan was entrusted with the OSS and able to build it up so rapidly no doubt owed a considerable amount to his long-standing relationship with the President, going all the way back to their time together at Columbia University's law school. Born to an Irish Catholic family, Donovan was a First World War combatant and recipient of a congressional Medal of Honor. He became a well-connected Wall Street lawyer and had amassed considerable wealth before making his name as head of the OSS.[19] While his nickname, 'Wild Bill', derived from his impressive sporting prowess as a student, the tag certainly seemed in keeping with his freewheeling leadership style.

Donovan was no political radical; he could not be described as remotely of the Left, although some of the OSS appointments he made led conservatives to wonder. In fact he had been a supporter of the Republican president Herbert Hoover in the early 1930s and had harboured his own political ambitions on the Republican side. But Donovan was amongst the old law-school classmates from 1907 that Roosevelt had invited to his fifty-first birthday celebrations in January 1933.[20] Despite misgivings about the huge government spending required by FDR's 'New Deal', Donovan had been assigned a variety of high-level diplomatic tasks in Europe during the early years of Roosevelt's presidency, including the brief to meet personally with Mussolini in December 1935.[21] Long before the United States formally engaged in the war, Wild Bill had anticipated that conflict would prove unavoidable. Evidently Roosevelt's and Donovan's personal understanding and alignment facilitated the latter's appointment as Coordinator of Information in 1941 and, the year after, as head of the OSS.

Whatever their political differences, the two men shared a belief in the importance of exploiting psychological knowledge in modern warfare and politics. Understanding the mindset of the German leadership necessitated application of the latest, most promising techniques for investigating the psyche. OSS intelligence-gathering would draw upon diverse strands of thought, and its research staff might apply anything from the metapsychology of the controversial Viennese professor to the dark arts of Madison Avenue advertising executives. The latter were deployed directly on occasion as 'black propaganda' specialists, with the aim of fomenting discontent behind enemy lines.[22]

Donovan was unabashedly an empire-builder, brazenly colonizing ground previously occupied by other agencies of government. His qualities aroused both admiration and mistrust. J. Edgar Hoover regarded the OSS as a hotbed of subversives, and rivalry between the OSS and FBI was intense. Hoover's mistrust of the OSS was well founded according to the official historian of MI5 Christopher Andrew, who has described Donovan's organization as 'the most penetrated intelligence agency in American history'.[23] Andrew describes intercept evidence suggesting that as many as 200 Americans may have been working for the Soviet Union around this time, adding that 'every section of the wartime administration of [Roosevelt] had been penetrated by Soviet intelligence'.[24] But between 1941 and 1945, when British, US, and Soviet interests in achieving the military defeat of the Nazi state had converged, Donovan was prepared to throw any resources he could find at the task and had no more compunction about employing able officers with leftist sympathies than he had about commissioning a psychoanalyst to study Hitler's mind. Evidently he broke from the 'waspish' and rigidly reactionary attitudes that had been commonplace at the MID.

———•———

Although the talking cure was naturally associated with anti-fascism (its Jewish founder was regarded in turn as a degenerate thinker by the Nazis), Freudian thought did not directly presuppose a political affiliation. It was, for many British clinicians, consonant with liberalism and democratic values. In American thought psychoanalysis often resonated with images of self-improvement and rugged individualism, a means of ensuring ego strength and even the unabashed pursuit of the American dream. At the same time, it did lend itself to particular kinds of leftist theory, in which the illusions of fascism or, for that matter, capitalism (with its unsentimental cultivation of greed, competition, and envy) could be understood as problematic features not just of social formations, but of unconscious psychic life too.

Herbert Marcuse, who would become especially well known as a radical intellectual in 1960s America, was one of several contributors to the Frankfurt School who pursued an interest in both politics and psychoanalysis in the war and through the post-war period. Like a number of his German émigré colleagues, Marcuse sought to combine elements of Freud and Marx in order to understand both fascism and capitalism, and more specifically he offered an assortment of observations culled from ethnography, historiography, and depth psychology in analysing the German situation as part of his remit for US intelligence.

Marcuse's willingness to provide reports for the OSS aroused occasional criticism later on from some on the Left: counter-culture gurus (as Marcuse became) were not supposed to be former American intelligence officers.[25] He had little trouble in justifying this aspect of his past, however: it was for him and his colleagues a necessary contribution to the struggle against the Third Reich. Nor was Donovan unduly worried by criticism from the Right of his appointment criteria that brought such assorted Jews, socialists, and radicals to Washington.

Marcuse produced papers for the psychology division of the OSS with titles such as 'The New German Mentality' and 'Private Morale in Germany'.[26] These aimed to harness history, economics, cultural theory, and psychology in identifying the peculiar nature of German development, thus providing a basis for both wartime and post-war planning. Marcuse pointed to the idiosyncratic nature of Germany's historical path, describing features of the economy, politics, and mythology that had combined to produce, as he put it, a 'catastrophic fatalism'. His approach moved between the identification of feelings and modes of relating to others that characterized German people at that time (for instance, grievance, hatred, envy, and idealization) and a more abstract kind of historical analysis. He argued that Germany demonstrated in an extreme form a collective state of abjection after 1918. On the other hand, as though anticipating the *Sonderweg* or 'special path' debate about the nature of Germany's modern history that would draw so much attention decades later, he was at pains to insist that the underlying group-psychological dynamic should not be seen as somehow a German preserve.[27]

Marcuse argued that the Third Reich was a *revolution* of the Right. It ushered in a new form of social order and it successfully played upon and exploited unconscious factors. It relied upon a seductive but also a terrorizing kind of group psychology.[28] Like Langer and Dicks, Marcuse made various kinds of practical intervention, including 'black propaganda' suggestions such as the proposal to spread a rumour of disastrous numbers of cases of TB among factory workers in Germany.[29] He also went on to draft the order that formally abolished the Nazi Party at the close of the war.[30] At the same time, though, he produced a series of more far-reaching reviews. For instance, he rejected the idea that Germany represented some aberrant and alien national form across the ages: it would not do to speak of the Germans' innate or constitutionally intolerant or especially murderous attitudes, as though there was some continuous illness in the body politic that ran from the time of Luther to Hitler. Historical perspective, not timeless psychology, was required. On the other hand, it was quite possible, he suggested, that conditions could re-emerge in Germany or elsewhere even after Hitler's defeat that would once again be conducive to fascism.

Although Max Horkheimer and Theodor Adorno, the two leading figures in the Frankfurt School, remained more remote from this kind of direct secondment (in part due to Horkheimer's heart condition, which had been a factor in the decision of both men to move from the East Coast to California by 1941), their work also returned over and over again to the German disaster. Like Marcuse, though, a number of other Frankfurt School associates contributed directly to intelligence research and analysis on postwar Germany, for the OSS or other government agencies.[31] Franz Neumann, for example, the author of *Behemoth*, a major study of the Nazi state, went on to play an important role for the OSS at the Nuremberg trial.[32]

———•———

Donovan's intelligence organization displayed a combination of academic seriousness, cunning, and wild ideas. Film and advertising executives rubbed shoulders with anthropologists, sociologists, economists, and psychologists. It drew on long-established Ivy League professors, whilst also recruiting in the worlds of business, law, journalism, and the arts. The OSS also employed actors and forgers, socialites, oddball artists, film stars, painters, even the head of Barnum and Baileys entertainments in various mysterious capacities. The term 'brainstorming' (a buzz-phrase of the 1940s, popularized by the advertising manager Alex Faickney Osborn) could have been designed for the house style of the agency. If anything was out of bounds, it was strict adherence to any standard operating procedure. Free-associative ideas at the organization ranged from a plan to make use of phosphorescent foxes to another involving incendiary flying bats that were to be flown into Japan.[33]

In Britain, comparable work was undertaken in several different branches of government. Both the Political Warfare Executive, a clandestine propaganda unit that reported to senior officials at the Foreign Office, and the Special Operations Executive, created by Churchill to focus upon guerrilla operations behind the lines, made use of officers (including some advisers with clinical backgrounds or specific psychological training) to develop ingenious forms of 'black propaganda'. British intelligence officers also assembled advice manuals that could be smuggled to enemy troops or civilians in a bid to help potential shirkers, deserters, and malingerers to absent themselves from duty. Detailed advice on how to fake the symptoms of flu, tuberculosis, or mental impairment was produced.[34]

Although Walter Langer was not given free rein in his research, and certainly no blank cheque, other schemes were apparently beset by financial irregularities and there were complaints that the OSS was tardy in investigating potential abuses and that money was wasted. But in noting such complaints of lax supervision, and the spectacular and at times even circuslike aspect of some projects, it would be wrong to downplay the gravity and urgency of the task facing the OSS. The incorporation of the human sciences into its operations evidenced the commitment of the Allies to bring all possible intellectual resources to bear against the Nazis.[35]

———•———

One line of investigation followed the suggestion that since Hitler's sexuality was so confused and his ego so peculiar in formation, his personality might be especially vulnerable to manipulation. He was not a 'normal' man, and had not resolved, it was said, the conflict between desire for his mother and fear of his father; he oscillated, so the argument went on, uncertainly between an unconscious identification with the denigrated, prostrate woman and the brutal sadistic man who would trample all before him: witness the fact that he was pathologically unable to find another woman to take his mother's place. His pathology, it was argued, was projected onto Germany, and this in turn fuelled his omnipotent quest to 'save' her. Particular significance was attached to the supposedly autobiographical components of Hitler's *Mein Kampf*.

As Erik Erikson, a pioneering and controversial psychoanalytic writer on matters of history, biography, and the stages of identity formation, warned soon after the war, it would be naive to treat *Mein Kampf* as simply the 'involuntary confession' of its author: this would leave out of consideration, among other things, the rhetorical, stylized aspect of its presentation and the orchestration of the 'personal' story by several other hands. The myth of Hitler's life was a work in progress through the 1920s and 1930s. Erikson drew attention to Goebbels' significant role in constructing public representations of Hitler's personal history and triumph over adversity; Erikson pointed to Hitler's particular abilities as actor and speechmaker, but also to Goebbels as the guiding force behind 'his barking master'. But such caution about the 'wild' analysis of the Führer through interpretation of *Mein Kampf* did not prevent Erikson (any more than certain ingenious 'dirty tricks' specialists at the OSS) from offering his own diagnosis: Hitler had 'hazardous borderline traits', yet he knew how to pull back from the brink of madness and 'exploit his own hysteria'.[36]

During the war the Boston industrialist Stanley Lovell, a leading figure in research-and-development work at the OSS, seized upon the view of analysts such as Langer that Hitler's sexuality was uncertain, and sought to find a practical application for such hypotheses. Notably, he described the attempt that was made to use drugs to tamper with Hitler's identity.[37] Apparently Lovell explored the possibility of slipping sex hormones into Hitler's meals.[38] It was typical of Donovan's style that his staff could so freely pursue such ideas: officials were encouraged to think of the impossible and waste no time in moving from half-baked plans to practical implementation. Lovell was advised on joining the organization: 'Never ask [Donovan] what to do. Do it and show him what you have done.'[39] Hence arose what Lovell called the 'glandular approach' to sabotaging Hitler.

This, Lovell confessed, was his own personal favourite among a host of unlikely schemes. He was inspired, so he said, by America's so-called 'top diagnosticians and gland experts'. They told Lovell that Hitler was 'definitely close to the male/female line', as was made evident apparently by the Nazi leader's poor emotional control, violent passions, and selection of companions such as the homosexual Ernst Röhm. Lovell's idea was to see if the Führer's sexual identity could be further confused. This scheme unwittingly echoed popular myth about Hitler; this was the time, after all, of the popular song that, to the tune of 'Colonel Bogey', mocked Hitler's 'one ball' and offered jibes about the deficient sexual equipment of Goebbels, Himmler, and Göring. (Claims that Hitler did indeed lack a testicle were made in the Russian autopsy report on the remains of his body—or at least the remains believed to be Hitler's—in 1945 and were subsequently built into various psychobiographical theories; they have since been debated, debunked by historians and revived in the press.)[40] Secretly infiltrated chemicals that could enhance 'the female side' of the German leader, the OSS officer believed, 'might do wonders'. Excited by thoughts of introducing hormones into Hitler's diet and thereby inducing, among other things, hair loss and a soprano voice (thus making the leader a figure of ridicule to his own people), the OSS, according to Lovell, endeavoured to find a corruptible gardener who worked in the vicinity of the Führer. He, in turn, would be bribed to inject a mystery product (somehow to be provided to him by an agent) into the food grown in the grounds of the Nazi leader's 'Eagle's Nest' at Berchtesgaden.

That this desperately unlikely ploy was unsuccessful is evident enough, although it makes Hess's concern with protecting his genitalia from excessive radiation during X-rays or avoiding certain drinks and foods that the British might have tampered with seem less outlandish. The details of the OSS scheme remain obscure: Lovell did not even know if the gardener in question was ever passed the money and if so, whether or not he had simply missed the chance, forgotten about the project, or had acted in bad faith all along.[41]

Lovell's reminiscences may have been somewhat overblown, but they convey the spirit that prevailed and illustrate the kinds of stratagems that were sometimes commissioned at the OSS: everyone from gland experts to booby-trap boffins to psychoanalysts had a place in this somewhat surreal espionage setting. As well as plans for using malodorous compounds to cause embarrassment and fear in Germany, mescaline to bend the minds of certain POWs, and bacterially infected stamps to produce illness, Lovell reported experiments that aimed at infiltrating a chemical agent into a vase of flowers in order to blind Hitler and Mussolini during a summit: unfortunately the venue of the summit was moved at the last moment and the plan was scuppered.

Lovell also described his investigations of the power of hypnosis, claiming that he had consulted distinguished psychiatrists such as Lawrence Kubie and Karl and William Menninger but was disappointed by their uncertain conclusions. Lovell wanted to know whether it would be possible to hypnotize a German POW then instruct him to kill Hitler, smuggling him back to Berlin where he would then carry out the task as soon as the opportunity arose.[42] It sounds like a scenario for *The Manchurian Candidate*.

————•————

The OSS sought exceptional talent; but it might also seem to offer a home for eccentrics of dubious sanity. Its own in-house psychologist, Henry Murray, was concerned that it was at risk of employing people who were seriously unhinged, and to avoid this he introduced elaborate screening procedures.[43] Looking back from 1950, when he was a witness at the trial of Alger Hiss, the American civil servant accused of spying for the Russians, Murray conceded that the OSS may indeed have employed quite a few 'psychopathic' characters.[44] For according to Murray, spying, with its much-vaunted requirements of disguise and double-dealing, borrowed identity papers, invented personal histories, licence to commit violence, and so forth attracted certain 'types' who might well bring the organization into disrepute or at least limit its efficiency.

Murray's selection procedures drew on behavioural science and also had a quasi-psychoanalytic aspect, having affinities with the new British army officer selection experiments pioneered around the same time by Wilfred Bion, John Rickman, John Bowlby, and other important contributors to psychoanalysis.[45] New methods of selection involved extensive observation of candidates. Sometimes they were required to live and work together for several days, to participate in group activities, undergo intelligence tests, and face stressful situations. The nature of the subject's social relationships, attitudes to army superiors, equals, and subordinates, capacity for insight, and ability to cope with adversity were monitored. Instead of a 'nod and a wink' form of interview or a rote exam, a crucial compass for selection bodies would be the nature of the candidate's emotional life and capacity to function in groups while being observed. Placed under pressure, how well could the subject in question think? Evidence of how individuals bore anxiety, how far they could 'digest' raw emotions, and the degree to which they shirked responsibility or took the lead was to be ascertained by close observation. This at least was the intention.

Such endeavours to screen and select the best officer-class 'material' on both sides of the Atlantic were dwarfed (in America at least) by the human resources devoted to diagnosing and removing 'unsuitable' cases from all ranks of the army, navy, and air-force. Psychiatrists gained a substantial role, screening vast numbers of potential GIs: marshalling a simplified version of psychoanalysis, spokesmen and lobbyists for the psychiatric profession in the United States promised far more than they could deliver: 'a revolutionary new approach to the cure of mental disorder' in the army.[46] It has been estimated that about 12% of army recruits (approximately 1.75 million of the men who applied) were indeed to be rejected as psychiatrically unfit.[47] Such assessments, notes the historian Andrew Scull, were often based on 'ludicrously superficial' examinations, lasting no more than a couple of minutes (thus quite unlike the elaborately conceived tests described earlier). Nor did such confident claims as to the acumen and scientific reliability of the psychiatrists in judging the soundness of the men before them in fact immunize the army against high rates of mental breakdown during the conflict.[48]

In Murray's eyes, the risk of mental breakdown was only one aspect of the evaluative task required at the OSS. Pen-pushers on the one hand and manic, sadistic, or melancholic types on the other were, in theory, to be weeded out. A premium was placed on leadership qualities, and it was stressed that the capacity to work collaboratively in a team, not merely to obey or embody authority, were required qualities. Those who failed to jump these hurdles were unlikely to be allowed to work abroad for the OSS.[49]

These recruitment procedures are further evidence of how far the discipline of psychology was central to the ethos of the organization, its self-conscious attention to how its own staff thought and functioned providing a counterpart to its prolific research on the mentality of Nazism. It may be, also, that working for an organization that employed disguises, spying, and subterfuge, led some OSS staff during the war to deepen their curiosity about issues of individual and group identity, or at least to become interested in the gap between stated intentions and unspoken motivations.[50]

If the OSS made use of 'depth psychology' in seeking to understand the behaviour and decision-making of Hitler and other key individuals within the Nazi regime, it also focused attention upon the myriad emotional factors that bind groups together and lead people to infect one another with fears and wishes. Undermining the sense of 'togetherness' of the German population was an aim of black propaganda and various other covert operations that were conducted behind the lines. Again the 'psy' professions were centrally involved in such endeavours.

———•———

This was a period when many artists, film-makers, and commercial enterprises sought to make use of Freudian discoveries. Advertising strategists, for instance, increasingly sought inspiration from Surrealist explorations of dreams and the unconscious that in turn owed a great deal to psychoanalysis. It was not unknown for business executives and public-relations consultants in mid-twentieth-century New York or Los Angeles to speak what the historian of psychology Graham Richard, looking at the cultural assimilation of psychoanalysis in Britain, has called 'Freudish'.[51]

This 'Freudish' language was seen by some as a vehicle by which people could be more successfully manipulated and persuaded to conduct themselves in 'desirable' ways, or rather to become commercially desiring subjects whose appetite for products—or for that matter, political causes—could be stirred up or dampened down by techniques of psychological propaganda.

Psychoanalysis could be adapted to commerce, promised Edward Bernays, the advertising guru and relation of Freud.[52] Tapping dreams, not needs, he argued, was often the best way into the wallets of consumers. The fact that Goebbels employed similar arts of persuasion and manipulation in an altogether more terrible form had increasingly exercised Bernays during the 1930s, although needless to say the Nazi propagandist showed none of the enthusiasm for Freud's work that characterized Bernays and was becoming commonplace on Madison Avenue.[53]

The superficial convergence between a culture of psychoanalysis that aimed at understanding of the unconscious and the unabashed exploitation of dream worlds, desires, and anxieties for corporate profit was made most apparent in America. Nowhere was the use (or abuse) of psychoanalysis for corporate advancement better illustrated than in the career of Bernays himself. How deep his knowledge of psychoanalytic ideas went is debatable, but he was able to combine certain of its terms with the findings of social psychologists and the *aperçus* of an earlier generation of crowd theorists such as Le Bon. A prolific writer on the science of identifying public opinion and of refining the arts of persuasion within corporate culture, Bernays became an influential figure in private and public image-management during and beyond the 1920s.

As well as producing books and speeches that explained the psychology of advertising and corporate public relations, Bernays also applied himself to the problem of securing the allegiance of millions to the liberal state. He was perturbed by the skill of fascist parties in exploiting modern media techniques, and was wary of the threat that a rampant extreme Right posed within America as well as abroad. He noted how demagogues in the United States were proving ever more adept at fuelling hysterical racial fears, often anti-Semitic in tone, through their diagnoses of the ills of modern life. Ominous tub-thumpers of the 1930s, such as the Catholic priest Father Charles Coughlin, echoed and endorsed Mussolini's and Hitler's diatribes against the supposedly linked menaces of Bolshevism, internationalism, Jewry, and capitalism. Coughlin followed in the footsteps of the European fascist vanguard in exploiting the medium of radio to reach large audiences with his populist, alarmist messages.

Such anxieties led Bernays into ever more active political advisory roles, and to writing works such as *Speak up for Democracy* (1940) and *Democratic Leadership in Total War* (1943). Without recognition of the unconscious attractions of the Duce or the Führer, he feared that American public opinion could take the wrong path and succumb to its own homespun demagoguery. In this he was part of a wave of writers and consultants who pointed to the fascist potential 'within'—in his novel *It Can't Happen Here* (1935), for example, Sinclair Lewis had presented the dangers of a fascist-leaning organization, the 'Minute Men', entrenching itself in power in America.[54] Like Bernays, Lewis insisted that it was necessary to bolster liberal democracy not only in the polity but also within the psyche of the electorate.

This kind of argument was not necessarily Freudian, at least beyond token reference, but the assumption that Freud *might* be relevant to political analysis of fascist attractions did become increasingly common during this period.[55] It is not surprising that in such a climate Donovan and his organization could be persuaded that commissioning psychoanalysts would be justified, and that Freudian thought would be a useful resource for understanding Hitler.

———•———

Donovan was well aware of the crucial role ascribed to mental attitudes by the Nazi Party itself, and above all by its leader. His files about Hitler included the translation of a speech from August 1939 in which he described the role of 'mental power' as paramount.[56] Anticipating the destruction of Poland, Hitler declared that for the German people there would be no retreat: a 'manly bearing' was essential. The state, he insisted, would always be victorious when united. In the final struggle, '[m]ental factors are decisive'.

In this speech the Führer cited Germany's military past as evidence of the role played by the will and the vital significance of maintaining absolute psychological strength. If there were vestiges of nineteenth-century ideas of the unconscious wrapped up in this—with the accent placed upon the wellsprings of 'race' and the power of instinct in shaping minds—there was also an insistence that, by dint of formidable personal volition, the self could master all obstacles or challenges. What was required, Hitler said, was the leader's total confidence in his own invincibility: 'Frederick the Great secured victory only through his mental power.' He went on to explain that the German defeat in 1918 had occurred because the 'mental prerequisites were not sufficient'.[57] In dozens of other speeches, not to mention *Mein Kampf*, this insistence on psychological strength and the fortification of the will could also be found.[58]

The Third Reich was based in reality on rather more material facts of life than the indomitable, masculine will. Industrial power and vast military force on the ground were of greater significance than airy appeals to mental power or the ghost of Frederick the Great. But Nazism was formidably effective at mobilizing hearts and minds; it produced deep and enduring identifications among a very wide electorate. (It also exercised, of course, terrifying powers of coercion for anyone inclined to dissent.)

Quite what the Führer signified for the German people was to become a research question at the OSS, just as it has remained for legions of political scientists and historians ever since. How had family structure and the particular patriarchal form it had taken in Germany affected mental development, and how did that in turn lend itself to political identification with such a bizarre figure? Culture and history could not be understood in isolation from the impulses of social psychology, it was argued. Unconscious terrors and desires shaped political allegiances all too often—perhaps always.

By 1943 the OSS's attention was becoming more closely focused upon the shape of a post-war settlement in Europe, potential arrangements for military occupation of Germany, and governance of the country. If there was a clear position within its research-and-analysis branch at this time, a recent historian of the organization has observed, it was to propose that government steer a course between the punitive attitude of Henry Morgenthau, Roosevelt's Secretary of the Treasury, who sought to break up post-war Germany, thereby destroying its economic and military potency, and others, notably Henry L. Stimson, who advocated a rapid rebuilding of Germany in order to create a powerful Western bulwark against the USSR.[59]

Researchers at the OSS had to try to predict the psycho-social consequences of such different approaches. The possible outcomes of policies that might cause 'humiliation', 'grievance', 'illusions', 'guilt', or 'persecution', issues that had already formed part of the discourse surrounding the Treaty of Versailles after the First World War, were now reconsidered. Fears of the emotional effects of a demand for restitution or heavy-handed international occupation and policing echoed through American and British debates on how to secure lasting tranquillity in Europe in 1945. In contributing to these debates the OSS drew not only upon its own staff members, but also upon a network of university teachers and researchers who were asked to give their views about the appropriate balance of 'carrot and stick' that should be employed. Among others, the historian of ideas Arthur O. Lovejoy and the influential social theorist Talcott Parsons were asked to circulate relevant ideas and proposals on such matters for the OSS and other wartime organizations.[60]

The OSS also played a significant role in the post-war prosecution of the
Nazi leadership, being designated as the official US investigatory unit for
the International Military Tribunal. Donovan served as special assistant to
the US Chief Prosecutor, Robert Jackson, and amassed much of the material that supported the prosecution case at Nuremberg.[61] Although Donovan
worked closely with Jackson at the outset, tensions soon emerged. Jackson
preferred to base the bulk of his case around documentary evidence, as this
was more reliable than eyewitness testimony. Donovan disagreed, arguing
that live witnesses would give the trial 'an affirmative human aspect' and
better enable it to serve its broadly pedagogical end.[62] They were unable to
resolve their differences and Donovan departed from the team only a few
days into the trial. It is not clear whether he directly supported the extensive
psychological profiling of the war criminals undertaken at Nuremberg, but
in view of his earlier role in promoting such studies it seems likely he would
have been as sympathetic as Jackson was to the need for close psychiatric
observation of the defendants.

In June 1945 eminent psychiatrists and neurologists had written to
Jackson pressing the case for intensive access to the prison, not only in order
to grasp the defendants' personal beliefs but also to learn more about the
German national character. Close study of the most important political culprits, declared one of the signatories, the psychoanalyst Dr John Millet,
would 'add to our information concerning the character and habitual desires
of the German people'.[63] It was claimed that such work was vital in order
to draw appropriate psycho-political lessons for the future. Some went as far
as to propose dissecting the brains of the Nuremberg perpetrators; this
would involve executing the men by a shot to the chest so as not to damage
brain tissue. Jackson replied that hanging was to be preferred to shooting as
a form of execution, since the latter might imply death with honour.[64]

Nuremberg was regarded as a unique laboratory, but the IMT had to balance the scientific and legal imperatives: should psychological interrogations
result in divided professional opinions, Jackson warned, the defence might
seek to use this conflict to undermine the prosecution case.[65] While the
judicial authorities did not grant all of the requests that were made for such
observational studies, a process of intrusive scientific investigation would
prove integral to the investigative procedure in several ways.

———•———

The OSS had many admirers but also some powerful detractors. Donovan
did not have the same close relationship with Harry Truman that he had

enjoyed with FDR. The organization was officially abolished in 1946, during the Truman presidency, and the CIA was established in its place on 18 September 1947.[66] However, a number of OSS initiatives and priorities (including psychological profiling and various techniques of psychological warfare) and many of its 13,000 former employees were incorporated in the new organization.[67]

7

Hitler's Mind

'What do you make of Hitler?' Donovan's question was to be the spur, in the spring of 1943, for Walter Langer, with the aid of a few of his colleagues, to compile a remarkably copious 'Source Book' and an accompanying secret report on the Führer for the OSS.[1] These remained classified documents for many years after the war. In an introduction to the later, published version of his wartime report, *The Mind of Adolf Hitler*, Langer recalled the furious speed at which he had proceeded: the text was submitted to the leadership of the intelligence agency that same autumn.

William Langer would later indicate the climate of hope that had surrounded psychoanalysis at the time his brother's work was commissioned. He described the inquiry that Walter was required to produce for the OSS 'into the mind, specifically into the unconscious and irrational forces that lay beneath the surface of mental functioning', and he noted how this research was designed for an urgent purpose at a time of war. Walter Langer's work was never envisaged as an academic, historical monograph, still less a psychoanalytical paper for a learned scientific meeting of the Boston Psychoanalytic Society, but as a piece of *intelligence*, written to a tight deadline, under considerable pressure. This was still, as William Langer ruefully observed, often overlooked.

Donovan's enthusiasm presumably overcame Langer's residual qualms about this form of psychobiography. The latter did not need to wait for the acerbic reviewers of his book, years later, in order to realize the scholarly and clinical limitations of such armchair speculation about Hitler's private fantasies or the secret passions that drove him: indeed, he was at pains to point them out himself. He never claimed to have written the last word on the matter, and much later, in correspondence with the American biographer of Hitler, John Toland, he drew attention to the fraught circumstances in which the report was originally compiled and cited its potential weaknesses as well as its achievements.[2]

In fact, Langer's report involved several different types of analysis: most notably, it provided a speculative account of Hitler's character and suggested how it might have come to be formed in his childhood. This is the 'wild' aspect of the work that has come to be most criticized. Langer also considered the perceptions of other people about the Führer, emphasized the symbolic role that Hitler occupied in German society, and explored the nature of his charismatic power. Langer's account sought to differentiate Hitler's own vision of himself from public perceptions of the leader, even though in practice it was clear that the two parts could not be kept fully distinct.

First came an account of Hitler as he believed himself to be; next discussion of the leader as the German people and his immediate associates regarded him. Such reconstructions of Hitler's views and prevailing perceptions of him were a preamble to Langer's own psychological analysis of the subject's mind, and predictions about the way he would conduct the remainder of the war. Thus Langer's brief was also to estimate, in light of his character, what Hitler was likely to do in the final reckoning, when even he might see that Germany's 'will' was no match for the external material forces pitted against it.

Some of Langer's interpretations are questionable, but much of the narrative that he spun might now be regarded as common knowledge and standard fare in biographies.[3] Here is the tale of the brutalized young boy, devoted to his mother Klara, dodging around his grim and punitive father Alois; Langer's tale is of a childhood and adolescence dominated by pipe-dreams, wretchedness, and sometimes terror. He describes the subject's early disappointments and thwarted ambitions, the failed mourning of his mother's death, the pathetic aspirations of the artist *manqué*, the squalid habitat of the loser and wastrel.

Certain aspects of Hitler's self-presentation struck Langer with great force: above all, the Nazi leader's determination to eradicate all doubt and to trust his own raw impulses. 'I follow my course with the precision and security of a sleepwalker':[4] Hitler's remark (made as the aggressiveness of his foreign policy escalated in the later 1930s) provided a dramatic rhetorical starting-point for the report. Langer was intrigued by the Führer's claim to feel such total certainty about the validity of his thought and his actions, and noted how Hitler used this rhetorical ploy in order to reassure his 'more wary followers' that he could not err.[5] Yet the reference to sleep-walking also intimated that he had no conscious control of his destiny, a fact that should have aroused intense anxiety in the German people. For if this blind assurance in the rightness of each new step led him to 'a pinnacle of success', it also 'lured him on until today he stands on the brink of dis-aster'.[6] Hitler believed that he was called to political action from sources that lay deep within himself: he spoke on occasions, Langer noted, of fol-lowing his 'inner voice'.[7]

In yoking the image of the sleepwalker to this sense of utter conviction Hitler made a revealing confession, according to the OSS analyst, that ought to have been taken more seriously. Evidently, for Langer, the ques-tion of whether or not Hitler was a self-conscious swindler (the kind of argument about his character and belief that divided post-war historians such as Alan Bullock and Hugh Trevor-Roper) was not the point.[8] The focus was instead to be upon the unconscious mind (in which contradic-tory views might well co-reside) and Hitler's relationship to his own unconscious processes. Langer was also interested in how Hitler seemed to induce or amplify the very states of mind in others that unconsciously flooded his own psyche.[9] What he communicated, it seemed, was far more than mere words or messages; inchoate emotions too were somehow 'got across'.

What kind of analysis did Langer make? On the one hand his methodo-logical tack was reminiscent of extant psychoanalytical approaches to remote historical figures, such as Freud's (much-criticized) account of Leonardo da Vinci.[10] Langer speculated about the infancy of the subject and investigated the meanings of Hitler's adult symptoms: the troubled sleep, violent rages and tremors, as well as the constant warnings of horrific prospective endings should his will be thwarted. If Langer, like Freud before him, focused his study upon a single mind and imagined what went on inside it, he also sought to pay attention to the way the Führer myth had emerged and the degree to which it was fashioned by others.

With regard to psychoanalytical theory Langer's approach now appears restricted or even antediluvian. Its approach might even have seemed rather dated at the time: it bore little trace of Freud's own later works or the con-tributions of psychoanalytical pioneers such as Karl Abraham or Sandor Ferenczi. Nor did it register British debates about psychoanalytical the-ory and technique of the 1930s and early 1940s, centred on the work of Melanie Klein, even though Langer would have had some awareness of these controversies while he was in London in 1938. In seeking to imagine Hitler's world Langer was, no doubt, influenced by some of Freud's case studies, but it would appear that his most important compass was Freud's *Three Essays on the Theory of Sexuality* of 1905. Langer took it as read that each of us must struggle through our psycho-sexual development, undertaking, if we are able, the rough passage from the 'polymorphous perversity' of earliest infancy to the genital sexuality that was said to mark the mature person. That the nature of sexual fantasy and indeed activity (or lack of it) might point the way to Hitler's pathological personality was also assumed. Langer tried to conceptualize Hitler's early struggles with the oral, anal, and phallic stages, and wondered how these would play out in his adult manner of relating to self and others.

But Langer's account was not confined to an isolated psychobiography; he noted how Hitler portrayed a carefully doctored version of his own history that also satisfied the wishes of his supporters. He suggested, in effect, how fantasies and projections bound Hitler and his followers together: Langer was concerned to demonstrate how the Nazi leader was infused with the desires of others even as he choreographed the legend, willingly allowing fantastical hopes to be invested in him. The Führer's 'charisma' was not simply to be explored by looking 'inside' Hitler's mind; it had also to be seen as a complex social and cultural concoction. Nonetheless, Hitler possessed or soon acquired crucial personal qualities, not least of maniacal conviction, dramatic speaking, and ruthless determination that enabled him to seize his chance as soon as it was offered. Langer understood that the removal of Hitler would not kill Nazism as ideology; but he believed it would in effect decapitate the regime. The Allies, he urged, should concentrate their fire upon the Nazi leader as quickly as possible.

————•————

Langer was not the only specialist who was asked to assess the Führer for the OSS during the Second World War, and by no means the only psychoanalyst who was working for American intelligence at this time. The OSS commissioned, simultaneously, another secret report about Hitler's mind which arrived at rather similar findings. The 240-page manuscript on the German leader that was eventually delivered by Henry Murray was eclipsed by Langer's 281-page submission, but the latter never forgave the former for leaving him in the dark about his separate undertaking. Murray's report was kept secret not only from the public but also from his erstwhile collaborator; and even as the two men struggled to make sense of Hitler's treacherous treatment of rivals, growing mistrust and resentment between themselves complicated and soured their inquiries.

Much intellectual ground was shared by these two analysts; their work covered Hitler's history, psychopathology, and likely attitude in the future should an Allied victory appear imminent. These similarities were not surprising: Langer had been a junior colleague of Murray at Harvard; both had undergone analysis and became practitioners (Murray seems to have abandoned psychoanalytical practice fairly swiftly after qualifying through the Boston Psychoanalytic Society in 1933; his career as an academic psychologist and innovative researcher clearly took precedence).[11] They worked from shared source material about Hitler and made many of the same assumptions. Both intuited that Hitler would pursue a scorched-earth policy in the final throes of the conflict. Murray's and Langer's accounts shared something else: the tendency to slide unnervingly from the particular to the general.

Murray had been interested in Freud's work for many years, but, more than Langer, he retained his independent position and freedom to criticize the psychoanalytical movement. Of the two he was by far the more senior figure in the world of the university and academic psychology. He sought to draw on what he considered best in the Freudian literature, alongside other approaches and ideas, in the development of an experimental psychology. One of his pre-war books had been dedicated to, amongst others, Freud and Jung.[12] Murray made his reputation in the 1930s by devising ingenious techniques to establish unarticulated beliefs, intelligence, and social attitudes. In order to standardize the form of his subjects' responses to his empirical inquiries he developed set procedures that proved widely influential: a plethora of questionnaires, ability gauges, registers to differentiate each person's hypnotic susceptibility, thematic apperception tests, ethical standard indices, and more.[13] In one experiment, involving a batch of student volunteers, he showed how anxiety could prove cripplingly severe, sometimes inhibiting work and ambition far more than the person in question consciously realized. He was able to illuminate how the tested figure remained unaware of the power and reach of his or her own thoughts and feelings of, for instance, inferiority, guilt, and dejection.

Murray's and Langer's studies of the German Chancellor's putative unconscious desires and defences drew upon the observations of several important fugitives, such as Otto Strasser, who had had first-hand knowledge of Hitler. Their views were gathered into a large archive of research material that became known as the OSS Sourcebook. Here Langer and his team assembled cuttings, gossip, recollections, articles, autobiographical snippets, medical bulletins, and so forth before proceeding to make their interpretations.

Langer believed that Murray was signed up as a part of the group he was coordinating for the OSS, only to discover in the course of 1943 that the Harvard psychologist was stringing him along; Murray was in fact writing his own account under separate instruction. In his correspondence with John Toland many years later, just in advance of the publication of *The Mind of Adolf Hitler*, Langer explained the fraught circumstances and sense of betrayal that had prevailed at the time of his original study.

There we learn how Langer gained the formal commission to write the Hitler study in May 1943. He and his assistants then amassed copious source material; they combed through literature and press holdings at the New York Public Library. As Langer admitted to Toland, this was not the ideal way to conduct research on a live subject—direct personal contact (still better, psychoanalysis itself) might reveal far more—but under the conditions of war second-hand records were better than none. More than a thousand pages of typed pages (originally produced in quadruplicate) of background information were produced. It came to be treated, albeit with some circumspection, as a substitute for case material. Or, at least, Langer tried to make some kind of plausible psychological narrative out of what he himself admitted was a mixed bag of news, opinion, and anecdote.

In his pursuit of Hitler's mind Langer had secured the services of several psychoanalytic colleagues, most notably Ernst Kris and Bertrand Lewin.[14] An intermediary, Arthur Pope, the chair of a committee of academics and intellectuals that offered various advisory services to government and to the OSS, had suggested that Murray too should be invited to join their study group. Langer agreed to this, assuming that he and Murray would pool data and work in partnership. Yet according to Langer, Murray mysteriously dropped out of the meetings that were convened in New York, and while he promised to send them a contribution in writing nothing was ever delivered. Langer confessed to Toland his amazement when he discovered that Murray had no documents to turn over in return for those that were shown to him. Having long glossed over what he regarded as the academic's shabby behaviour, he was especially furious to find, many years on, Murray's report turning up in the Roosevelt Presidential Library, where it might, he thought, gain unduly in reputation. His conclusion was that Pope and Murray had been involved in a conspiracy to access his own source material.

It is unclear what contribution his other psychoanalytical colleagues made to what was in the end decidedly Langer's project. It is quite possible that many of the psychoanalytic ideas contained in the report were theirs: nothing in Langer's post-war career suggests he was an innovative psychoanalytical writer, while Lewin and Kris, by contrast, went on to produce many other papers and reports. After several further meetings with his associates the OSS set a firm deadline for submission, and Langer had to work long hours to finish the text. He had no opportunity for elaborate editing, but managed to complete the manuscript just an hour before the Federal Express left from Boston to Washington, the night before the deadline.[15]

Confronted by Langer's accusations of filching source material, Murray is said to have replied coolly that he had made no direct reference to the OSS material in his own report.[16] This still rankled with Langer in the 1970s, but in fact he had felt let down even before Murray's departure from the team in 1943, after a larger network of clinical colleagues (known as the 'Psychoanalytic Field Unit') he had put together for intelligence purposes was regarded as not cost-effective and his budget was curtailed.[17] Despite this setback and Langer's temporary resignation, Donovan had called him back and redeployed him on the Hitler study.

—————•—————

The OSS Source Book remains an interesting artefact of the time, a repository of images and insights, clichés and personal opinions about Hitler from the 1920s through to the 1940s. Langer's Hitler study was not simply the product of his own particular psychobiographical perspective on the Nazi leader, but was of necessity a collage of contemporary impressions and micro-analyses of the Führer's personality, as much a dictionary of received cultural ideas as the royal road leading to the private fantasies of the leader. The hundreds of pages of material comprised individual testimony and speculation, critical opinion and reportage, remarks on Hitler's special, fascinating way of looking at or through his audience, talk of his self-mastery and opacity, and attempts to explain his mysterious capacity to evoke tumultuous emotions in others.[18] There are interviews with the Hitler family's physician Dr Bloch; reports from diplomats, notably William Dodd, who had headed the US Embassy in Berlin from 1933 to 1937; extracts from journalists' assessments, such as those by the CBS radio reporter William Shirer, who had spent much of the 1930s in Germany tracking the horrifying course of events (Shirer returned to the United States in 1941, the same year that he published his memoir *Berlin Diary*); and a mass of miscellaneous observations and memories.

Langer assumed that the source of Hitler's political and ideological pathology could be found by uncovering the sexual secrets of the bedroom or recovering the lost memories of the nursery. For this purpose he made use of any information he could glean about Hitler's early years, as well as Strasser's and Hanfstaengl's depictions of Hitler's private life and the comments of another Nazi insider-turned-exile, Hermann Rauschning. Langer also took note of the 1924 report on the Nazi leader that had been produced by the prison psychologist at Landsberg, who had been asked to determine if it was safe to release Hitler after he had served a minimal sentence following the Munich Putsch attempt. This report gave Hitler the all clear, thereby also granting him licence to continue his political career upon the completion of his lenient sentence.[19] In the context of the comfortable conditions Hitler enjoyed in Landsberg prison, where he was allowed to receive guests and had ample leisure to work on the the manuscript of *Mein Kampf*, it seems unlikely that the tame deliberations of that first psychologist would have caused him too much stress.[20]

Hitler's personality was characterized, according to some of his more admiring witnesses, by selflessness of conduct, simplicity of manner, and sureness of touch. Evidently here Langer was dealing with emotional projections that were made onto Hitler by sympathetic viewers, as much as or even more than with Hitler's self-fashioning or self-perception, but the two aspects were anyway confused. His supernatural talent and demonic will, Langer observed, were likened to those of some supposedly 'Asiatic' genius of destruction. Hitler manifested a strange quality of otherness, not quite European perhaps, nor quite modern—certainly not quite 'normal'. The Führer had great skill, Langer remarked, at remaining closed off, opaque in his dealings, whilst exercising an ability to arouse passions—of adulation, rage, perplexity, love, or fear—in his audience.

The Source Book is full of references to Hitler as hysterical, changeable, perverse, feminine, illogical, sensitive, slippery, oily, dogged, and prone to fits of crying. Some of Langer's informants detected incipient signs of hysteria in his behaviour in the trenches during the Great War, or at least noted how a company commander at the time had said that this 'hysterical' private would never make an officer.[21] Another commented that Hitler was like a bad imitation of an ideal cultural type; he sought to actualize a figure that really exists only in fantasy.[22] Such characterizations of Hitler's personal perversity, chameleon-like qualities, powers of performance, and omnipotent delusions are bound to have had a shaping influence on Langer, Kris, and Lewin in their deliberations.[23]

Observations of Hitler's life-style, his fads and fashions, concerns about weight and appearance, and the like were included in Langer's compilation, alongside more generalized remarks about his ideology, the sources of his inspiration, his hypnotic effects on others, and much besides.[24] Langer and his associates collected anecdotes about Hitler's capacity for concentration, the nature of his typical conversations, his attitudes to noise, idiosyncratic manner of speech, likes and dislikes in music, art, fiction, and cinema, as well as accounts of his posture and dress sense. Oral testimonies, not just written reminiscences, were sought; Langer had managed to get himself placed on a priority-travel list by the OSS so that he could undertake a fast, fact-finding mission and talk to informants and colleagues in other parts of the country.[25]

In these interviews the Freudian intelligence analyst sought to take into account the prejudices of his informants, but perhaps was not sufficiently alert to their desire to please and satisfy, or perhaps on occasion to titillate, disappoint, and frustrate him.[26] The precarious position of these émigré witnesses meant that they would consciously contrive to use the interviews to their own advantage, for instance as leverage in negotiations for better treatment and greater privileges, or as a convenient platform from which to disavow their earlier political support for the Nazi regime.

The colourful Princess von Hohenlohe, who (despite her reputed Jewish origin) had once been in direct personal contact with Hitler and Göring, was a case in point. This extraordinary adventuress apparently conducted affairs and espionage (for Germany) with remarkable aplomb as she moved around in high society at home and abroad. She talked to Langer about Hitler while she was held in a detention camp in Texas. Not for the first time, she sought to arrange a favourable deal and secure her position, this time from authorities at the OSS. She made it clear that she wanted her information about Hitler to be traded for her release, even asking that Donovan place her on the staff of the OSS. Langer could not oblige her, but still managed to gain some information. Langer also travelled to Canada to interview Hitler's former associate Otto Strasser, who with his older brother Gregor had been an early member on the left of the National Socialists, before being expelled from the party by Hitler in 1930. Strasser was to be influential in building up a picture of Hitler's pornographic imagination.

As well as conducting interviews Langer did his best to dig up material about Hitler's parents and speculated about their approach to child-rearing, as well as about his more extended family. Much of the data was ancillary to the main task: thus titbits about Brigid Hitler, the wife of Hitler's half-brother Alois, who had faced trial in Britain for tax-evasion found their way into the Source Book, although the investigation was not taken much further.[27] Other stories of delinquency among Hitler's relations were also noted, for instance cases of theft and bigamy,[28] including that of the half-brother Alois himself, who had settled in Liverpool in 1910 then left in 1914, abandoning his wife and a son, William Patrick Hitler. The father re-emerged in the 1920s, living bigamously with a German wife, with whom he also had a child. Stories about the Liverpool branch of the family and the connections between the half-nephew and Hitler were recorded in the briefing documents, although it was not clear what light they might cast on the main subject.[29]

A further source for the analysts was 'Putzi' Hanfstaengl's seventy-one-page report about Hitler supplied to the OSS. Hanfstaengl had played a significant role as a coordinator of press information for the Nazis, before fleeing Germany for England.[30] Donovan pulled strings in order to obtain his transfer to US custody,[31] where he was moved to a detention camp before being paroled by Roosevelt. Hanfstaengl, who provided information to the OSS and other government agencies of a vivid and provocative kind, appeared to have a foot in both camps, or at least to express mixed sympathies. The son of an American mother and speaking fluent English, as a young man he had studied at Harvard. Even as he had risen through the Nazi hierarchy in the 1920s, in close association with Hitler (who apparently particularly enjoyed his company), he still kept in touch with American colleagues and friends. He fell from favour in the 1930s and eventually, in fear of his life, managed to escape Germany. Interned as an enemy alien in Britain after the start of the Second World War, he was subsequently moved to Canada where he was again imprisoned before being handed over to the Americans in 1942. The German informant's code-name was 'Dr Sedgwick'.

Hanfstaengl's accounts of the leadership, including the long profile of Hitler, were closely studied by OSS interpreters and were known by Roosevelt himself, whose interest reflected his concern to glean as much information as possible about the psychology and backgrounds of the Nazi elite. To this end presidential advisers had been entrusted with compiling elaborate biographical résumés of German ministers, senior administrative officials, and high-ranking soldiers. The anthropologist Henry Field, who accepted an invitation in 1941 to become a member of Roosevelt's personal staff, organized (under the supervision of one of the president's aides, the journalist John Franklin Carter) a trawl of information about the German top brass. Nearing the end of the task in March 1944, Field dashed off a memorandum to explain that there were still 'about 100 more records of these skunks to come!'[32]

Roosevelt followed the Hanfstaengl debriefings especially closely, writing a note on 10 June 1943 regarding payment and other arrangements, and adding: 'I don't think I should see "Putzi". I would, however, like to read the manuscript.'[33] Hanfstaengl was even allowed to contribute advice on US propaganda leaflets to be dropped over Germany.[34] A report to the President about Henry Murray's manuscript came with a note attached by Carter: 'It is an interesting and important confirmation of the material on Hitler prepared by Putzi Hanfstaengl and is thus an unexpected vindication of the value of his work. Putzi is now being put to work on a commentary and analysis of this document for use in official circles concerned in psychological warfare.'[35] Carter's remarks involved a degree of circular reasoning—it was unsurprising that the OSS reports tallied with Hanfstaengl's account since the Murray and Langer inquiries were indebted to his and similar views from émigré witnesses in the first place.

Further assessments of Hitler by Hanfstaengl were regularly passed on to the President. A representative example is this report from an official working for Roosevelt, dated 11 September 1943:

> Doctor Hanfstaengl telephoned this morning with an analysis of Hitler's speech. He said there was no sign of hysteria or of defeatism in his voice. On the contrary, he seemed full of grim determination and of confidence. Doctor Hanfstaengl added that in voice and in manner Hitler sounded precisely as in the days of his greatest power. He thought that any attempt to read defeatism into what Hitler said would be to grossly misjudge the character of the speech.[36]

A couple of months later the analysis had changed; Hanfstaengl referred to more recent evidence about the Führer, suggesting that he had now revealed himself as a desperate man heading wilfully towards destruction. He believed that Hitler displayed signs of psychological deterioration and the unmistakable symptoms of a pathological building mania. Hitler, he suspected, had come to relish the bombing of his cities and responded to the destruction with 'almost libidinous gusto'. The German leader's manic talk of millions of cubic metres of concrete that would be produced to rebuild ruined homes was but his 'latest pseudo-Messianic outburst'. It was as if Hitler was saying, in his madness: 'Let them tear down my Father's temple, I shall rebuild it in three days.' Hanfstaengl concluded on an optimistic note: the Nazi leader's indifference to the human consequences of the bombing—not only for enemy populations but for his own people—would no doubt convince millions of German men and women that a 'deranged individual is guiding their destinies'.[37]

Like other Nazi fugitives, Hanfstaengl briefed the OSS about his first-hand experiences of Hitler's exceptional charismatic power during the 1930s, information which the organization was eager to acquire, despite the fact that an OSS report acknowledged that this German informant was not entirely stable himself and was, as one intelligence official put it, 'whacky' about the Jews—although his personal attitude and emotional condition were said to be improving.[38] Hanfstaengl offered copious character sketches and psychological interpretations, recalling how the leader would enter into states of what he called 'destructive madness'. As a general assessment he claimed that Hitler was a 'madman' who understood life through the 'muzzle of a gun'.[39] His followers were little better: for German culture, he warned, was producing a nation of 'Machine Beasts'.[40]

Meanwhile, this loquacious source spoke to Walter Langer of Hess's and Hitler's early intimacy (they called each other 'du' until a certain moment when Hess began to call him the Führer) and offered intriguing stories about the leader's odd sexual life. Hanfstaengl referred to Hitler's Oedipus and Narcissus complexes, and portrayed him as a sado-masochistic type with homosexual leanings. He referred to conversations in which Hitler had told him that he could only be married to the people as a whole. Hanfstaengl claimed (in a rather mangled recollection) that Hitler had declared: 'Politics is a woman; he who loves her unhappily she bites off his head.'

Much of this material about Hitler's sexual behaviour and fantasy life was hearsay and speculation. No less contentious, but ultimately more compelling, was the analyst's emphasis on the perverse kernel of Hitler's thought: there was a sadistic and 'pornographic' quality to his imagination that fuelled the political rhetoric. This was most evident, of course, in his obsession with the Jews and their putative power to desecrate and pollute the 'Aryan race'. It is a characteristic feature of anti-Semitism and other forms of racialized fantasy to project the subject's own 'dirty' sexual, destructive, and/or deadly thoughts onto the imagined other, who must then be punished, segregated, or even eliminated in order to protect the subject from contamination.

While Langer viewed Hitler as being 'elusive to the diagnostician', he nonetheless thought he exhibited a curious mixture of sexual pathological traits stemming from infancy. Actual sexual engagement, let alone any sense of fulfilment, it was said, was impossible for him. Hanfstaengl stressed how Hitler's fondness for the whip was a fetish, a 'memory residue' linked to a sadistic father. It was suggested that the whip was used as an exciting substitute for a person, and that beneath Hitler's bravado he may have been impotent. Hanfstaengl, who had hosted parties that Hitler attended during the 1920s, frequently witnessed him carrying one of his whips; several of these were presents from his patronesses, and they become part of his get-up. As Ian Kershaw remarks: 'In his gangster hat and trenchcoat over his dinner jacket, touting a pistol and carrying as usual his dog-whip, he cut a bizarre figure in the *salons* of Munich's upper crust.'[41] Hanfstaengl remembered seeing Hitler inflamed by a particular woman, strutting up and down, cracking his whip in an attempt to impress her: 'the whole performance seemed hopelessly pubescent and empty.' Some onlookers, he recalled, were revolted by Hitler's display.

In fact, Langer surmised, the situation was more complex still: Hitler, he suspected, identified with his denigrated mother, and sought to occupy the place of the 'masochistic' woman: here he cited gossip about how Hitler, in a brief private encounter with an actress, Rene Mueller, had fallen to the floor, begging to be kicked. When she did as he asked, it 'excited him greatly and he begged for more and more'.[42] Other occasions when Hitler had supposedly grovelled 'in a most disgusting manner' at the feet of women or even exhibited 'coprophagic tendencies' were also cited.[43] To defend himself against such propensities, Langer believed, Hitler had isolated himself from any intimate relationships and identified with the aggressor, embodying in his fantasy and political performances, the role of the omnipotent, strutting man:

> Unable to enter into a 'give-and-take' relationship with other human beings that might afford him an opportunity of resolving his conflicts in a realistic manner, he projects his personal problem on great nations and then tries to solve them on this unrealistic level. His microcosm has been inflated into a macrocosm. . . . his relationship to Germany was, in effect, the sexless, idealistic marriage he longed for.[44]

Yet it was a cruel 'marriage' if ever there was one: he sought to dominate the other in merciless fashion; just as his whip gave some clue to his sadistic fantasies, so his dominating voice and terrifying will were employed to subjugate the crowd, which he associated explicitly with a woman.[45]

Like Hanfstaengl, other of Hitler's former admirers made assumptions about the nature of the leader's troubled psychological interior, describing a man haunted by sexual feelings, weird dream states, and repressed violent desires. Some saw Hitler as a lonely unhappy man, unable to form a meaningful human relationship; others, as practically impervious to ordinary feelings—more like an automaton who was able to invoke strange psychic states in his followers.[46] Various witnesses were clearly tuned in to Freudian thought, but other approaches (for example, based upon inquiry into the subject's physical nature, including most notably the brain) were also apparent, as were observations reminiscent of late Victorian criminology and sexology, with their assumptions about race and degeneration. Among the authorities cited in the Source Book is one 'Kurt Krueger', described as a specialist in racial hygiene who claimed to have studied Hitler's physiognomy. It is not clear how the OSS came by this material, but it may have been taken from the writings of 'Samuel Roth', the author of the wholly unreliable *Inside Hitler*. This 'authority' on race declared the German leader actually to *be* a racial inferior, not only to be haunted by the perception of himself as such—in this (perhaps facetiously intended) deployment of Nazi racist terminology against itself Hitler was revealed as the very opposite of his own Aryan ideal.[47]

Langer's sources more typically focused on phases of Hitler's psychosexual history and the nature and consequences of his immediate environment as child, young man, and soldier in seeking to pinpoint how this background had shaped his psychic formation, with the confusing and unhappy home-life of the infant Hitler regarded as particularly significant. Langer's model of his development came to be based on the assumption that Hitler's underlying nature, whatever that may have been at the start, was exaggerated and perverted first through his familial and social experience, and then through the traumatic and brutalizing effects of war. This view, though, did not discount the possiblility that the violence of Hitler's own unconscious attitudes reciprocally coloured and distorted these difficult life-experiences at the same time.

In considering Langer's account, it is important to note how much had changed in the language of 'clinical' biography during the first half of the twentieth century. Psychiatrists who made their name before 1900, such as Cesare Lombroso in Turin, Valentin Magnan in Paris, Henry Maudsley in England, or Richard von Krafft-Ebing in Vienna, would have conceived the problem of writing the life of a political tyrant differently—they were more interested in biological make-up and the vicissitudes of personal ancestry than in unconscious fantasy—and of course they lacked the Freudian concepts that were to become so influential in Western cultural understanding of human 'inwardness'.[48] While Murray and Langer, with their academic backgrounds in psychology, were both well versed in these earlier traditions, their priority was to get 'inside' the mind of the leader and to assess his psychological impact upon others, for example by investigating aspects of Hitler's speeches and writings such as the metaphors used in *Mein Kampf*.

Admittedly, Murray reverted on occasion to the language of organic psychiatry and a racialized form of anthropology, whereas Langer was more consistently focused upon the psychological meanings—for Hitler—of his ancestry. Murray noted, for instance, Hitler as a man of 'illiterate peasant stock', drawn from 'a mixture of races', 'no pure German among them'.[49] Almost immediately, however, his attention shifted from Hitler's actual (supposed) pedigree to the Führer's 'complex about impurity of blood'.[50] He referred on one occasion in clear-cut terms to Hitler's symptoms of 'paranoid schizophrenia', and on another stated as a matter of simple fact that the Führer was impotent. The psychologist actually devoted more of his attention, as did Langer, to Hitler's feelings about himself, his neuroses, inferiority complex, sense of shame, 'repression of conscience', 'unconscious need for punishment', and so forth.[51]

Murray claimed that the investigation of Hitler's mind was also, by virtue of his special place in the national imagination, tantamount to the first stage of an investigation into the psychology of the German people at large, or at least of those who had supported the Party: 'The proper interpretation of Hitler's personality', he declared, is important as a step in understanding 'the psychology of the typical Nazi'. Since this 'typical Nazi' 'exhibits a strain that has, for a long time, been prevalent among Germans', this would, Murray hoped, provide a 'step towards understanding the psychology of the German people'. Murray believed that whilst other leading Nazis should be brought to trial, Hitler, if finally caught, should be committed to an asylum, where he could be filmed, monitored, and analysed by a committee of experts, since he represented the case *par excellence* of modern morbid political psychology.[52]

Nonetheless, the elevation of Hitler to the status of a 'demi-God', Murray went on, could only be explained 'on the hypothesis that he and his ideology have exactly met the needs, longings and sentiments of the majority of Germans'.[53] Langer was more circumspect here, remarking, for instance, that Hitler's speeches invited such an identification: thus the listener 'seems to identify himself with Hitler's voice, which becomes the voice of Germany'.[54]

The enigma of Hitler was linked by Murray to the larger question of the psychopathology of Nazis or even the German people as a whole, and, notably by Langer, to the question of unconscious identification with the Führer as the supposed embodiment of Germany's spirit. How far Hitler typified and exploited a certain strain in the national culture was also extensively considered. Some of those who were quoted in the Source Book, for example, suggested that Hitler could be classified as an exemplary *form* of psychological being, a particular, representative type, marked both by his psychopathy and his peculiar asexual attitude. As with the British psychiatric investigation of Hess, the accent fell at some points on what was seen as typical, at others on the individual's oddities.

Like Murray, Langer was interested in how Hitler encapsulated or deployed certain pathologies of the nation that he led, whilst at the same time noting that the image of the Führer was carefully contrived through Nazi propaganda. He devoted considerable space to the analysis of this contrivance, in short, to Hitler 'as he has been pictured to the German people'. Hitler was identified as a megalomaniac who claimed to speak for Germany and through the acquistion of such tyrannical power had indeed come to do so. He claimed to embody in his person the will of the state. In so far as he had done so, Langer observed, others must bear responsibility. Hitler's own rhetorical self-identification with the state was noted, as when he declared on one occasion that the war is conducted by 'me', and on another that 'I was the supreme court of the German people'.[55]

Langer was particularly struck by how Hitler's obsession with cleanliness fed into his sense of himself as a godlike figure and the belief that he embodied a kind of divine will. Had not the Führer sometimes likened himself to Christ, and pictured himself as a redeemer who would put paid to the vice and corruption of Weimar-era Berlin? Had he not implied that he would seize his whip and scourge the 'money lenders'?[56] Of course, Hitler's particular identification with Jesus, Langer noted, was with the agent of divine authority, the cleanser of temples, not the prophet who advised his followers to turn the other cheek.

—•—

Typically, the interviewees for Langer's project would be asked to talk freely about their impressions of Hitler or the attitudes of his acolytes. Occasionally Langer sought to steer the speaker more precisely, in search of concrete details about certain episodes in Hitler's life, but mostly he liked to let his sources talk without interruption.[57] It was not quite 'free association', but the analyst was nevertheless looking out for unguarded comments and unexpurgated memories. Much sifting was then required to get at nuggets of usable information.

Arguably, such an approach always lends itself more to the concoction than the retrieval of fantasy. Given Langer's professional identity and the scope of his psychological interests, it seems likely that those who talked to him about the Nazi past had assumptions about what he wanted to know and were influenced by this in what they told him. Did they feed Langer the sexual material about Hitler that they knew he was so eager to 'discover'? How far did the sources accommodate themselves, consciously or unconsciously, to the analyst's desire for a particular *story*? Did the informant perhaps share with Langer certain underlying psychological assumptions, however little he may have known directly of Freudian thought? Similar 'co-productions' would emerge during the preliminary investigations to the Nuremberg trial, when some of the Nazi leaders and their psychiatric observers sought to reveal the psychological interactions that had culminated in Hitler's total ascendancy.

While Langer's earlier intelligence reports about Hitler's speeches had been relatively sober affairs, concentrating on the rhetorical devices employed, the obvious subtexts of their message, and their use of 'projection',[58] his OSS analysis of Hitler tended towards the spectacular, perhaps reflecting the way in which Langer and his team were encouraged to come up with the 'goods' and show how far a clinical reading of Hitler could go beyond the banal observations of non-specialists. Langer seems to have been impressed, for example, by Otto Strasser's lurid account of the relationship between Hitler and his niece Geli Raubal,[59] describing the pressure to which Hitler had subjected her in the run-up to her death on 19 September 1931. Geli had died following a gunshot wound to the lung. The official cause of death was listed as suicide (her door having been locked from the inside). No autopsy was conducted.[60]

Competing tales about Geli and her uncle were in circulation in Germany before and after her death. Since she had, apparently, been killed by a bullet from Hitler's revolver, it was whispered that he had probably shot her himself, or ordered her to be assassinated, on account of her 'infidelity'. Claims, denied by Hitler, that Geli was engaged to someone in Vienna and that her uncle forbade the relationship emerged. Hitler's political success, nonetheless, continued unabated; he gave speeches a few days later, working himself up, as Ian Kershaw puts it, into 'an orgiastic frenzy'.[61] Hitler's relationship to Geli and his reactions to her death have been the subject of speculation ever since the early 1930s; they continued to intrigue biographers long after Langer and his colleagues pored over the details during the war.

In Langer's report and Source Book there are many descriptions of how body and mind, as well as individual and group, interact and transform each other. It is unconscious attitudes to body, not just the actual organic body, that shape the person. There was speculation about whether Hitler's supposed abnormalities (referring, for instance to the rumour that he had only one testicle) affected his view of the world and of himself. Such fascination with the physical speaks, as Ron Rosenbaum has put it, to a futile anatomical search for Hitler's inwardness.[62] (Consider the cultural gossip surrounding the putative Russian autopsy conducted on the Führer's remains, especially his brain, or tales about vestigial bits of the dead tyrant that were locked away in vaults, for the edification of mysterious teams of scientists in Moscow or Leningrad.[63]) It shows how 'conflicting embodiments of competing visions' always surrounded the representation of his life and death.[64]

The idea of some primal event or singular fantasy as the decisive determinant is equally spurious. Speculation in post-war literature that a bout of syphilis might have been responsible for Hitler's obsessive resentment of the Jews, that provocations at the hands of a Jewish prostitute drove him to a frenzy of hatred, or that the failure of a Jewish doctor to save his mother was *the* psychic turning-point are also wide of the mark. Psychic development is not so easily reducible to a series of staging-posts, and what is often striking is not so much the event, or even the fantasy of the event, as the way it comes to be charged with new unconscious meanings. In the same way it is misguided to see Hitler's bout of 'hysterical' blindness and his subsequent treatment at the Pasewalk military hospital in 1918 as the fundamental transformative experience that turned this 'nobody' into a 'megalomaniac'. All of these aspects of Hitler's life are intriguing, but it is wrong to claim that it was any one of them that definitively twisted Hitler's mind into a different shape.

On the one hand, Langer sought to excavate the nature of Hitler's hidden character; this drew him into various speculative and rather dubious claims that the infant Hitler's experiences (in so far as they could be inferred) somehow explained the adult politician's choices. If it was relatively uncontroversial, perhaps, for him to suggest that 'the present character of an individual is the product of an evolutionary process, the beginnings of which are to be found in infancy', it was surely more problematic for him to claim that the missing gaps in his knowledge of Hitler's personal history (and fantasy life) might be inferred from 'our knowledge of what goes on in the minds of [certain] patients together with a knowledge of their histories'.[65] Thus he freely speculated about the meaning of the birth and death of Hitler's siblings, and in particular his horror and intense jealousy at the arrival of his baby brother Edmund (who died in infancy in 1900): 'Again we can imagine that Adolf reaped an additional harvest of affection and again became the apple of his mother's eye.'[66]

Langer sought to portray the essential character of Hitler's parents and to gauge their unconscious effect upon their son; for example, he invited the reader to consider the father's drinking and violence, and suggested its deforming psychic impact. Hitler had already hinted at such pathological consequences himself, so Langer argued; this was one of many such claims that have been made as to the autobiographical elements of *Mein Kampf*. Hitler, he thought, hated and yet identified with his father; he also felt himself to be bound up with the mother that the father abused. Langer also described the kinship group, the role of the culture and thought of the time (Vienna 'low life', the trenches, Munich and so forth) in making the political outlook of the man. When considering the period of the First World War and its aftermath, Langer had rather more evidence to rely upon than in his account of the Führer's infancy: the analyst sought to study the mysterious nature of Hitler's interactions with like-minded ex-soldiers after 1918, and to show how many hands had been involved in producing the mythic figure of the Führer who ruled Germany. In general terms these experiences evidently marked Hitler's attitudes. But less anodyne and ultimately more suggestive and persuasive than the familiar background story is the analyst's concentration upon the perverse and repetitive fantasy structure involving masochism and sadism, soiling and purification, that, he believed, lay at the core of Hitler's thought: 'The greater the demands of his perversion became, the more he hated the Jews and the more he talked against them. Everything that was bad was attributed to them.'[67]

Whatever else the Nazi leader expressed in his political ideology, Langer highlighted the rabid outpourings about Jewish pollution. He also invited the reader to consider how the content of Hitler's political messages and the manner in which they were then relayed were heavily invested with Hitler's own emotions and a kind of erotized horror. These racial visions were not simply the Führer's fantasies, of course: they were embedded in a certain kind of culture and ideology of his time. Countless other anti-Semitic pamphleteers made similar points about the sexually rapacious Jew who penetrated and desecrated the pure Aryan body.

Historians have long debated the role the Führer played in promoting the various racial laws of the 1930s and in encouraging the massive escalation of racial persecution and then genocide in the 1940s. But what Langer wanted to get at was not so much the precise decision-making process within the Nazi government (in so far as any of this was already known at the time that he wrote), but the symbolic world in which Hitler lived and which he sought to impart to his followers. Much of what is now known about Hitler's outlook confirms, of course, Langer's basic premise about the Führer's heavy personal requirement for ever greater radicalization of the cause. Many of his public utterances sought to inflame others with the same intense excitement and revulsion, and to require unflinching and ever more extreme action in response.

Before turning to the particular perverse scenario in which he believed Hitler was caught up, Langer paints a picture of a seedy and empty figure, an impoverished man who, from an early stage of his development, revealed a certain relish for sadistic scenes. The report also laid particular stress upon the oral and anal world in which Hitler was caught up; these were his 'fixations', the obsessive areas within which his normal developmental process had stalled. He was deemed incapable of normal genital satisfaction. Hitler expressed his unresolved Oedipal feelings, so it was said, in displaced symbolic form, for example in the image of the damaged homeland (from whom the hero, of course, in myth is so often tragically separated) that was to be redeemed and cleansed. The corrupt and disgusting hybrid other power (the Hapsburg 'father') was contemptuously cast aside and then triumphantly repossessed. Langer tracked the development of what he called Hitler's 'Messiah complex' after 1918. According to this account, Hitler's fanatical desire to purify the race had to be understood in relation to unconscious fears of his own 'pollution'. It was as though in purging the nation of all the bad objects that plagued him, he made a vain attempt to achieve a kind of self-cure.

Langer's presentation invites the reader to consider whether the Führer, curious about his own origins or, more concretely, excited by the wish to see into or be inside his mother's private parts, was in turn driven to enact and seek punishment for that curiosity. The writer speculated here about the supposed wish of his subject to be soiled, or rather, Hitler's need to ero-tize the soiling process that both stimulated and horrified him.

At the root of Langer's particular rumination on the Führer's mind was the story of Geli Raubal. As their relationship had become closer in the years before her death, or rather as Hitler became ever more con-trolling and obsessively jealous of all other potential rivals or suitors for his niece, he required (so it was said to Langer, most notably by Strasser) her collusion in a particular perverse scenario that he craved: she was apparently required to squat over and relieve herself upon him in order to excite him. In this way he could both indulge his desire and suffer for it all at once; suf-fering and enjoyment were bound together.[68] No firm evidence that such events actually took place exists, and it would be naive to place too much credence on Strasser as a witness. But certainly Geli occupied a crucial role in the mythopoetic story of the Führer's life that Langer controversially put forward.

Although a sceptical eye is required when reading this account of what may or may not have occurred behind closed doors in Hitler's Munich apartment, the analyst was surely onto something more important about the perverse role that the Führer played as a public figure and ideologue in inter-war Germany. If we consider the idea that a certain imaginary scen-ario was entailed in this looser sense, it becomes less important to determine whether the Nazi leader's secret dealings with his niece, as sketched by Langer, actually took place or not. The scene was rather a suggestive illustra-tion of his macabre thought world. After all, Hitler facilitated and partici-pated in an orgy of whipped-up blame and brutality. Was it perhaps the case that the Führer called on many others to join him in an erotized excitement and to enact the most deadly 'solutions' to Germany's problems? The most squalid and disgusting thoughts were manipulated and exploited, even as the semblance of probity and high-minded rectitude was preserved. Nazism was an invitation to turn grievance into grandiosity and gave a green light to destructiveness and hatred of monstrous proportions. It enabled support-ers to project fantasies into Hitler and to identify with his dreams and hopes;

to feel themselves part of this new resurgent power whilst also remaining abject in submission and loyalty, joyously passive tools in the hands of the master. The deadly political 'seduction' that he offered was broadcast loud and clear. In that sense, the perverse quality of his mind and of the party's political message was not hidden at all.

Langer suggested (in similarly speculative terms) that Hitler constantly sought to fend off a persecutory form of guilt and was beset by visions of the dead (including his mother and niece as well as comrades in war). As his defences against knowledge of the horrific consequences of his own perverse wishes became more frenzied and desperate, so the need to find, project into, and destroy his 'enemies' grew ever more intense. For Langer, the paranoid style of Nazism was equally evident; he believed that both perverse and persecutory modes of thought were in operation throughout. Again, this is suggestive even now for the analysis of Nazi ideology, regardless of whether Langer's particular argument about the deleterious intra-psychic effects of Hitler's childhood or perverse sexual activities is accepted or not. Hitler's political discourse was shot through with fantasy; he promised omnipotent solutions to prevailing anxieties, fears, and resentments, and sought to locate all weakness, dirtiness, and humiliation in particular reviled objects who could be attacked and even destroyed with impunity and cruel satisfaction.

————•————

According to Langer, one outcome was highly likely: the German leader would carry on to the end, staying true to his desire. But in the face of the contradiction between his wishes and reality, his mind would collapse altogether, even as his political regime and military organization came apart around him. In face of the disintegration of the omnipotent delusions that had carried Hitler along, Langer envisaged a final total breakdown.

Langer and his collaborators anticipated the downfall clearly (let it be recalled that this was in 1943, not 1945): there would be a nervous collapse and an ever more desperate retreat inwards, away from a persecuting reality. There was acumen in this to be sure; but Langer, Lewin, Kris, and Murray were not by any means the only ones to foretell the shape of things to come. Sebastian Haffner, author of a critical diagnosis of Germany in 1940, predicted that Hitler might eventually commit suicide.[69] George Orwell also wrote in 1943 of his belief that Hitler would never surrender, but would 'perish in some operatic manner by suicide at the very least'. Orwell then added, facetiously, another possibility: the Führer might in fact cut and run, with a suitcase of securities, to retirement in Switzerland.[70] Langer suspected that the last redoubt would be the 'Eagle's Nest' on the Kehlstein. Suicide would occur within this 'symbolic womb'. Here the Führer would defy the world one last time and destroy himself.[71] In fact, Hitler had threatened individual or collective destruction throughout his political career: in the putsch attempt of 1923, for instance, he had intimated that suicide would be the price of failure.[72] He had on that occasion, as so often thereafter, elevated the will as the supreme principle. It was cast as an indomitable force; defeat was treated as though unthinkable, or as tantamount to death itself. Thus he had spoken, in what turned out at that stage to be a mere rhetorical flourish, of shooting himself in the head if victory was not achieved.[73]

In fact, as the historian Christian Goeschel shows, images and acts of suicide proliferated in Nazi Germany; motives, or at least the stated reasoning for such behaviour, took many forms: from proud identification with Hitler and his regime, through hopeless depression at the catastrophe facing the nation, to (well-founded) dread of what the Red Army would do to German women (the perpetration of rape on a massive scale).[74] A number of high-profile suicides marked the end of the Reich: those of Goebbels and his wife (together with the murder of their children), for instance. Himmler took his own life once in Allied captivity, and both Robert Ley (head of the German Labour Front) and Göring were to commit suicide during the Nuremberg trial.[75] Above all, it had been Hitler's decision to end his own life that signified the end of the regime. While Langer could not know of that final act with Eva Braun, in 1943 he dwelt prophetically upon Hitler's stylized manner of performance and anticipated that his death would constitute a final drama.

————•————

Langer's report was circulated within the higher echelons of the OSS, but was soon left to gather dust. The author knew little about its subsequent reception.[76] It is unlikely (given both his workload and low opinion of psychiatrists in general) that Churchill would have read it, although William Langer did report back to Walter that Lord Halifax, the British ambassador to Washington and former Foreign Secretary, had polite things to say about the study. William evidently was not able to elaborate, so it is hard to tell whether Halifax was being more than merely courteous.[77] There is no evidence that Roosevelt read Walter Langer's account, although he was broadly aware of OSS research in this area, knew about some of the key material on which Langer's analysis was based, and was cognizant, at least, of Murray's report.[78]

Among those who were directly influenced by the idea of applied psychoanalysis was William Langer. Whatever its flaws, his brother's report, William enthused later, was a powerful reinforcement of the argument for the importance of studying unconscious factors. In this context, he claimed, psychoanalysis was a key tool for the historian. By the time of his appointment as President of the American Historical Association in 1957, William was vigorously promoting the case for psychoanalysis in historical research, and he tried to demonstrate its efficacy in a new interpretation of the terrors surrounding the Black Death. Psychoanalysis, he enthusiastically told (perhaps somewhat bemused) colleagues in his presidential address, represented the 'new frontier'.[79]

Looking back years later, Walter Langer felt that, despite all the limitations of his study, it would have been helpful if such work had been produced at an earlier stage: if so the course of the 1930s, he believed, could have been different—the illusions of Chamberlain's abortive peace mission to Munich of 1938 might even have been avoided. Going further, he proposed that a study of Stalin along the lines of his interpretation of Hitler might have produced a different Yalta,[80] implying that Churchill and Roosevelt would have treated their Soviet counterpart in the discussions about post-war spheres of influence with greater circumspection and resisted his plans more vigorously had they been in possession of a proper psychological 'profile'. With Soviet troops by then dominant in Eastern Europe, it was surely somewhat fanciful to imagine that even the most insightful psychoanalytical study of Stalin could have dramatically affected such outcomes on the ground.

When Langer's book *The Mind of Adolf Hitler* (reproducing verbatim his OSS report) eventually appeared in 1972 his collaborators on the OSS team were not credited with co-authorship; the absence of Murray's name is understandable given Langer's feeling of betrayal, but it is not clear why the roles of Kris and Lewin were marginalized. Neither their archives, nor Langer's, reveal much about what became of the original ideas of collaboration nor the provenance of specific psychoanalytical ideas within the report.[81] On the other hand, the use of psychoanalysis and allied professions in American intelligence continued apace in the years after military victory over Germany was achieved: Langer and Murray's OSS profiles, along with the other wartime endeavours of the clinicians in intelligence, were in that sense important precedents for future (sometimes morally queasy or even utterly grotesque) developments in the Cold War period

and after: senior American intelligence officers sometimes sought advice
from psychologists, psychiatrists, and psychoanalysts, for example, regarding
the most effective means of breaking down the resistance of subjects during interrogations.[82] Psychological profiling of foreign leaders also became
commonplace. Those wartime assessments of Hitler and Hess by Langer
in the United States and Dicks in Britain were part of this lineage of profiling. Although the wartime analysts had laboured in relative obscurity,
'Nuremberg' brought such questions to wide attention: for the remarkable
post-war war trial of the German leadership was to be conceived both as a
site for the investigation and punishment of the war criminals, and as a
laboratory for the study of Nazi minds.

8

So Plainly Mad?

Conspicuous amongst those on trial at Nuremberg was Rudolf Hess, whose case here entered an important new phase. A number of psychiatrists were asked to assess the prisoner's mercurial mental state for the International Military Tribunal. Inquiries into Hess and the other prisoners were in part driven by forensic and medico-legal considerations; but they were also efforts to produce psychological portraits of the leading Nazis for the benefit of posterity. Although Nuremberg was a judicial process, a clinical gaze was never absent. Nor was that gaze confined to professional psychiatrists. The psychological condition of the individual 'conspirators' and the nature of their interactions were assessed by doctors and by fascinated (and horrified) onlookers. These Nazis were discussed as discrete psychiatric entities, but also as a pathological group. The psychiatrists were interested in specific cases, but also in the 'chemistry' of the Nazi elite as a whole.

To understand the significance that was attached to Hess's behaviour at the trial, it is useful to sketch the broader setting and to note the psychiatric assessments that were made simultaneously of other major defendants. These inquiries often took place with the active participation of the prisoners. The present chapter concentrates on the story of Hess at Nuremberg. Chapter 9 widens the discussion, considering the charge that was laid of conspiracy and suggesting how this resonated with post-war discussions of pathological groups. In all of these cases psychiatrists sought to move from the particular to the general: the stories of individual 'Nuremberg minds' were regarded as clues to larger psychological and political truths.

The Allied prosecution of the Nazi war criminals took place at the International Military Tribunal in the largely undamaged Palace of Justice at Nuremberg. Courtroom 600, the location inside the Palace that was used for the trial, became 'a venue of world history'.[1] This legal entity was, as the President of the court, Lord Justice Lawrence, declared, 'unique in the history of the jurisprudence of the world'.[2] As the prosecutions unfolded, news of proceedings was relayed regularly, not only to the defeated German population, but also via print and newsreel around the globe.[3]

Nuremberg remains a key repository of evidence about the decision-making process in and casualties of the Third Reich. It marked the beginning of a large-scale post-war effort to document Nazi atrocities, above all 'the Final Solution'. Although genocide was not among the specific charges brought against the defendants at the IMT, the vast crimes against the Jewish people featured strongly in the prosecution account. Other international war-crimes trials in Japan and in Germany (although not in Italy or Austria) would follow, but they remained, for public consciousness, always in the shadow of this first, well-publicized, marathon set of hearings.[4] Thus Nuremberg came to provide the most familiar post-war images of the defeated entourage. The line-up of defendants, including Hermann Göring, Joachim von Ribbentrop, Albert Speer, and, of course Hess, remains, along with Hitler's mental chaos and suicide in the bunker complex in Berlin, the emblem par excellence of the ending of the Nazi state.

At Nuremberg Hess found his place once again beside the rest of the leadership in a public setting. He seemed by then to symbolize the deflation and even disintegration of the once omnipotent regime. He had featured strongly in visual propaganda of the 1930s (often by Hitler's side) as an exemplar of utter belief and ceaseless devotion. He was found to have shared significant responsibility for many criminal decisions that were taken in the 1930s. Yet he was also regarded as an anomaly amongst his peers. This was not only because he had not been available in Germany for much of the war, and thus not present when so many of the fateful choices were made— including those to implement the Final Solution—but also because of his behaviour.

Hess and his companions were only a fraction of the senior governing personnel, but as individuals and as an aggregate they had contributed vastly to what Rebecca West, who observed some of the process at first hand, called 'this nameless evil'.[5] 'West', author of some of the best reportage to emerge at Nuremberg, was in fact the nom de plume of the prolific English writer Cicely Isabel Fairfield. A masterpiece, Black Lamb, Grey Falcon, the record of her pre-war journey through Yugoslavia published in 1941, had already conveyed the brooding menace and madness of Nazism. In that monumental piece of travel writing West offered memorable images and formulations of what she took to be a collective fascist pathology. Mussolini and Hitler, she wrote, 'came to power because they offered the victims of capitalism a promise of relief by a magical rite of regimentation'. Nazism revealed how individuals (weak and impotent when alone) were intoxicated and strengthened in large company. They could become, she warned, 'a seething and desperate mass'. Describing Austria's attitude to its neighbour Germany before the Anschluss, West diagnosed 'a suicidal enthusiasm for imperialist and internationalist Fascism'. 'Insane impulses', she declared, led certain governments—and their peoples—to the abandonment of all honour, decency, and humanity.[6] In West's narrative of Nuremberg, madness and deathliness are again powerfully evoked, nowhere more so than in the cameo descriptions of Hess.

West was not alone in this. Practically everybody who wrote first-hand accounts of the trial dwelled at some length on the startling case of Hess. Questions about the nature and authenticity of his illnesses were present from the start: no sooner had Hess arrived at Nuremberg than interrogations became bogged down in the mystery of his symptoms, including most notably his amnesia. The American officer Colonel Amen, who conducted an interview with Hess on 9 October 1945, brought Göring into the room to try to engage his former colleague. 'Listen, Hess, I was the Supreme Commander of the Luftwaffe', insisted the Reichsmarschall, before referring to other common experiences and memories he hoped would animate Hess.[7] The latter offered only his by then familiar refrain: 'This is all a fog.'[8]

Before the court proceedings got underway, the defence sought the exclusion of certain prisoners on grounds of mental or physical illness; Hess's lawyer was quick to claim that his client's amnesia was so complete that it constituted grounds for his removal from the trial. In the case of the long-ailing industrialist Gustav Krupp von Bohlen, who was among the charged men, the court agreed with the defence, or rather with the psychiatrists who reported on the matter, that legal action should be waived: his facial paralysis, loss of bladder and sphincter control, heart problems, and 'senile softening of the brain' had led the doctors to a clear conclusion. In the words of one of the judges, a distinction had to be made between this defendant and the missing Martin Bormann, who was in fact tried *in absentia*: 'Where nature rather than flight or contumacy have rendered such a trial impossible, it is not in accordance with justice that the case should proceed in the absence of a defendant.'[9]

Hess's and Julius Streicher's lawyers were not successful in similar bids. One issue was their mental state at the trial; another was whether they were sane enough at the time of the crimes of which they were accused to justify their prosecution thereafter. The judges concluded that both should face prosecution, although the image of mental derangement stuck. The ghastly Streicher, notorious as publisher of the anti-Semitic and quasi-pornographic magazine *Der Stürmer*, had long aroused not only revulsion but also psychological and forensic interest: William Shirer, for example, had described years earlier the 'sadism of his face'.[10] Hess's condition was by far the larger story though, in part because of his behaviour and in part because of the especially intimate relationship with Hitler he was thought to have enjoyed before the war: the court heard that he had previously been the 'closest confidant' of the leader and had real influence, which he could have used for good instead of for ill.[11]

For West, Hess's physical presence at the trial was especially startling. Her description of his case stressed his eerie facial appearance, bodily spasms and rigid postures, as though drawn from the annals of the Salpêtrière hospital in Paris, where in the late nineteenth century the neurologist Jean-Martin Charcot had impressed so many European doctors, including the young Freud, with his demonstrations of patients' dramatic hysterical symptoms: 'His skin was ashen, and he had that odd faculty, peculiar to lunatics, of falling into strained positions, which no normal person could maintain for more than a few minutes, and staying fixed in contortion for hours.'[12] Many other observers singled out the desiccated figure of Hess, the one-time sidekick to the Führer, as painful and yet strangely compelling. His bizarre gestures and performances drew the eye, and his remarkable quality of hollowness and indifference isolated him from the ranks of fellow defendants. In the dock or around the gaol yard, the prisoner's apparent clown-like turns—smiling inappropriately to himself, marching up and down, swaying back and forth, ignoring the court, even as his sentence was finally declared— helped to make him the special object of psychological inspection and of public attention.[13]

Hess was 'so plainly mad', according to West.[14] This snap diagnosis was understandable, although not everyone agreed with it or thought that Hess was so 'plainly' anything at all. It took some effort to imagine the ravaged psychic interior. How had he become this emptied-out wreck now before the court? All that was left, West surmised, was a shell, and yet she suspected the man was still haunted by the darkest of dreams: 'He had the classless air characteristic of asylum inmates; evidently his distracted personality had torn up all clues to his past. He looked as if his mind had no surface, as if every part of it had been blasted away except the depth where the nightmares lived.'[15]

West's description conveys more than the prisoner's banality of mind; it dwells upon the ghastly legacy of his psychic destruction. In a curious turn of phrase, she evokes a 'distracted personality' that had 'torn up' clues as to its own history. During the legal process Hess was prodded again and again by doctors or other officials with reminders of his former life, but to little avail. As Hess, on some occasions, swayed this way and that, apparently out of his head, he conveyed, precisely, *unconcern*. He remembered nothing, or at least presented himself this way. The psychiatrists struggled to make much sense of his views or experience of the trial, although occasional bursts of renewed devotion to the Führer or disgust with the legal proceedings did occur, as though in anticipation of his strange, self-exculpating final statement on 30 August 1946.[16]

—•—

Measured by deaths directly caused, more heinous criminals than Hess faced justice at Nuremberg. But for all that, it was this prisoner who was the most carefully scrutinized. In the courtroom he prompted feelings of perplexity and embarrassment, even in his fellow defendants. The soldier, intelligence officer, lawyer, and Conservative politician Airey Neave recalled his own involvement at Nuremberg and the sight of Hess on the grim patch of ground, on the north side of the court building, 'wild-eyed' as he insisted on 'goose-stepping past the windows'.[17] Inspecting Hess at closer quarters, Neave was struck by the man's gaunt appearance and those deep sockets of his blue eyes that 'gave the look of a skull'. This army office, who later became an ardent campaigner for Hess's release, noted how he had immediately felt sorry for him.[18] The prisoner, he observed, 'aroused the greatest interest and speculation', and the British felt somewhat 'possessive' of him.[19]

By 1945–6, when the trial process brought Hess back to public attention, a dense, secret clinical archive on his case had already been established. British doctors had long noted Hess's narrowed horizons, paranoid fears, and narcissistic absorption. There was no evidence, according to the clinicians, that he possessed much—or perhaps any—capacity for empathy. He viewed the world as if it was made up of discrete parcels of goodness and badness, remedies and poisons, even as he dreaded the infiltration of the one by the other. He perceived himself to be dealing with constant threats of contamination.

On Hess's transfer from Britain to the Palace of Justice in Nuremberg in October 1945, primary responsibility for his care had passed to the Americans. A number of records about him, such as the British medical orderlies' note-books, were also apparently handed over to the US authorities. (At any rate, they are now to be found in the National Archives in the United States rather than in Britain.[20]) Specialists—seven in all—drawn from the four occupying powers were asked to gauge his condition and produce reports. These unanimously concluded that he was a suitable case for punishment, even if they all found in him a cornucopia of disorders.[21]

For the British, the War Crimes Executive in London dispatched a team to re-examine the prisoner. Alongside Brigadier Rees, there was Lord Moran (Churchill's personal doctor and President of the Royal College of Physicians) and Dr George Riddoch (Director of Neurology at the London Hospital).[22] Their fact-finding trip to Nuremberg was brief, but the doctors could also draw upon material derived from Hess's time in his English and Welsh prisons. The Americans and the French made further assessments; some of their findings were in turn relayed to colleagues at home.[23] The team from the United States was led by psychoanalyst and psychiatrist Nolan Lewis and supported by Dr Ewen Cameron. The French authority was Professor Jean Delay (a former pupil of the illustrious pioneering French psychologist and philosopher Pierre Janet, and a specialist at the Salpêtrière hospital).[24] The Soviet line-up comprised Eugene Krasnushkin and Eugene Sepp, from the Medical Institute of Moscow.[25] The Russians denied that Hess showed signs of schizophrenia and were quick to dismiss any idea that he might be excused or that his potential punishment should be mitigated. The British reported Hess's paranoid and hysterical behaviour, but similarly rejected the idea that he was unable to understand proceedings. He had, they said, a 'psychopathic personality'.[26] The report signed jointly by the US and French doctors concurred that he was not insane: they recognized sev-eral of his symptoms as more than just malingering, but considered that Hess had exaggerated those symptoms for his own ends.

The American army psychiatrist Douglas Kelley, who monitored Hess closely in the early period of his captivity at Nuremberg, was struck by his intense suspiciousness and desire to confound his interrogators and doctors. Hess refused to sign his name to anything, objecting, for instance, to provid-ing a signature when requested to do so by Dr Delay and similarly refusing

Kelley's request that he write a short autobiographical sketch. Yet when Kelley asked for a sample of his handwriting, Hess readily complied, saying graphological analysis was important.[27] He appeared willing to oblige an American guard who requested, in more than dubious taste, a signature for his personal collection. Hess signed it but then ripped it apart, with the words, 'Our German signatures are precious'.[28] He remained convinced that he had been systematically infiltrated with some mystery venom, and he had come to Nuremberg seeking proper inquiry and redress. Indeed, turning the tables, he offered his own bizarre assessments on the pathology of his British diagnosticians, even as the distinguished group of psychiatrists was busy scrutinizing him on behalf of the court.

Dr Lewis retained in his personal papers the prisoner's drawn-out descriptions of the cruelties he had suffered in his captivity in Britain: the men who had treated him there were themselves, supposedly, mad *and* malign. Implying, perhaps, that he was sane, Hess described how he had lived for years in a veritable madhouse. Hess referred presumably to the hospital in Wales that had indeed been a mental hospital, but the remarks also airily suggested that the entire regime with which he was dealing, whilst a prisoner of war, was characterized by its delusions and cruel tyrannies. This was what required forensic investigation at Nuremberg:

> I have been imprisoned for four years now, with lunatics and [have] been at the mercy of their torture without being able to inform anybody of this, and without being able to convince the Swiss Envoy that this was so, not to mention my being unable to enlighten the lunatics about their condition. It was worse than being in the hands of criminals, for, with them, there is some little reason and some obscure corner of their brain—some feeling and some obscure corner of their hearts, and [a] little bit of conscience in them. With my lunatics, this was out of the question one hundred percent. But the worst [were] the doctors, who employed their scientific knowledge for the most refined tortures.[29]

This account ignored the actual situation in which Nazi doctors and psychiatrists had committed crimes after 1933, from enforced sterilization to 'euthanasia' of the 'unfit'.[30] Although he may not yet have known of the crimes committed by doctors in concentration camps after 1941, Hess reversed all such accusations and regarded the British doctors as the true abusers and torturers. Psychoanalysts would call this a 'projection' of guilt onto the other party. Reference to the barbarism of the Nazi state seemed to puzzle Hess at the trial. He intimated that he was the victim of a hateful conspiracy, not a party to one, and demanded that tests be conducted into the condition of the food he had been made to eat whilst a prisoner of war. He had brought with him, so Kelley recalled afterwards, various parcels sealed with red wax, including drugs and food (bits of chocolate, sugar, condiments, and so forth), and insisted that an impartial expert should submit these for chemical analysis.[31] The pharmacological investigation that Kelley wanted to do, however, was rather different. The proposal that he and others floated, that Hess be given 'truth drugs' (repeating the experiment that had been conducted in Wales in 1944) was turned down by the American authorities.[32] It was regarded as vital to ensure that the prisoners had no grounds for legal complaint about the use of any such involuntary measure (Hess himself showed no inclination to repeat the truth-drug experiment). One of the prosecuting lawyers tartly remarked that if Hess had been struck by lightening it would have been blamed on the way officials had mal-treated him.[33]

Hess, like his co-conspirators, was observed constantly, night and day, following the first prison suicide—of Robert Ley—towards the end of October 1945. Hess must have been more familiar with such close observation by this time than his colleagues. Reunited with his fellow defendants, Hess continued to make claims about the impenetrable mental obscurity in which he lived. Brought in to interrogation meetings handcuffed to a US soldier, Hess maintained his blank stance; he betrayed no flicker of recognition, for example, when Dr Rees (whom he had known in Britain) abruptly marched in.[34] Confronted with his erstwhile mentor Professor Haushofer, Hess said that he did not know him, and failed to react to the name of Haushofer's late son, Albrecht.

In another attempt to cut through Hess's amnesia, on 8 November 1945 he was shown newsreel film of himself and other Nazis in their time of power. The only result that could be discerned, however, was that Hess's hands tensed up as he watched particular sequences. The prisoner suggested that he could not recognize himself in these images; it was a long time, he claimed, since he had even looked in a mirror. (Whether this was true or not isn't known.)[35] On 16 November Hess was unexpectedly confronted with his former secretaries Ingeborg Sperr and Hildegard Fath, to see what he made of them. They expressed some emotion, but he seemed to show no interest.[36]

Hess spoke good English; whatever his capacity with the language before the war, four years in custody had strengthened it. But once back in Germany he insisted that he could only follow court proceedings if remarks were made to him in his own language through an interpreter. It was thought that this might reflect anxiety as well as truculence, or more cynically, that it might provide precious time for him to prepare himself between question and answer.[37] When pushed, Hess acknowledged that he recognized the name of the Führer. As was noted by one of the assembled commentators: 'it almost seemed that Hitler, like God, had in some curious way escaped the oblivion of most men and events in Hess's past life.'[38] Shown footage of concentration camps on 20 November 1945, Hess said, 'I do not understand.'[39] His responses to Rorschach ink-blots, it was claimed, betrayed signs of his aggressive and violent impulses, tinged with hysteria; there was a 'flat', lifeless quality to his attitude and certain signs that were deemed to be congruent with psychopathic tendencies.[40] The US army psychologist Gustave Gilbert conducted a battery of examinations, including Rorschach, Wechsler-Bellevue, and thematic apperception tests.[41] He observed that Hess gave only the sparsest responses. It was the *poverty* of his imagination that struck this observer. Hess would average only about forty words in response to the pictures he was shown, where the 'normal' adult would give 200–300. When urged to try, Hess protested his 'lack of aptitude for fantasy' and insisted, 'I can't see any further than what is here'.[42] Of course, another explanation would be the prisoner's reluctance to cooperate; Hess's attitude to tests and questioning was obstructive, one of the lawyers complained in open session. Yet Hess was found to be capricious: even his refusal to participate could not be taken for granted. The US army psychiatrist Dr Leon Goldensohn stressed Hess's hyper-fastidiousness and hypochondria. He noted the prisoner's carefully recorded messages to himself urging the greatest caution in what he ate, and underscoring the importance that he ascribed to avoiding sleeping-pills and eggs. He would accept marmalade and bread, but preferred to avoid other food or drink in the morning.[43] There was a flamboyant and clamorous quality to his complaints, as the doctors sometimes pointed out. There was also a bizarre disjunction between the gargantuan crimes and world-changing events that were being discussed by the court on the one side, and Hess's preoccupations with the minutiae of his dietary intake on the other.

Hess's lawyer, Gunther von Rohrscheidt, had claimed to the court from the outset that his client suffered from a 'reduction in mental capacity' due to faulty memory, and that he could neither be tried in person nor *in absentia*.[44] But Hess dismissed the argument that he was incapable of facing trial, even if he also rejected the authority of the court as such. He implied that no cure of his condition was necessary, at least not unless it was the ministrations of the doctors and officials themselves that was *making* him unfit to plead.[45] Expert psychiatric opinion, however, was united against the defence lawyer in arguing that Hess could understand the course of the proceedings against him and must face trial.

Sir David Maxwell-Fyfe, the British Solicitor-General who had become the chief British prosecutor at Nuremberg, noted in response to von Rohrscheidt's arguments that the Soviet doctors concurred with their Allied colleagues in finding Hess's speech coherent enough. The issue then turned on the significance of a partial loss of memory. Maxwell-Fyfe sought to bolster the argument for trying Hess by pointing out that in English law the fact that a person suffered a problem of memory did not lead to exemption in cases where the charges had been understood and the defendant had a normal intelligence.[46] He referred to other examples, including cases of manslaughter, where defendants had claimed amnesia but were held to account nonetheless. Maxwell-Fyfe suggested that the defending lawyer had slanted Hess's psychological symptoms to his client's advantage. He turned to psychiatric evidence in support of this point: the doctors, it seemed, had shown how Hess's 'hysterical amnesia' displayed a 'subconscious inclination toward self-defence'.[47] The arguments of the prosecutors prevailed: the prisoner's amnesia was not deemed to have rendered him incapable of following proceedings.[48]

Even after this furore the saga of Hess's addled mind and ambiguous motives was far from over. On 30 November he announced to the court that he had the use of his memory after all and that his previous amnesiac appearance had been merely tactical.[49] Hess insisted that his counsel had not colluded in the subterfuge. He emphasized that he bore 'full responsibility' for everything that he had done, signed, or co-signed. It was a perplexing new twist to the case. Some onlookers remained unconvinced that either the claim of amnesia or its weird retraction resolved the matter.

The prisoner's apparent recovery and further decline were to produce as much consternation among the other defendants as among the court authorities.[50] Göring declared (at least, if we rely on Gilbert's account) that Hess simply had him 'licked'.[51] According to the Rees report, when Hess's flight to England was discussed at Nuremberg, Göring slapped his old colleague on the back in mock congratulation.[52] Göring was also upset, according to Kelley, by Hess's antics in the court. He was at first nonplussed by Hess's signs of madness then amazed at his sudden *volte-face*. In Göring's view, his former colleague was an 'inadequate personality', or just extremely odd.[53] Göring recalled to Goldensohn that Hess had been 'slightly off balance for as long as I can recall', and wondered why Hitler had kept him close to the pinnacle of the Party when he was clearly not up to the task and lacked the necessary mental stability for this role. Göring painted a picture of the Deputy's past eccentricities, including the excessive preoccupation with health matters. Hess liked to play the alternative doctor, for example, turning up to treat Göring himself once when the Reichsmarschall had neuralgia with an assortment of pots and pans for preparing his own special treatments.[54] On another occasion Hess was said to have used a pendulum in his office to detect whether the letters he received were worth answering or not: 'If the pendulum swung in one direction, the letter was all right; if it swung another way, the letter was a bad one.'[55] One or two other defendants wondered if Hitler might have put Hess up to his flight in 1941, but most saw him as a renegade.[56] The Gauleiter of Thuringia and plenipotentiary for labour deployment, Fritz Sauckel, thought Hess's mission had been, at least, well intentioned; he suggested that Hess had been a good influence on Hitler.[57] But Ribbentrop saw Hess as pathetic and deluded, a man devoid of logic.[58] As to Hess's announced recovery of his memory, fellow prisoners declared themselves astonished; Streicher called his declaration shameful; the one-time architect and later Minister of Armaments in Hitler's government, Albert Speer, considered him a 'screwball'.[59]

Shortly after Hess's astonishing statement to the court he was interviewed again by Kelley: the prisoner was found to be elated at the impression he had created, proud of his ability to fool everyone. Hess, it now appeared, had hoped all along that the British might repatriate him as an insane person.[60] He was able to recall his flight to Scotland, his period of depression in captivity, his suicide attempt, and more. On 16 December Hess seemed to express some doubt about the Nazi system, even acknowledging, according to the Rees report, that its racial ideology was probably a mistake.[61] He was able to recall quite long strings of numbers when tested. But a few weeks after the *volte-face* Hess once more started to complain of lack of energy and to display new forms of secretiveness, nerviness, and paranoia. He described his condition using psychiatric language, commenting upon his own *idée fixe* in believing his headache and stomach-upset stemmed from a bad cracker he had eaten. Nevertheless, he required that other prisoners such as

Ribbentrop should first eat a snack and report on how they felt before he would touch it.[62]

Observing Hess in this period after his supposed recovery had faded into renewed apathy and paranoia, Gilbert thought that he was hysterically rejecting reality again because he was faced with the unbearable disintegration of the ideology that had held him in one piece: the smashing of his political dreams and self went together. He could not bear to accept a share of the guilt, nor could he bring himself to reject the Führer, so his mind once more collapsed.[63] Hess insisted, Gilbert observed, that 'I don't understand: I don't understand'. He reorganized and blurred all sense of reality in order to avoid taking in what had happened in Germany.[64] Soon Hess reached the point of claiming not to remember even the events of the previous day. He was by then unable or unwilling to corroborate the testimony of others, to the chagrin of several detainees. He would apologize with phrases like 'I am terribly sorry... but I cannot keep my memory intact'.[65]

The day before Hess was due to take the stand in March 1946, he told Göring he would not speak to the court. Next day, apparently changing his mind, he unexpectedly pulled notes from his pocket and made a speech that was deemed both grandiose and somewhat paranoid. It intimated that mysterious influences explained Hitler's abnormal condition, but quite what he intended by this description is unclear.[66]

Hess's final statement to the court was given on 31 August 1946 (reprinted as Appendix 2 below). It expressed no guilt, contrition, or regret and gave vent to his fears; he spoke of how he was faced by men with 'strange eyes'. Hess also referred to how Hitler (according, he added, to reports which had reached him) had changed and how his eyes had grown cruel. Hess seemed to allow a large public audience access to his own personal phantasmagoria. Sinister, glassy-eyed creatures appeared to him then reverted to an illusory normality: their 'symptoms' 'lasted only a few days', before the 'completely normal impression' returned. At this point, '[t]hey could no longer be distinguished from normal human beings'.[67]

Hess was found guilty on two of the four counts against him, the judges reading out their conclusions on 1 October 1946: he was declared to have been a willing and informed participant in German aggression against Austria, Czechoslovakia, and Poland, and was judged to have supported Hitler's policy of rearmament and known of its violent intent. Hess, they noted, had actively worked to promote laws discriminating against the Jews. The judges took care to refer to the medical examinations that were conducted into Hess's mental state and acknowledged that it might be true that he 'acts in an abnormal manner, suffers from loss of memory, and has mentally deteriorated during the Trial'. Even so, he understood the charges and was deemed 'completely sane' at the time the acts charged against him were committed.[68] He was sentenced to life imprisonment.

According to Rebecca West, Hess underwent a further stage of psychic disturbance during the period of the verdicts, September–October 1946. Watching him face the legal judgement, on a bleak Monday afternoon, West recalled how the 'darkened mind' of Hess 'passed through some dreadful crisis'. He ran his hands over his brows repeatedly, 'as if he were trying to brush away cobwebs, but the blackness covered him'. Then '[a]ll humanity left his face':

> it became an agonized muzzle. He began to swing backwards and forwards on his seat with the regularity of a pendulum. His head swung forward almost to his knees. His skin became blue. If one could pity Ribbentrop and Göring, then was the time. They had to sit listening to the judgement upon them while a lunatic swayed and experience a nameless evil in the seat beside them. He was taken away soon, but it was as if the door of hell had swung ajar. It was apparent now, as on many occasions during the trial, that the judges found it repulsive to try a man in such a state; but the majority of the psychiatrists consulted by the court had pronounced him sane.[69]

Hess's own valedictory statement was hard to square with the idea that he was anything but mad, with those references to glassy-eyed people plunged into a sea of poison. That Nazism was immersed in venom was the truth, but Hess's vision turned this upside-down. He saw the corrosion and persecution as constantly coming from shadowy forces outside himself, the Party, and the nation.

9

Nuremberg: Conspiracy and Confession

'Conspiracy' got the prosecutors at Nuremberg out of a fix; it also encapsulated the nefarious group processes at stake in Nazism and resonated with the diagnosis, prevalent since the 1930s, that Hitler and his acolytes were a bunch of sinister gangsters.[1] Sharp-eyed journalists and chroniclers such as William Shirer and Rebecca West covered the trial and sought to delineate at one and the same time individual characters and the human interactions that had led to catastrophe. They also did much to convey the atmosphere of this judicial and quasi-clinical process, where horrific disclosures and flashes of procedural uncertainty were combined with long stretches of tedium.

The charge of conspiracy that became a central feature of the prosecution case at Nuremberg had a long and vexed history in jurisprudence, but the fact that it was adapted to form the basis for key indictments of the war criminals owed much to a New York lawyer and US army officer, Lieutenant-Colonel Murray Bernays (who, like the advertising guru Edward Bernays, happened to be related to Freud).[2] He had gained the ear of the chief American prosecutor, Justice Robert Jackson, as well as a number of key figures within Roosevelt's government, who seized on the 'conspiracy' idea as a clear and efficient means of proceeding. During the last years of the war various politicians and advisers at the White House, keen to create a judicial framework, worked to persuade the President that a viable trial system could be established, without the risk of widespread acquittals or a dangerous aura of martyrdom for the men in the dock. It had in fact fallen to Truman, not Roosevelt (who died suddenly on 12 April 1945), to confirm that such court proceedings would be endorsed by the United States. On 6 May 1945 the first agreements were made between the different Allied delegations as to the shape of the tribunal. The question of whom to try, and by what process, had yet to be finalized. In practice, the British and Americans played more important roles than the French or Russians in resolving matters. Above all, the Americans ran the organization and, once the decision was taken, expressed the most enthusiasm for the task.[3]

The very existence of the court was in some ways a surprise. Churchill had not initially supported it, and other major statesmen and several of their advisers also changed positions before the final compromise was reached. Many had expected negotiations for the creation of the court to collapse in the same way as had plans, after 1918, to establish an international tribunal to deal with crimes committed by the German army and politicians in the First World War.[4] But despite much division within Roosevelt's cabinet, the United States eventually led the way to creating 'Nuremberg' in 1945.[5]

The juridical solution that was found broke new ground, although it owed something of its spirit to attempted negotiations in the 1920s and a range of earlier initiatives that had aimed to civilize military conduct, prevent wars of aggression, and challenge the arbitrary exertion of power in the European empires. Liberal humanitarian responses to outrageous acts of violence and retribution within the British Empire, for example, had stirred intense political and cultural debate in Victorian times. Calls by the great liberal philosopher John Stuart Mill and others for the impeachment of Governor Eyre of Jamaica, after he had suppressed a rebellion by large-scale reprisals, mass killings, and brutal punishments, divided many of the most famous intellectuals of the day. Historians have listed many 'stepping-stones' to Nuremberg, including the creation of the Red Cross in the 1860s, growing debate about war atrocities through the second half of the nineteenth century, major set-piece conferences (Geneva 1863, the Hague 1899 and 1907), and journalistic reports about outrages in the Crimea and during the American Civil War and Franco-Prussian War. All might be regarded retrospectively, as germane to the new and ever fragile, law-bound world that was constituted after the Second World War.[6]

Nuremberg was to prove a more elaborate and cumbersome judicial process than some of the diplomats had originally envisaged when the terms were first mooted and negotiated in 1943 and 1944. Some claimed that there was no need to establish German guilt for the war or to document atrocities, since these were already evident: the task of the IMT, according to this line of thought, was to determine the measure of culpability of each case, whilst the criminality of the regime and its associated agencies could be assumed.[7] Other counsel prevailed, and a more costly system was put in place in order to demonstrate that thorough examination of the facts had occurred. Claims of fairness were instantly disputed, but the IMT did require that the prosecution set out each story in detail whilst defence lawyers were allowed to represent the interests of the prisoners as best they could. Those arraigned were given opportunities to participate, indeed were required to contribute to the process in a variety of ways. None of them opted to remain entirely mute.

In proposing the use of conspiracy charges, Murray Bernays drew on a controversial area of American law; he was in part inspired to pursue this line by the wartime work of Raphael Lemkin, a Polish lawyer who (unlike many members of his own extended Jewish family) had escaped his native land to find refuge in America. Here he began a successful academic career and campaigned to ensure that Nazi laws, beliefs, and atrocities were not forgotten; the notorious Nuremberg laws on race, for example, ought to remain in the spotlight; all the more so the horrific final outcomes of the Nazi policy they embodied. It was Lemkin who coined the term 'genocide', and he went on to contribute to the United Nations in its deliberations and declarations over universal human rights in the late 1940s.[8] An important advantage of using the notion of conspiracy was that it obviated the need for prosecutors to proceed, in an impossibly time-consuming fashion, from first principles in the case of each defendant. The criminal nature of the key Nazi organizations (such as the Gestapo and the SS) would be established once and for all, and then assumed in subsequent hearings.[9]

In all likelihood the Harvard-trained Bernays, who promoted the conspiracy approach, would have known of the major review essay dealing with the problems and opportunities such law presented in the *Harvard Law Review* of 1921–2.[10] One point that had been stressed there by the legal scholar Francis Sayre was how the deleterious activity and potential criminality of a *group* was often more than the sum of its constituent parts. Groups had the potential vastly to magnify the powers of individuals and to bind them in a process for which nobody was singly responsible, but in which everybody concerned had a certain share. He cited a judgement from a New Hampshire court in 1844 that had turned on immoral acts 'committed by numbers' in furtherance of a 'common object'. The advantages and strength that determination *and union* impart to them altered the complexion of certain acts immeasurably. Voluntary participation in that union made members co-responsible for, say, a murderous outcome, even if they had not individually pulled the trigger. Sayre, in fact, had high-lighted such cases with the aim of noting the risks of legal abuse; he was concerned with criminal law in the United States rather than international law and crimes of war. He warned of the risks of curtailing individual free-dom through the inappropriate use of conspiracy legislation in situations where the subject's direct hand in an unlawful action was ambiguous, and where the mere fact of endorsement of an organization could all too easily be equated with criminality.[11]

In November 1944, though, three members of Roosevelt's cabinet, Cordell Hull, Henry Stimson, and James Forrestal, summarized for the President several practical advantages of adopting the conspiracy approach: it avoided any possibility that defendants could rely on saying they had just obeyed orders, and it also shifted the focus from discrete criminal acts towards the underlying group plan to dominate the world, transgress against humanity, and violate the laws of war. It was, they added, the 'purposeful and systematic pattern' of illegality that needed to be exposed; the prosecu-tion would need to reveal the 'continuing conspiracy' that governed the Nazi state. Initially it was said that only one major trial would be required. The procedure would be manifestly judicial and not obviously political, and it could not but fail to impress the wider world for 'generations to come'. One potential stumbling-block was whether the Nazi leadership could be successfully prosecuted, if no prior international law had existed to outlaw their specific actions before 1945. The 'no law, no crime' defence would not apply, however, Roosevelt's advisers explained, since it would be clear that major treaties and conventions had been breached, and the atroc-ities would be understood to have flown in the face of accepted standards of humanity and military conduct. (In fact the defence lawyers at Nuremberg did indeed claim that, as the laws under which the men were being tried were not in place before 1945, the crimes were not admissible; the judges rejected the argument.) Weeks later a further memo to Roosevelt clarified that perhaps a few trials rather than just one might be needed, but not more.[12] Justice Jackson and other prosecutors seized upon the notion of conspiracy as a crucial plank of their argument, since evidence was not necessarily available to prove that defendants had personally murdered or tortured anyone. Under the conspiracy charge, Jackson only needed to demonstrate that the accused authorized, or agreed to, actions that pro-duced the crimes alleged; this, they believed, could be established where necessary by circumstantial evidence.[13]

The American judge at the International Military Tribunal, Francis Biddle, reminisced that 'Hitler's ghost haunted the courtroom'. He also described the Führer as 'a mass psychologist of really diabolical genius, who finally fell victim to the spell he cast over the masses, for whoever seduces them is finally led and seduced by them'.[14] The assumption that the culprits in the dock had mental competence and had committed 'malice afore-thought' jarred, at times, with these evocations of ghosts as well as with other depictions of the men as bureaucratic automata, robotic figures. Free will was, of course, key. Jackson made references to the men's volition and yet also conveyed how a kind of moral disease had set in. He acknowledged that the dead Hitler was the mastermind, but eloquently showed how others could and should have stopped him. All of the prosecutors strained to find words for the enormity of the crimes. The French lead counsel, François de Menthon, suggested that what was at issue was a 'crime against the spirit'.[15]

Outside the courtroom Nuremberg was a city of dust and rubble, ever after a 'haunted city',[16] but within the walls of the Palace of Justice the idea of due process was to be quickly restored. The military guards, stenographers, lawyers, translators, clerks, psychiatrists, and psychologists all worked to a new routine. The doctors went about their daily business here, using their close contact with the prisoners to offer ancillary sources of information about the war criminals. According to Major Kelley, who had taken charge of Hess from his British counterparts upon his arrival, this entire cadre of high-ranking officials was nothing less than 'psychological treasure'; the psychologist Gustave Gilbert also called the prisoners 'laboratory mice'.[17] Cross-examined about his role at Nuremberg whilst giving evidence years later at the Eichmann trial, Gilbert recalled the care he had taken to ensure the intelligence and personality tests he had conducted on the prisoners were valid, 'because of the supreme importance' that had been assigned to the psychiatric aspects of the case.

At times the entire German people were brought into the proceedings. According to the French prosecutor, for example, advancing his own 'German peculiarity' thesis, the nation had reverted 'of her own free-will...to the primitive barbarity of ancient Germany'.[18] Yet the trial also led some to perceive the perpetrators in other ways, for instance, as akin to cogs in a machine or as hypnotized subjects who had, to an unprecedented degree, lost all capacity to think. To be sure, some defendants took advantage of this idea in order to confess their helpless fascination with Hitler, as though thereby to exonerate themselves. The senior Nazi lawyer and governor in Poland, Hans Frank, conveyed this sense to Goldensohn, laying stress upon the 'hypnotic personality' of Hitler.[19] This was not an excuse, he said, although it sounded self-exculpating enough.[20]

Hitler's magnetism became a common trope in the confessions that were made to the doctors around the courtroom and in a vast accompanying literature. Smooth Albert Speer, talking much later to the writer Gitta Sereny, echoed the point when he described his experience of the leader's strange personal 'fascination'. What he called the Führer's charisma, charm, and mystique could only be explained, he believed, via the power of mesmerism.[21] Many of the defendants spoke in a fashion that suggested their egos were simply in thrall to Hitler and insisted on the duty of obedience—questioning, in the process, the notion that they were free to act other than the way they had. Göring was incredulous at the idea that soldiers could *ever* legitimately subvert the instructions of their superiors, although in his own case—and unlike many of his colleagues—he did not shrink from acknowledging the central role he had played in the conduct of the regime, even if he disavowed all detailed knowledge of the horrors of the camps. Göring had long embraced the view that life was a violent, pitiless struggle. As his biographer, the historian Richard Overy, observes, he sought to function in a manner commensurate with his vision of man as a 'beast of prey'.[22]

Gilbert and other designated listeners took every opportunity to assemble information about the prisoners' attitudes to responsibility and duty, and to identify the underlying cultural and unconscious attitudes on which such claims were based. They clearly had the ear of some of the prosecutors, notably Robert Jackson, who also took a close interest in recent social scientific literature on the psychology of the Nazi perpetrators and their victims. He was informed about the New York psychiatrist Richard Brickner's study of the paranoid features of German culture and thought, and also of Bruno Bettelheim's account of the extreme psychological situation of inmates in the camps.[23]

Bettelheim, born in 1903, became a significant, and later contentious, figure in post-war America. After studies at Vienna University and a period of psychoanalysis in the 1930s, Bettelheim emerged as a champion of Freud. As an Austrian Jew he found himself interned at Dachau and Buchenwald in 1938, although an unexpected policy decision led him and some other prisoners to be released the following year.[24] This enabled Bettelheim to leave Germany and escape to the United States. His wartime article on Nazi mentality and the psychology of camp life proved swiftly influential, as did his therapeutic work with children suffering from aphasia and other disturbances. But it was revelations, following his suicide in 1990, about his personal behaviour that turned his reputation in America on its head. The wealth of his publications on politics, parent–child relations, totalitarianism, mass society, and so forth were placed in the balance against the harrowing reports that he became, in the words of his biographer, 'a sadistic brute'.[25] How much his behaviour owed to his own painful experiences under the Nazis became a matter of subsequent inquiry.[26]

Published in the *Journal of Abnormal and Social Psychology* in 1943, Bettelheim's article described the author's own grim experiences of, and acute reflections on, his internment by the Nazis. He spoke of the psychology of the inmates, albeit basing his account on a period before the camp system had plunged towards its full and final horror in the 1940s.[27] Bettelheim wrote of the physical and mental torture of the prisoners, the fear and prospect of death, the loss of dignity, and of contact with hope. Reality outside the camp world, he suggested, gradually receded and the very sense of self was swiftly transformed: intense regression to infantile feelings of helplessness and terror occurred in victims, as their defences were overwhelmed by the most primitive and uncontainable feelings. Most shockingly, he suggested that a shift commonly occurred in the prisoners' orientation, from secret aggressive feelings against their captors towards covert identification with the values of the guards. Many long-term inmates, according to Bettelheim, gave themselves over in fantasy to their jailors and tormentors; they 'took over the Gestapo's attitude towards the so-called unfit prisoners'.[28]

This claim was based on Bettelheim's own direct observations of himself and those who agreed to talk intimately about their experience, but not, of course, on any widespread and reliable survey (whatever that could have meant at the time). Accurate or not, however, Bettelheim's thesis was significant as an early example of a much larger mode of inquiry into the unconscious psychic life of power. Brickner's *Is Germany Incurable?* and Bettelheim's work on camp inmates, 'Individual and Mass Behavior', pointed the way towards two different trajectories of post-war thought: the former concerned with localizing the horror of Nazism to the German 'case'; the latter suggesting that, under given conditions, certain victims—perhaps any victims—might start to think and even function like perpetrators. Bettelheim believed that he retained his sanity by somehow managing to become interested in, and observant about, the very process of identification he was caught up in as an inmate.

Bettelheim also aimed to show how the treatment of prisoners in the camps of the 1930s illuminated the way the Nazis exerted social and political control more generally. He described the camps as 'an experimental laboratory', a 'training ground'. The aim was not only to break the prisoners, to spread terror and to produce a 'docile mass' inside the camps, but to 'study the effective means of breaking civilian resistance' at large and thereby to create *more useful subjects of the Nazi state*'.[29] This argument clearly reflected the particular kind of camp that Bettelheim experienced, and a particular phase of Nazi history. The camp system that Bettelheim described, in other words, was regarded here as part of a terrifying disciplinary mechanism, an important means of producing conformity inside the state: as options for rebellion or open dissent dwindled, an extraordinary corrosion occurred, with the capacity for personal hesitation, resistance, or even individualized feeling by the denizens of the Third Reich replaced, he argued, by 'mass mentality'.[30]

In 1945 Eisenhower arranged for the distribution of Bettelheim's work to American officers in occupied Germany.[31] It was suggested at one point that he might even usefully be called as a witness at the IMT.[32] This did not happen, but Bettelheim's paper on the psychology of camp inmates anticipated and sometimes influenced post-war literature concerning the trauma of Nazism's victims: the sense of shame, the loss of individuality, the unconscious identification with the aggressor, and so forth. It also resonated with contemporaneous reports of so-called loss of self among the perpetrators, anticipating how the German leadership was seen in two distinct ways at Nuremberg: as responsible, calculating subjects who had freely entered into a malignant conspiracy; and as examples of a group pathology that eroded all capacity to think as individuals and exercise freedom of mind. (Hannah Arendt would take this line further still in her seminal account of the Eichmann trial roughly fifteen years later.)

Scrutiny of the prisoners at Nuremberg was extremely intense. After Ley's suicide the guards were required to practice physical observation at one-minute intervals, hence those famous photographic images of Allied soldiers on constant watch outside every cell. The risk that prisoners would harm themselves enabled Colonel Burton Andrus, the American commandant of the military prison, to justify close psychological observations as well as inspections by guards, so that alongside the direct gaze of the military police a variety of psychological and psychiatric assessments were arranged. In December 1945 the psychiatrist Colonel Paul Schroeder made a confidential assessment of the defendants, and as historian Paul Weindling has pointed out, by June 1946 five medical inspectors were at work at the IMT: the psychiatrists Kelley, Goldensohn, Schroeder, Lewis, and Cameron, together with the psychologist Gilbert, were all collecting 'data'.[33] Whatever distaste some later critics have expressed for this kind of close psychological interest in the Nazis' personal motives or psychic formations, Nuremberg abundantly facilitated it.[34]

———•———

The first Nuremberg trial combined obvious punitive and educational purposes: the potential of rehabilitation for those given long jail sentences, and the production of a documented history of the Third Reich's criminality. The psychological discourse of the trial was always important—it was the characteristics of the men and the chemistry of the group, not just the acts committed, that were explored. In the National Archives in Maryland it is still possible to hear some of those original figures talking to American interviewers about their roles in the war. From old, scratchy tape recordings, conducted by Colonel Amen of the OSS, emerge the sounds of Göring, Hess, and other prisoners in detailed conversation just before the trial. Amen interrogated these men about their former activities, their views of Hitler, the conduct of the war, and their personal beliefs and ethical attitudes. The interviews, evidently, were preliminaries to the task of prosecution, providing information, furthermore, that could be of interest to the security services. But they also disclosed a certain fascination with the defeated political leaders themselves, as if what was at stake was the discovery and revelation of Nazi fantasy as such, and the way this crystallized in the minds of the subjects. In Hess's case, as ever, the taped interview was dominated by the riddle of the prisoner's amnesia.[35]

What induced the defendants to speak to the psychologist Gilbert, the psychiatrists Kelley and Goldensohn, and the others? Vanity? Despair? Self-righteousness? Garrulousness? Sheer boredom? Nuremberg was a long-drawn-out affair, not an event; the first trial lasted many months and the attendant personnel had ample opportunity to talk to the Nazi prisoners and to build up some kind of relationship. Whatever drove the defendants to speak, the content of these scripts, and the process of their construction is striking. Nuremberg turned into an elaborate fishing expedition to capture the personality traits and convictions of the surviving leadership before it was too late.

Psychiatrists documented the subjects' responses to the Nazi regime, the meaning of defeat by the Allies, the experience of imprisonment, and the anticipation of verdicts against them. These first-hand observations contributed to the larger stream of information about the Nazi past. The IMT, as Richard Overy puts it, provided 'oral evidence of an entire leadership corps'.[36] In many cases, given the passing of death sentences in 1946, it was to be the first and last such oral history. Those Nuremberg commentaries were part of a larger psychological literature that was produced by the Allies in occupied Germany. Political and military analyses by American and British intelligence experts in 1945 and 1946 (direct from Nuremberg or from other parts of Germany) often shaded into overt psychiatric diagnosis.[37]

Rebecca West was among the first observers to take critical note of this dimension of the Nuremberg process. Pondering the suicide of Göring (an act that pre-empted his imminent execution), she observed: 'Like all the Nazis, he had been plagued by the attentions of the psychiatrists who haunted Nuremberg Jail, exercising a triple function of priest and doctor and warder hard to approve.' She noted how these functionaries had visited the men in their cells on frequent occasions, offering themselves as sounding-boards whilst actually performing their duties at the behest of the court authorities.

> When some of the defendants seemed to be taking an unrepentant pro-Nazi stand in their line of defence, one of the psychiatrists worked out, at the commandant's request, a plan for a new seating arrangement at the lunch table in order to break up this group and expose them to other influences. It is not easy to think of an accused person on trial before a national tribunal being subjected to such manipulation by prison officials. There was no silver lining in this cloud. One of these psychiatrists has related, without humorous intent, that when Göring asked him what a certain psychological test had revealed about his character, he replied that it had shown that he lacked the guts to face responsibility.[38]

Psychiatric inquiry was certainly pervasive; even critics of this language such as West were tempted to make diagnoses. 'The Nazis', she wrote, 'were maniacs who plastered history with the cruelty which is a waste product of man's moral nature, as maniacs on a smaller scale plaster their bodies and their clothes with their excreta.' Göring, she complained, should not have been allowed to die by his own hand, since: 'It is unfair, not only to Germans, but to all the world, if the vileness of the Nazis be extenuated; and it was unfair that this Nazi of all Nazis should have been allowed to disguise his gross dementia.'[39] By taking his own life he disguised his sick *and* depraved condition under a carapace of 'courage'. Execution, West believed, was necessary in order to bring home to the public the sheer squalor of his mind and actions.

At every stage in the proceedings the drama in the courtroom was observed in close detail. Thus, as the men were made to watch Allied film of the liberation of Belsen and other camps their reactions were monitored and recorded as evidence of each individual's capacity for contrition, grief, and compassion, or conversely, for pathological defences against shouldering any of the burden of guilt. The following account reveals the double process of watching, as various doctors and analysts scrutinized the prisoners while they in turn faced the film of the concentration camps:

> Funk covers his eyes...Sauckel mops brow...Frank swallows hard, blinks eyes, trying to stifle tears...Frank mutters 'Horrible!'...Rosenberg fidgets, peeks at screen, bows head, looks to see how others are reacting...Seyss-Inquart stoic throughout...Speer looks very sad, swallows hard...Defense attorneys are now muttering, 'for God's sake—terrible.'...Fritzsche, pale, biting lips, really seems in agony...Doenitz has head buried in his hands... Keitel now hanging head.

Airey Neave also recalled the prisoners' 'twisted guilty faces...with tears on their cheeks', as they saw these terrible scenes. He added: 'I sometimes dream of it.' Not all of the observers agreed with these accounts: some presented the Nazi defendants as cooler than this, or as actively turning away their gaze.[40]

Reflecting upon the trial two years later, anthropologist Margaret Mead suggested that rather than guilt, the behaviour of the Nuremberg defendants indicated instead a new form of compliance: 'The fact that certain of the Nuremberg prisoners were described as "beginning to feel some guilt," should, I believe, simply be interpreted as a shift of moral allegiance—under pressure of the trial conditions—so that these particular prisoners began to feel that they had not been accepting the correct authorities under whom to act.'[41] In other words, they tuned into the requirements of their new masters, the Allied victors. Mead and Henry Dicks both suggested after the war that it was a mistake often made by psychiatrists to attribute individual guilt feelings to people without paying proper heed to the nature of the culture in which they lived: if rote obedience and duty were far more valued social qualities than individual choice and responsibility, this would, in all probability, profoundly affect the entire outlook of the subject; researchers brought up in a different, more individualistic culture, they warned, might well be barking up the wrong tree when they sought to interpret the mental state and motivation of the leading Nazis.[42]

In fact the situation was still more complex. Both interviewers and interviewees may have had fundamentally different political views, but they were not in fact from mutually uncomprehending cultures. They also shared a number of preconceptions, not least about the significance of the role of the psychological interview: often it appeared as though the prisoners anticipated the expectations of their psychiatrists regarding the function of such discussion. The psychiatrists endeavoured to let the subjects speak for themselves, to obtain authentic opinions. In this respect their approach had something in common with the style of Langer's interviews with former Nazi insiders, or of the many verbatim accounts of conversation with Hess and other prisoners of war conducted by British and American officers. As a reviewer from the *New Yorker* put it (the quote served as a puff on the paperback edition of Gilbert's *Nuremberg Diary*, which appeared not long after the trial): 'The author lets the defendants talk for themselves and introduces himself into the picture very little'. And yet the result, as this enthusiast admitted, was somewhat confusing, 'a mass of quotations that have the phantasmagorical quality of a sinister "Through the Looking-Glass" in which reasoning and logic run backward'.[43]

As with some of Langer's witnesses for the OSS Hitler study, it is striking that prisoners often seem to have spoken in a manner that might be likely to interest, or even impress, their psychologically minded interviewers. Certainly there was an attempt to talk to the 'professionals' about psychopathology. According to Göring, Himmler was undoubtedly 'a criminal' and Bormann 'a primitive criminal type'.[44] As for Goebbels, here was a 'fanatic of an abnormal calibre'.[45] Schmidt referred to Göring as 'a dope addict'.[46] Hans Fritzsche, in a semi-confession, said: 'I was used as a tool for evil by Goebbels.'[47] Goebbels, Fritzsche added, was a 'completely ruthless, conscienceless fanatic'.[48] Hans Frank, an educated figure, was loquacious in his account of Hitler's complex psychology and sought to match the interviewing psychiatrist on his own terrain. He engaged in a discussion of the possibility that Hitler suspected he had a Jewish grandfather. This was a story that easily lent itself to a 'Freudian' reading: Hitler's ferocious denial of Judaism linked to his unconscious horror that he was so directly implicated.[49] Frank also spoke of Hitler's psychic abnormality, sadism, and so on, suggesting (with direct reference to Freud) that frustrations of love might have warped the Führer:

I think that Hitler was abnormal in his sexual needs. That is, he needed too little from the opposite sex. He considered women as objects of beauty, and he often talked with affection about his own mother. I obtained the impression that he disliked his father, because he never mentioned him. But it is a bad thing if a man has too little Eros in him. It makes him insensitive, and probably leads to cruelty. Freud, Sigmund Freud, the last of the great German [sic] psychiatrists, who died in England, pointed out the relationship between frustrated love and cruelty. I believe it is what you psychiatrists term sadism. I'm convinced that a man who does not need the love of a woman, and thinks he can forgo it, or who does forgo it, can turn to cruelty and sadism as a substitute.[50]

Asked whether he had read Freud, Frank is reported to have replied: 'Not his works, no books of his, but I have read many articles about what he said and about his work.'[51]

Göring discussed with Goldensohn his understanding of the differences between psychologists and psychiatrists, suggesting that the former were concerned with book knowledge, the later with the treatment of human beings. The Reichsmarschall also let it be known that he did not believe that his own childhood had affected his adult personality. He then appeared to defer to the doctor for an expert opinion. Göring suggested to the psychiatrist that he believed there were in effect two Hitlers: a charming and approachable leader (evident until the end of the invasion of France), and a tense, withdrawn, and mistrustful character (from the Russian campaign until the time of his suicide). This served, if nothing else, to focus the psychiatrists' attention back upon Hitler, the vicissitudes of his character, and the strange power that his personality exerted over others.

The 'psy' professionals no doubt gave clues as to the theoretical background that prompted their questions. They were interested, for instance, in reminiscences about childhood and evidence of brutally violent, ferociously misogynistic, and/or simply absentee fathers. For example, Paul Schmidt, Hitler's translator, told Goldensohn: '[Father] used to spank me whenever I deserved it but he never went to extremes.'[52] On the other hand, the doctors sometimes spoke as though free association was really the aim. Here too they echoed something of the psychoanalytical situation by proposing that prisoners say 'whatever comes into your head'. Thus invited, some interviewees fervently rejected the idea that they personally had been ruthless, felt hatred of enemy nations or of the Jewish people, indeed denied that they had personally ever been influenced by anti-Semitism; they were more inclined to pin the blame for all horrors on others. How far some of these men sought specifically to ingratiate themselves with the Jewish army officers, Gilbert and Goldensohn, by insisting on their lack of anti-Semitic feeling is open to conjecture.

Some of the defendants were prepared to cast Hitler as a great criminal; others praised his tremendous mind and remarkable memory (the view, for example of the German naval commander, Karl Doenitz). Göring continued to call Hitler a genius to the end, and saw himself as 'standing in' for the leader at the trial. In others, self-pitying or rueful pseudo-confessions such as 'I should have cleared out and not had anything to do with these criminals in the first place' or 'I am not guilty of crimes against humanity' were the norm.[53] General Jodl insisted that he was 'very normal'. Otto Ohlendorf, who led one of the special task forces (*Einsatzgruppen*) responsible for countless murders in the East declared knowingly that Goebbels might have suffered an inferiority complex due to his club-foot.

In the interviews Goldensohn was able to tease out one or two of Streicher's fantasies about circumcision, and in addition noted the prisoner's squinting eyes and frequent wetting of his tongue as he spoke. The psychiatrist concluded that Streicher was a psychopath of limited intelligence, caught up in his own pornographic obsessions. Many Nazis had long ago concluded the same thing, disgusted by his rabid ranting, empty posturing, and unreliability; he fell out with so many colleagues that he had been stripped of his Party reponsibilities in 1940 and forced to adopt a lower profile. Ernst Kaltenbrunner (Reinhard Heydrich's successor in the SS) referred to his boss Himmler as being 'primitive mentally' and revealed that he considered other colleagues, such as Kurt Daluege and Heydrich, insane and wantonly cruel.[54]

Perhaps the diagnoses that were eventually made by the psychiatrists may now seem less striking than the cool willingness of the war criminals to enter into forensic analysis, and to intersperse discussion of Germany's historical responsibilities with occasional comments, in response to prompting by the psychological evaluators, regarding first sexual experiences, marital difficulties, psychosomatic symptoms, or disturbed sleep patterns. To be sure, certain high-ranking Nazi prisoners were disinclined to contribute to, or were even quite incapable of, entering into such psychological discourse in the first place. Some gave the stark message that they had no dreams or even fantasies that they could recall at all: this, for instance, was the gist of the response by Rudolf Hoess, the commandant of Auschwitz, as recorded by Dr Goldensohn in his notes. Cross-examined at Nuremberg (where he was called as a witness by one of the defendants' defence lawyers) about the millions of deaths that had occurred, Hoess gave matter of fact answers, said he had had some doubts about the killings but 'the only one and decisive argument was the strict order and the reason given for it by... Himmler'.[55] Hoess was to be tried the following year in Poland and was executed on 16 April 1947, in the vicinity of a crematorium at Auschwitz.

———•———

Hess was one of several of the arraigned men at Nuremberg who escaped with their lives, albeit to face long custodial sentences. Three defendants were acquitted (Schacht, Fritzsche, and von Papen) and ten were executed on 16 October 1946. The Soviet judge dissented from all of the acquittals and the life sentence for Hess.

No wise person will write an unnecessary word about hanging, wrote Rebecca West, 'for fear of straying into the field of pornography'.[56] She was alert to the prurient satisfaction that the observer might feel, as though savouring the executions of some of the Nazi war criminals, and she condemned such propensities: 'the strain of evil in us, which, given privileges, can take pleasure in the destruction of others by pain and death, taking delight in dreams about hanging, which is the least dignified form of death. That delight emits the strongest of all the stinks that hang about the little bookshops in the backstreets.' West's discussion of methods of capital punishment seemed to be as much about the disturbingly perverse emotions that might be evoked by the contemplation of the act as about questions of justice and retribution; hence the references to the 'strain of evil in us', 'pleasure in destruction', sordid 'delight'. Nevertheless, if there must be capital punishment—and West seemed to believe that, for these guilty men, there was no alternative—it had better take the form of hanging than any other method, she suggested. She rejected the view that murderers should be killed by lethal injections; for this could not be efficiently done without recourse to the aid of doctors, who could not give such assistance without breaking the Hippocratic oath and thus losing their 'sacred characters as the preservers of life'.[57] The electric chair, she said, was an 'obscene retrogression', for it raised up in the minds of the vulgar a vision of 'regal stoicism'; the sedentary posture of the condemned could be made to appear throne-like.[58] The firing squad ('the happiest of executions') might enable the accused to gain the good opinion of the executioners; she regarded it as altogether too noble a solution. Decapitation, with its accompanying 'grace notes of horror', was also rejected. Hanging

PLATE 1. Into exile . . . 1938. Sigmund and Anna Freud on their journey from Vienna to London after the Anschluss.

PLATE 2. Picture of Hess and his sister Margarete, as children. This image was reproduced in *The Case of Rudolf Hess* (1947). Hess's early interpreters wondered if the roots of his Nazi beliefs might lie in the deformations of his childhood experience.

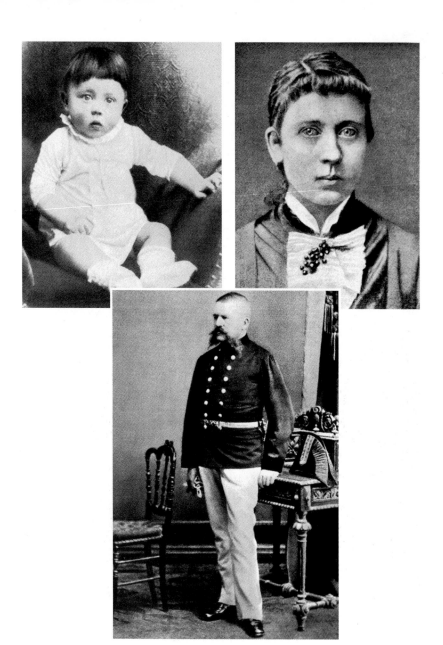

PLATES 3, 4, and 5. The Führer as a baby, alongside his parents, Klara Poelzl and Alois Hitler, recycled in Walter Langer's *The Mind of Adolf Hitler* (1972). An important question for Langer and his peers was how far Hitler's infantile experience and early psychological struggles might serve to explain the monstrous 'authoritarian personality' of the adult Nazi leader.

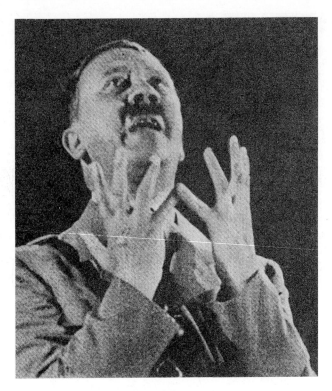

PLATE 6. Hitler's messianic performances. Langer used such illustrations in his book and made much of Hitler's dramatic rapport with his audiences in his wartime OSS report.

PLATES 7, 8, and 9. From a postcard series in the 1920s, 'Adolf Hitler Speaks, 6 Photographic Moments', by Hitler's official photographer Heinrich Hoffmann.

PLATES 10, 11, and 12. Stills from Leni Riefenstahl's *Triumph of the Will* (1935). Hess silently enjoys for a moment the audience's adulation.

PLATE 13. A Nuremberg rally, 1934.

PLATE 14. Hitler addresses the SA, Dortmund, 1933.

PLATE 15. Walter Langer.

PLATE 16. Henry Dicks.

PLATE 17. 'Wild Bill' Donovan.

PLATE 18. Rebecca West.

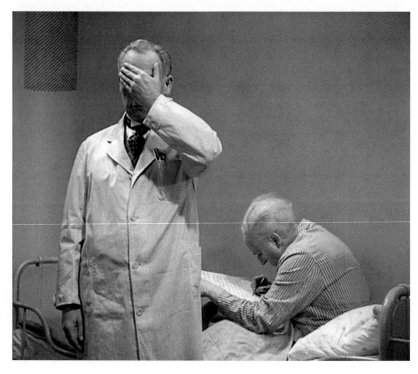

PLATE 19. In this scene from Fritz Lang's *The Testament of Dr Mabuse* (1933), the psychiatrist Prof. Baum is witnessed falling prey to the mesmeric power of his dangerous patient, the eponymous criminal mastermind.

PLATE 20. Baum and the ghost of Mabuse, on the road to perdition.

PLATE 21. A spectral Mabuse opens the gates to the asylum.

PLATE 22 and 23. The hero Stephen Neale in Fritz Lang's *Ministry of Fear* (1944), at the moment of his discovery of the mysterious Dr Forrester's tome, *The Psychoanalysis of Nazidom*.

PLATE 24. Hess at the International Military Tribunal, interviewed by Col. John Amen and other officials, Nuremberg, October 1945.

PLATE 25. Hess, Göring, and Ribbentrop in the dock.

PLATE 26. Hess in old age, imprisoned at Spandau.

PLATES 27 The site of Spandau prison, after the building was razed to the ground following Hess's death in 1987.

it had to be. Yet West observed how the executions were handled incompetently and did not always provide the swift and clinical end to the perpetrators' lives that was expected: Ribbentrop, for one, was reputedly left to choke for a full twenty minutes.[59] Hess, by contrast, survived Nuremberg, but was never to be released.

10

Sane Futures?

Ideas of democracy and of collective sanity were closely bound together after 1945; the 'mental health' of nations had never seemed of more pressing public concern. Congresses of health professionals, developments in group therapy, and interdisciplinary research efforts such as those that were made shortly after the war at the United Nations Educational, Scientific and Cultural Organization (UNESCO) all illustrate this striking trend.

An obvious context for these debates was occupied Germany: after the defeat of the Third Reich certain key psychoanalytical and psychiatric models and ideas were adapted (and criticized) in discussions of denazification, re-education, and regeneration. A number of influential commentators linked the language of sanity and madness to the recent titanic struggles against Nazism, some even seeing the forces of freedom and of tyranny as locked in perpetual battle for the human soul. Psychoanalysis and the other 'psy' professions lent themselves again to political diagnoses of the Third Reich and, especially, with the coming of the Cold War, to the study of totalitarianism.[1] Some feared liberal democracy was dangerously vulnerable not only to foreign invasion or espionage, but also to renewed bouts of popular authoritarian 'sickness'.

This impetus to safeguard democracy can be seen at the International Congress on Mental Health held in August 1948. This strikingly large-scale event in London assumed that mental illnesses in individual cases *and* in the human aggregate were essential considerations for the consolidation of post-war liberty, peace, and international cooperation. The psychological state of the citizen and the robustness of the polity were seen as intimately linked.[2] Recurrent debates at the congress concerned the nature of aggression, the social role of guilt (and the defences against facing it), and the problem of the management and treatment of madness. Insanity, it was widely argued, lurked not only in individuals but also in groups, communities, and nations.

Patrons of the congress included British Prime Minister Clement Atlee and the former Foreign Secretary Anthony Eden. With such concerns about war and peace, cooperation, and aggression at stake, luminaries from the psychoanalytical world, including Anna Freud and Melanie Klein, and anthropologists such as Margaret Mead spoke to the assembly about the latest findings of their disciplines. Mead and Anna Freud had star billing, whilst Klein spoke from the floor (albeit at some length). Anna Freud opened the congress with an address entitled 'Aggression in Relation to Emotional Development: Normal and Pathological'.[3] Other psychoanalysts, including John-Carl Flügel (president of the congress programme committee), also contributed their thoughts on the problem of violence and the possibility of enhancing cooperation between nations.

Present alongside the contingent of psychoanalysts were large numbers of academics and health professionals from Britain and the United States, including assorted sociologists, anthropologists, physicians, psychotherapists, psychiatric social workers, and nurses, along with teachers and members of the clergy. Nearly sixty countries sent one or more participants.[4] Staff from newly created international bodies such as the World Health Organization and UNESCO were also present.[5] This was but one of a series of high-profile international meetings in the second half of the 1940s that explicitly set out to pool academic, political, and clinical expertise, encourage collaborative work across disciplinary boundaries on behalf of liberal political ideals, and guard against the plagues of fascism and militarism.

A specific section of the London gathering was devoted to 'Mental Health and World Citizenship'. Its chairman, John Rawlings Rees, reminded his audience that here they were not dealing with sick individuals so much as 'sick groups and sick communities'.[6] In fact, a number of speakers stressed the relationship between early life experience, family values, social care, and the general harmony or disharmony of states. There was not much attention paid in this particular intellectual context to the formal apparatus or legal systems of political states; there was, however, much talk of 'culture' and the psychic formation of babies and children.

Henry Dicks, for instance, in response to Mead's plenary lecture on human aggression, agreed that character structure and culture were closely bound up. What had to be understood, he emphasized, was how culture inhabited and was affected by the subject's interior life. He suggested that what was required was a study that focused on the nature of the formation of the superego in a range of different countries. He was interested in identifying the particular social structures that provided status and reward, and, conversely, with rituals of shaming and humiliation, and how these affected the mind.[7]

It would be fruitful, Dicks suggested, to interpret Nazis ideology not only as a terrifying manifestation of the superego, but also as the (false) promise of freedom from it. Thus, whilst the Third Reich required mass obedience, it also exploited the youthful wish to wage war against the authoritarian figures epitomized by the traditional pre-Nazi 'elders'. Although it installed in Hitler a supremely cruel and domineering father figure, it presented itself as an ecstatic liberation from the old order; hence its captivating aura of romantic revolt.[8] Turning his attention to the future health of nations, Dicks proposed that certain goals should be held in mind, such as a shift from egocentric attitudes towards 'sociality'; from unconscious to conscious; from superego to ego; from aggression to tolerance; from fear to security; from emotional and moral prejudice to psychological-rational judgement.[9]

The vital importance of motherhood was stressed repeatedly at the mental-health congress and in similar venues after the war. Where the accent had so often fallen in Freud's work upon the role of the father, post-war clinicians shifted much of their attention to the nurturing role of the mother and the consequences of maternal deprivation. Congress participants tried to imagine the kind of society that would be most likely to eschew the aggression, militarism, and racial hatred that had been epitomized by the Third Reich. The psychoanalyst John Bowlby—another of the contributors to the congress—exemplified this. He was to gain prominence in Britain and abroad (notably through the World Health Organization, for which he wrote substantial reports) as a campaigner for child mental health; he stressed the vital importance of allowing the close bond between mother and baby to develop without hindrance; conversely, he warned about the serious, long-term psychological consequences of callously disrupting the emotional 'attachments' that developed throughout childhood. Bowlby referred (perhaps with a nod to Melanie Klein, who was also present) to the infant's powerful and often unmanageable feelings of hatred and aggression, at the same time stressing the crucial role of a benign family environment.[10]

Although Bowlby would later be accused by some psychoanalysts of losing touch with the role of the subject's own unconscious fantasy, especially in its more destructive aspects, and of stressing the importance of external experience to the exclusion of all else, he did a great deal to consolidate the view that human personality was created in the cradle and the nursery, and that disregard of the tender feelings of the infant and child had disastrous psychic *and* social consequences. Whatever precise balance psychoanalysts struck in describing the internal world and its social context, there was wide agreement that political attitudes were first forged through the earliest experiences.

These contributions formed part of a transition in theories of human nature in the post-war period. The emphasis upon care, nurture, attachment, and security in infancy resonated with British Labour welfarism and continental social democracy. After the horrors of Nazism, eugenics was largely out of favour; indeed, for many it was now regarded as a permanently toxic brand of belief.[11] Visions of the psyche and of the care it required in order to thrive changed markedly; environmental and cultural theories of the personality gained much greater purchase. The critique of biologically determinist models was not, of course, invented *ex nihilo* in 1945. Anthropologists such as Franz Boas had already challenged a number of ideas about race and human nature that had been commonplace in earlier decades of the twentieth century. He also questioned the implicit value judgements about 'good' or 'bad' cultures and superior or inferior civilizations that were sometimes made in the human sciences of the past. After 1945, accounts that referred to 'inborn' human nature were often challenged; statements about the innate qualities pertaining to particular individuals and groups, classes, or—especially—'races' were increasingly to be regarded as outmoded and suspect—inconsistent, at least, with mainstream progressive opinion.

In the immediate wake of Nazism such accounts acquired near-pariah status amongst liberal commentators and the social-democratic elites of many countries. This rejection of what had once passed for 'nature' can be seen in the programmatic declarations on race and human rights at the United Nations in its early post-war years. Further afield, admittedly, old ideas about natural difference and the dread of miscegenation persisted unabashed: witness, for instance, the rise of the Nationalist Party and the pursuit of 'Apartheid' policies in South Africa. Ideas of innate natural difference and of racial 'contamination' were also championed by various politicians in the Deep South of the United States, to be challenged by the Civil Rights movement in the 1960s. Racial theories of the Victorian variety were not banished entirely to the realm of folklore in Britain either: they continued to lurk on the fringes of respectable politics.

Ideology is at its most toxic when it grounds justifications of dictatorial power and social exclusion in the presumed facts of nature. Nazism brought this lesson home. For liberal thought after 1945 there was growing uncertainty about the boundaries of the natural and the unnatural, the normal and the pathological, not least in relation to the problem of the human passions that had been exploited by Nazism itself. To be sure, there were disputes between psychoanalysts in the post-war years about how far 'constitutional' factors could be assumed in theory in any given individual case. Controversy in British circles, for instance, sometimes focused on Melanie Klein's assumption of the existence of a rudimentary ego at birth, of innate envy, or of the supposedly given, rather than environmentally determined, loving or hating endowments of the infant. But the dominant images and concerns of psychoanalysis in the public sphere were congruent with the messages so often sent out by the social sciences after the war; the focus was upon the vicissitudes and inequalities of nurture, rather than of born nature.

The London mental-health congress illustrates this powerful post-war mood and commitment to the politics of infant nurture and the recognition of human interdependency. Minds, it was shown, were substantially shaped in the earliest years by the capacities, values, and emotional attributes of their primary carers, even if it was also the case (as psychoanalysts sometimes reminded social scientists who treated the infant as a blank screen) that the baby and the child seek to transmit powerful unconscious feelings and fantasies into their picture of those who nurture them. Parts of the self could indeed be 'projected'. This serves partly as a way to disown unbearable feelings and locate them in the mind of someone else, but may also be a means (as Klein's follower Wilfred Bion noted) to get through to the other, to communicate—unconscious to unconscious—what it feels like to be 'me'.

There is no such thing as a baby, the influential British psychoanalyst Donald Winnicott once famously remarked, as he cast his keen and intelligent eye upon the constant interaction of the mother and her newborn. By this he meant that it makes no sense to talk of a baby as though it was a discrete entity, in isolation from the primary carer who enables it to survive, to play, to tolerate pain, and to think. His regular 1940s BBC radio broadcasts had already sought to make a wider public both curious about infancy and proud of 'good' empathic parenting. His talks had titles such as 'A man looks at motherhood', 'Getting to know your baby', 'Infant feeding', 'Why do babies cry?', 'Weaning', 'What about father?', 'What do we mean by a normal child?', 'Visiting children in hospital', 'Instincts and normal difficulties', and so forth. These user-friendly accounts, mostly free of technical psychoanalytical jargon, did much to promote the case for the lasting importance of early nurture. Winnicott stressed the intuitive understanding of the baby that occurs spontaneously in the 'good-enough mother', and of the mother's vital importance to individual and social well-being. (How far this kind of argument was progressive or reactionary within the sexual politics of the post-war period has been much debated since.[12])

The widespread adoption, without due qualification, of environmentalist views about human nature caused another of the participants at the London mental-health congress, the Director-General of UNESCO Julian Huxley, increasing discomfort: he fired off various broadsides in an attempt to counter what he saw as an over-reaction in the social sciences against the very discussion of race, or even genetics. Huxley repudiated 'uncritical racialists', but suggested that environmentalism was at risk of turning into a new form of zealotry.[13] He clearly saw himself as on the defensive, not only regarding prevailing intellectual attitudes to 'race' but also in relation to the legitimacy of genetics as a science that might be relevant to understanding human character. In the immediate post-war years, in other words, the idea that people were made by social forces, not born with given dispositions, attitudes, or abilities, became a dominant form of discourse.

Of course, not everybody within the psychoanalytical organizations in, say, London or New York, let alone beyond them, sang from the same hymn-sheet. There were to be many debates about the extent of human malleability and the connections between neurosis, psychosis, and social systems. The accent, however, was frequently to fall on the possibility of effecting deep-seated change in cultures that could in turn support the psychic health of individuals and groups, and vice versa. Freudianism, it was argued, could help to identify and remove the fetters inside people that kept them from thriving. It could also help to make a better post-war world through its understanding of psychic life and social processes, and through its form of therapy. The British psychoanalyst Roger Money-Kyrle caught the wider mood when he observed in 1947 that psychology (within which he evidently included psychoanalysis) might trump both biology and economics in confronting what he, like so many of his peers, called the world's 'illness':

For more than three decades, psychologists have been saying that the problems of the world are not purely economic, but also partly psychological.
They have been saying, in effect, that it is ill. And behind their words, there
may have been a *phantasy* that it ought to come to them for treatment. At first
there was no sign of the world recognizing its illness, or of accepting the
implied advice. But, by degrees, and especially since the Second World War,
there has been an increasing tendency to turn to them with rather more
attention. It is this new attitude of a society, now more than ever aware of its
discomforts, which presents psychology with its present challenge.[14]

Or, as an enthusiastic participant-observer at the congress, John Millet,
observed: 'mental health cannot exist in a family, community or world which
is at war... the first task of scientists, therefore, was to find ways to expedite
the achievement of peace'.[15] Both Money-Kyrle and Millet, in other words,
expressed similar hopes that psychoanalysis might contribute to the task of
shoring up peace, democracy, and freedom after the Nazi defeat.

Millet, a psychoanalyst working in Manhattan, had been closely involved
in the Allied struggle against Germany and chaired the Committee on
National Morale established by American psychoanalysts in response to the
wartime emergency.[16] A member of the New York Psychoanalytic Society
since 1935, he had moved to the breakaway organization that was established
during the war by the Hungarian émigré Sándor Radó, along with David
Levy, Nolan Lewis, and others, at Columbia University. Millet wrote approvingly of the public role of the clinicians and noted how psychoanalysts had
joined forces with health professionals for a task larger than the treatment of
individual neuroses. If the aim was to regenerate the old continent, the most
substantial resources, he believed, now lay in the United States, which had
become a 'Mecca for psychiatrists, social scientists, and educators from every
corner of the free world'.[17] Millet's rhetorical juxtaposition of the free and
the unfree harked back to hallowed American ideals ('land of the free'). In
the New World, he went on, the talking cure is more strongly entrenched
and has a larger body of active practitioners 'than the rest of the world put
together.'[18] In view of this, he suggested that his American colleagues must
show proper sensitivity when engaging with their counterparts abroad, give
generously of their time, and cooperate with social scientists and enlightened lay researchers 'in the direction of promoting the cause of mental
health on the local, national, and international scenes'.[19] Millet perhaps
implied that the 'soft-power' of American analysis could spread benign and
effective psychological values, in much the same way that, after 1945, the

United States sought to project visions of the 'free world' through ambitious new forms of cultural and educational outreach programmes, funded by the intelligence services and the State Department.[20] One commentator at the time pinpointed the precise moment of this monumental shift in the role of the United States: President Truman's confirmation on 27 January 1948 of an Act of Congress which, 'for the first time in our history committed our government, in time of peace, to conduct international information and educational exchange activities on a world-wide, long-term scale'.[21]

Millet also illustrates a conviction that was evident in many of the contributions to the London meetings that summer of 1948: the restoration of something approximating to collective sanity was the task at hand. But what was sanity? Nobody pretended that defining it or even identifying what was sometimes called the normal mind was as easy as describing gross pathology (Ernest Jones, for example, had struggled when called on to identify the normal mind before the war).[22] But the congress suggested that without success in inculcating a certain kind of enlightened humanism in the majority if not the entirety of populations, there could be no political security. It was vital, according to this ethos, to ensure that people in every powerful state were brought up and educated as far as possible to be wary of Manichean thought—the division of the world into absolute 'good' and 'evil' forces—and the 'magical' promises of would-be tyrants and totalizing ideologies. To be sure, such urgent psychotherapeutic advice about the importance of eschewing polarized thinking often fell on deaf ears, especially as the political rhetoric of the Cold War was increasingly cranked up in the 1950s.

How far such a 'mental-health' ideal in the Anglo-American world was used (or misused) to excoriate *all* political radicalism or 'extremism', not merely the twin terrors of Hitlerism and Stalinism, is still a matter for research. The immediate context of this post-war politics of collective psychic life, however, should not be forgotten: concern with the catastrophe of the Third Reich and the problem of post-war recovery. To say that the stress fell on the importance of environmental factors in the making of the child, and on the need to help individuals and groups to own and bear responsibility for their own 'pathology', is not necessarily to suggest that clinicians were always optimistic that benign change could be effected in popular attitudes to freedom and tyranny. But many psychoanalysts believed at least that they were on the right track in seeking explanation for the political disasters of the twentieth century in the vicissitudes of mental experience and human relationships; when populations turned towards psychopathic

leaders, it was said, an important place to look for an explanation was neither in timeless ethnic destinies nor in our genes. Of course, economic
tsunamis such as those of the 1920s and 1930s were not to be dismissed, but
what had to be understood, it was remarked again and again after 1945, was
the interaction of adverse economic and social circumstances with particular features of the 'internal world'.

Contributors to post-war international bodies such as UNESCO, the
World Health Organization, and the World Federation for Mental Health
(which emerged in the context of the International Conference on Mental
Health of 1948) sought to place collective mental pathology high on the
political agenda, and to draw psycho-political lessons from the fight against
fascism. It did nothing to harm the case for the political importance of
mental health that the director of the WHO was the Canadian psychiatrist
Brock Chisholm; he saw mental illness as scarcely less dangerous to the
world than the killer diseases whose eradication was, admittedly, his primary
brief. Appointed to lead the WHO in July 1948 with resounding backing
from his colleagues, Chisholm fought malaria, typhus, yellow fever, cholera,
and diphtheria, whilst also emphasizing the social and political consequences
of the scourge of the neuroses and more serious mental disorders.

Chisholm had a personal interest in psychoanalysis, promoted the ideal
of frank and open discussion (for instance, regarding sexuality), and insisted
on the interconnections between moral, physical, and mental well-being. In
the same year in which he took on the leadership of the WHO he gave a
keynote speech to the American Psychiatric Association, suggesting that if
politicians and the staff of international organizations were successfully to
work together to steer the world away from disaster this would require a
role for psychiatrists. Chisholm was increasingly exercised by the political
dangers and psychic terrors of atomic and biological weapons. Whatever the
actual, very considerable, risk of geopolitical disaster ahead, he warned, it
was deleterious to the nurture of the next generation to live in a world
bristling with such appalling instruments of war: they made people feel
profoundly 'insecure'.[23] The concept of 'insecurity' was a key word: and it
resonated powerfully, both in the language of infant mental health and in
the political discourse of the new atomic age.

————•————

The emergence of 'the group' as a unit of study and analysis after the war
was heralded enthusiastically by a number of the participants at the
international congress on mental health in 1948. Group therapy, consoli-

dated as a distinct field after 1945, in fact owed a great deal to the pioneering work of psychologists, psychiatrists, and psychoanalysts over the previous decade. The early history of group analysis was inextricably linked to the struggle against authoritarian forms of government; Nazi Germany formed the overwhelming backdrop to this emerging therapeutic tradition, as can be seen in the experiments and papers of Kurt Lewin.

This Jewish psychologist had left Germany and moved to the United States in 1933. Despite the short-lived nature of his American career (Lewin died in 1947), he was to influence numerous colleagues in the human sciences. Lewin paved the way for later important developments in group analysis and organizational theory through his experimental work at the University of Iowa between the mid-1930s and mid-1940s. Here Lewin, along with his students Ronald Lippitt and Ralph K. White, created various forms of laboratory work to study the effects of different organizational structures upon behaviour and thought processes in groups. Lewin was concerned to investigate how authoritarian forms of governance affected what he called the 'space of free movement' inside the mind and within the group.[24] Experiments to test the effect of democratic, authoritarian, and laissez-faire styles of organization were created in a confined environment to see what happened and thereby to draw psycho-political lessons.

In a paper for the *Harvard Educational Review* in 1939 Lewin described a system of observation that he had developed in Iowa to test the effects of leadership: this had involved creating several different clubs for 11-year-old boys. The focus of the project on boys was not by chance: it was the making of men, rather than women, that dominated (albeit not exclusively) such experimental inquiries at the time. The psychologists monitored the children as they met together once a week for social and leisure activities. The groups were run by adults who were required to 'role-play' different leadership approaches. The authoritarian leader always made decisions unilaterally, without input from the group, remained aloof from members, and praised or criticized them without explanation. Under a 'democratic' regime all decisions were to involve the views of the youth-group; the chief was encouraging, friendly, took note of the opinion of others, and gave guidance and reasons for his evaluations. The laissez-faire leader left things to the assembly but provided no active guidance or support.

In fact, Lewin said rather little about the outcome of the laissez-faire model, other than to note that the impact on the mental functioning of the boys was less impressive than in the democratic club. The authoritarian leadership, he reported, led to domineering behaviour between the group members, apathy, a failure of 'spontaneous sub-grouping' to deal with necessary tasks (meaning that the leader was constantly relied upon to create micro-organizations within the organization), scapegoating, and a lack of cooperation and of liveliness. Children who were transferred from the democratic to the authoritarian club quickly began to 'mirror' the atmosphere of the circle in which they moved.[25] He concluded that '[t]o believe in reason means to believe in democracy, because it grants to the reasoning partners a status of equality'.[26]

Lewin was interested in systems of leadership and their impact on the group's capacity to think and to cooperate. His findings had certain affinities with the applied work of post-war psychoanalysts, even though Lewin eschewed the Freudian concept of the unconscious and confined himself to observable behaviour before drawing political conclusions. (How far he was predisposed to find certain outcomes in the experimental situation he created because of his own prior political predilection for liberal democracy and his admiration for the United States is, of course, open to question.) A number of psychoanalysts during and after the 1940s sought to show that the unconscious dynamics within the group could be pinpointed in much the same way that aspects of the individual patient's inner world could be revealed (and modified) through the work that took place in the consulting-room. A method was devised to investigate what was thrown up by the experience of being with a number of others in a distinct and boundaried therapeutic setting. The analyst would endeavour to be abstinent, witnessing, experiencing, and perhaps occasionally commenting, but without moralistically judging the group. Thus was the situation constructed in a fashion that resembled the kind of open inquiry promoted in the psychoanalytic session: the question was what might emerge, what surprises might lie in store inside this structure when 'normal' service was not provided (through educational teaching, medical advice, and so on) by the group analyst (or, to borrow Jacques Lacan's useful phrase, by 'the subject supposed to know').

Post-war, there was in short a growing fascination with the analysis of groups and a belief that they might serve not only the therapeutic needs of individuals but also the advance of social knowledge. This can be seen in the work of one of Freud's admirers, the sociologist Norbert Elias, author of *The Civilizing Process* published in 1939. He emerged as an important champion of group therapy after 1945. Elias is most famous for his insistent demonstration that what we regard as natural tastes, expectations, and revulsions have changed over time. The sociologist indicated that our modes of behaviour, even our most seemingly natural sense of disgust, is contingent on the social order within which we live. History, Elias argued, has witnessed a continuing and general transformation in manners. Moreover, what was once external constraint, encouragement, or compulsion comes to be internalized and is eventually experienced as if it was natural.

Elias argued that his account of the civilizing process offered no particular moral evaluation of the changes that he tracked over time. He claimed it was neither an optimistic nor a pessimistic vision. His critics, on the other hand, suggested this was a new version of an old 'Whig' story about enlightenment and benign advances in the conditions of human life, since he had so often shown tastes, customs, and manners moving in the direction of sensibility and refinement, or as some would add, improvement.[27]

It was not without irony that Elias should have concentrated so much attention and pinned so much faith, even in the 1930s, upon a civilizing process that brought with it a progressive limitation of outward danger, and thus also a limitation and channelling of fear of such external dangers. Even if life appeared uncertain today, he claimed, the outward risks to human life had become more calculable and the paths and scope of fears had grown more regulated over time. This control of sources of fear had been slowly established in the transition to modern social structure through the concept of civilization.

Elias's own family fell victim to Nazism, his parents refusing to leave Germany and dying in the camps after he had found refuge in London.[28] During the war Elias worked with British intelligence to help identify Nazi incorrigibles amongst German prisoners of war. Subsequently new lines of thought emerged in his work, and one of his later preoccupations lay in explaining the exceptional nature of the German historical case.[29] Strikingly, however, the final note in the 1939 edition of *The Civilizing Process* had already exposed the cross-current of fear and foreboding in Elias's story of the cultivation of manners and the 'civilizing process':

> The armor of civilized conduct would crumble very rapidly if, through a change in society, the degree of insecurity that existed earlier were to break in upon us again, and if danger became as incalculable as it once was. Corresponding fears would soon burst the limits set to them today.
>
> However, one specific form of fear does grow with the increase of civilization: the half-unconscious 'inner' fear of breaching of the restrictions imposed on civilized men.[30]

In the late 1940s Elias participated, with the psychoanalyst Siegfried Heinrich Foulkes and others, in establishing group therapy in Britain. Key wartime experiments provided the immediate impetus for Foulkes and his colleagues as they pioneered this development.[31] Having undertaken some training, Elias even conducted therapeutic groups himself.[32] He insisted ever more strongly that the individual is enmeshed entirely in social relationships. In the new preface that he wrote for *The Civilizing Process* in 1968 he argued that it was crucial to recognize that individuals are never really discrete entities at all: 'So long as the concept of the individual is linked with the self-perception of the "ego" in a closed case, we can hardly conceive "society" as anything other than a collection of windowless monads', he complained.[33]

Elias's post-war views of human connection and dependency bear comparison with those of Tavistock-based researchers, such as John Bowlby, on the vital significance of the earliest human attachments.[34] Elias's suggestion that the reality of interdependence tended to be underestimated or even blindly ignored was also reminiscent of the psychoanalytic view that powerful defences (for instance, involving omnipotent fantasies and manic 'solutions') may prevent people from acknowledging vulnerability, neediness, and reliance on others to survive. Although Elias did not take much cognizance of the notion that unconscious attitudes may shape, as well as reflect, our encounters with others, he echoed an argument made by Freud in his study of group psychology in 1921: it made little sense to speak of personal psychology in contrast to group psychology, since 'someone else' is present in constituting and sustaining the self from the start. 'In the individual's mental life', Freud had remarked, 'someone else is invariably involved, as a model, as an object, as a helper, as an opponent; and so from the very first individual psychology, in this extended but entirely justifiable sense of the words, is at the same time social psychology as well.'[35]

Freud's account of the self presupposed inevitable conflict not only between unconscious desire and 'civilization', but also between different parts of the mind. Although Freud was a child of the enlightenment who assumed that factors such as bigotry and intolerance were harmful to individuals and to society, increasingly it was the splits, fetters, and warring agencies within the mind (even in a potentially benign social order) that most concerned him.[36]

After 1945 problems of authoritarianism in psychic life were considered by Arthur Schlesinger Jr, a former OSS officer and Harvard academic who would later become an important adviser to President Kennedy. Schlesinger was especially impressed by the applicability of Freud and Fromm to the post-war struggle to secure and bolster political liberty. He cited both authors approvingly in his study of modern systems of belief and the clash of ideologies, *The Vital Center: The Politics of Freedom* (1949). Taking note of Freud's account of the mind, he argued that psychic conflict is natural and inevitable; it followed therefore, he believed, that society could only be healthy where it ensured multi-party arrangements, and guarantees of tolerance of conflicting political points of view. He made an analogy between the healthy mind—that is, a mind capable of owning up to and tolerating its own divisions and conflicts—and the healthy polity.

Such references to Freudianism in political thought on liberty were more evident in America than in England. The Austrian philosopher Karl Popper, among the most influential émigrés based in England and author of *The Open Society and its Enemies* (1945), dismissed psychoanalysis as an example of pseudo-science; he did not see Freud's work as a useful tool for either political or scientific thought.[37] Isaiah Berlin, another key exponent of the idea of liberty, showed precious little enthusiasm for the talking cure. Nor was F. A. Hayek, the Austrian-born economist and philosopher, professor at the London School of Economics, and winner of the Nobel Prize in economics in 1947, tempted to draw upon Freudian literature in his warnings about the dangers of political tyranny.[38]

Hayek's *The Road to Serfdom* (1944) bore some comparison with Schlesinger's *The Vital Center*, but showed no such interest in ideas of the unconscious mind. Hayek was resident in England, and his work was to be taken up on both sides of the Atlantic in later decades, although at the time of its publication it was decidedly contrarian in its wholesale antipathy to state planning.[39] Like Schlesinger and Popper, Hayek saw socialism and fascism as twin dangers for liberty. But he took a notably uncompromising stance regarding the moral value of laissez-faire policies, and was deeply hostile to all vestiges of 'collectivism'. For Hayek, state interventionism was the path towards moral and political ruin, and he wanted to get back to the classical liberalism of the mid-nineteenth century, not the 'new liberalism' of the *fin de siècle* that had already conceded so much of the argument to 'statism'.[40]

It was the use of psychoanalysis, not simply the political interpretation of the appropriate balance to strike between personal freedom and state interference, that distinguished Schlesinger's message from Hayek's. Here the

Nazi or the Soviet model was not only viewed as a political and moral
affront to civilization, but also the foundation for, and perhaps the consequence of, intra-psychic disaster. Systems that stifled internal opposition
also invited people to accept and enjoy their own passive submission to
authority. Schlesinger warned that tyrants oppressed 'the people', but that
hostility to democracy also stemmed from within the human mind. In this
regard he followed Erich Fromm's line of thought, suggesting that we all
too easily crave subjection and abase ourselves before charismatic, supposedly omniscient figures, thereby relieving ourselves of uncertainty and
ambivalence.[41] Outright tyrants, he believed, exploited this psychic propensity all too well, and so too did slick, populist politicians in democracies.

Fromm was one of a select band of post-war psychoanalytical writers
whose reflections on politics reached wide readerships. Erik Erikson was
another. Both sought to show how the psychological dramas of infancy
were significant factors to reckon with in understanding the formation of
adoring fascist subjects. Erikson clearly admired much about modern
America, although he warned his readers of the dangers of popular conformism there, and set out his fears that democratic structures and liberal
ideals would be eroded by powerful vested interests.[42] Fromm spoke more
caustically on the subject of American values and rampant capitalism,
inspired, as he continued to be, by Marx as well as Freud. An enthusiasm for
Marx had also led a number of notable American and British radical voices
of the 1930s to reach for the language of psychiatry when insisting that the
Soviet Union was the only major country following the 'sane' path of planning and equitable distribution. By the 1950s, though, the fault-lines in such
political diagnosis were generally different: 'authoritarianism' or 'totalitarianism', in their Nazi and Soviet incarnations, were to be twinned again and
again with the representation of minds that were fundamentally distorted
and impoverished within.[43]

The practice of group therapy came of age after the Second World War.
Although there were some precedents for this work in the 1930s, group
therapy was by and large an outcome of psychiatric and psychoanalytic
experimentalism in the 1940s, most notably in work conducted with psychiatric casualties in the army. One psychoanalyst to track this development
was the upper-class Englishman, writer, and psychoanalyst Roger Money-
Kyrle. This intriguing figure had links with the 'Bloomsbury group' of writers and artists, and long-standing personal interests in anthropology, Freudian
thought, and politics. His penchant, like that of so many inter-war liberals,

for exploring eugenics was to prove less enduring. After the Great War (in which he had served), Money-Kyrle had become a follower of Freud and later of Klein (he had personal analysis with both, as well as with Ernest Jones). 'Humanist' became Money-Kyrle's shorthand term for describing the character traits of the democrat and anti-fascist. His writings on psychoanalysis and politics were designedly accessible; critics might put this less favourably, and note how he was prone on occasion to make debatable jumps from describing 'minds' to assessing 'nations'.

Money-Kyrle could be seen as a barometer of many of the broader psycho-political ideas that have been traced here so far; he shared with Erich Fromm and Henry Dicks, for instance, an acute awareness (in principle) that states were far more complex entities than individuals 'writ large'. Nonetheless he believed that terms such as 'sanity' and 'psychosis' were just as applicable to the social order as they were to individual minds. His accounts sometimes implied that minds and societies could relatively easily be likened to one another, according to the quality of the superego that shadowed them, and the power to face reality (or what he sometimes called simply 'the facts of life').

Like Dicks, Money-Kyrle contributed directly to, and then wrote about, the Allied task of denazification.[44] In fact Money-Kyrle acknowledged that he had followed in Dicks's footsteps with regard to his work in 1946 for the German Personnel Research Branch (GPRB) within the Allied Control Commission.[45] Looking back upon his career, Money-Kyrle noted the enormous impact of Klein's major discoveries; however, he came to reflect self-critically upon his excessive optimism about both politics *and* psychoanalysis, noting that (like others, including, as he pointedly added, Klein herself), he had overestimated the social benefits of treatment—particularly the analysis of children—and underestimated the difficulties involved.[46] Later he wanted to offer a more sober reflection on the propensities of the mind, the limits of therapy, and the terrors of modern politics, as though to underline the fact that in none of these domains was 'cure' guaranteed. Groups, he showed, sanctioned or stimulated (but did not create *ex nihilo*) ferociously aggressive, manic, or anxious affects. States too could amplify or modify infantile feelings, and thus political science needed to pay attention to the findings of the psychoanalyst.

Money-Kyrle's later accounts of the sources of Nazism were influenced not only by his direct encounters with Nazis in Germany, as part of his work for the GPRB, but also by the findings of Wilfred Bion and others regarding unconscious processes in groups. If psychoanalysts showed how powerful unspoken beliefs could bind people in the most disturbing forms of complicity, denial, and projection, 'working through' might also assist people to recover their sanity.[47]

The wartime clinical work on groups was extensively reported at the London congress on mental health, to which Bion directly contributed.[48] During the war he had participated in a therapeutic project with his colleague (and recent analyst) John Rickman. This experiment in applied psychoanalysis concerned military casualties, sufferers from so-called 'war neuroses', at Northfield Hospital in the English Midlands. Bion had endeavoured to create conditions in which members of the group could say what they liked. He sought to eschew the requirement to embody 'authority', and this often led to a build-up of tremendous hatreds within the group. Indeed, while Bion became increasingly interested in creating what came to be known as 'leaderless groups', the assembled men would sometimes unite in anger at his refusal to direct them. With normal instructions suspended and the internal structure of the gathering left so much more fluid than in standard army procedure, tensions quickly mounted. If this was found liberating by some patients and illuminating for the group organizers, it was regarded as somewhat scandalous and dangerous by more senior officers and the experiment was soon shut down. Nonetheless related experiments were soon under way that had ramifications both for therapy and for methods of staff selection.[49]

Money-Kyrle tried to draw out some implications of this work in an article of 1948. He considered first what unconscious factors draw individuals into allegiances with particular kinds of group. He suggested that the child forms an imaginary picture of the family, which is more or less distorted and which is preserved in fantasy throughout life. This picture contains good parent figures 'to protect, to follow and to imitate', and bad parent figures 'against whom they have to be protected'. Moreover, the child tends to reproduce this pattern in the external world. For Money-Kyrle, individuals find common political symbols that express their own unconscious preoccupations. If the members of the group have severe internal conflicts, he explained, they are apt to create enemies for themselves by suspecting enmity where none at first existed, or to become depressed if they fail to get 'the fanatical leadership they need'.[50] According to this account, the group develops in ways that reflect the inner conflicts of its contributors, but may also become so powerful that it overrides the scruples, doubts, and constraints that ordinarily complicate and 'check' each individual's primitive impulses: either way, Money-Kyrle warned, '[a] group like an individual may be either pathological or sane'. Although less subtle than Bion's developed account of the life of the group, Money-Kyrle's eloquent, broad description, just after the war, of the *potential* for acute phobic anxiety, paranoid projections, and visceral hatreds to move within and between people illustrates one of the broader implications of this body of work.

Bion went on to make an important distinction between what he called 'work groups' and 'basic assumption groups'; under the sway of basic assumptions, the group is governed by unconscious beliefs and fantasies that corrode actual hard-won thought; indeed, in the world of 'basic assumptions', thought is a misnomer, and the communications at stake are better understood as un-reflexive forms of *action*. What passed for thoughts were often more like the outcrop of the most primitive primary processes of the mind.[51] Bion was fond of analogies between thinking, containing, and digesting. In considering different types of group, or at least different possible moments within the life of a group, Bion drew upon Klein's work and showed how hard it was for the group to learn, to face guilt (for instance, in the face of its own acts of aggression and cruelty), to integrate people into communities, or, for that matter, to bring unwelcome knowledge into consciousness. Often, he showed, groups become infected with a kind of malaise, feel passive and hopeless, or angry and sullen, expecting structure, rules, and enlightenment to be gifted to them by the edict of the leader, whilst collectively taking no heed at all of external realities. The 'work group', by contrast, possessed a capacity for intellectual and emotional integration, and some tolerance of differences within its own ranks; his account of this structure and process (published in book form as *Experiences in Groups, and Other Papers*, in 1961) was, by implication, a useful guide to what might enable a democratic community to thrive and what might destroy it from within.

————•————

Ideas about individual psychology and group functioning were also applied in the immediate aftermath of the war in programmes that set out to change minds and root out Nazi incorrigibles. Conditions in Germany after the war were bleak in the extreme; ensuring the physical survival of the defeated enemy population, responding to threats of epidemic diseases and other health emergencies, providing food, water, and shelter in a period of massive population movements and displacements, and achieving a basic restoration of law and order were the most pressing problems. Nonetheless, considerable effort was expended upon psychological assessments of the defeated population. To contain, if not 'cure', the Germans would involve, so it was often claimed, a deep psychic as well as economic, cultural, political, and social transformation. In practice, though, such endeavours to change minds and root out unrepentant fanatics were riddled with difficulties and inconsistencies.

Various British and American clinicians who worked in the post-war occupation forces sought to make use of psychoanalytical concepts and techniques in this task. It was argued, for example, that 'an authoritarian environment' awakened people's unrealistic and 'ferocious' superegos; the new 'humanist direction' of German society would require that such tendencies be submerged, if not replaced, by 'a more realistic [superego] based to a great extent on the actual character of tolerant and kindly parents'.[52]

It is important to remember the context in which Allied 'denazifiers' worked and to acknowledge the enormous power they held. In the chaos of the first years of peace, above all in the morass of confusion, misery, corruption, and desperation that prevailed in the camps that held German refugees or in the vast displaced-persons camps containing people of many nationalities, British and American staff were faced with the task of identifying hidden high-value Nazis from among the German rank and file, spotting Soviet moles, and cultivating 'stool pigeons' or informants with military data to trade. Where hard evidence to determine suitability was not available, motley forms of psychological testing came into play in order to help sort out the merely morally compromised person from the irredeemably tarnished hard core. Small wonder that the term *Persilschein* became a widely used—cynical—slang term for the clean bill of health provided by certain denazification certificates.

George Orwell, who visited occupied Germany and sent back reports for the *Observer*, described the gap between English myths of Aryan types, who would be visible immediately to the untrained eye, and so many of the actual people he saw before him who did not conform to the image. The Germans he encountered, Orwell wrote, were usually no different in the flesh from the Belgians.[53] As the historian Jessica Reinisch observes, large numbers of people within Nazi officialdom simply 'melted away', leaving the Allies to sift through identities, not just identity papers, in a quest for promising, democratically minded subjects.[54]

—•—

It was in this context that both the American and the British zones of occupied Germany provided a test-bed for new experiments in human observation, evaluation, and screening. The aim of such projects was not so much to adjudicate on innocence or guilt, but to provide more elaborate information on the underlying attitude of particular German individuals. Henry Dicks played a leading role in this enterprise, as a consultant in the screening programme that was set up at the British military government's headquarters at Bad Oeynhausen in the German Personnel Research Branch. Dr David Levy, a New York psychoanalyst and army officer who was sent to Germany to lead a key American screening programme in 1946, provided an admiring account of the British efforts to root out Nazi 'types' and singled out Dicks's contribution as especially important.[55] Levy made a point of meeting the British officer in person, noting that he had done most to pioneer new approaches to screening.[56]

Such programmes were aimed at identifying the underlying psychological tendencies as well as conscious beliefs of German applicants for significant post-war civil-service jobs, or for commercial or other sensitive posts. The premise was that 'persons of "democratic" character' might be distinguished from 'persons of "fascist" character' through the process of interviewing and the close monitoring of group activities. What had passed for the 'norm' in the Third Reich (a certain level of paranoia; uncritical acceptance of all orders, however mad; manic endorsement of the leader; and so forth) would now have to be made to seem 'abnormal'.[57]

Levy wrote in some detail about the procedure that the British installed at the GPRB. The organization, he noted, had thirty-two staff, including a psychiatrist, a few psychologists, administrators, testing officers, and others, under the command of Oscar Oeser, an officer who had worked at Bletchley Park in one of the great decryption projects and who was himself, in civilian life, a social psychologist.[58] Levy saw the aims and (largely) the methods of screening by the British and Americans as similar, although the former developed a greater specialization of roles and made use of lay analysts. At GPRB twelve candidates for post-war employment were studied at a time, being kept under scrutiny for a full working week; at the end of this process they were discussed and assessed by the staff. Written questionnaires, mutual introductions (that is, self-descriptions by candidates in the presence of the rest of the group), intelligence and other psychological examinations (such as word-association, thematic apperception tests, and the like) were arranged. Participants were required to describe themselves through the eyes of an imagined best friend and strong critic. Each member of the group was also subjected to psychiatric and political interviews lasting ninety minutes. Further material, Levy noted, was to be gleaned from the reports of the group meetings, in which each person would be asked to discuss themes such as personal happiness, relationship to family and state, and Germany's contribution to European reconstruction.

Following this, each of the candidates was asked to give an unprepared five-minute lecture to the group on topics that might include, for example, the legitimacy of corporal punishment or the nature of the black market. Questionnaires were employed to gauge more directly the social and political outlook of each participant, and to compare these with the other evidence that had been gathered. A miniature interview was then set up, but with the twist that one candidate would quiz another in the presence of the British staff. Topics covered might include the applicant's hobbies, interests, or recreational activities. Each participant was then asked to imagine facing a difficult situation, and also subjected directly to criticism and frustrating behaviour on the part of the examiners. The group was required to collaborate in formulating the solution to a problem relating to the administration of the country. It was also split into two negotiating teams (one representing the British military government, another the German people) obliged to deal with the solution of a given problem. This was followed by mutual evaluation of one another by the candidates in terms of leadership, friendship-worthiness, and reliability.

The purpose of all this, as Roger Money-Kyrle explained, was to expose those 'with the strictest type of paternal superego'. These 'authoritarians' were likely to be 'obsessionally painstaking and meticulous in their work', and governed by a 'sense of duty... [that] outweighed whatever other moral feelings they had'. Their conduct would be dominated by anxieties pertaining to the safety of their own person or their narrowly conceptualized subgroup, which became akin to a narcissistic extension of the self. Through the various exercises devised, the analysts hoped to identify '[t]he humanists, to whom Germany was the "fatherland" no less than to the authoritarians, but in a much smaller degree. And because they experienced it to a much lesser extent, they were able to be conscious of a different, and this time predominantly depressive type of guilt at having failed, or been impotent to protect, the victims of a tyranny.'[59]

These efforts to harness modern psychological techniques in denazification were, in many instances, eclipsed, forgotten, or deliberately shelved amidst more pressing problems for the Allied forces, although some screening and profiling of individuals within the British and American armed forces continued to be fine-tuned after 1945.[60] Certain programmes that were established during or at the end of the war endured for years thereafter. One of the most notable examples was conducted at Wilton Park in southern England. This major experiment in the rehabilitation of German POWs was brought into being by the Political Warfare Executive and the Political Intelligence Department of the Foreign Office, and was inspired, founded, and directed by the Jewish émigré and Oxford-educated historian Heinz Koeppler. Although no psychoanalysts seem to have participated in this project, there were affinities of approach with the contemporaneous group experiments of Bion, Dicks, and their colleagues. Briefly, the aim of the experiment was to make the life of the group politically 'therapeutic', while also serving as the basis for evaluating the democratic potential of the participants.

Such courses continued in various guises at Wilton Park well into the 1950s, and in the first instance aimed to do far more than to indoctrinate ex-soldiers and civilians with new official messages: rather, they sought to effect a deeper change in outlook, to inculcate, through lived experience, the liberal psychological attitudes that were seen as essential to the post-war future. A number of later German politicians, business-people, journalists, lawyers, and academics were alumni of this residential programme. It was hoped that the participants would realize that a spirit of questioning, doubt, criticism, and dissent would not be scorned by the organizers, and might well be valued. The vision here seemed to be based upon that of a university—perhaps an idealized image of the Oxford colleges from which several of the tutors came—in which probing arguments were valued far more than mere acquiescence and rote learning. German political developments in the twentieth century were thus to be explored rather than merely condemned, and British institutions and practices were to be examined 'warts and all'. Contributors to the staff group at Wilton Park included the classical scholar Gilbert Murray, the historian A. J. P. Taylor, and their fellow Oxford don (and later a prominent Labour cabinet minister) Richard Crossman. Not all the talks were directly political and historical; Murray, for example, spoke to one group of German participants on the programme about 'The Problem of Hopelessness'.[61]

As Koeppler recalled: 'Our methods of work are not those which have made "re-education" a term of abuse. We do not lecture our students; in fact there are no lectures, as such, only introductions or discussion.'[62] The POWs were organized into 'working parties', required to participate in the life of the group. Germany's intellectual reconstruction, it was felt, must be achieved primarily by the Germans themselves: hence many of the presentations came from native speakers and émigré intellectuals. Above all, Koeppler thought the required moral and emotional transformation would be wrought from within the thinking of the group itself. The assumption of personal responsibility was to be the key. As at the Nuremberg trial, footage of the concentration camps was shown to the residents, but they were invited to consider the material, debate it, and draw their own conclusions, rather than to sit passively whilst hectored by the instructors.

Major-General Kenneth Strong, Director-General of the Political Intelligence Department, set out the blueprint to the assembled German participants on 17 January 1946. This work, he declared, is:

> an experiment that has no precedent in previous war and post-war periods... We believe that an attempt must be made to bridge the gap in trends of thought between victor and vanquished... We hope that this... will assist to build up, within a well-ordered social and economic framework, a peaceful and co-operative Europe.... a large part of the course will be devoted to working out with you the main points of German development during the last eighty or hundred years. I say purposely 'with you', for your active co-operation in everything which happens here is an indispensable condition for the success of the experiment.[63]

Strong (whose speech may have been directly crafted by the subtle Koeppler) emphasized to the POWs that the Allies recognized how much Germany had contributed to the arts, science, philosophy, and technology: but 'Beethoven cannot excuse Belsen, nor Goethe the Gestapo'. Nor did the national pathology originate with Hitler. He added the following quip regarding the geography of Berlin: 'It seemed to me to be not without symbolical meaning that the Bismarck-Strasse led, via the Kaiserdamm, to the Adolf Hitler Platz.'[64]

Many POWs apparently did respond well, but Koeppler was dismayed when one of the first German civilians to take the course at Wilton Park, a pre-war teacher who was now on a path to become the headmaster of a large secondary school, maintained in seminars the point of view that in about 1740 'something went "click" in the tortured and sensitive German soul'. This was the year in which the reign of Frederick the Great began and an extended period of military conflict between Prussia, Austria, and other powers was unleashed. Thereafter, the teacher continued:

> [I]t is not good discussing <u>facts</u> with Germans; they must be given psycho-therapeutic treatment until with some sudden stroke of magic their souls click back again to where they were in 1740 and all is well. It must be said for the other students that they protested almost as a man...But it would surely be a pity if his charm and polish should lead him to a responsible position where he could instil into German Youth theories that would make them more convinced than ever that whatever happened or might happen in the future, they or their poor little Fatherland could in no possible circumstances bear any of the blame.[65]

For some critics, the entire panoply of denazification measures was viewed not only as inconsistent or inadequate, but as a distraction, an irritant, and an unnecessary extravagance when the menace of the Soviet Union loomed so large. It is important to differentiate here between short- and long-term outcomes, for denazification continued to have reverberations decades later, even if many judged the direct measures of the 1940s too limited and generally disappointing. In light of the secret Cold War redeployment of German officials (scientists and intelligence specialists among them) by the Americans, Russians, and others, some denounced denazification as a scandalously hypocritical affair.

A recurrent concern in the post-war period was the presence of so many old (unreconstructed?) Nazi officials in positions of power in Germany, as well as in safe havens elsewhere. It is well known that various key fields within the Federal Republic (the judiciary and the medical profession, for example) remained largely untouched by denazification; some former Nazis were appointed to government posts, and fugitives from justice were able to find new homes and identities in Europe or beyond (notably in Latin America). Senior members of staff escaped the legal net and were redeployed in a variety of posts in order to ensure the functioning of the new German state. Only gradually was the scale of the continuity of personnel disclosed and vociferously challenged. The measures taken between 1945 and 1948 to 'detoxify' the population became less and less of a priority for the Allies thereafter. Moreover Konrad Adenauer, leader of the Federal Republic from 1949 to 1963, came under significant internal pressure to soft-pedal or even reverse the limited measures that had been put in place. Domestic and international political concerns derailed those preliminary efforts at denazification.

Under Adenauer, many old Nazi figures did indeed slip back into senior positions. But even earlier there were signs that denazification strategies were being curtailed by the practical problems of getting German
systems running again, and hence of making use of personnel who had
fought against the Allies, with more or less fanatical conviction, for years.
The onset of the Cold War placed West and East Germany at the heart of
post-war international politics, diplomacy, and espionage. The Americans
required the support of the West German population for the Berlin air-
lift and the measures that followed it. This is not to suggest that the
Western powers, in conjunction with the government of the Federal
Republic, pursued a policy of total 'amnesia': some important trials of
officialdom from the camps and other Nazi criminals did take place in
the 1950s and early 1960s. However, the limitations of denazification and
anti-renazification measures in post-war Germany came under criticism,
of gathering seriousness and intensity, during and after the 1960s. A sense
of silent conspiracy, cover-up, and complicity of the elders was explored
in memorable works of cinema and literature, and eventually in substantial investigative works by German psychoanalysts that exposed the vexed
history of their discipline.[66]

The decision to wind down the international military tribunals and
limit the importance of screening and other counter-Nazi measures was
bitterly decried in the final sequence and captions of *Judgement at
Nuremberg*, the great 1961 Hollywood educational blockbuster, featuring
Spencer Tracey and an all-star cast, that charted the demise of the
American denazifiers. There has been much debate about the political
efficacy and later consequences of the measures that were taken, post-
war, to secure the liberal, democratic settlement in Germany (from school
education programmes to the banning of the dissemination of *Mein
Kampf*). There is certainly a case to be made that, limited and flawed
though the efforts evidently were—with so many accommodations made
and ruses employed in order to spirit away useful officials or turn a blind
eye to someone's criminal past—the endeavour to transform social and
political structures, and to place Nazi ideology beyond the pale, was nevertheless an important contribution to the entrenchment of liberal
democracy in the long term.[67]

———•———

Other measures were also put in place at an international level. No sooner
had UNESCO been created in Paris than it announced a major collabora-

tive research and educational initiative that would address 'Tensions Affecting International Understanding'. In 1946 UNESCO officials began to assemble research and teaching teams to take forward this multi-pronged inquiry. This was to involve a large 'summer school' (held in 1947) and, for the next few years, was extended to include conferences, colloquia, committees, research groups, fact-finding missions, circulated internal UNESCO reports, opinion-polling, social surveys, informal cross-disciplinary seminars, grants, and publications. The 'Tensions' project offers a further illustration of the importance of the 'psy' professions in policy debates and political thought of this period, and at the same time provides evidence of academic criticism of the excessive and sometimes facile use of psychological models in social and historical analysis and so-called 'culture and personality' studies. Dicks again played a significant part in this story: in 1947 the American sociologist Ed Shils keenly recommended him to UNESCO's Director-General Julian Huxley, as just the man to lead this major research initiative.[68]

This recommendation and several other endorsements gave Dicks the edge over the Harvard psychologist Henry Murray and other potential candidates for the post. By then a professor of psychiatry in Leeds, Dicks was unable to take up the job offer, however, as it would have involved a long stint in Paris. Nonetheless, he contributed extensively to the UNESCO summer school, seminar, and conference programme as well as other research organizations. He produced a stream of publications on the human personality under Nazism and Stalinism, and was regarded as an especially well-qualified commentator on the problem of human aggression.[69]

The UNESCO 'Tensions' project drew upon a number of eminent American, English, and French intellectuals. Contemporary psycho-political phenomena were explored in several ways in order to identify and thus to facilitate change in both conscious and unconscious militaristic and fascistic attitudes, so as to ensure there would be no repeat of the war.[70] A central argument of the 'Tensions' project was the importance of taking children at a very young age and moulding their characters, in a modern and secular, psychological version of the old Jesuit belief that moral fashioning was best accomplished in the early years of life. It stemmed in part from the realization that Fascist Italy, Nazi Germany, and the Soviet Union paid enormous attention to inculcating political attitudes in children. Although the sex of the child was by no means entirely neglected in anti-fascist work of this period, nor specifically in the contributions of Dicks and his peers at UNESCO and other post-war agencies, it was taken for granted that the key problem in countries such as Germany was to transform the psychic life of boys.[71]

In a statement to UNESCO on 26 January 1949 Dicks pulled together his thoughts on German wartime behaviour and considered its implications for post-war thought. He stressed the relationship of character structure to the social climate of the time, noting in particular the consequences of the depreciation of the social status of women and the overvaluation of tough masculinity in Nazi Germany. Love, he observed, was 'canalized' into the adoration of Hitler and a strong emphasis placed on gang solidarity. Dicks also asked how far women shared the same political views as men. He wondered if Hitler held an especially strong 'erotic charge' for German women; underlying 'sexual motivations', he suspected, were a stronger factor for women than men in their initial wish to support the Führer. It was curious in one sense, however, that he made such play of this, since elsewhere it was clear he saw the entire national relationship to Hitler as highly erotized. The majority of German women, Dicks concluded, acquiesced in the subordinate status that was assigned to them during the Third Reich: 'Accordingly they have found their main fulfilment in devotion to home duties and, looking up to their lord and master, have accepted his political views.'[72]

Dicks speculated that women's political attitudes would have revealed a similar spectrum to that which he had discovered among German POWs, but clearly he could not do wartime empirical research to demonstrate this in the same way. He went on, however, to suggest that the morale of women (especially wives and mothers) in Nazi Germany had been subjected to greater strain than that of men; he argued that they suffered the deepest sense of emotional loss as the war went on; they were the primary mourners of the dead; this and the ever-more desperate struggle to feel safe and to find basic resources for sustenance were likely, he surmised, to have induced in many women 'a fairly violent swing towards disillusionment and apathy'.[73]

It was, nonetheless, primarily the political identifications of boys and men, and the disastrous consequences of their—and their society's— combined idealization and utter denigration of women, that became a central preoccupation for Dicks, and more generally for the research agenda of the 'Tensions' project. Dicks may not have seen the entire locus of fascism as being bound up with patriarchal values and male subordination of women (in the manner that, for example, Virginia Woolf set out in a celebrated critique of the 1930s, *Three Guineas*), but he did insist that a fundamental transformation of sexual attitudes would be required to avoid the recurrence of

fascism in post-war Germany. He repudiated the extreme forms of hierar-
chical and paternalistic culture and the pathologies it fostered, such as a
'tendency to gloating and to other manifestations of deep destructiveness
towards objects of hate'.[74] He particularly emphasized the disastrous
consequences of the formal and informal constraints upon women's freedom in this profoundly disciplinarian culture. There was, he remarked, a
pronounced and excessive preoccupation with status, hierarchy, and 'losing
face' in front of others that would have to be challenged in the future.[75]

Numerous discussions, surveys and interpretations ensued under the
umbrella of this eclectic research project, which continued for several years
at the Paris-based organization. In various key colloquia politics was related
to people's search for solutions to mental pain and conflict, emanating from
the confusions of infancy and, in part, from the influence of parents and
other childhood educators. Anglo-American contributors produced the
bulk of the work. Some of the participants were critical of the approach
taken, and expressions of dissent, for instance, from various French and other
European experts who were consulted gave the discussions more edge.
Critics complained about the tendency of some speakers to bandy about
general psychological terms regarding authoritarianism, politics, and the
unconscious with insufficient precision or much sense of history.

Many of the themes that dominated the 'Tensions' project for the next
few years were already clearly set out in the inaugural summer school held
in July and August 1947. The aim was to define the agenda of UNESCO's
research efforts and educate the participants in current thought on demili-
tarization and international cooperation. The summer school took place in
a building provided by the French Ministry of Education at Sèvres, a suburb
in Paris. Much of the six-week course of seminars was devoted to thinking
about how family life, education, and social care could be enhanced to promote mature forms of understanding and cooperation rather than aggression and enmity. The eighty participants were hand-picked 'mature
professional leaders' (in the words of the organizers), and included school
head-teachers, sociologists, social psychologists, professors of education,
anthropologists, clinicians, and political scientists. Meetings were to be
arranged with abstract thinkers, experimental scientists, and hands-on practitioners whom UNESCO officers regarded as important contributors to
post-war social science, the judiciary, the diplomatic world, or the clinic.
Where such advisers could not attend in person, their work would at least
feature on the informal curriculum or as circulated reports.

The participants came from over thirty countries and were invited to read the work and listen to the contributions of Jean Piaget, Anna Freud, and Margaret Mead. They were also addressed by jurists (a judge from the recently constituted international court at The Hague, for example, was sent to talk to the group) and by the moderate socialist politician (and former Prime Minister of France) Léon Blum. As a French Jew, Blum had first-hand experience of violent anti-Semitic attacks at the hands of his own countrymen long before he became a prisoner of the Nazis at Buchenwald. Other visiting speakers included the poet and essayist Stephen Spender, who had personal experiences to report of inter-war and newly liberated Germany, the political scientist Herman Finer, and the philosopher and social theorist Raymond Aron. The majority of advisers to the UNESCO project were from America, Britain, and France, but although these three countries provided the most personnel, the trawl of professional opinion was substantially wider. Thus UNESCO solicited a contribution from Dr B. S. Guha, an anthropologist based in Calcutta. Professor Torgny Segerstedt, from Uppsala University, was amongst several other professors who were consulted.[76] Advice was sought on health matters from officials at WHO and, later, the World Federation of Mental Health. Findings of the GPRB were noted and there was some contact made with polling organizations (particularly Gallup). Side projects to explore intelligence-testing and Rorschach results were also undertaken and some people proposed that it would be useful to collate daydreams contributed by sample groups in various social milieus. Among the highlights of the presentations, according to the feedback questionnaires returned by the participants at the summer school, were the talks given by Blum and Dicks.[77] Dicks's particular credentials were appreciated and attention was drawn to his prior 'fundamental investigations of a pioneer kind into these problems in relation to Germany'.[78]

Some of those who took part felt that the organizers of the summer school had got the balance of the agenda wrong, or had made insufficient effort to focus on particular topics, most notably how to resist the return of fascism and Nazism. Thus, in the opinion of one participant the Third Reich was present as the elephant in the room: Vilhelm J. Scharp (a schoolmaster from Stockholm) remarked upon the lack of practical attention to the monstrosities of recent German history, and in polite terms criticized the tendency of speakers to resort to pious generalities. There was always the risk that research projects designed by committee would end up with a somewhat diluted and incoherent agenda. Scharp complained of 'the practically

total absence of reference to the existence of this [German] problem—the
most urgent and actual of all in the field of "international understanding" '.
There was another question of the same difficult but imperative kind, he
suggested: anti-Semitism. This too, he objected, had not been deemed 'ripe'
for full and frank discussion in these meetings in Paris, and he believed
it ought to be dealt with urgently on a scientific and historical basis.
Furthermore, casting his eye especially towards America, he recommended
more attention be paid to what he called 'the negro question'.[79]

US race relations were not, in fact, completely ignored. Nor was the
immediate political history of Germany. Several field studies of social attitudes were commissioned; but the aim was to widen the terms of reference
and thus consider intolerance, racial tensions, and militarism in a global
context. The Swedish schoolmaster was not alone in his impatience with
the airy and imprecise discussions that ranged across all manner of subjects:
the rising tensions in the Indian subcontinent, for instance, were mentioned
but not systematically explored. A number of the instructors and advisers
also came to similar conclusions, warning that general speculation was all
very well, but close attention to social structures and precise historical trans-
formations would lead to more productive discussion. The historian Lucien
Febvre (co-founder of *Annales*, the celebrated journal that looked at the
structuring factors that shape long-term historical developments, produce
changes, or ensure continuities) voiced his scepticism about the project in
January 1949. He wrote to the organizers urging that a more definite, historical perspective be adopted.[80]

Some UNESCO officers were also dubious about the value of rehears-
ing over and over again the psychological accounts advanced by people
such as Dicks and Fromm at meetings in Paris; they felt that there was no
need for more of the same, especially since the Americans would in all
probability dominate the field.[81] In fact, the British vied with the Americans
for leadership of this UNESCO agenda: senior figures at the Tavistock
Clinic and the British Psychoanalytical Society, for example, were closely
consulted about the terms of reference of the research, and a delegation
from Paris visited London in the spring of 1948 to learn about the dynamics
of what one of the organizers called 'attitude change'.[82] Plans were under
way for a conference under UNESCO auspices to be held in England, in
pleasant surroundings near Windsor Great Park in November 1949. Among
the miscellaneous range of specialists invited to the event were the psychoanalysts John Bowlby, J. C. Flügel, Edward Glover, and John Rickman, the

anthropologist Margaret Mead, and the historians Michael Postan, E. H. Carr, and G. D. H. Cole; but UNESCO records are unclear as to whether the meeting proved fruitful, or precisely who did attend.[83]

Anna Freud had been invited to present her work at the summer school in 1947 but declined, citing the short notice and the difficulty of cancelling appointments with her patients. She was subsequently asked to write a report, to which she readily agreed,[84] and in April 1948 received the request from UNESCO representative P. W. Martin for a paper of between 5,000 and 10,000 words on 'Techniques of attitude change which you regard as of particular importance in relation to tensions between nations'; advice on 'the next step for further development and practical application of these techniques', he added, 'would be appreciated'.[85] In her report she spoke of the work conducted during the previous few years at the Hampstead Nurseries which had provided sanctuary to approximately one hundred children, many of whom had been made homeless and sometimes orphaned in the Blitz. Anna Freud developed a particular system for their care, basing her approach upon her psychoanalytical understanding of child development. Wherever possible she invited parents to involve themselves in the life of this refuge and ensured consistency of care; the same member of staff would work with the same child throughout to alleviate anxiety. She even sought to create small, 'family-style' groups of children and staff within the wider community. The nurseries provided nurture and also an opportunity for Freud and her colleagues to undertake close observation of child development in a time of war. She stressed the importance of the psychoanalytical outlook in helping each child, especially each war-torn child, to face the anxieties that beset it. Human aggression, she warned, could not be abolished; indeed, harsh prohibition of infantile aggressive impulses might well be counter-productive. Anger and hostility, she implied, are integral parts of human nature and of all relationships. Nonetheless, such raw feelings might be modified and perhaps sublimated, if not eliminated, in the course of ordinary development or therapy. Looking to the future, she suggested that knowledge of infant mental life needed to be disseminated more broadly in society, above all to parents themselves: 'Without such enlightenment, the majority of parents and other educators will continue to handle the next generation in a manner which will produce the very attitudes they are attempting to eliminate from the nature of the child.'[86] Anna Freud recommended that UNESCO should try to enlist the services of able and experienced analysts in every country that it could, to as many oversee the work in orphanages, hospitals, children's homes, crèches, and nurseries.

Looking back at the history of their discipline, present-day psychoanalysts tend to be alert to the animosity that had developed between some of its major figures. There was indeed bad feeling between Anna Freud and Melanie Klein in the Freudian movement during this period, and genuine, substantial differences between their outlooks and those of other publicly influential psychoanalytical commentators of the post-war era such as John Bowlby and Donald Winnicott. Seen from outside the field, however, what may seem equally, if not more, striking was the degree to which psychoanalysts at large linked the question of infant mental health with the 'good society' or, conversely, with fascist polities. Whatever their other disagreements psychoanalysts at least shared this passionate conviction, that the experience of infancy was fundamental not only to the well-being or malaise of the individual, but also to the nature of future communities.

Important innovations by psychoanalysts in the study of groups were also discussed at UNESCO. Erich Fromm, for example, who attended at least one meeting of international researchers at the 'Tensions' project in Paris in 1948, proposed that the best way of studying the relative degree of nationalistic aggression and xenophobia in different contexts was to arrange empirical observations, based on recent clinical work on groups: 'The experiments with group therapy have shown that it is possible under the proper guidance of a psychiatrist or psychologist to bring a group of 5–10 people together and to create an atmosphere in which they are able to speak as frankly and unconventionally about their own problems as people do in the normal psychoanalytic interview.'[87] He proposed that UNESCO or other research organizations should arrange small gatherings of appropriately selected people to discuss race and religion. The setting, he felt, must be as free as possible, so they could air their views without fear of moral disapproval. Meanwhile Dicks and his colleague from the Tavistock, the anthropologist Adam Curle, attended further sessions in Paris during May 1949, designed to train field-workers from overseas in interviewing techniques that would tease out deeper beliefs and assumptions from more superficial and compliant responses to questions.[88]

Usually it was the English and American contributors to the 'Tensions' project who laid greatest stress on psychological, and specifically unconscious factors, rather than sociological and political explanations for inter-group hatred and violence. They also sometimes focused upon the significance of the emotional experiences that arose in the course of interviews they had conducted. One of the Americans, for instance, insisted that in research involving interviewing the key issue was to try and grasp 'what is going on in oneself and the other fellow, without any let or hindrance'.[89] The authors of a paper submitted to the project organizers in 1949 pointed to the significance of the theory of 'unconscious envy', in grasping what is at stake in anti-Semitism: '[t]he possibility suggests itself that there is a strong unconscious identification with and envy of the Jew, particularly among more prejudiced individuals'.[90]

The UNESCO project was in the end to become so capacious that it lost whatever coherence had existed at the outset. Its officials, as noted, canvassed an extraordinary range of opinions about how to avoid future wars and overcome other violent social antagonisms. Not only did the project draw upon diverse experts and disciplines, but its precise research objective was also increasingly diffuse. Nonetheless, what so many of the commentators seemed to be arguing about, explicitly or implicitly, was the value of psychoanalytical ideas, and the very idea of the unconscious, in post-war political inquiry. This can be seen in the commentary of the Austrian physicist Hans Thirring, still another luminary to give his opinion to UNESCO on these matters. He too underlined the unconscious factors that afflicted politics not only in Germany and Russia, but also in the United States, in an account seasoned with references to death instincts and sado-masochistic processes. Thirring was 'ready to agree that a formidable hell of destructive and sadistic impulses is being let loose in quite a significant percentage of all combatants once a war has begun'. The 'fatal chain-reaction of violence and brutal counter attacks', he warned, is always hard to stop once it has started. But he cautioned against placing too much store on psychological motivations, since these were as much, if not more, the consequences of war rather than the ultimate causes: 'All these horrid manifestations of perverted, displaced or projected instincts are, however, of a secondary nature; they do rather break through under war conditions than act as the primary cause of war.' Thirring sought to widen the range of emotional states of mind that he felt needed close attention:

> That is why we must not restrict our attention to the psychic phenomena connected with destructive instincts, but study as well—or rather first of all—those mechanisms of human nature which are responsible for the arising of a hysterical atmosphere of confusion, blind zeal, hatred, misconceptions and

misunderstandings between men who are not at all neurotics in the clinical sense.[91]

It is not always clear from the archives who only contributed to the planning stages rather than taking part in the formal seminars themselves, but it is still intriguing to find that as well as Dicks, Anna Freud, and Mead, corresponding members and invited guests to various events within the 'Tensions' programme included, *inter alia*, E. E. Evans-Prichard, Lucien Febvre, Erich Fromm, Geoffrey Gorer, Max Horkheimer, Daniel Lagache, Claude Lévi-Strauss, Alfred Métraux, Henry Murray, Joseph Needham, Franz Neumann, Henry Stack Sullivan, and Henri Wallon, although in at least some cases the input of these various psychoanalysts, legal scholars, scientists, social theorists, anthropologists, and psychologists was restricted to occasional appearances or letters. Whether the American and British authors of the Hitler and Hess studies described earlier, Murray, Rees, and Dicks, met directly through these channels is also unclear; all, however, contributed to the project.

This UNESCO inquiry ran on (in increasingly repetitive fashion) into the early 1950s, unable satisfactorily to resolve its methodological uncertainties or to turn endless reports and communiqués into any settled conclusions. Whilst some contributors spoke as though Freudianism held the most important key to understanding 'international tensions', others emphasized that neither particular psychoanalytic formulae nor general reflections on 'human nature' could substitute for precise historical, economic, or sociological knowledge in the interpretation of fascism, militarism, or nationalism. Whatever the theoretical debates that remained, few if any of the participants doubted that the political world could easily descend once again into monstrous forms of collective psychopathology.

II

Legacies

Historians have provided various explanations for the resilience of the Nazi state; amongst the reasons given for the survival of the regime is the high level of personal loyalty and public approbation that Hitler enjoyed not only during the 1930s and the early triumphant period of the war, but even during the final phases of the conflict. This 'answer' in turn prompts further questions, for instance regarding the extent of the Führer's actual popularity amongst civilians or in the armed forces by the last two or three years of the war. The degree to which faith in his wider cause was in fact eroded, and the myriad factors that prevented schemes (most notably the bomb-plot of 1944) to topple the leadership from succeeding or other means emerging to end the lunacy and nihilism of Hitler's 'vision', have been much discussed in the literature. The vagaries of public opinion and the depth of allegiance that the leader and the Party enjoyed during the war remain of great interest to historians.[1] That it was necessary not only to pulverize Germany from the air, but also to send armies from east and west across its territory meant that the attitudes and beliefs of the population and the psychological state of Hitler's army had remained of major concern to Allied intelligence analysts right up until the final surrender was achieved. Indeed, these issues were of importance long afterwards too. British and American surveys of German mentality continued apace during the years of occupation.

Interest in such matters has never simply been the preserve of politicians, military strategists, and intelligence officers, or even of professional historians. Broader psycho-political 'lessons' were sought and the views, beliefs, and passions at stake in what Wilhelm Reich had called this 'mass psychology of fascism' were examined and considered in a plethora of general psychological discourses and in particular clinical studies much later in the twentieth century. The sketches below may serve to indicate how elements of Freudian theory and methodology were brought to bear in culture and thought on fascism in the last years of the conflict and *a fortiori* in post-war accounts of political fanaticism and the 'authoritarian personality'; the significance of the 'talking cure' was also to be debated by a number of commentators on military intelligence. A sample of those discussions, alongside vignettes from film, literature, social theory, and clinical writing, can offer some indication of developments over the longer term.

In one sense critique of 'psychologism' within the human sciences made the pursuit of the unconscious dynamics of Nazism (at least in the terms set out during the war) look increasingly outmoded. Many researchers came to the view that the attempt to understand Nazism through the lens of psychoanalysis was best discarded altogether, like some rusty relic of the past. New endeavours to use psychoanalysis in interpreting the Third Reich continue to emerge, but to make much intellectual sense now these must register, if not actually endorse, the well-rehearsed critique of 'psychologism'.[2] The post-war period was in fact marked by numerous criticisms of all of the 'psy' professions as forms of therapy, theories of mind, and adjuncts to social or political inquiry.

When British and American psychoanalytical interpreters used individual cases of leaders and followers, or even larger groupings of such cases, to define the entire field of the Nazi constituency they lost credibility. Such work often came to be criticized by later generations of historians and social theorists for its generalizations and lack of attention to social context. Wartime interpreters of the Nazi mindset might have done well to pay more heed to the warning of the nineteenth-century pioneer of sociology, Émile Durkheim: 'whenever a social phenomenon is directly explained by a psychological phenomenon, we may be sure that the explanation is false.'[3] Although the aspirations of some wartime clinicians to explain Nazism's triumph in Germany through the pursuit of individual profiles such as those of Hitler, Hess, and the other major war criminals were overblown, a far larger set of issues—regarding, as it were, the boundless potential of Nazi-like processes in ordinary people, groups, and organizations—ultimately proved more enduring and perturbing. If the Third Reich could not be explained away by psychology, the charismatic allure of the Nazi leader and the subterranean attractions of his cause continued nonetheless to be examined and interpreted by many post-war writers.

Discussion of Rudolf Hess after the war was always to be overshadowed
by the question of his madness, and his pathetic collapse from frightening
henchman to amnesiac patient and bizarre defendant. In the case of Hitler
too, what seemed so striking with hindsight was the disparity between the
gargantuan evil leader, whose will had held such sway, and the diminished,
shaking, ashen figure confined to an underground life in Berlin towards
the end of the war. These two pictures of his personality were hard to square
up. Already by the late 1940s published inquiries into those 'last days' in the
bunker evoked the sense of a troglodyte existence and provided a perplexing counterpoint to earlier visions of his vast magnetic power, political
reach, and daunting visibility in the 1930s.[4] Some investigators argued force-
fully that these two aspects of Hitler might be seen as part of his charismatic
allure in the first place, not simply as two sequential 'chapters' in his life or
two phases of his image.

In a remarkable essay on Freudian theory and fascist propaganda published in 1951, Theodor Adorno considered the oscillation between ordi-
nariness (or even tawdriness) and utterly exceptional power (even
superhuman gifts) in the portrayal of the Nazi leader. He suggested that
fascist belief systems may always rely upon this double aspect of the representation of its own leading figure: to understand the appeal of Hitler
required a grasp of the unconscious position that the fascist follower
characteristically yearned to occupy. Adorno believed that many people
sought narcissistically to identify with the Führer, and hence he presented himself successfully as the outsider or the 'little guy' who understood the grievances of common folk and took revenge on the old powers
on their behalf. Hitler wore his unconscious resentment, Adorno suggested, on the outside, and invited others with similar feelings to share
and endorse his bitter complaints and envy-ridden 'analysis' of the contemporary world and of the Jewish conspiracy that he held responsible
for so many modern ills.

Simultaneously, it was recognized and insisted on that Hitler was entirely
out of the ordinary—'abnormal' in the eyes of his enemies, messianic to his
followers. This peculiarity was in turn made into a fetish. He was cast as
preternaturally gifted and presented as utterly alone, in a separate stellar
space, as in the opening sequence of Riefenstahl's *The Triumph of the Will*,
where he descends to Nuremberg from the skies. Here he was the gigantic
master of souls who would dominate the 'ordinary' person completely and

take away any need to think. He invited the follower to share with him in a sense of superiority, whilst at the same time requiring masochistic submission to his will. Yet Hitler also seemed to be guided by a will or force that lay beyond him, or at least that was unconscious in him, hence his belief that he was akin to a sleepwalker. He was cast as all-powerful and astonishingly mundane. To put it another way, Hitler, Adorno suggested, was a composite of the fearsome King Kong and the suburban barber. Fascist propaganda, he argued, played on the pleasure principle. It gratified narcissistic wishes, the joy of belonging to an aggrieved and yet spiritually superior 'in-group', whilst also requiring each subject's obedience and self-abasement. This functioned all the way down the chain, with each little man or woman in thrall to 'superiors' whilst lording it over 'inferiors'. People were 'taken over' by this mindset, he argued, but only up to a point. Somewhere the voters knew it was a sham (not truly believing in the demonology of the 'out-group' that the propaganda provided). There was a willed suspension of disbelief required in this transaction between the leader and his admirers, a quality of make-believe: Adorno called it the 'fictitiousness' of fascist group psychology. For if people would stop to reason for a second, Adorno mused, the whole edifice of such an ideology would fall apart.[5]

In the wake of the Nazi defeat, many commentators would come to remark upon this ordinary/extraordinary, normal/abnormal, inflated/deflated dichotomy. If the Nazi war criminals were viewed on occasion as anomalous specimens, they were also, almost immediately, seen as pathetically reduced, brought down in size, shockingly inadequate specimens of humanity. Some stressed their inner emptiness, or at least their gross incapacity. What if there was nothing demonically 'special' about any of them at all? Here it was the *machine* of the state and the chemistry of the group that was most horrifying, whereas the particular operatives were in many, if not in all, cases (so it was sometimes argued) of no particular psychological or philosophical interest. The subjective dimension—the sense of the system as driven by the special minds and indomitable wills of individual 'leading' people—was perhaps required by the ideology, but it was not, for many theorists, including Adorno, the key point about how fascism or Nazism really worked. The question of evil entered into the discussion to be sure, but it could not satisfactorily be explained by or confined to a psychology, still less a demonology, of the leader or his closest entourage. And yet, the special personality of Hitler could not be ignored in any reckoning of what had occurred: he returned again and again to the fore, even much later in the twentieth century, the 'hot' issues of his mind and charisma breaking in amidst cooler discussions of 'structures', 'systems', 'processes', and 'discourses'.

———•———

During the war itself popular culture and visual propaganda often still sought to identify the evil of Nazism through demonic images. It thus came as a surprise to some commentators that German POWs did not usually look or behave like their wartime caricatures. More significant even than the acknowledgement that appearances might in fact hold no clue to the character within was an emerging argument about Nazi banality. George Orwell's remarks after visiting a POW camp in southern Germany in 1945 pointed in this direction, and also suggested the fascistic treatment which Allied soldiers and indeed civilian victims were capable of meting out in revenge. A man Orwell described condescendingly as a 'little Viennese Jew' (who had enlisted in the American army) showed him around the camp. Here Orwell saw a former SS man with deformed feet, who had clearly been badly beaten already and who was then further attacked by the guide (with the justification: 'That's the real swine'). The SS prisoner had a 'scrubby, unfed, unshaven look'; he was a 'disgusting specimen', but appeared 'neurotic', a 'low intellectual', rather than an obviously 'brutal' figure. He was apparently rather akin to many people Orwell had seen in London (including, he pointedly added, in the Reading Room of the British Museum): 'So the Nazi torturer of one's imagination, the monstrous figure against whom one had struggled for so many years, dwindled to this pitiful wretch, whose obvious need was not for punishment, but for some kind of psychological treatment.'[6]

Cinema has continued for decades, of course, to code German villains as visibly brutal types, whose moral nature can be read off from their appearances and mannerisms. Nonetheless, already in the 1940s films could also suggest the gap between the surface appearance and depths of the fanatical figure; superficial social traits and personal manners might well hide rather than reveal the dark nature of political fantasy locked inside the self. Moreover, just as some films located the entire moral evil that had generated the catastrophic violence entirely within the geographical limits of Germany (or at least the Third Reich and its political allies, most notably Japan), others complicated this picture, suggesting the tremendous, barely repressed violence and/or treachery that may lurk inside the 'civilized' 'decent' antifascist person elsewhere as well. These representations relied on older tropes of the concealed monster, but they were now also inflected by the enigma of Nazism and its spellbinding, explosive power. Lethal forms of cruelty were not simply the preserve of some designated category of lunatics or wrongdoers abroad. Several Hitchcock films of this period, for example, directly connected the psychology of Nazism with the everyday psychopathy, or outright inhumanity, that exists in ourselves and in our midst: comrades, family, or friends, not just obvious national enemies, may behave with horrible callousness and malice—witness *Saboteur*, *Shadow of a Doubt*, *Lifeboat*, or *Notorious*.[7]

Numerous later Hollywood films and television dramas nonetheless continued to evoke familiar German stereotypes, to dramatic or, at times, comic effect. Some drew upon religious languages to address this history. Even for the secular onlooker, 'evil' still seemed the necessary and unavoidable word. One way to encode what had happened, without recourse to theology, was to reach back to the naturalistic imagery of forensic psychiatry and criminology in the previous century, thereby to describe the Nazis as psychopaths, degenerates, and atavists. But this was harder to do when characterizing the millions of people who supported Nazism.[8]

The question of how Nazism caught the subject's desire and how it might remain a lifelong (secret) passion was explored again and again; it was as though this very question might itself be a traumatic problem to resolve, requiring us repeatedly to return to the 'mystery' of how it all begins and how it is then sustained in hearts and minds. Several Hollywood films of the 1940s put psychiatrists and psychoanalysts into the frame, reprising those politically charged images of madhouses, madmen, and mad doctors that had already been extensively explored in Weimar cinema of the inter-war years. Even the doctors, as shown here, were not immune to the lure, the tempting siren voice, of the terrible 'master criminal'. Fritz Lang, who left Germany and resumed his career in Hollywood, provided an important bridge between the two worlds of cinema. In Lang's *Ministry of Fear* (1944), based on a story by Graham Greene, a particularly equivocal character called Dr Forrester appears. The viewer is left in doubt for most of the time as to whether he is orchestrating a Nazi cell in London or working in good faith for the British government's security services. This psychoanalytic practitioner and psychiatrist treats patients in a mental hospital and also authors a popular work, shown in close-up, entitled *The Psychoanalysis of Nazidom*. But it may well be, the viewer discovers, that Nazidom is his organizing belief system, and psychoanalysis merely a masquerade.

Carol Reed's film-noir masterpiece *The Third Man* (1949), again based on a story by Greene, offered an unforgettable snapshot of the residues of Nazism in post-war Vienna. It brought American actors and the old continent setting together, with Harry Lime (played by Orson Welles) epitomizing just that contemptuous indifference to—even glee in—the death of others that had characterized the recent past. There was no need to be German, in short, to espouse such attitudes. Lime describes people as mere 'dots', to the consternation of his ever-more alienated friend Holly Martins (Joseph Cotten). The story culminates in a chase through the sewers of Vienna. On the other hand, the need for psychiatric experts to analyse the particular features of the German national case was picked up wryly in another film of the time also starring (and this time directed by) Welles: *The Stranger* (1946). Here we see Edward G. Robinson, playing an investigator from the Allied Control Commission, in search of hidden Nazis. He quips at one point that it would indeed take a psychiatrist to understand Germany. The film reveals a Nazi fanatic (played by Welles) embedded in a peaceful village in America, pretending to be a good citizen but unrepentant still in his allegiance to the cause.

The terrifying reach of political dictatorship into the furthest recesses of the psyche became the stuff of dystopian fiction between the wars and again after 1945. The most celebrated representation of all, after the war, was Orwell's *Nineteen Eighty-Four*. 'Big Brother' was shown to be irresistible; the work has come to be regarded as the defining literary monument to the horrors of totalitarianism and enjoyed enormous sales, especially in the United States.[9] Here the monster state was immortalized: there could be no end to it; it had subdued the minds, not just the freedom of expression, of practically everyone, save temporarily for one or two eccentric lone resisters.

Some stories highlighted existential moments of defiance or escape from such totalitarian conditions; others the collusion of minds, or of groups, in generating their own tyranny. Many theorists explored authoritarian processes within groups and considered the relationship of the emerging child's mind to the politics of intolerance and hatred. It was not by chance that one of the most discussed novels of the 1950s should also depict a group of children who create states of fascist terror for themselves, even without (or perhaps especially without) adult interference. William Golding's *Lord of the Flies* (1954) was obviously influenced by knowledge of what people had done to one another during the 1940s. Nonetheless it drew the reader's attention away from Germany to a larger fable of childhood. The tale relied on the old trope of physical isolation—the island—and the struggle for survival. The marooned youths of this story are not so much budding Robinson Crusoes as creatures drawn into allegiance with charismatic and destructive leaders; their malleable minds are overwhelmed by violent and hateful powers. Psychopathology grips the group. Splits emerge within the band of children; ferocious totems and taboos are constituted. The capacity to pursue collective interests (in this case to keep a fire going in order to maximize the chance of being seen and thus rescued) is lost. Increasingly terrifying manic, phobic, and sadistic wishes hold sway. The tormentors of the weak, vulnerable, and outcast figures (epitomized by the character Piggy) dominate. As forms of delusional thinking triumph over reason and compassion, murder and torture become possible. The central protagonist, Ralph, is spared his fate at the hands of the frenzied gang only thanks to Golding's less-than-convincing *deus ex machina*: the naval officer who arrives on the beach to end the children's isolation. The officer's obtuse underestimation of what has ensued complicates this moment of narrative solace. Golding makes it hard for the reader to treat this as a fable exclusively of feral children: the adult war raging elsewhere is also heavily signalled.

————•————

The contributions of Langer, Murray, Dicks, and their peers to the analysis of the Nazi mind were part of the stream of intelligence information that emerged about the Nazi leadership and the mentality of the German population in the 1940s. Langer's predictions in 1943, for instance, that Hitler would never give in, would pursue a scorched-earth policy and ultimately kill himself, entered into a much larger conversation about the likely resolution of the war; these analysts and intelligence officers were preaching to the converted by the time they published these findings: Allied leaders were hardly in any doubt by now that the campaign would have to be fought to the bitter end. Some especially prescient observers, of course, had reached this conclusion as soon as Hitler entered into government in 1933.

If these analysts sometimes voiced doubts about the legitimacy of extrapolating from the specific case (or even from hundreds of cases) to the entire field of the German mind, they made such assumptions too. Close observation of the Führer or of the Nuremberg prisoners alone could never be a basis on which it would be possible plausibly to explain the rise and fall of the Nazi Party. Whatever claims were made at the time regarding the so-called 'psychological treasure' that was locked away in the minds of the defendants at the International Military Tribunal, it could not substitute for detailed social history or empirical research. Some of this more precise evidence about actual viewpoints emerged during the war, for instance attempts to pinpoint and differentiate attitudes among POWs. Soon afterwards such research was widened, and increasingly the focus shifted from German mindsets to human propensities. Perhaps the most famous example of the endeavour to test the prevalence of fascist-style assumptions in the population at large was the work by the Frankfurt School on psychology and fascist politics that culminated in *The Authoritarian Personality* (1950).

This lengthy book stemmed from the collaboration between Adorno (and, behind the scenes, several of his colleagues from the Institute for Social Research) and the Berkeley Public Opinion Study Group. The latter provided detailed surveys for the project. Although swiftly hailed as an original and important contribution to knowledge, some critics in the 1950s complained that the research focused too narrowly upon the pro-clivities of the ultra-right and should have spent equal time considering the psychic life—and pathology—of communism.[10] Nonetheless, even if it was attacked by some Cold War figures for this 'bias', *The Authoritarian Personality* remained by far the most discussed and best known of the items that appeared within a series entitled 'Studies in Prejudice', sponsored by the American Jewish Committee and directed by Max Horkheimer and Samuel Flowerman, a psychologist and member of the scientific research department of the AJC.[11]

A key aim of the Studies in Prejudice was to bring together social science, history, and political theory in order to provide a deeper understanding of modern ideologies and practices, above all of Nazism. Many of the Frankfurt School stalwarts produced work under the auspices of this project, as did looser affiliates of the group such as Bruno Bettelheim. Characteristically, studies combined research on social background and psychological traits with analysis of ideological convictions. Psychoanalytical concepts were then brought to bear to understand the irrational aspects of political beliefs.[12]

The Authoritarian Personality exemplified this approach. It attempted to apply something of the methodology and theory of the talking cure. Dauntingly long and replete with many scales and measures, the book was organized around an underlying theory of mental life derived in the main from Freud. Adorno and his co-workers offered the compelling picture of a mind in which (as Horkheimer later summed it up) a 'mechanical surren-der' had taken place to certain unquestionable 'values'. The 'authoritarian' mind was marked by 'blind submission' coexisting with 'blind hatred of all opponents and outsiders'. Anyone who challenged the system of belief was profoundly hated. The authoritarian subject in question was characterized by resistance to introspectiveness, rigid stereotyped thinking, a penchant for superstition, a tendency to vilify others, and an orientation towards human nature that managed to combine extreme moralism and deep cynicism.[13]

This account became an important catalyst for other works of political psychology. It presented the picture of a struggling ego navigating external reality and powerful aggressive and sadistic drives within. This ego was obliged to cope with—or, failing that, to seek to circumvent—the superego. Much of this struggle inside the self took place unconsciously. Although *The Authoritarian Personality* provides numerous descriptions of individual (albeit anonymous) interviews, at its core are composite portraits, depictions of certain types likely to be drawn towards dictatorship. Hostile to (and ill-equipped for) the encounter with psychic anxiety, guilt, or uncertainty, the person with authoritarian proclivities, according to Adorno *et al.*, gravitates spontaneously towards the party of action, the politics of scapegoating, the 'man of destiny', and automaton-like obedience. In formulating the project Adorno drew inspiration from research conducted earlier, notably by Erich Fromm, on social attitudes in 1930s Germany. Adorno's post-war commentary was also informed by and preoccupied with the kind of officialdom that operated the concentration-camp system and organized the genocide; the terminus of the Third Reich, in other words, was known, whereas the 1930s researchers on Nazi mentality had sought to second-guess where Hitler and his government were heading, even as they documented existing horrors of intolerance, violence, and persecution.[14]

In their preface to *The Authoritarian Personality* Horkheimer and Flowerman remarked upon the post-war lull in anti-Semitic persecution, but suggested this more benign settlement might prove short-lived. Anti-Jewish hatred, they observed, 'is not manifesting itself with the full and violent destructiveness of which we know it to be capable'.[15] Other forms of racial fantasy and prejudice, however, were neither ignored nor assumed to be on the wane. Horkheimer and Flowerman conceptualized such deep-seated attitudes to race as an illness that was now merely in its period of 'quiescence'. It was sure to erupt again. Even so soon after the extermination of millions, they complained 'the world scarcely remembers'.[16] Psychoanalysis informed their understanding of this phenomenon: 'forgetting' is viewed as an active, motivated process, a convenient 'getting rid' of unwanted knowledge. Without remembering and 'working through', Freud had suggested, people might well find themselves repeating the past. Erik Erikson offered a similar warning in *Childhood and Society* (also from 1950): 'I do not think we are improving the chance of human progress in Germany or anywhere else by forgetting too soon what happened.'[17]

The assumption that German commentators, let alone world opinion, simply 'forgot' Nazi horrors after 1945 is clearly exaggerated, although it is true that historical interpretations that placed the Holocaust at the centre of the story of Nazism, war and even twentieth-century history, became far more apparent during and beyond the 1970s. If much of the horror of the war and the camps was actively avoided during the late 1940s and 1950s, it is a cliché to imagine that Germany, still less the world, was simply 'amnesiac'. Historians more plausibly record particular cultural moments of engagement with Nazism, and of willed blindness to the past, rather than a simple passage from post-war forgetting to later twentieth-century commemoration; thus the historian Jane Caplan observes that, shortly after the war, various journalists, independent authors, and historians in Germany produced a considerable amount of work that focused attention upon the Nazi period and sometimes involved open expressions of guilt; at other points writers complained in more self-exculpating terms of Germany's 'wrong turnings' or of 'fate'. 'It was not until the 1950s', Caplan adds, 'that fuller rein was given to popular desires to repress the recent past.'[18]

Precisely because of the risk of airbrushing the Nazi past from view, a succession of ingenious post-war researchers sought to develop forms of social survey, polling, and psychological experiment that would glean the extent of fascist or Nazi attitudes that most people, at least in liberal societies, are unwilling to admit to. This endeavour to prise open unacknowledged or actively repressed beliefs (or what the psychoanalyst Christopher Bollas has more recently described as the 'unthought known') was presaged by the sophisticated approach to interviewing displayed in *The Authoritarian Personality*, whose methodology proved to be as significant as the resulting 'types' that were sketched out in the book. The form of this psycho-social inquiry into attitudes bears comparison with endeavours by Dicks and others during the war. In the work of Adorno and his team a clinical gaze was turned upon America's own population. Well aware that few Americans were likely, in the late 1940s, to endorse fascism or Nazism directly, the interviewers sought to tease out the real views towards authority that lay behind the superficial stance of the subject. The purpose of the inquiry was thus disguised and questions were put obliquely.

Interviews lasted about ninety minutes and were divided into 'ideological' and 'clinical' sections.[19] The researchers sought to test personality variables such as commitment to convention, submission to authority, tolerance of subjective, imaginative, and tender-minded feelings, superstition and stereotypical thinking, love of power and 'toughness', evidence of destructiveness and cynicism, and so on. Adorno noted how the authoritarian type tended to blame 'malfunctioning' exclusively on factors outside the self. The capacity to acknowledge 'symptoms' as stemming from one's own self and to relate this to personal life history tended to be characteristics of the democrat. The ability to speak with relative frankness and freedom from moralism was also regarded as a good indication of the more democratically inclined form of subjectivity.[20]

Adorno and his colleagues also described the authoritarian's prurient fascination with, and horror at, the secret 'goings on' (sexual or otherwise) of other people. They showed how 'negroes' were used as repositories for denigrated and discarded aspects of the bourgeois or white working-class self; the Jew too was presented as full of unwanted 'dirt', but also contained the anti-Semite's fantasies of a race that was mired in secrecy and conspiracy, marked by its own supposed superiority, domination, and omnipotence. The Jew was seen as the gloating possessor of the real 'goods', the all-powerful plotter, the manipulator of capital (or of communism) or the exemplar of free and dangerous movement itself: hence the legendary Wandering Jew, the rootless figure, belonging everywhere and nowhere. Social and historical reality (the actual positions of black people and Jews in a given society, faced by persecution, regulation, and constrictions of many types) became fused—and profoundly confused—with the figures of unconscious fantasy. Furthermore, *The Authoritarian Personality* aimed to understand the interaction of specific political, racial, and social stereotypes as they congealed into set beliefs and views about the world.

It is apparent that for the Jewish Horkheimer and the partly Jewish Adorno, as for several of the other interpreters of Nazism within the Frankfurt School, the nature of the Nazi racial obsession was of theoretical and immediate personal concern. The German rather than the Italian case dominated discussion of fascism's pathological core. In Nazism the most virulent form of anti-Semitism had been of crucial significance from the start. This was far less apparent in Mussolini's Italy, where the most flagrant persecution of Jews that did occur, including the policy of deportation to the camps, was powerfully (although not exclusively) determined by the

Duce's more powerful northern ally. The study of anti-Semitism had been regarded as of urgent importance and central to the original formation and funding of the Institute for Social Research in Frankfurt in the 1920s. That these writers sought again and again to explain the unconscious dimensions of Nazi racial hatred no doubt owed something to the immediate personal stake they felt in the matter, though it is true Horkheimer and some of his close colleagues also downplayed the significance of Judaism in their own intellectual formations and in their published writings.[21] It would be misleading, of course, to say that such analyses were the preoccupation of Jewish commentators alone; a number of the key theorists who contributed to the interpretations of the Nazi psyche during the 1940s and 50s were gentiles. It is noteworthy, nonetheless, that a substantial variety of the figures who shaped this field of theory, reportage, and practical endeavour (such as Arendt, Bettelheim, Fromm, Gilbert, Goldensohn, Koeppler, Levy, and Marcuse) were Jewish, and many were also in enforced exile. In short, a number of those who shaped this field of inquiry into the Nazi psyche were directly the targets of the racial political fantasies and phobic beliefs that they studied: how far this may also have affected the nature of the face-to-face clinical encounters of army psychiatrists and prisoners during and after the war, however, often remains unclear.

————·————

Elements of psychoanalysis also found their way into the toolkit of some of the intelligence officers who interrogated or sought to rehabilitate suspect officials, soldiers, and civilians in post-war Germany, Austria, and other liberated territories. Those, such as Dicks or Money-Kyrle, with direct clinical training and detailed knowledge of psychoanalytic theory and practice were a small minority among staff involved in denazification and screening in the British zone of occupied Germany, but some of their ideas were also to be taken up and adapted by other army and intelligence officers with no direct training in psychoanalysis or psychotherapy. Methodologies were makeshift. Frequently, tried-and-tested approaches of interrogation prevailed; for instance, direct enticements were often made by staff in order to gain the trust of desperate erstwhile enemy officials seeking the restoration of their posts or at least to avoid imprisonment and trial. Personal favours were often traded for information. Menaces and savage assaults were also resorted to by some of the interrogators for the British and American intelligence services in Germany in and after 1945. Speaking off the record, one former MI6 officer who had come into the service a few years after the war declared: 'The reality of most interrogations in those days was a lot more brutal than scientific from all one hears.'[22] He recollected that some of the best interrogators for the security services were former policemen. Powers of memory, acute observation, painstaking preparation in advance of interrogations were, no doubt, more valued skills than familiarity with psychiatric, psychoanalytical, or psychological textbooks.

A separate inquiry would be required to assess in any detail the combination of working practices (inducements, threats, acts of violence, outright torture, pharmaceuticals, lie-detectors, and the rest) and implicit assumptions about the minds of others that governed interrogation methods in post-war western intelligence. Nonetheless, expert psychological knowledge was sometimes declared to be a key requirement, especially on the American side.[23] Various documents now publicly available demonstrate the degree to which officials at the CIA not only discussed the case for torture in interrogations, but also emphasized the greater efficiency that could be achieved by deploying staff well trained in the latest psychological theory and techniques. The history of collaboration between certain post-war psychoanalysts, psychiatrists, psychologists and intelligence organizations, hitherto insufficiently studied, is a subject of current, timely, academic research.[24]

A rather different legacy of wartime work by the 'psy' professions was long-distance 'profiling'. The concern with political psychobiography described in this book continued to find favour in intelligence briefings on the private behaviour, covert fears, and scandalous secrets of foreign leaders (mad or otherwise) after Hitler, but long before security consultants made the mental state of Saddam Hussein, Muammar Ghaddafi, and Osama Bin Laden the stuff of regular bulletins and detailed diagnoses.[25] Kremlinology, of course, became an industry in its own right during the 1950s.[26] The work of the wartime analysts was also one source of inspiration for later developments in 'psychological warfare'.[27] The shape of things to come can be discerned in an American study by Paul Linebarger in 1948 of Allied intelligence and propaganda operations and the lessons that could be drawn for the future. Linebarger's overriding argument was that 'psychological warfare' would remain hereafter an immensely important consideration for Western governments.

Linebarger had worked for the Office of War Information in Washington—he would become better-known later as the author (under the pseudonym Cordwainer Smith) of works of science fiction. He suggested that it was important that interrogation and other information-gathering techniques go 'down into the *unconscious* mind'.[28] He added: 'Some of the worst blunders of history have arisen from the miscalculation of the enemy state of mind.'[29] The

Second World War showed—so he claimed—how a cross-section of German POWs could help intelligence analysts to estimate the mentality of an entire theatre of war at a given period. The task was to adhere to 'scientific psychology', for unless 'we aim at exterminating the enemy, then in the end, we must effect a change in the enemy's mind'.[30] It was important to try and let sources (such as POWs) speak in their own terms, freely:

> When processing prisoners of war, it is an excellent idea to deal with them for [intelligence on] morale as well as for general and assorted military information. Questions should not aim at what the prisoner thinks he thinks about God, his leader, his country, and so on, but should concern themselves with those things which most interest the prisoner himself. Does his wife write that the babies have enough diapers? How is the mail service? Is he worried about war workers getting his pre-war job? [...] Does he think that anybody is making too much money at home?[31]

Another participant-observer in US intelligence, Daniel Lerner, also emphasized the need for depth analysis of 'morale' in modern war and the importance of deploying sophisticated techniques in order to draw out the actual views and general orientation of prisoners of war. Lerner, who had worked for the psychological warfare division of the Supreme Headquarters Allied Expeditionary Force, published a book on psychological warfare in 1949. Here he sought to learn lessons from the campaign that had been designed to soften up German opinion before the required total surrender.[32] Such work, he enthused, must be based on the closest possible understanding of enemy thoughts and feelings. An 'opinion' voiced, for instance, by a prisoner could be regarded as a 'mis-expression' of an attitude; it was the latter that was often the crucial point to glean for intelligence purposes: 'That is, the person giving an opinion may, consciously or unconsciously, be mis-representing his "real" attitude.' In societies such as Nazi Germany, he argued, where nobody had felt free to express dissent, opinions by men in Allied captivity were a poor yardstick of deeper convictions. Reports of the utterances of POWs were not to be regarded as the end of the story; rather, they were the raw data for analysis.[33] Thus, although major Allied propaganda and intelligence operations relied heavily on the expressed attitudes of German POWs, it would be facile, he warned, to take the material at face value. Dicks's ingenious questionnaires were singled out for praise: they sought to get behind opinions to uncover entrenched beliefs.[34] By careful classification of interrogated subjects and collation of responses within each category, Lerner explained, it was possible to gain reliable and useful insights into the trends of opinion.

Lerner recommended that in undertaking a systematic interview the gathering of standard information (name, rank, unit, task, former occupation, circumstances of capture, experience, age, place of residence, and so forth) should be just the start. Drawing on his experience of the most in-depth interviewing that was conducted of German POWs, he noted how the interviewer might also want to consider the personal reliability of the interviewee as a witness, attitudes towards 'last ditch' warfare, and responses to various hypothetical possible outcomes of the conflict. The interview should seek to glean the subject's views of the Allies, idiosyncratic personal concerns, and moral attitudes (for instance, regarding acts of revenge against the civilian population, looting or destruction of property). Other subjects that could usefully be covered included rape, the predicament of people on the home front, the human consequences of air-raids, the status of foreign workers, underground opposition, commitments to social justice, and unemployment. In best practice, interviewers of German POWs would have been interested to discover the individual's assessments of Hitler and other Nazi leaders, to consider what capacity the person showed for tolerating the idea of German war guilt and acknowledging responsibility. How far did the POWs fear ill-treatment, and on what basis? What did they reveal of their frame of mind when entering into discussion of Allied weaponry? How did they relate to the immediate superior officers in their group? Did they participate in squabbles and rivalries? The interviewer, he made clear, had to ask searching questions about the underlying aims of the interview before even approaching the POW. The exercise might do far more than simply establish hard facts; it could also identify the amorphous cluster of beliefs, hopes, and fears that lay below the surface.[35] Interestingly, Lerner considered the wartime surveys that the Allies conducted into German opinion reassuring: there was 'democratic' material to work with; many people, it was argued, could 'recover'.

——•——

Despite the stated enthusiasm of some historians, especially in the United States—such as William Langer—for the application of psychoanalysis, the majority of professional historians on both sides of the Atlantic ignored or actively rejected the work of Freud and his followers, regarding it as irrelevant or inimical to their subject matter. Nor were other psychological models explicitly placed in the foreground or regarded as of vital relevance *in theory* by most Anglo-American historians, although many have implicitly adopted versions of rational-choice theory or models that are reminiscent of behaviourism. In one sense psychological factors receded into the background: in the vast post-war literature that emerged on the Third Reich historians increasingly concerned themselves with the particular structural conditions or systemic features of German society, rather than psychoanalytical accounts of the individual or inquiries into the dynamics of groups. Nonetheless, the various accounts of German social structure that emerged were soon subjected to critique as well, not least because they failed to account for the irrational, subjective dimensions of political allegiance and identification.[36]

Experimental psychology, psychiatry, and psychoanalysis were all regarded for different reasons with considerable suspicion in later twentieth-century historiography. The naive construction of apparently value-free experiments in supposedly neutral laboratory conditions by certain psychologists was much criticized, as were various forms of supposedly apolitical testing of personal ability or intelligence. Meanwhile the claims of psychiatry to be scientific and objective were also reappraised. How far, it was asked, were psychiatric diagnoses and treatments shaped by unacknowledged culturally determined considerations of gender, skin-colour, age, class, or ethnic provenance? Psychoanalysis, it was said, had broadened its observations of the Viennese bourgeoisie *circa* 1900 into an untenable theory of the human condition at large. Each of these disciplines were seen as especially prone to insensitivity regarding the shaping impact of culture, ideology, and socioeconomic forces: the subjectivity of boys and girls, men and women—even the very idea of 'the self'—should not be treated as 'givens'. Instead of assuming that people must always return to the same deep intra-psychic problems, historians were to investigate how the most apparently timeless beliefs or structuring assumptions of life are constituted in and through history itself.

Critique of 'psychologism' came from several quarters. In *Les Mots et les choses* (1966, translated as *The Order of Things*, 1970), Michel Foucault lyrically described 'man' as an historical construction, a figure in the sand who might be washed away. Here he caught and profoundly influenced a sceptical historicist mood regarding the supposed naturalness of the categories of knowledge that organize our experience. Psychoanalysis was in itself a critique of extant psychology and need not, in principle, deny the shaping impact of culture (Dicks, for instance, could not be accused of ignoring the way culture affected personality), but certainly many of its discussions were couched as though it was obvious that minds always in the end struggled with the same 'universal' problems. Thus it was to be frequently criticized for suggesting that the most basic features of identify formation (most notably the negotiation of the Oedipus complex) were timeless: the matter of what, if anything, is simply a shared predicament of being human, across time and place, and what changes through and through remains a matter of debate. Freud was increasingly to be challenged, post-war, for his 'normative' account of the differences between the sexes, the putative clinical inefficacy of his practice, scientific shortcomings of his method, misrepresentations of his own past, self-aggrandizing mythologies, and reputed personal pathologies and hypocrisies. Freudianism was equally vigorously reviewed and criticized for its forays into anthropology, history, religion, and politics.

Some critics complained (not without reason) that although prominent psychoanalytical writers on history, such as Erikson, opened up exciting and important new questions in the 1950s, they encouraged the adoption of simplistic schemas in which adult political attitudes could be derived directly from (inferred) childhood experiences, or complex social processes from the psychic life of any one person. Could the unconscious struggles of Martin Luther really be retrieved from the records, and could this in turn plausibly be used as a basis to interpret key aspects of the Reformation?

Psychoanalysis, according to a variety of later polemics, was insufficiently sensitive to historical differences. Critics had vociferously pointed this out since at least the 1920s, but such debates were reignited in the final decades of the twentieth century. Psychoanalysis was Janus-faced in relation to the idea of the 'normal'. Freud and many of his key followers profoundly challenged the conventional 'Victorian' distinction between the normal and the abnormal person, the sane and the mad, the healthy and the ill, the law-abiding citizen and the criminal. They invited scepticism about such binary terms, and thus many of the shibboleths of organic psychiatry and late-nineteenth century criminology were probed and disturbed by psychoanalysis. But Freudian practitioners also often remained close to that normalizing psychiatry, seeming at times even to lose sight of the interrogative spirit that had marked what was most revolutionary in the talking cure. They could sound, on occasion, morally, politically, and sexually prescriptive, prone to resort to prognostications that now seem highly dubious and suspiciously like the old forensic style of psychiatry from which psychoanalysis had broken away. This can be seen, for instance, in Ernest Jones's general assumption in 1941 that 'Quisling' types were quintessentially homosexual in outlook—what psychoanalyst would want to defend such a claim now?[37]

A distinction between normality and deviance had indeed been too readily assumed by some of the wartime and immediate post-war clinicians; such 'normative' characterizations of sexuality and morality on the one side, and of broad historical development toward 'civilization' on the other, faced overwhelming intellectual challenges. The field of psychiatry became the object of intense political and historical scrutiny in the 1960s and 1970s. Sometimes psychoanalysis was seen as the benign alternative to this 'repressive' psychiatry; at others, it was cast as its accomplice. 'Anti-psychiatry' became a movement, and powerful critics decried not only the stigmatization, institutionalization, and regimentation of the insane, but even the invention of the very categories that 'produce' what we mean by madness, crime, or perversion.

Despite all of this, intellectuals continued to study the Nazi problem as a feature of both history and human psychology at large, and in pursuit of answers they continued to draw upon Freud. David Astor (the editor of the *Observer* newspaper between 1948 and 1975), for example, took a close interest in work that might help post-war societies to learn lessons from the history of Third Reich. The Eichmann trial was one catalyst for his invitation to a group of academics and clinicians to work on such problems throughout the 1960s. Astor had undergone psychoanalytical treatment with Anna Freud and became a champion of the talking cure.[38] Norman Cohn (who directed research on the horrors of the Nazi regime and of fascist, racist, and 'totalitarian' belief systems at large courtesy of the Columbus Trust that Astor created and funded for these purposes) considered him a zealot in this regard: 'He thought the answer [to explaining the Third Reich] had to lie with psychoanalysis....He went so far as to describe Nazi Germany as a study in collective psychopathology. That's absurd. It's a country of 60 million people. They were not all Hitler worshippers.' Cohn nonetheless was also convinced that a kind of Nazi mentality had set in, marked as much, if not more, by a robot-like state of mind as by sadistic wishes and malevolence as such. Like Arendt, Primo Levi, and other influential writers on the psychology of the camps, he described one terrible aspect of this process as the Nazi descent into 'bureaucratic automatism'. He observed: 'Just as you write out your income tax form, so you drive the trains. I don't mean there were no perverts in the concentration camps, where people were beaten to death, but it's amazing how perfectly ordinary people can obey instructions

if they are at a certain distance and not bothered by bureaucratic apparatus.'[39] Under Astor's patronage, Cohn, Dicks, and assorted historians, anthropologists, and clinicians met frequently to discuss the 'potentialities for
murderous destructiveness in members of so-called "advanced" societies'
that are 'close to our own ethically and historically'.[40]

The 1960s and 1970s witnessed a variety of new psycho-historical projects
on both sides of the Atlantic, as well as the rising tide of methodological
doubts.[41] Suffice to say here, regarding debates about the relevance of psychoanalysis within the historical profession, that after the 1960s it was primarily via works on gender and politics that the wheel turned again;
psychoanalysis gained fresh attention, inspired, for example, by innovative
work that linked the sexual and political fantasies of men of the far Right
during the 1920s. During and after the 1970s feminist historians pointed out
how impoverishing the renunciation of any consideration of psychoanalysis
often turned out to be: histories that concern human subjectivity and identity cannot simply jettison the unconscious.[42] And if a task of the historian
is not only to reconstruct what the actors of the past consciously intended,
but also to interpret what they have been *doing* and signifying through their
own actions and communications, historical interpretation may well also
require intellectual tools, such as psychoanalysis, that were unavailable to
those historical agents themselves.[43]

Post-war historians sought to move from abstract political science or
general social psychological models of democratic or authoritarian systems
to the minutiae of the national case: hence, a more complex picture gradually emerged of the myriad factors that marked the rise of Fascism and
Nazism. Moreover, so it has often been argued, it was the particular con-
junctures of politics and economics, social circumstances and ideology, that
came together after 1918 that best served to make sense of the emergence of
Nazism. The psychological aspect was not entirely erased even here; charismatic forms of authority were still acknowledged as an important additional
factor to reckon with, but the mainstay of historical explanation lay elsewhere. If, however, the field of charisma was to be considered by historians,
it was more likely to be in the terms of the great German sociologist Max
Weber than in dialogue with Sigmund Freud and his *Group Psychology and
the Analysis of the Ego* of 1921.

There was far greater scepticism later in the century about claims that it
made sense to speak of German psycho-cultural peculiarities, any more than
it made sense to treat nations as following or failing to follow some presumed

'normal' path to modernity. To be sure, not all historians agreed, immediately
post-war or even in the last decades of the twentieth century, that the notion
of a collective German mindset had been superseded. For example, Daniel
Goldhagen's polemical *Hitler's Willing Executioners* (1996) argued that the
intention to destroy the Jews was especially widespread in the German population long before, as well as during, the Third Reich. This account, along
with the literature of often furious debate and criticism that surrounded its
argument and supporting scholarship, shows, if nothing else, that the issue of
social psychology and the question of German exceptionalism retain the
power to channel the most intense and painful emotions.

Meanwhile, a quite different kind of political literature emerged to
prominence in the 1990s and 2000s, masquerading as sober history, intent
upon the very denial of the worst horrors of this Nazi past, and the rehabilitation of Hitler and other leading Nazis, including Hess, often under the
guise of relativist arguments.[44] A term with a certain psychoanalytic resonance entered common parlance—Holocaust *denial*—except that in this
context (unlike in Freudian use) 'denial' implies a conscious, politically sinister, and calculated rejection of reality.[45]

Madness is not usually a term that respectable historians would now want to
deploy to make sense of complex historical processes.[46] The notion that groups,
even vast numbers, of people may behave in deluded fashion would often be
regarded as a failure of explanation, not an explanation. Historians have sought
the underlying logic and reason of seemingly insane activities, and have attempted
to identify 'the moral economy' that operates even in the most violent and frenzied of crowds. Yet as Ian Kershaw remarks in his outstanding biography of
Hitler, even historians who eschew psychological terms of explanation, and
who are wedded to identifying the social and economic rather than the emotional or indeed unconscious factors that shape the past, have viewed Hitler's
particular character and the enormous allure that the Führer held for so many
people as a limit case for conventional forms of understanding.

———•———

How best (if at all) to make use of psychoanalysis in accounts of Nazism
whilst considering the historically contingent nature of concepts of self or
group will, no doubt, remain a matter of debate, but in some ways it is clear
the pursuit of the Nazi mind was a time-bound model that rose and fell
during the middle decades of the twentieth century. The intellectual context has changed dramatically since the time when Langer, Dicks, and
their colleagues set out to investigate the unconscious minds of Germany's

ruling elite. The categories that a previous generation of human scientists had assumed in discussing such problems—for instance 'the mind', or 'the unconscious', still more 'the normal mind' or 'the healthy self'—came under combined fire. It is worth emphasizing again the important role of Foucault in reshaping this debate. Here Freudianism was a particular object of scrutiny, part of Foucault's genealogy of systems of thought, not the compass for his own methodology. Freud, it seemed, initiated what was only the latest mode of confessional discourse to have afflicted the West. This so-called discovery of the unconscious portended a world in which, as Foucault once put it, people even lend out their ears for hire. Foucault's work was widely discussed, if not necessarily accepted *tout court*, by historians, but either way, it contributed to the view that the endeavour to use psychoanalysis or other psychological approaches to understand key aspects of culture and society, or even the minds of individual people in the past, was an antiquated approach, and categories such as 'the abnormal' should not be reproduced but rather historicized and analysed.

In considering the intellectual offensive against psychologism it is also worth alluding here to the Canadian sociologist Erving Goffman, whose key work on the self, social stigma, and the politics of incarceration was contemporaneous with the early researches of Foucault. Instead of looking 'inside' the self, it was important, Goffman argued, to look at how selves were constructed, and also to focus attention on the dramaturgical roles that social actors are required by convention to play in their dealings with each other. He set out these ideas in an influential book, *The Presentation of Self in Everyday Life* (1956). It was one of several forerunners of the tendency (indeed the vogue) later in the century to explore all aspects of performance in the making of social identities.

Goffman also considered the role of asylums and other 'total institutions' in shaping selfhood. The sociologist's analysis of the modern asylum inmate's 'institutionalization' was linked to still more extreme evidence about the political fashioning of subjects in Third Reich.[47] Goffman, like Foucault, challenged entirely the presumption that 'selves' were the property of the person to whom they were attributed. Each self, Goffman declared, 'occurs within the confines of an institutional system' and within the networks of 'social control'; 'the self dwells in' the system that surveys it; indeed, special kinds of institutional arrangement, such as, *in extremis*, the asylum or the concentration camp, '[do] not so much support the self as constitute it'.[48] Goffman cautioned against analyses that claimed to fathom the 'depths' of the mind; rather, the task was to situate selfhood in the network of social arrangements.

It was probably not by chance that at around the same time Hannah Arendt offered her own challenge to the idea that analysis of deep fantasies and wishes—for instance murderous desires, joy in destruction, seething hatred—necessarily held the answer to explaining the officialdom of the Reich: rather, it seemed, what was most disturbing was the evacuation of the self in a kind of automatism: what was monstrous was the utter superficiality of motivation, even the emptiness inside.[49] Her focus on Adolf Eichmann's banality was to remain highly controversial, but it sought to move attention away from the idea of some mysterious hidden realm that could explain such atrocities. By the last three decades of the century, and despite the appearance of several further avowedly Freudian interpretations of Hitler and his regime, lines of inquiry that laid weight on the unconscious minds of the key historical actors were out of fashion. Challenges to *any* psycho-analytical approach that encroached upon or presumed to interpret the historical past were also commonplace in this period.[50]

The more subtle psychoanalytical accounts, as well as historical and fictionalized biographies of particular Nazis, invite us to speculate about the remote and proximate psychological causes of murderous political practices, without claiming definitively to understand the nature of this critical path. Some psycho-historical literature on the Third Reich, however, problematically assumes in advance that individual events cause much later ideological outcomes, or suggests that evidence of, say, psycho-sexual 'deviance' in childhood or adolescence carries obvious explanatory weight in understanding later 'perverse' political attitudes. The trouble is that the same set of antecedents might well have produced quite different outcomes. This can be seen, for instance, in a study of Himmler in 1971 by the pioneering writer on history and psychoanalysis Peter Loewenberg.[51] This placed considerable emphasis on the notion that Himmler's adolescence followed what Loewenberg took to be an abnormal path, devoid of what we ought to expect: the normal turmoil, colour, and passion of youth. Placing much store on Himmler's juvenile diary, the author suggested that he could be characterized as an incipient schizoid personality, with clear obsessive, compulsive featured which featured in his later career; he cited in support of his thesis Anna Freud's 'important distinction between the usual process of repression and the abnormal phenomenon of asceticism that must be considered psychotic'. Whilst Loewenberg is well versed in historical methodology and his 'diagnosis' of Himmler was suggestive, it would be a mistake to follow him in rushing to any conclusion about causality here. Moreover, since 'asceticism' obviously has had many different cultural (and no doubt psychic) meanings over time, to assume that it constitutes evidence of abnormality and in turn bears upon the political pathology of the particular Nazi subject under investigation begs crucial questions.

Questionable value judgements, in other words, are often embedded in the psychiatric or psychoanalytical approach to this history. And yet, biographers of the Nazis suggest that we cannot but turn to the clinical, pathological vocabulary if we are to find any semblance of explanation. Thus Joachim Fest, amongst the most influential of Hitler's biographers, wrote of the significance and complexity of Hitler's morbid psychic make-up, describing the Führer's 'neurosis', 'nervous breakdown', 'erotic fervour', and fixations, whilst diagnosing his oratorical 'discharges' as 'largely instinctual', a peculiar combination of 'delirium and rationality'. The sound recordings of the period, Fest mused, convey clearly 'the peculiar copulatory character of the mass meetings'. The death of Geli Raubal, he argued, is the event that 'seems to have fixed forever his relationship to the opposite sex, which was curious enough in any case'. [52] For Fest, a mere glance at Hitler was enough to indicate the exceptional pathology beneath: 'criminal features' were written, it seems, upon 'this man's psychopathic face'. [53]

Much historical writing on Nazi Germany remains rife with speculation that is reminiscent of Langer, or at least echoes elements of psychoanalysis and/or psychiatry that were commonplace in the 1940s. Such terms of explanation do not simply disappear, it could be argued, because the idea of the complex, multilayered, conflicted psychic 'interior' is so essential to what we assume by 'the person'—the person, at least, as understood and imagined in our own historical epoch. In that sense it is not surprising to find these features recurring, even though many contemporary historians eschew psycho-history as a methodology and make no reference to Freudian thought. If some insist on Hitler's psychic 'abnormality', others reassert the contrary, declaring with—as Loewenberg puts it—'truly stunning confidence' that he was in fact 'normal'. The German historian Werner Maser, for example, declared '[t]here is no doubt about the fact that Hitler's sexual life was normal'. [54] Either way, discussion of Hitler's sexuality, putative perversions, and unconscious fantasy life remain central features of discussion. The historian Norman Stone returns to this territory, remarking on the pattern that linked Hitler to other Germans of his time, of remote, often absent, irascible, uniformed fathers and crushed dormouse mothers. Hitler, he suggests, was horribly lonely and sexually inexperienced (here he cites Putzi Hanfstaengl's view that the Führer was a 'repressed masturbatory type'). Stone's Hitler was perhaps latently homosexual in orientation, a fuss-pot hypochondriac, a sufferer from hormonal defects that impaired his masculinity, and certainly one of a 'type' that despised whoever accepted him—including, ultimately, the German people. His love of Prussia was 'almost psychotic' and his oratory a 'strange blend of the masculine and feminine'. He took up with the nondescript Eva Braun, who 'looked uncannily like his mother', and was an obsessive hand-washer and insomniac. Stone warned against drawing any deduction from such factors, but also noted that, once in power, 'Hitler acted out his fantasy'. Turning from Hitler's psychopathology to that of the masses, he concluded that the enduring German infatuation with Hitler, after it was clear that the cause was lost and the Führer had 'passed into a world of fantasy', 'defies analysis'.[55]

Another British historian, Andrew Roberts, wonders if Hitler 'might still have been a virgin at thirty-five'.[56] In recounting 'secrets of leadership', he makes large claims not only about Hitler's real nature but also about that of the British Prime Minister who led the war against him; these were, it seems two utterly contrasting inward lives. Roberts states firmly that 'neither envy nor resentment' formed any part of Churchill's nature—a remarkable claim to make about anyone.[57]

Not every historian, to be sure, claims firm 'insider' knowledge of the mindset of the leaders or suggests that the character of totalitarian rulers can somehow be traced back to *and* explained by the psychopathology of the child. In a fine survey of Hitler's Germany and Stalin's Russia, Richard Overy observes that both dictators were closely attached to their mothers and were 'beaten unmercifully by a tyrannical father', before pointing out that in most other respects the two men were quite different.[58] Ian Kershaw is equally, if not more, wary of over-exuberant psychological speculation and alert to the shortcomings of applied psychoanalysis in some previous accounts of his subject. He provides careful explorations of Hitler's development and avoids any claim to have grasped the totality or found the secret psychological key. Nonetheless, in his bid to bring the protagonist alive Kershaw also speculates creatively about his hidden emotional states and relies upon various terms that are freighted with psychiatric and/or psychoanalytic connotations.

In the face of the murder/suicide of Geli, Hitler, Kershaw notes, succumbed to a 'near hysterical state' before falling into a 'depression'.[59]

Elsewhere he refers to the astonishing 'grandiosity of [the leader's] fantasy'.[60] He describes well Hitler's prostration following his mother's death from breast cancer,[61] and shows how the young man floated around 'in an egoistic fantasy-world' in Vienna.[62] Kershaw also probes the 'phobia' that the Führer developed, in relation to Vienna and how it contrasted with his love of Munich, where he was based for fifteen months before the Great War and then again after it. Munich was for Hitler a properly *German* city; in contrast, Vienna was a Babylon of races.[63]

Kershaw evokes the sexual underworld of Vienna and the erotized way in which Hitler perceived the city that became a source of both disturbance and excitement to him. The 'city' becomes an active player in the story of the developing self; an outside world shot through with fantasies and myths which in turn are shown to influence Hitler as he moves unhappily through it. Kershaw examines the interaction of self, city and culture, demonstrating how the subject's mind is influenced by the urban environment (its underworlds, squalor, dark recesses, horrors), even as the psyche imbues these spaces and experiences with its own particular obsessions and beliefs. Rarely though, in a manner reminiscent of an earlier generation of psychobiographers, even he can be found making categorical statements about feelings or hidden behaviour that can only be entirely conjectural; suggesting, for example, that Hitler at a certain stage abstained from masturbation. This seems to be based on a report of Hitler's early friend August Kubizek, but while such indirect testimony might establish that a person did something, it can hardly be taken as firm evidence for what he did or did *not* do behind closed doors.[64]

One more observation about shared psychobiographical assumptions: it is now commonplace in the literature to show how anti-Semitism worked like a kind of cancer unconsciously inside Hitler's mind. Its metastases are to be seen across his thought and policies, and throughout Nazi ideology as a whole. Langer was a forerunner in this regard, describing how the Führer was haunted throughout by the Jewish question and showing how he would twist his relentless aggressive attacks upon the Jews into the claim that what was proposed was a *defence* against pollution, corruption, and above all against envious and aggressive attacks upon the Aryan race. The 'Jew' was the phantasmagorical figure haunting the Nazi mind. Once freed of restraint this montrous imagined object would cause havoc: thus Himmler would invite an audience to think of the damage Jews would inflict if they were ever let off the hook.[65] Jewish children too had to be destroyed so they would not become avengers of the future.[66] The Jews, Hitler wrote, would put 'insane plans' into effect, if given the chance.[67] The manipulation of public opinion through propaganda was justified, it was argued, because otherwise the Jews would accomplish their world conspiracy, poisoning the minds of gullible Germans through their own supposed control of radio and the other public media.[68]

Fascism and Nazism signify political movements and ideologies, but 'fascist' and 'Nazi' also serve as metaphors for (or sometimes as insults to describe) certain pernicious states of mind and group process. Post-war, the term 'little Hitler', for example, became a common figure of speech for authoritarian qualities in people who might have had no sympathy with Nazism itself, and 'fascist pig' became a generalized term of abuse on the Left. Fascists and 'little Hitlers' lurked in unlikely places. Meanwhile, invented tales of Hitler's interior thoughts (as a child and as an adult) complemented occasional news reports of actual embedded Nazis in Europe, the Americas, or elsewhere. For example, George Steiner's controversial novella *The Portage to San Cristobal of A.H.* (1981) presented a Führer finally captured in his hideout in Latin America. Put on trial by his captors, Hitler defends his anti-Semitism as being inspired by the Jews' own sense of themselves as chosen: 'My racism was a parody of yours, a hungry imitation.'[69] According to Steiner's Hitler, the Jews' own 'bacillus of perfection' 'infected our blood and brains'.[70]

More recently, a novel by the young Franco-American writer Jonathan Littell, *Les Bienveillants* ('The Kindly Ones', 2006), explores the mind of an SS officer, Max Aue, who after years in hiding speaks about his involvement in the Russian campaign and his role as an official in Albert Speer's ministry making more productive use of concentration-camp inmates in industrial and arms production. The narrative assumes the relevance of the subject's unconscious motives: his sexual confessions and masturbatory fantasies are juxtaposed with his revelations of murderous actions, cynical indifference, and brutal political outlook. Writing of an earlier *succès de scandal*, D. M. Thomas's *The White Hotel* (1981), that similarly juxtaposed sexualized narratives and graphic descriptions of the mass murder of the Jews, cultural critic Susanne Kappeler coined the phrase 'the pornography of representation'.[71] The novelists' counter-argument might be that the aim of such narratives, through their very excess, is to discomfort and subvert our assumptions, drawing us into the intimate workings of a Nazi mind, or at least into those workings as conceptualized in the psychiatric and psychoanalytical literature. The interior life that is presented invites a psycho-analytical reading; it is replete with evidence of an elaborate defensive psychic structure that enables the Nazi subject to repudiate guilt and shame, to give an appearance of utter moral indifference, ennui, emptiness, and yet also stupendous officious 'zeal'. According to Klaus Theweleit, author of the controversial work *Male Fantasies*, 'Littell has extracted hundreds of personality traits from the biographies and literature on this kind of man in order to stitch them together into Aue'. He is a composite, a figure that bundles together countless received images, indeed, 'the greatest number of traits of "the Germans"'.[72] How far such novels and other works dealing with Nazi relationships (the controversial film *The Night Porter* (1974) would be another case in point) use scenes of tormented sexual activity or sadistic fantasy for prurient and exploitative purposes of their own is always open to question.[73]

———•———

Two distinct currents of thought ran through the Allied literature on the Nazi mind of the 1940s. Psychoanalysis was deployed in order to gain some insight into the precise nature of the enemy mentality that the Allies faced, but it also encouraged discussion of a more general 'Nazi' potential. Meanwhile, historians and journalists also complicated the picture: if the tendency of much of the research was to underscore the *differences* between the thought-worlds, emotional tendencies, and conduct of individual people on the warring sides (first the Allies and the Axis powers, then the Cold War superpowers), other reports and interpretations came to suggest certain discomforting *affinities*, if not necessarily equivalences.

Studies of the history of eugenic thought in a number of European countries, the United States, and elsewhere, for example, invited comparison with the particular German case. Although policies varied from country to country, certain of the core ideas regarding the dangers of reproduction by 'degenerates', 'the unfit', the 'feeble-minded', and so forth proved to have been widely shared. How far social Darwinism and eugenics in Germany had an especially sinister aspect, well before 1933 has been extensively debated. To equate any other racial discourse or set of political acts with the Nazis' responsibility for the Shoah, however, was to break a taboo; for this has always remained for very many people, above all for many Jewish people, a catastrophe of the twentieth century of unique significance and scale. If it was thought to be clear evidence of anything it was of a recalcitrant, or perhaps even ancient anti-Semitism colliding with modern means of destruction. Even to enter into comparison between these and other events proved problematic. Nonetheless renewed historical attention post-war to earlier gross atrocities, for instance, the vast massacres of Armenian people in the Ottoman Empire during the First World War, complicated the group-psychological representation that had sometimes prevailed in which Nazi evil and the Final Solution were isolated entirely from other historical tragedies.

For Hannah Arendt, one of the most widely discussed commentators to reflect upon the meaning of Nazism, it was ultimately not the German question but the trajectory of modern history, in all its brutal imperial aspects, that was cast into stark relief by the barbarism of the 1940s. Whilst some witnesses at the Nuremberg trial and elsewhere were quick to con-clude either that they had faced a gaggle of freakish madmen and sadists, or characteristic 'types' of Germans, others—more unnervingly and ultimately more importantly—suggested that what had to be understood was what a 'normal' human being is capable of thinking and of doing under certain historical conditions.

The post-war psychological literature on Nazism frequently split, not only between geographically limited accounts and broader reflections on modernity or the 'human condition', but also between two different psy-chological images. Some accounts stressed the massive, willed cruelty and destructiveness that produced Nazism; others emphasized mental states akin to robot-like blankness—although it could be argued that such states are not mutually exclusive, or even that so-called blankness and moral insensi-bility act as camouflage, masking the real hatred and enjoyment of that hatred beneath. Arguments regarding Nazism's bureaucratic mentality proved particularly influential in the case of Adolf Eichmann, and it is worth looking at the role of Gustave Gilbert as witness and authority at Eichmann's trial (1961–2) in Jerusalem, which revealed, among other things, the scepti-cism of at least some senior judges as to the relevance of the psychological specialist and the possibility of scientific classification of pathological polit-ical types. At the time of the trial Gilbert was a professor of psychology in Long Island, New York, and author of several influential texts, notably *The Psychology of Dictatorship*.

During the trial Eichmann sat awaiting judgment for his substantial role in the genocide of the Jews in a specially constructed glass booth. This structure protected him from physical attack but also marked out his juridical and psy-chological isolation, or even—as implied by the prosecuting lawyer at one point—his status as specimen of the unnatural. Since the presiding judge rejected the arguments of the counsel for the defence that the psychologist's recollections of his conversations with Nuremberg prisoners fifteen years earlier were mere hearsay, the court thus took note of Gilbert's evidence when he recalled what Göring and others had said about Eichmann, evidence which emphasized his senior role in the administration of 'the Final Solution'.

The judge made a distinction, though, between Gilbert's recollections and his more abstract speculations.[74] It was Gideon Hausner, the Israeli attorney-general and chief prosecutor, who invited Gilbert to brief the court about the Nazi personality type. Gilbert had come to the view that such functionaries as Eichmann were best understood not as atavistic savages but as mechanical executioners, possessed of inhuman personalities. The idea that the Germans had a machine-like mentality was not new,[75] but the notion of psychic 'mechanization' was powerfully reinforced in the political inquiries of this period. Either the idea of the ordinarily human now had to be enlarged to take account of such features, or the perpetrators had to be cast outside the discourse of the normal, and seen as being devoid of what we call 'our' nature.

With Gilbert on the witness stand, Hausner mused: 'The question is: How can it be that a man born of woman can perform these acts? . . . I know that I, and possibly many others, have been looking at this glass cage for the past six weeks and asking myself the question: How could this have happened from the point of view of the man himself?'[76] If 'this man' was a rare *type*, then it made a certain sense to ask Gilbert, as an officially certified expert on the subject, to explain it. But the judge was decidedly wary of this approach, noting that although this may be 'a very interesting psychological question', it was less clear that it was relevant to the matter at hand. As Laurence Douglas observes in his recent study of the Holocaust trials: 'in refusing to admit Gilbert's theory of SS character, the court added an important new twist to its efforts to conventionalize the extraordinary trial'. The judge voiced doubts about the utility—in this setting, at least—of such abstract and definitive scientific answers as to the psychology of the perpetrators and 'impossible horrors of the Holocaust', or at least of regarding them as admissible evidence.[77]

The meaning of the Eichmann trial was framed for many people by Arendt's remarkable reportage. She sat through a number of weeks of the hearings and wrote about the experience in her articles for the *New Yorker*.[78] Although Arendt insisted that such courts should not be transformed into laboratories or educational events—they should simply administer justice— others heralded both Nuremberg *and* the Eichmann sequel as (in the words of one eye witness) 'the greatest history lesson in the history of the world'.[79] Arendt dryly noted how several psychiatrists who had examined Eichmann before his trial had declared him 'normal': 'More normal, at any rate than I am after having examined him', one of the doctors was said to have remarked. Another psychiatrist found Eichmann's whole psychological outlook, his attitude toward his family and friends, 'not only normal but most desirable'.[80] Apparently he was not 'morally or legally insane'. Arendt was interested in how Eichmann was at such pains to insist that he had retained his moral compass:

> he was perfectly sure that he was not what he called an *innerer Schweinehund*, a dirty bastard in the depths of his heart; and as for his conscience, he remembered perfectly well that he would have had a bad conscience only if he had not done what he had been ordered to do—to ship millions of men, women, and children to their death with great zeal and the most meticulous care.[81]

Arendt's courtroom portrait of that quintessentially obedient Holocaust 'manager' became a classic, an indispensable starting-point of discussion. She described how such automatic propitiation of rules and regulations (of 'authority', however mad) can become the governing condition of the mind, even where external conditions cannot explain it. In short, external tyranny or the social conditions of terror should never be underestimated; but, according to this line of thought, nor should the fact that many people like it that way. Historians have frequently pointed out that those in the killing squads of the SS and other deadly organizations did usually have the chance to opt out and be transferred to services elsewhere, without major punishment. This has complicated debate about the normal and the abnormal, suggesting, for instance, that many unexceptional people did heinous things in the murderous Nazi process for rather 'ordinary' reasons: thus Christopher Browning's important research on one particular band of killers was entitled *Ordinary Men: Reserve Police Battalion 101 and the Final Solution in Poland* (1992). Browning suggested that group ties and loyalties, passive acquiescence, cooperation, and obedience to the higher command (however outrageous) may have been more evident than deeper and more active murderous desires in the particular battalion that he studied. His account tells us much more about what these men consciously declared and felt, or what they knew themselves to want, than about what they may unconsciously have sought to do—the question that, in the particular setting of the consulting-room, psychoanalysis would seek to explore.

At Eichmann's trial there was detailed discussion of his options during the war. The prosecutors convincingly argued that the official did have a choice: he could have desisted from his key role in orchestrating the logistics of the camps, should he have so wished. For Arendt, the phrase 'banality of evil' was not intended to suggest that the outcomes of Nazism were mundane (far from it), but that the operations of conscience, empathy, and imagination that might produce even a modicum of doubt and conflict in the subject had been almost entirely snuffed out. It was the 'satisfactory' completion of duties and tasks, it seemed, that Eichmann was concerned about, however insane and obscene they may have been. How far this psychic state accurately characterized Eichmann and, if so, how common it may be, have been much debated since. Psychological experiments, such as those conducted by Stanley Milgram (also in the early 1960s), drew many to the stark conclusion that people's willingness to perform tasks, regardless of the cruelty of the outcome, in total obedience to the edict of the master was a widespread phenomenon.

Milgram showed what could occur when volunteers (assembled at Yale University, not some denazification centre or psychiatric clinic in Germany) were asked to participate in certain 'educational' tests. According to this researcher, the majority of the participants acquiesced knowingly (albeit to varying degrees) in the torture of a human guinea-pig so long as they were told to do so by a convincing and commanding power in the wings. The volunteers did not know that an actor played the role of the tortured subject. The experimental interest lay in seeing what most, if not all, people proved capable of doing voluntarily, regardless of the pain and devastation inflicted on the victim. A particular inspiration to Milgram was the ingenious experimental work that had been conducted before the war by Kurt Lewin, such as his study of 'democratic' and 'authoritarian' styles of leadership in boys' clubs in Iowa, which showed how the latter approach eroded the capacity of group members to think.[82] Milgram referred to the Third Reich and mentioned Dicks and Freud (as well as Arendt) approvingly in the published book-length version of his research, *Obedience to Authority* (1974). However, he did not make a sustained attempt to integrate his experimental work with the language of psychoanalysis.[83] Milgram was more interested in the impact of social factors, the consequences of particular situations on decision-making, than in 'the internal world'. Some people have reinterpreted Milgram's experiments, suggesting that they demonstrated unconscious aggression rather than simply rote obedience. In other words, the appearance of the accomplice's mere compliance with official instructions might well disguise more active wishes to dominate, control, and/or to hurt; according to Freud, after all, there are aggressive and destructive wishes inside us that continually press for release, held in check because society and the 'moral' order that is installed within us (usually) impose certain constraints.[84]

Either way, the mentality of Milgram's volunteers, who were for the most part so willing to please the authorities that provided the instructions, was not to be understood as the *state of exception* to some norm, but as an extreme instance of more regular (and parlous) human propensities.[85] Milgram's work was to stimulate further research, for instance the well-known prison experiment by his friend, the Stanford psychologist Philip Zimbardo, in 1971. In this case, volunteers were assigned roles as guard and prisoners. The sadistic actions of the former and desperation of the latter became so extreme that the planned fortnight-long experiment had to be curtailed.[86]

Following psychoanalytical wartime experiments, new contexts emerged in the second half of the century in which participant-observers could study the impact of groups, as well as gain therapeutic treatment within them. The aims were not always directly therapeutic; sometimes they were more loosely educational and instructive. At the Tavistock Institute of Human Relations (an offshoot of the Tavistock Clinic that emerged soon after the war and went on to become a distinct enterprise), a mini-industry of writing and research was set in motion. It relied on soft funding from various philanthropic institutions and increasingly from commercial sponsors. The fact that, at the outset, the Institute's key funders included the American-based Rockefeller Foundation gives an indication of the traffic of ideas, not just grants, across the Atlantic. Psychoanalysis was not the only inspiration for this work; other influences were also apparent, notably the social psychological experiments that had been conducted in America in the 1930s and 1940s by Kurt Lewin. Through his influence a new development, the National Training Laboratories, emerged in the United States in 1947. Lewin died the same year, but under the direction of other psychologists, the NTL's work continued. Originally based in Maine, these experimental laboratories in human behaviour soon spread elsewhere, and a number of links were established between psychologists at NTL and researchers at the Tavistock Institute.[87]

Among the best-known examples of such investigations of groups were the celebrated 'Leicester Conferences'. Inspired, *inter alia*, by Freud, Klein, and Bion, and guided by staff from the Tavistock Institute, this annual residential event (initiated in 1957 and still continuing) allows participants to work together and observe what happens in the large and small group formations that comprise the conference. The procedure is structured up to a point. There are specific configurations of the participants into sub-groups, large gatherings, and inter-group meetings; 'consultants' are present to observe and occasionally interpret the process; clear boundaries mark the start and end of proceedings. Nonetheless, these are experimental situations, opportunities for the emergence of unexpected feelings and communications. Among the more common findings has been the very powerful nature of the anxieties that are stirred up when there is no clear authority dictating the rules or the task. This kind of work drew inspiration from, but also radically extended, the group experiments of the 1940s at Northfield and the pioneering approaches to army officer selection that were described earlier in this book. Psychoanalysis has also made a major postwar contribution to understanding how intense anxieties, feelings of indifference and despair, and even at times the most callous and sadistic wishes, may be managed, split, denied, and amplified in the modern workplace, not least within the organization of health services themselves.

———•———

No national borders could entirely isolate *their* psychic propensity to barbarism from *ours*; something like Nazism might be commonplace in 'us': this thought has always had to be balanced against the fact that there is no equivalent of, or precedent for, Auschwitz. Even so, revelations of the scale of atrocities systematically committed within various other modern states and in conflicts around the globe (including, of course the numerous actions undertaken in violation of international law by the victorious powers that shaped the post-war order) make it harder to regard such systemic policies and practices of inhumanity as entirely foreign or as transient. Evidently modern, leading democratic governments, not just old totalitarian regimes, violate with alarming frequency, and too often with utter impunity, the boundaries of the permissible, at least the permissible as understood in key international laws, treaties, and conventions after 1945.[88]

We must be wary, in considering what the Nazis did to their victims, either of treating the Third Reich as a phenomenon entirely apart from the rest of history, or conversely of making untenable moral equivalences between the conduct and ideology of all modern states. Nonetheless, there has been no shortage of evidence of heinous crimes of war committed by other powers. The rationale of the strategies that were used within the Allied war with the

Axis powers has not been exempt from tough scrutiny. Above all, the fateful decisions to drop atomic bombs on Japan have been frequently questioned in terms of their morality, regardless of their efficacy. Historians also debate how far the policies that laid waste to the German cities were justified on military grounds alone, or how far they constituted by the last year of the war something closer to acts of vengeance and collective retribution.

In post-war thought Nazism increasingly came to connote a possible psychic danger everywhere, not just the specific ideology that triumphed (in specific historical conditions) in inter-war Germany. Erik Erikson warned in 1950 that 'it is our task to recognise the black miracle of Nazism was only the German version—superbly planned and superbly bungled—of a universal contemporary potential. The trend persists: Hitler's ghost is counting on it.'[89] This was a curious juxtaposition, to say the least. Erikson evokes the ghost of Hitler, whilst envisaging the Nazism he led as a mixture of masterful efficacy and total hopelessness and folly, all at the same time. Erich Fromm went further than Erikson in insisting on the pervasiveness of the Nazi mind. In *The Anatomy of Human Destructiveness* he declared: 'There are thousands of Himmlers living among us.' He made the case again for developing what he called the field of 'characterological studies' in order to learn more about the exterminatory logic that is so easily accepted, or at least to which such indifference is shown. This was needed because 'the potential Himmler looks like anybody else, except to those who have learned to read character and who do not have to wait until circumstances permit the "monster" to show his colors'.[90] He might have gone further still by asking whether anyone was entirely free of Hitlers and Himmlers 'within'.

Hans Askenasy, a German psychologist writing in the 1970s, placed various Western and Soviet military atrocities alongside revelations about the Third Reich and asked still more bluntly, *Are We All Nazis?*[91] This was a deliberately challenging and uncomfortable essay on psycho-politics, but a similar argument was to be the basis of the maverick Marxist lawyer Jacques Vergès's controversial argument for the defence in the case of Klaus Barbie, the notorious Gestapo chief in Lyon, who was put on trial in France in the 1980s. Vergès's tactic was not so much to deny the defendant's vile war crimes as to generalize them into the common practice of the great powers: 'they were of a kind', as one historian explains the lawyer's position, 'with the normal excesses of war'.[92] Hence myriad activities by other Western powers that claimed to be democratic and liberal in spirit were all, for Vergès, akin to the actions of the Nazis.[93] Barbie was sentenced to life imprisonment and died in 1991, but not before the argument was put to the court that the involvement of so many Frenchmen in the type of crimes attributed to the prisoner might make the fact of his singling out hypocritical.[94]

What is apparent in many recent responses is how the *cordon sanitaire* that held Nazi pathology apart from the rest of history has slipped. Some writers now invite us to share this thought experiment: imagine there was nothing in Bormann's, Himmler's, or Eichmann's inner worlds that could sufficiently differentiate them from those of innumerable other people who, in different circumstances, carried out their activities without grave political consequence or who at least came, serendipitously, to be constrained by other factors. Seen from this angle, could it be that 'moral luck' rather than stupendous abnormality in the make-up of the personnel might explain the drastic differences of outcome?[95] Despite this argument, there is a striking tendency to make exceptions—of Himmler perhaps or, all the more, Heydrich—as though we require psychological and moral categories that differentiate the true abnormal monsters and must place them in a category apart even from the rest of the terrible war criminals.

The acts were monstrous to be sure, but suppose that after all the horrific circumstances are charted, all the documents read, all the deciphering work completed, we are left with no satisfactory psycho-social explanation, but just 'radical evil' in all its monstrosity? Yet to leave it there would also be problematic and glib: Nazism should not be somehow placed beyond analysis, exempted from the reach of the human sciences, or excluded on principle from historical and psychological comparison as though it constitutes some ultimate, transcendent mystery.

There is no comfortable, settled intellectual position that one could safely adopt in relation to the psychological endeavour to track Nazi states of mind; if there is something too reassuring, even crass, in all the wartime profiling of Hitler and his acolytes as special cases, the opposite path may also lead to mystification: the Nazis become banal, 'ordinary', a mere product of 'the age', the empty recipients of historical discourse. Still less acceptable is the road that presents this history as a necessarily inaccessible 'traumatic' terminus of the modern age. Here the psychological process at stake for the perpetrator is disregarded, but in a kind of homage to the mystery—Nazi motivation as the point that can never *begin* to be explained. Here it easily becomes the embodiment of metaphysical horror. As Primo Levi, one of the victims, suggested, Auschwitz defies 'understanding', or at

least understanding in terms of the culprits' rationality. Yet he also rejected
the idea that the perpetrators could be categorized, for the most part, as
abnormal, especially sadistic, individuals.[96] To eschew all temptation of
understanding this human history, or rather the human elements of this
history, for fear of falling short is no less questionable than the claim to have
encompassed the meanings of that history through psychoanalysis, economics, ideological critique, or any other frame of reference.

Rather than thinking of the mentality of the Allies and the 'incurable'
Germans as being in a binary opposition, post-war human scientists, in fact,
often stressed how actively 'fascistic' wishes as well as automaton-like obedient attitudes may reside to be exploited anywhere, in particular circumstances. This, again, need not mean the equation of actual political outcomes
in post-war history (which would be fatuous) but would involve recognition of the constant potential for such crimes to be enacted. It would then
entail exploring what social, civic, psychological, or other structures contain and modify such (perhaps ubiquitous) propensities in human groups.

Perhaps no other modern political phenomenon has been so widely
studied by clinicians or possessed the same imaginative purchase upon psychoanalysts as Nazism. The meaning that Hitler possessed in post-war
Germany itself was taken up in numerous ways. A landmark here was the
Mitscherlichs' book *The Inability to Mourn*, which appeared in 1967. Massive
denial and failed mourning for the once-beloved Hitler were key terms of
their analysis of the common response of the German people. The enormous post-war shame and opprobrium that was attached to Hitler meant
that the German people's love of the Führer and ensuing sense of loss was
never worked through.[97] Their work led to extensive debate in Germany
and has remained influential, a point of reference for many historians and
social theorists.[98] Substantial psychoanalytical attention has also been paid,
of course, to the massive psychological damage that was wrought upon surviving victims of the camps and their descendants.[99]

———•———

Although, post-war, a number of psychoanalytic writers directly addressed
the history of Nazism there were also indirect connections and affinities
between many other clinical papers and discourse on the psychopathology
of the Third Reich. Take the example of New York psychoanalyst Phyllis
Greenacre's paper of 1958, 'The Impostor'. The most immediate context for
this work had nothing to do with the politics of fascism in Europe but
rather concerned Greenacre's first-hand experience of a disturbing cover-

up that had taken place during the 1920s of the work of an insane mental-asylum director much closer to home, the psychiatrist Henry Cotton, superintendent of the Trenton State Hospital in New Jersey. He had become obsessed by an unproven theory that certain pus-producing infections damaged the brain, leading to madness, and that the patients in question required surgery. Convinced that he had uncovered the single source of psychosis, Cotton undertook invasive and entirely unnecessary operations on many people. His patients suffered the consequences for years; substantial numbers were maimed or died under the knife. Despite the controversial nature of this treatment—Greenacre had at the time written a critical report on Cotton's methods—investigation into the matter proceeded at glacial pace, hampered by the reluctance of senior colleagues to face what was happening, let alone stop Cotton's outrageous experimental practices.[100]

Henry Cotton was not named in this paper on imposters, but his work had so disturbed Phyllis Greenacre that we may well detect its presence in her essay. One might say the same with regard to Hitler, who is also arguably so present in his absence in this account. In fact Greenacre presented a number of other historical examples as well as vignettes from the consulting-room in the course of the paper. 'In some of the most celebrated instances of imposture,' she wrote, 'it indeed appears that the fraud was successful only because many others as well as the perpetrator had a hunger to believe in the fraud, and that any success of such fraudulence depended in fact on strong social as well as individual factors and a special receptivity to the trickery.' She considered how far fraudulence sometimes only works because the victims of the fraud are in effect 'unconscious conspirators'. The success of imposture, she added, 'is partly a matter of timing'. 'Such combinations of imposturous talent and a peculiar susceptibility of the times to believe in the swindler, who presents the deceptive means of salvation, may account for the great impostures of history.' Among the basic constellations of symptoms that mark the true impostor, Greenacre surmised, are an active family romance, in which, in fantasy, the subject belongs to a 'high'-birth family, not to the lowly so-called parents; second, an intense and circumscribed disturbance of the sense of identity and a serious distortion of reality; 'third, a malformation of the superego involving both conscience and ideals'.[101] The correspondences between this schema and events in Nazi Germany are suggestive.

The history of the Nazis weighed heavily for many post-war psychoanalytical writers, not only for those who had fought against the Reich and/or fled from Germany. Whatever the impetus for new directions in psycho-analysis after 1945, it is striking how often the historical investigation of Nazi ideology on the one hand and clinical ideas of psychopathology on the other converged. The point here is not that there was always a direct causal relationship in which post-war literature on the Third Reich can be shown to have led to a transformation in the substance of psychoanalytical discourse. Rather, it could be said, clinical writings that emerged on severe narcissistic disorders, paranoid psychosis, borderline personality disorders, perversion, and so forth have at times powerfully resonated with the polit-ical literature of the time. Nazism and the camps cropped up in post-war theoretical discussion, but a sense of the history was registered in other ways too, not least in reports of patients' material.

The Kleinian psychoanalyst Hanna Segal has recalled, in explaining her ideas about sadism and the death drive, the moment when a patient turned towards her and said coolly that people like her should be put in a gas chamber.[102] In a paper on 'Cruelty and Narrow-Mindedness' (1970), Eric Brenman described his work with a woman patient in which it seemed as though 'inhuman' states of mind were the only ones possible. The patient expected the analyst to view her with a kind of merciless perception and tended to view him in the same way.[103] She was described as an East European refugee whose family had fallen victim to the Nazis. Gradually some change in the patient's outlook was effected, but not before many sessions had elapsed in which the atmosphere in the room seemed to approximate to the intolerant, brutal, tyrannical, and omnipotent attitudes that were in turn so redolent of Hitler's regime that had destroyed her par-ents.[104] In a related vein, another British psychoanalyst Robin Anderson wrote a paper (entitled 'Putting the Boot In') describing a depressed and isolated patient who lived in a pitiless, perverse, and violent world of fan-tasy, and whose fetish for boots was linked to 'very powerful men like Hitler and the Nazis, Stalin, Saddam Hussein; and sometimes less obviously tyrannical figures like policemen, soldiers, horse-riders, or motorcyclists'.[105] Across the Atlantic, Otto Kernberg wrote in a different idiom of a clinical situation he faced in which a patient was governed by extreme and relent-less pathological hatred. No surprise that here again the analysand revealed dreams of a sadistic world of mass murders and concentration-camp guards.[106] The point is not that such states of mind are confined to those who suffered under the Nazis. Rather, these writers suggest how the patient brings his or her inner world, with all its tangled history, to the session; in the analysis many fragments of the past (infused with the patient's own unconscious fantasies and current purposes) are played out—'relived'— and hopefully also modified in the course of the treatment.

How far such rigid 'authoritarian' modes of functioning are required by certain people in order to fend off full-blown psychotic or depressive breakdown is a moot point. Rather than thinking of single defences that are constructed against the awareness of painful feelings, an influential trend since the Second World War has been to explore whole clusters of defences, or as they are now sometimes called, 'pathological organizations' of the mind. Here the patient functions within an elaborate internal economy of unconscious beliefs that save (or at least are somehow imagined to protect) the self from pain and horror, but that also have been likened to the grip that a criminal organization holds over a captive society. However destructive and constricting they may be, in the emotional life of the patient they may serve, as psychoanalyst John Steiner has put it, as 'psychic retreats'; that is to say, they serve a crucial function, offering a kind of shelter in which the self can operate and survive, albeit massively impaired.[107]

Steiner's various rich accounts of pathological organizations drew on earlier work, crucially by the late Herbert Rosenfeld, an influential figure within the British Psychoanalytical Society. Rosenfeld had studied medicine in Germany (his MD thesis examined the problems of multiple absences in the lives of children) but was forced to leave the country because of Hitler's rise to power. He managed to move to Britain during the 1930s, where he trained as a psychotherapist at the Tavistock Clinic and then as a psychoanalyst in private practice. Rosenfeld also worked in mental hospitals, including the Maudsley. In addition, he and some of his colleagues expressed the ambition to treat long-stay psychotic patients in hospitals directly by means of the talking cure.[108] Encouraged by Melanie Klein, Rosenfeld, in parallel with Bion and Segal (among others), pursed this line of thought boldly in the post-war years. Although he was later self-critical of his own approach, noting the naive and idealistic aspects of his early therapeutic endeavours, such work was an important new venture: the psychoses, it seemed, could now not only be understood but also be treated via psychoanalysis, something Freud himself had doubted.

Such innovative work generated much excitement and hope and led to new theoretical formulations, although the enormous difficulties and sometimes failure of psychoanalysis in such cases also led to renewed debate about the limits of therapy. The nature of the superego in its most disturbing and destructive forms has been a particular area of focus. Here Bion's work also proved especially influential: he considered how, in certain instances, the superego might serve to destroy, rather than to judge, the ego, leading to drastic fragmentation in the mind. This 'ego-destructive superego', he surmised, might stem in part from constitutional factors in the individual, but also reflected problems that had emerged in the earliest relationship of the baby and mother: if the latter was incapable of 'taking in' (and thus modifying) the raw terrors experienced by the baby or infant, then the nature of the superego would be duly affected: the mother that was 'taken back' inside the mind of the child might well be experienced as part of the hostile, implacable, impenetrable, and murderous superego, rather than as the helpful force that served to reshape it into a more benign form, or at least to help the ego cope with it. 'In pathological development', according to a recent account of the Kleinian approach, 'the early severe superego does not become modified'; in extreme cases, the superego is characterized by 'terrifying and idealised defused aspects of the primary objects', 'and banished into an area of [the] deep unconscious'.[109]

Meanwhile, problems relating to the superego within the psychoanalytical encounter also led to new scrutiny of psychoanalytical institutions in the second half of the twentieth century. Several important studies not only charted flagrant abuses of power that have sometimes occurred in the psychoanalytical setting, but also the manner in which training schemes have tended to encourage timid, subservient attitudes to authority and power to flourish. One symptom might be the tendency of psychoanalytical candidates anxiously to ape the views and mores of their elders (and for the elders subtly to encourage such conformism), rather than to sift, learn, and develop in more independent and questioning fashion. It has sometimes been said that innovation and critique are hampered by the very structures of allegiance fostered by training. Much of the process, as Freudian theory would lead one to expect, is unconscious.[110] The compelling nature and painful ironies of Jacques Lacan's endeavours to prevent the ossification of hierarchy and power inside the psychoanalytical organizations that he built up—and then disbanded—in France have been especially closely examined in these terms.[111]

No doubt problems regarding authority and authoritarianism in the psychoanalytic movement and its consulting-rooms—problems that have haunted psychoanalysis throughout its history—are apparent and even systematic in countless other professional organizations and practices too. But psychoanalysis, by definition, invites heightened interest in how such processes occur, so it is of interest that these problems persist in the very psychoanalytical societies that explore these issues. The danger of despotic mastery of hearts and minds, or conversely, of the will of 'the mass' to allow itself to be enchanted by charismatic, dictatorial certainty has been a theme in psychoanalytical theory for many years. Where does creative and helpful loyalty and passionate commitment tip over into masochistic and subservient 'blind' allegiance, including messianic faith in the cause of psychoanalysis? How far can a leader resist the pressure from self or others to enact the role of the omnipotent saviour? Such concerns are evident enough already in many of Freud's own writings, including in his last major and still-debated work of the 1930s, *Moses and Monotheism*, in which he wrote:

> We know that in the mass of mankind there is a powerful need for an authority who can be admired, before whom one bows down, by whom one is ruled and perhaps even ill-treated. We have learnt from the psychology of individual men what the origin is of this need of the masses. It is a longing for the father felt by everyone from his childhood onwards, for the same father whom the hero of legend boasts he has overcome. And now it may begin to dawn on us that all the characteristics with which we equipped the great man are paternal characteristics, and that the essence of great men for which we vainly searched lies in this conformity.[112]

Freud once spoke of the aims of psychoanalysis as enabling the patient to love and to work. The talking cure seeks to free up thought through the extraordinary—indeed unique—setting it provides. In more recent parlance, the encounter tends to be conceptualized above all in terms of the constant shifts that occur 'here and now'. Thus the primary focus is placed upon what goes on and is enacted in the consulting-room; this is used to understand the patient's own shifting states of mind. But throughout the twentieth century it was clear that the space of the analytic session created a radical new opportunity for the close and detailed investigation of what goes on unconsciously when two people talk and listen to—or fail to hear— each other; it is no surprise, then, that this strange and asymmetrical two-person setting was to become an inspiration for various kinds of social and political application, as has been shown in this book.

Freud remarked in a very early publication that the goal of therapy might be to help the patient replace hysterical misery with ordinary, everyday unhappiness; another stated aim of treatment is to help the patient to less crippling subservience to the superego. Among its many concerns, psychoanalysis has always made the study of dire mastery, as it operates within and between people, an object of study. The vexed interplay of coercion and freedom (conscious and unconscious) is another consideration to bear in mind when looking at what occurs, as some analysts like to say, between the ego and its internal objects, or between the patient and analyst.

Critics make an important point when they argue that 'the narcissism of minor differences', esoteric theoretical disputes, personal rivalries, and so forth have frequently dominated and vitiated psychoanalytic proceedings. Moreover, by comparison with the heady days in which Freud and his most illustrious followers set out the foundations of the discipline, it now often appears that the intellectual horizons and ambitions of the movement have shrunk inwards. Yet it would be a travesty, nonetheless, to imagine that after Freud's death in 1939 psychoanalysts talked only amongst themselves or confined their attention entirely to the clinic. On the contrary, the wider history has cast an enormous shadow over their work and psychoanalytical findings have in turn percolated into accounts of politics. If there have indeed been important, and sometimes crippling, conflicts inside psycho-analysis during the 'age of extremes', there have also been significant battles on behalf of psychoanalysis as a form of understanding psycho-social—or, as they are sometimes still called, human—relations, and the problems of power, love, and hate that they entail.

12

Afterword

Henry Dicks's and Walter Langer's lives ended at around the same time, but not before both produced significant books in the 1970s that reprised their wartime intelligence work on Nazi mentality. Between the 1940s and 1970s Dicks continued to write papers on international affairs, psychotherapy, matters of social policy, and how best to work with couples in order to help them survive their conflicts together or to part amicably. He also participated in a BBC television documentary about Rudolf Hess and was at pains to ensure that his views would not be distorted and simplified by the programme-makers. Here he reiterated his opinion that the Hess whom he had come to know in wartime Britain was a very ill figure, haunted by obsessional thoughts and paranoid fears.[1]

Dicks's major work from this period was *Licensed Mass Murder: A Socio-Psychological Study of Some SS Killers* (1972). It appeared as part of the project on race and genocide directed by Norman Cohn and funded by David Astor, which set out to commission a range of scholars and clinicians to investigate mass hatreds, racial mythology, genocide, fascism, the history of anti-Semitism, and related topics.[2]

Licensed Mass Murder aimed to test the received view that Nazi atrocities were necessarily the work of insane people, perverts, sadists, fanatics, or psychopaths. These preconceptions might well turn out to be mere stereotypes, Dicks implied, and would not do. Instead he wanted to get a sense of what went on in the minds of individual perpetrators and what it was like to talk with those perpetrators about this past. The aim, as he put it, was to gain 'a first-hand professional "feel" of at least some of these "fiends"'.[3] Sadism existed, to be sure, but Dicks sought to move beyond the mere labelling of the offender, or the description of the subject's crimes, and to provide a more nuanced account. He intended to make use of his acumen as a clinician and at the same time to develop a particular form of oral history. Following negotiations with the London embassy of the German Federal Republic, Dicks was given permission to interview a number of mass murderers, mostly from the ranks of the SS, who were serving jail sentences in German prisons. Much of his account, admittedly, traversed familiar ground; thus the character types presented echoed earlier research findings such as those of Adorno and his co-workers in their 1950 study of the authoritarian personality, and the wartime reports on POWs produced by Dicks himself. Of far more interest is the way in which the author charted his specific work with each man individually; he described sometimes bewildering and unexpected experiences during these live encounters that complicated his theories and preconceptions.

One of Dicks's cases was a man referred to only as 'S2', a multiple mass murderer. Dicks noted that S2 had been known even among his peers, and certainly by surviving victims, as an especially sadistic Nazi official. He had taken a lead role, for instance, in one of the camps in setting up whipping-blocks for merciless beatings; he had also been known to trample people to death. The author revealed horrific details of the man's imagination and how this had been enacted in atrocities, for instance, how he had inserted a fire-hose into a victim's mouth then ran water under pressure until the body burst open.[4] When Dicks interviewed S2, however, he 'seemed to make an appealing, boyishly open, naïve rapport with me', and appeared not to be paranoid at all.[5] Gradually, as the interview unfolded, a range of more sinister features emerged. S2 attempted to 'woo' Dicks, revealing a quality of masochistic 'faithfulness' whilst also conveying a 'childlike lack of guilt'. Dicks noted, however, that the prisoner was not marked by those 'self-pitying persecuted feeling[s] such as I had seen and was to see in other SS killers'.[6] This ferment of different, sometimes contradictory qualities makes the pages dealing with S2 more vivid and troubling than the schematized 'types' provided elsewhere in the book. Here, one could say, Dicks's account became more obviously psychoanalytic than psychiatric in style, closely attentive to the atmosphere in the room. The researcher attempted to avoid crude prompts, to remain opaque and yet alert to each inflection in the discourse of the interviewee.

Dicks's work was well regarded by some scholars in his field. As Norman Cohn recalled: '[Dicks's book] remains I think in its [own] way authoritative. It was an extraordinary thing to have done. He was not young ... when he went back to Germany and he did this job, which can't have been terribly pleasant, of interviewing these former concentration camp guards. He was critical of his own book. He said that he should have taken longer now, thinking it over, should have done this or that. But his book in a way was unique.'[7] *Licensed Mass Murder* remains a substantial example of the endeavour to bring a psychoanalytical and historical sensibility together.

In the later years of his career Dicks retained a keen interest in how the Oedipal dramas of individuals and families related to authoritarian outcomes in culture and society. Many years after the war Michael Briant, who had just completed a doctoral thesis on applied psychoanalysis, interviewed him about his work and asked how Nazism could be prevented from ever happening again. The psychotherapist took the young inquirer over to a table on which lay a copy of his newly published work, *Marital Studies*: 'He asked me to read the last two pages, which linked together his work on Fascism and his work with couples. Then he turned to me and [in answer to the question of what means might best safeguard society against Nazism] said "anything that undermines the image of the harsh, authoritarian father as a model with which boys should identify".'[8]

—•—

Whilst Dicks continued to research and publish widely on various clinical and political questions after the war, Langer disappeared from view without much further public trace, at least beyond the immediate milieu in which he lived and worked. He produced no notable post-war psychoanalytical papers or further applied Freudian works; until, that is to say, the appearance of his book, a tremendous publishing success that took him and his family greatly by surprise. The repackaging of Langer's original OSS report of 1943 as *The Mind of Adolf Hitler* received numerous media bouquets, as well as brickbats from historians.

Langer always had interests outside the psychoanalytical profession, and he had made money from ventures as a developer and property speculator. By the time he was made a life member of the Boston Psychoanalytic Society in 1969 he had changed direction and had in fact already withdrawn from his clinical practice in Cambridge, Massachusetts, preferring to spend his retirement in Sarasota, Florida, where he had settled in 1961. It was the career and family fortunes of his much-loved nephew Leonard, and his participation in regular golf matches, rather than in debate about Freudian thought, still less participation in psychoanalytical institutional politics, that proved to be great passions of his senior years. He died in 1981.

Perhaps because *The Mind of Adolf Hitler* appeared in print for the first time in 1972, some reviewers appear to have treated it as a recently created interpretation, thereby losing sight of the conditions of its production during the war despite William Langer's pointed reminders in his preface that this context should be taken into account. This old study of Hitler's psycho-political development is not, of course, the place where the student would now turn for the authoritative version of 'the life'; as we have seen Langer's work was prepared in some haste, and without access to key documents that only became available after the war. But his agenda anticipates the narrative structure and speculation to be found in many of the major historical biographies that followed.

————•————

For all its defects, *The Mind* was enthusiastically fêted; possibly Langer's book was a beneficiary of the burgeoning American interest in and commemoration of the Holocaust in the 1970s. The prescient account that he had given of Hitler's suicide added to its lustre. Moreover, it could be admired for pioneering the forms of psycho-political profiling that became commonplace in the second half of the century at intelligence organizations such as the CIA. Langer, who was privately modest about the quality of his research, was astonished to find himself invited for chat-show interviews, featured in *Newsweek* and numerous other magazines and papers, and his work translated into a number of languages. One New York paper declared the book: 'A powerful study, remarkable for the scope of Dr. Langer's understanding and the depth of his research.' *Newsweek* wrote: 'Fascinating. Langer outlines Hitler's various manias (wolves, severed heads, pornography), phobias (horses, germs, moonlight, syphilis), and contradictions.' The *Herald Tribune* admiringly described how '[o]thers cite it as a pioneering model in applying modern psychoanalytical techniques to the understanding of historical figures. Although still controversial, this technique has since been applied by Erik Erikson, the psychoanalyst, in a monograph on Hitler and in books on Martin Luther and Ghandi.' Another specialist on Hitler, the writer John Toland, offered the publisher the perfect puff: 'Amazing. This is an intriguing and significant book that helps explain our century's greatest enigma.'[9]

In correspondence with a Massachusetts doctor, John Abbott, Langer declared his surprise and pleasure at the popular response: 'I am amazed at the interest this study has aroused in recent times,' he confided, before adding self-deprecatingly: 'Personally I never thought too highly of it. To me it was the product of one of those rush-rush assignments that are common during wartime and I always felt that I could do infinitely better if I had had more time and space in which to elaborate.' Langer added in this letter some previously undisclosed background information. Before his death in 1947, an Austrian émigré colleague in Boston, Hanns Sachs, 'was interested in the project'; apparently he was so enthusiastic about the Hitler study that he wanted to see it published swiftly in serial form in the psychoanalytical journal *American Imago*. 'Since it was still classified', Langer pointed out, 'as "Secret" this was impossible.' Busy with other things in the years that followed: 'I practically forgot about its existence until a couple of years ago when I began receiving letters from scholars who had discovered it in the National Archives and urged its publication.'[10]

Despite his own long-standing interest in this kind of Nazi 'interior' exploration, and even his occasional forays into psychobiographical speculations that had their own tinge of Freudianism, the historian Hugh Trevor-Roper had no truck with Langer's efforts to probe the nature of Hitler's psyche.[11] He regarded *The Mind of Adolf Hitler* and, it seemed, by extension other psychoanalytically inspired work as vulgar, hopelessly flawed, indeed inimical to history itself. His hostile review is worth citing here as an example of the wider contempt in which Langer's report was to be held by a number of professional historians.[12] Trevor-Roper's review in one of the broadsheets, 'Re-inventing Hitler', dismissed the book as wild and unwarranted conjectural analysis, a secular version, he suspected, of older superstitions about the human heart, albeit spiced up with titillating sexual details. The approach was fatally marred by its tendency to reduce 'complex problems' to 'simple explanations'. Langer, in short, was one of the tribe of 'psychoanalysts who have recently invaded the field of history' and who explain great events by imagining the infantile experiences and secret perversions of chosen individuals, conveniently dead'.[13] Curiously, however, this historian did not place Langer 's endeavour *in history*: he effaced the wartime context and purpose (for better or for worse) of the project in the struggle against Nazi Germany.

——•——

Hess survived at Spandau prison for more than four decades after the war. Many commentators debated the ethics of his endless incarceration. For example, towards the end of his career Norbert Elias declared: 'I myself am an old man and find it inhuman that... an old man like Rudolf Hess who can no longer harm anyone is still being held in solitary confinement. To me, it would appear to be a symbolic gesture of humanity if he were set free.'[14]

Nowhere is the eerie afterlife of Nazism in post-war culture more vividly evident than in the countless representations of Hess, the long-term solitary prisoner in Berlin. Prison officials, even a priest at Spandau, penned their reminiscences. The doctors who monitored the prisoner's health (and reported regularly to the various diplomatic authorities) were more reticent, and there were no landmark publications of this type after the appearance of the casebook of 1947. Detailed historical essays in learned journals, newspaper articles, and full-blown popular studies of the Hess 'mystery' continue to appear, the latest being Stephen McGinty's investigative account *Camp Z: The Secret Life of Rudolf Hess*. McGinty describes vividly the dilemma faced by the British authorities in May 1941, and portrays Hess's relationships with the various MI6 officers and his retinue of guards, orderlies, and doctors, including Rees and Dicks. *Camp Z* makes much of the setting of Mytchett Place, playing nicely upon the tradition of English 'country-house' dramas and detective stories (even offering sketches of the three-floor layout, with its hall, library, drawing room, billiard room and wine store), whilst offering the reader what he calls a 'locked room mystery', at whose centre is Hess's mysterious mind.[15]

Meanwhile Hess haunts some of the more unsavoury recesses of the internet. He continues to arouse a certain ghoulish fascination, as well as—for some—the aura of history's victim.[16] Certain writers have focused their fire upon the captors—including 'perfidious Albion'—as much as if not more than upon the role of Hess in Nazi Germany. That Hess may have been duped by the British secret services, before or after his arrival, would not be very surprising, especially given the timing of this hare-brained mission at the direst point of the war for Britain. His treatment by the Allied powers in the long decades of his imprisonment after 1945, including for so many years as sole inmate at Spandau, were, however, in some people's eyes, another matter entirely. Prominent campaigners for his release, such as the *Times* columnist Bernard Levin, were ultimately stymied by a Cold War logic that led to the prolongation of his imprisonment.[17] Hess was even dubbed (to cite the title of one of the many books about him) *The Loneliest Man in the World*. The elderly and ailing Laurence Olivier portrayed Hess in a dubious adventure caper, *Wild Geese II* (1985). In one of Olivier's last roles the actor (by this time suffering memory problems himself) played the part of a pathetic figure so institutionalized that he refuses to cooperate with the gang who successfully secure his release from Spandau. Instead, Hess asks to be returned to die an inmate.

Hess's wife and son made numerous protests about his treatment and enduring captivity over the years, and attempted to gain publicity for the campaign. But, save for occasional hospital visits, Hess never left gaol. The views of all the occupying powers shifted over time, but in the end it was the Soviet side that remained the most obdurate. It was thought in the Kremlin that the Western powers did not fully appreciate the case from the Soviet point of view. Given the scale of Russian losses in the war and the fact that Hess, as a high official until 1941 and confidante of Hitler, bore some responsibility, why, it was argued, should he be shown clemency? Hess remained a political headache. Diplomatic files bulged with correspondence about the problems involved in his treatment and the uncertain prospects connected with his eventual demise and its public reception.[18]

Discussions of potential funeral arrangements cropped up regularly from the 1950s onwards; the bodies of prisoners, it was said, must be retained in the territory of Spandau. The ceremonial form to be adopted after Hess's death, the site to be used for his grave or cremation, and the number of people who might be permitted to attend were often considered. Fears that neo-Nazis would build a shrine on an identifiable burial-site were—quite understandably—taken very seriously. (Only in July 2011 was it finally announced that Hess's remains had been exhumed from the cemetery of the Lutheran church in the town of Wunsiedel in Bavaria; they were then cremated and the ashes scattered at sea. As had been anticipated, Hess's grave had indeed become a hallowed site for the far Right.[19]) Inquiries regarding the theft of some of Hess's personal property during the 1980s, and prisoner number 7's own periodic appeals for release on grounds of old age, illness, and infirmity, together with medical bulletins and the rest, occupy further files in the archives.[20]

A hopeful memo by one US diplomat in July 1975 declared that the 'time is not only ripe but overdue for a new effort'. The effort he had in mind was not the liberation of Hess, but the procedure required to ensure swift, orderly, and dignified action in the event of the inmate's sudden or lingering departure.[21] Officials of the occupying powers monitored the vicissitudes of Hess's health over the years. After the release of other prisoners, most notably of Albert Speer in the 1960s, he seemed ever more isolated, the focus for historical work, campaigning, and neo-Nazi adulation. Sometimes news headlines brought the case back to the fore, as when unexpected events—at one point even a firebomb—threatened to interrupt the clockwork of Spandau, with its routine changing of the guard as the Allies rotated their command. A further concerted effort to secure Hess's release, orchestrated by family and assorted sympathizers, occurred in 1982, five years before his death, accompanied by Hess's latest petition for liberty that detailed the many injuries he had suffered and insisting, plausibly enough, that he no longer posed much of a threat.[22]

In 1987 came the news that the old Nazi had managed to kill himself by rigging up a noose from the electric cord of a lamp he had found in a small building within the grounds of Spandau. The official version of events was swiftly contested and became the catalyst for a new round of ingenious, if unproven, conspiracy stories that turned, for instance, on his possible murder by British secret services or through the covert action of other powers. These tales take their place in the larger literature of suspicion that has surrounded the case since 1941. Spandau prison was razed to the ground after Hess's death—this unprepossessing corner of Nazi and Cold War Berlin subsequently housed a branch of the Kaiser supermarket chain as well as a bowling alley, a discotheque, and a vast parking lot.

———•———

The problem of how to deal with places of memory is nowhere more carefully and well considered than in post-war Berlin, but at Spandau the new buildings that were hastily constructed by the British authorities and temporarily known as 'the Britannia Centre', providing shopping facilities, seem designed to kill the past with banality. A few commercial signs and advertisements to be glimpsed around the site herald material goods and promise a bright future.[23] Visitors encounter no sober plaques, nor any other historical information, still less sculpture or other forms of art. Rather, the street signs point exclusively to the new facilities, including shops and various health services in the old outbuildings, offering such treatments as hypnotherapy, cosmetic medicine, and psychotherapy. It is not hard to see the genuine and understandable dilemma for the military and civic authorities as to how best to deal with this unsavoury location. Perhaps a combination of motives might explain the removal of any obvious references to what took place here. Yet despite the demolition of the main prison building, material traces of that history can still just be discerned. Clearly a political decision was made to avoid explicit signs and descriptions, so only a line of old trees and a few forbidding outhouses remain, like so many unwanted remnants of the past.

Much has been written about the problem of commemoration in post-war Germany. The architect Daniel Libeskind, whose work includes the remarkable extension to the Jewish Museum in Berlin that deals with the Holocaust, argues the case for creatively relating to, rather than endeavouring slavishly to freeze, the historical past.[24] His account has affinities with Freud's distinction between a kind of remembering which could be seen merely as repeating or even re-enacting the past, and that more painful and elusive process of facing internal and external reality known as 'working through'. In his paper of 1914, 'Remembering, Repeating, and Working Through', Freud described the aim of helping the patient to hold on to a thought and face it, whilst overcoming (to some extent) the resistance to which that thought or feeling gives rise. 'Working through', as Laplanche and Pontalis put it in their dictionary of psychoanalytical terms, 'is taken to be a sort of psychical work which allows the subject to accept certain repressed elements and to free himself from the grip of mechanisms of repetition.'[25]

The analyst's task, wrote Freud in his paper 'Constructions in Psycho-Analysis' (1937), is to try and make out what has been forgotten from the traces which are left behind, 'or, more correctly, to *construct* it'. The time and manner in which the analyst conveys such constructions to the person who is being analysed, as well as the explanations with which he accompanies them, Freud added, 'constitute the link between the two portions of the work of analysis, between his own part and that of the patient'.[26] Like the archaeologist, the analyst draws his inferences from the fragments of memories. In addition, the analyst draws upon the behaviour and responses of the subject of the analysis, which are discernible in the present. Psychical objects, Freud adds, are incomparably more complicated than material ones, and there is still much mystery about what we may find in the mind. Freud had from early on expressed scepticism about the human capacity to retrieve past memory, doubting, for instance, that the patient could be induced directly to remember forgotten early childhood experiences.[27]

Nations, it has been said, like people, are founded on complex patterns of remembering and forgetting the past. A nation's architecture is in many ways a record of such choices and omissions about what is worth monu-mentalizing and what must be forgotten. In a famous essay, 'What is a Nation?', the French philosopher Ernest Renan in 1882 made the impor-tant observation that to form into large entities, nations enter into a com-munal process of forgetting.[28] We may well endeavour, individually and collectively, to forget or repudiate what is traumatic, wrote Freud, years after

Renan, but our minds often dwell obsessively on painful pasts, even on specifically traumatic images (witness his concern to investigate why certain
'shell-shocked' soldiers in the First World War compulsively returned in
their dreams to the scene of their trauma).[29] Our wishes to remember and
to forget, Freud wrote on another occasion, do not cancel one another out;
nor does one wish fully overpower the other; instead a compromise occurs
and the result is somewhat like 'a parallelogram of forces'.[30]

Many historians and psychoanalysts these days would share the conviction that the present and the future are active agents in reconfiguring the
meaning of the past. In a reflection on the concentration camp as 'site of
memory', Libeskind stepped into the debate about how to represent the
Nazi past, challenging two extremes: on the one hand, antiquarians who
would freeze history and retain every last vestige of the camp; on the other,
modernizing demolishers who would simply begin again from scratch. The
latter approach, he suggested, was too reminiscent of the totalitarian impulse
to complete rationality, the utopian fantasy of an architecture that would
bring a world gleaming to perfection. Instead, he argued that urban spaces
might better be seen as collective, unfinished structures, hybrid, and *in process*, inscribed with and transformed by the conflicts that shape them.[31]
History, Libeskind adds, 'is not a story with a happy or unhappy ending'.

In the years immediately after the Second World War a number of important commentators feared not so much that the Nazi past would become
petrified in nostalgic and obsessive evocations, but that it would be conveniently marginalized or even altogether forgotten. In her preface to *The
Origins of Totalitarianism*, Hannah Arendt warned that 'we can no longer
afford to take that which was good in the past and simply call it our herit-
age, to discard the bad and simply think of it as a dead load which by itself
time will bury in oblivion'. In the 1940s, Arendt believed, '[t]he subterranean stream of Western history' finally came to the surface and 'usurped the
dignity of our tradition'. By 'subterranean' Arendt did not mean to signify,
in Freudian fashion, the unconscious mind, but rather the forces of modern
barbarism that lay beneath the surface of 'civilization' (imperialism, militarism, racism, genocide) and that led to Auschwitz. Arendt's account of 'totalitarianism' sought to encompass both fascism and Stalinism in a single
account, but, writing in 1951, it was above all the world of the Nazi concentration camps that provided the core of her concern. This history, she
declared, is now 'the reality in which we live . . . And this is why all efforts to
escape from the grimness of the present into nostalgia for a still intact past,

or into the anticipated oblivion of a better future are in vain'.[32] Arendt thought that studied efforts by writers such as herself were required to keep the political processes that produced Nazism before the public gaze.

There are affinities in this regard between historiography, social theory, and psychoanalysis, perhaps even a shared endeavour to integrate Nazism into accounts of 'the mainstream' of history and psychic life.[33] Psychoanalysis offers a rich vocabulary, partly inspired by that political history. It is certainly a vocabulary that could be used to think about that history. Its concepts should not serve to 'explain away' the wounds of the continent as the consequence of a few madmen, but rather to consider the unconscious fantasies that are mobilized in and perhaps also reshaped by, the process of politics.[34]

The 'logic of the illogical' (as Arthur Miller put it) is one way to describe what psychoanalysis has always sought to grasp.[35] To allow for unconscious factors in historical interpretations of Nazism was not necessarily to deny that economic and other contingent historical determinants are of vital importance: neither the Great War, the Versailles settlement, nor the financial crash of 1929 were always downplayed by the best writers in this genre (although they were not always sufficiently highlighted). Nor did the analysts or the historians who drew upon Freudian thought in the middle and later decades of the twentieth century necessarily assume that the majority, let alone the entire mass, of German people voted enthusiastically for 'the Final Solution' and the precise blueprint of war and conquest that Nazism produced in the 1940s. Nonetheless, as many people acquiesced in these outcomes, tacitly supported them, or more actively and willingly allied themselves (from the late 1920s and 1930s onwards) with a cause that could only lead to escalating international conflict and internal repression, violence, cruelty, and hatred, it is certainly true that they shared in that historical responsibility for Nazism's outcomes.

Many of the commentators described in these chapters focused upon the interaction of Hitler and German society. They needed no reminding that the former was a ruthless opportunist, who manipulated the position granted to him when first invited to lead the government in 1933 in order to fashion the conditions for subsequent dictatorship. He was not cast simply as a 'reflection' of those who elected him, although he did, according to this line, offer up sentiments and opportunities that keyed in with the wishes of many millions.

Ideas of the unconscious attractions of fascism and Nazism were increasingly congruent with the views of influential political theorists beyond the ranks of the psychoanalytical movement. In fact psychoanalysis was

eagerly seized upon to help explain why previous more optimistic assessments of human nature and historical progress had foundered. It became a
truism to argue that political subjects desire and dread far more than they
consciously know when they exercise 'choice'. The unconscious, after all,
according to Freud, bears contradictory thoughts and wishes, and it is, at
least in part, from the place of the unconscious that our political identifications arise and our selections are made.

The cultural reception of psychoanalysis has gone through many phases
over the last hundred years. Not only has the standing of Freud and his
movement changed dramatically over time, but so too has the reputation of
psychoanalysis as a tool for modern historical and political interpretation.
Freudian thought had always paid attention to the murderous wishes that
lurk inside the 'civilized' self: witness the Oedipus complex that, from the
1890s onwards, Freud contentiously, even scandalously, placed centre-stage in
his account of normal psychic formation. According to Freud, the wish to
murder one parent and possess the other is not just the preserve of some
outlandish psychopathic (or tragic) class of being, but a universal condition,
a problem to be negotiated by every child in one fashion or another. From
this radical and soon hotly disputed idea there followed a host of others. The
wish to devour and destroy, and the dread of being annihilated, is never,
according to this approach, ever fully surpassed: behind every vegetarian a
raging carnivore, as Freud once quipped (although not with reference to
Hitler). Psychoanalysis set out to explore not just what we are capable of
doing to ourselves and to others, but the power of the desire not to know
about any of this, even when it is revealed. Our myriad propensities to seek
solace in omniscient and omnipotent (hence mad) leaders have also constituted an important part of its field of investigation in the twentieth century.

'The struggle is not yet over': Freud's famous remark in an interview
with the BBC, shortly after his arrival in London in 1938, sought to describe
the predicament of psychoanalysis in an ever-resisting world. It may serve
equally well to suggest the continuing danger of the return to new forms of
fascism in contemporary politics. That the unconscious minds of ordinary
people might contain not only illicit sexual desires but also aggressive and
destructive propensities aimed at both self and other became a commonplace, albeit uncomfortable, notion in the age of Freud; by the wartime
period considered in this book psychoanalysis was an important resource in
the culture. It remains so now.

Appendices

Appendix 1. Extracts from Henry Dicks's Clinical Notes

Visit to Maindiff.   Feb. 44.

26.2.44. Collected pass from D.P.W., arrived late owing to trains.

27.2.44. Conference c̄ Ellis Jones. Psycho-pathologically, present case considered a pseudo-dementia, allied to Ganser syndrome. Both agree that clinical management is likely to get more difficult if pushed till successful, but that general policy reasons make an attempt not necessary. Pt classified now as P.O.W., hence liable to re-patriation.

Ellis Jones assigns pride of place to precipitating cause of loss of exercise under stress of security.

Clinical Obsⁿˢ Saw pt at 12.30. Had just risen. Cold, huddled figure, simian features have pronounced. Eye dulled and vacant. Nutrition fair. Demonstrated a curiously affect-less attitude towards amnesia. With v. good grasp & v. good vocabulary. Showed no signs of recognition though there were 2 moments when eyes became flickering: once when referring to my previous insult which I related, & once when some other heavily charged topic was alluded to. Cannot remember his son's or wife's names. Bland "indifference", with show of shallow affect. Introduced by E. Jones, who slipped in idea of curability of this condition, reinforced by me. It had to be said that it involves giving an injection.

Seen again 4 p.m. long chat, in which I reminded him of main features of his past life & chief associates. Bland grin – "I suppose you are telling the truth – but you could just as well tell me fairy tales."

Describes his condition as awareness of the present, but with any but the most recent past slipping into a fog. There is a sense of continuity of personality but it is lost in the mist. Occasionally asks "what do you mean by nature cure" etc. Slips in his sense of aversion from all drugs – says "have I always used ...?" Impression is that the dissociation is a superficial one. Attention & concentration well maintained, but occasional sense of wandering – e.g. at some remark of mine. Says he cannot read ... letters sent to him from home: that he lapses into a dozing ... state. Introspection is adequate, & sense of judgment well maintained. E.g. when I discussed causes of amnesia in terms of functional + organic (e.g. concussion), he reverted at once (after ½ hour's interval) to topic of a possible concussion sustained on arrival, proving acute attention. There is certainly no loss of essential hold on reality.

Eating habits still peculiar. Wavers between greed and guilt: e.g. verse on window to remember to abstain from breakfast + tea: Keeps food + reheats it in own time. Devours masses of potatoes + greens.

Daily colic spasm - saw one at 6.45 p.m. Groans + says it is v. exhausting: "but only has a tablet if it is very bad."

Rapport fairly good, but some ties. Keen follower of papers + radio.

28.2.44. V. brief visit before lunch as pt. rose very late. Quick glance of resentment when I alluded to his earlier habit of taking some milk for breakfast. Only bowed to Jones. Fell greedily upon lunch.

In afternoon Jones + I made a definite attempt to get his views on amnesia. We brought out old letters + a manuscript of his to show what background knowledge was there + demonstrate needless painful impoverishment of mental content. Pt. in very good humour + pleased at compliments of to past mental achievement. Also used argument of his inability to contact his relatives through poverty of ideas for letters.

He asked if there were no system of practice for his memory. When told this was no good in his case, he turned the tables by saying: "My present state is good enough for my purposes here. So long as I can kill time by reading + drawing - that is all I need. It doesn't really matter whether I remember what I read. When I get back home perhaps this trouble will pass, or I can find some treatment. Maybe it is even a merciful dispensation of fate that it makes me forget. If I got back my memory I may suffer nine. So I don't want anything done."

we both pointed out that it was he who had complained
of his disability, but he said if he was not reminded of it
he could "doze away" quite happily. During his remarks about
the possible purposive nature of the amnesia he broke into
mischievous laughter. It was left that he should think it
over during the next 24 hours, that the help was there, that
the remedy was a safe and even pleasant one, frequently used
to restore normal consciousness etc., but that there was no desire
on anybody's part to do anything but to help him.

Reported to be in very good mood later on, at dinner, and
free from abdominal pain. Rang up J.R. told to wait orders.

<u>29. 2. 44.</u> Pt reported in s. aggressive, fault-finding mood.
run at lunch time ∴ Ellis Jones; he stated he had had a very bad
night, full of pain. Pt. occupied the time by petulantly retailing
the omissions of the N.Os & other grievances. E.J. reminded him of
his condition & need for therapy. Pt clearly stated he wished to wait
now, as he had apparently had his amnesia for so long, whether & in a
few months or weeks it might not go of its own accord.

Accompanied him on afternoon excursion. Escort Officer remarked
afterwards he was more silent & tense than usual. I was
conscious of an "atmosphere"; & he walked less than normal.
In evening I went in to say good-bye, very briefly & formally.
He professed to be sorry, "as I was a German speaker."

1. 3. 44. Reported to J.R. verbally.
2. 3. 44. Top S. report to Commandant sent off.

6. 3. 44. Having had verbal orders to the effect that Pt had consented
to Evipan Tt, I arrived at Maindiff at 6.30 p.m. Conference ∴ D.
Jones. Decided I sh? not appear until post-narcotic state.
Pt stated to be still willing.

7. 3. 44. Final arrangements. Evipan 5.5 cc. given, at pt's request, late
in evening. 9 p.m: by D. Ellis Jones, in presence of D. Phillips, &
Cpt. & Cpl. RAMC. Smooth, normal first stage. Total unconsciousness &
complete muscular relax." 12 min. Then as per verbatim notes.

note worthy that pt had prepared, before session 2 glasses
of water standing in hot water ready for his use, + further
he called solidly throughout the session. Jones expressed
the opinion "she was determined to cheat us by that pain."

Subsequent conference re WP, Jones + Phillips on undesirability
success of further attempts. Trunk-called J.R.

saw pt.- he was fairly bright + said it was most comforting for him
to know that, as Jones had told him, the session had proved
his memory was intact underneath.

8/3/44. Stated to have had a fair night. Seen at lunch-time. Said was
very unhappy. Asked what view he took of further procedure
he said he hated drugs in his system - even a rabbit - + wd one
repeat if absolutely essential. Nervy + restless.
Jones later saw him + argued advantages of further injection.
Told to think it over.
This evening I saw him for a long time. Discussed the
disadvantages to himself, his family, his appreciation of the
political + military situation + flattered him = the pity so
rich a mind was being needlessly starved.
He said it didn't really matter - he wd sooner stay as he
was - my arguments were cogent etc - but while he was
alone it wd save him much torment + boredom; he now
knew that he wd recover sometime in the future. And anyhow
it was nicer than he could screw himself up to for a second
time to have poison injected and especially squirted - worse
than the mouth. He felt sure he must refuse.
He thanked me + offered to shake hands.
was more alert + did not ask for any verbal explanation
of quite stiff medical terms.
Phoned J.R. - told to return.

(Gwann) Schmerzen! im Darm! (more Gwann) 1/3/44. began S.S E.C. at 8.45 pm Begins to respond 9.10 pm Verbatim Notes

Leibschmerzen . Ich weiss nicht — Durst —

Wenn ich nur gesund würde — Wasser —

(Re past) — Wasser — Schmerzen im Leibe — im Hebel —

What is yr son's name? Ich weiss nicht . (Your wife?) — Ich weiss nicht — (Do you know my voice) — nein.

(Homöopa) — nein (Willi Messerschmitt) — nein —

(Gwann) — Leibschmerzen! — Ach gott (Why?) —

(Alex audrien) — nein :— (Adolf Hitler is father): Nein .

(Putsch in München) — nein.

(what do you think) — Leibschmerzen . (Why?) — Ich weiss nicht . (repeated)

(wife's name) … Ich weiss nicht . —

[Jones: speak & answer] — Answer the question (echolalia) — Leibschmerzen — (Hatten sie jahrelang) .. jahrelang (echo) Leibschmerzen — (An alles Erinnern) — An alles erinnern :— (Sie Ihren Ereignisse) … Ereignisse (echo) —

(You boy? his name) Der Bruder — wie heisst er.

(Gwann) — Leibschmerzen — [loud Gwann]

[Jones] — Leibschmerzen — (rep). — Leibschmerzen —

[??? Warum diese Selbstaufopferung? Warum geben sie sich diese Schmerzen? Gwann + + b. hnd.

[wie kam das böse Ding in den Leib] — "Wasser."

[You speak it will do you good — says Jones] — Gwann again .

[Warum sollten sie sich — was hissen sie?] "Wasser"! quälten etc

[Wer hat ihnen weh getan?] — Ich weiss nicht?

[Phillips also asks in v. falling voice] — Renewed Gwann. — Schmerzen — "Wasser."

[Jones returns to boy & wife] — [echolalia]

Top Secret.

Subject: Report of Visit to Maindiff Court.
To :   D.P.W., The War Office.
From :   Lt Col. H.V. Dicks, R.A.M.C.

I visited Maindiff Court on 12 and 13 Feb. 45, in place of
Brigadier J.R. Rees, at present overseas.

I learnt from the physicians in attendance the recent medical history
of the case. I found arrangements for the patient's comfort and review
of the case & strict supervision as good as they could be made (leaving nothing to be desired.)

I was able to see, and talk to, the patient for considerable periods.
interviews The patient He has made a very dramatic recovery from the temporary
affection of his memory which now functions very fully and accurately.

I cannot accept his own statement that the memory loss never
existed. There was at that time a true partial dissociation of the
personality, which permitted the patient to "take in" what was going
on around him, with difficulty of recall. It is a case of preferring to have
duped us to having shown temporary weakness.

His present physical condition is good. Appetite and intake
of food are returning to normal after a recent protest which was
overcome by peaceful persuasion from Dr. Phillips and Major Ellis
Jones. His superficial wound is healing satisfactorily.

The recent acute phase of suspicion and associated excitement,
during which he has launched a number of reports and appeals, has
now been followed by a much calmer phase. He is very rational,
discusses his suspicion as a symptom; i.e. is prepared to consider
it as a creation of his own imagination. In evaluating the recent
episode, certain national cultural influences must be borne
in mind in toning down the impression of his personal mental abnormality.

The action taken, highly reprehensible and anti-social to our
ideas, is almost the normal way out of indignity and loss of face
in his ethical code. At present honour is satisfied, after an
appeal through the Protecting Power to his own government in
whose hands he leaves the decision whether to eat or to starve.

Thus I find the patient at much the same level of mental
and physical health as I left him three-and-a-half years
ago: i.e. intellectually vigorous and alert; somewhat grandiose
and overbearing when acting 'officially', simple and rational in
private, rather egocentric, fussy and suspicious. this suspicion follows
lines a stereotyped formula in his normal
milieu, and the patient has some insight into them, as before.

I do not consider it necessary to recommend any changes in
regimen. All concerned are aware that a certain risk of impulsive
action exists, but short of making his life intolerable these must
continue to be taken. At the moment tension has been relieved.

I recommend, however, as a matter of urgency, that steps be
taken to provide the patient with light reading matter as
repeatedly, and very reasonably, requested by him &

~~[illegible]~~

The granting of such modest requests will do much to help in the management of what is always a difficult personality.

I consider that all concerned are to be congratulated on their devoted skill and patience.

H.V.D., MD., MRCP
Lt.Col. RAMC

Copy: Consulting Psychiatrist to the Army
AMD 11.

Appendix 2. Rudolf Hess's Final Speech at Nuremberg

From IMT, Trial of the Major War Criminals, Nuremberg 1947, vol. 22, pp. 368–73. Spelling mistakes have been silently corrected.

THE PRESIDENT: I call on the Defendant Rudolf Hess.

RUDOLF HESS (Defendant): First of all, I should like to make a request to the High Tribunal that I may remain seated because of my state of health.

THE PRESIDENT: Certainly.

HESS: Some of my comrades here can confirm the fact that at the beginning of the proceedings I predicted the following:

(1) That witnesses would appear who, under oath, would make untrue statements while, at the same time, these witnesses could create an absolutely reliable impression and enjoy the best possible reputation.

(2) That it was to be reckoned with that the Court would receive affidavits containing untrue statements.

(3) That the defendants would be astonished and surprised at some German witnesses.

(4) That some of the defendants would act rather strangely: they would make shameless utterances about the Führer; they would incriminate their own people; they would partially incriminate each other, and falsely at that. Perhaps they would even incriminate themselves, and also wrongly.

All of these predictions have come true, and as far as the witnesses and affidavits are concerned, in dozens of cases; cases in which the unequivocal oath of the defendants stands in opposition to the sworn statements of the former.

In this connection I shall only mention the name Messersmith: Mr. Messersmith, who, for example, says that he spoke to Admiral Dönitz at a time when the latter was, to my knowledge, in the Pacific Ocean or the Indian Ocean.

I made theses predictions, however, not only here at the beginning of the Trial, but had already made them months before the beginning of the Trial in England to, among others, Dr. Johnston, the physician who was with me in Abergavenny.

At the same time I put these statements down in writing, as proof. I base my predictions on some events in countries outside of Germany. In this connection I should like to emphasize now that, while I mention these incidents, I was convinced from the beginning that the governments concerned knew nothing about them. Therefore, I am not raising any accusation against these governments.

In the years 1936 to 1938 political trials were taking place in one of these countries. These were characterized by the fact that the defendants accused themselves in an astonishing way. For example, they cited great numbers of crimes which they had committed or which they claimed to have committed. At the end, when death sentences were passed upon them, they clapped in frenzied approval to the astonishment of the world.

But some foreign press correspondents reported that one had the impression that these defendants, through some means hitherto unknown, had been put into an abnormal state of mind, as a result of which they acted the way they did.

These incidents were recalled to my mind by a certain happening in England. There it was not possible for me to get the reports of the trials at that time, any more than here. However, the corresponding years of the *Völkischer Beobachter* were at my disposal there. While looking through these numbers I came upon the following passage in the number of 8 March 1938. A report from Paris dated 7 March 1938 reads as follows:

'The big Paris newspaper *Le Jour* made revelations about the means which were apparently used in these trials. These are rather mysterious means.'

I quote literally what the *Völkischer Beobachter* reprinted from *Le Jour*.

'These means make it possible for the selected victims to be made to act and speak according to the orders given them.'

I emphasize and point out that this report in *Le Jour* not only says 'to make them speak according to orders given them,' but also 'to make them act according to orders given them.' The latter point is of tremendous importance in conection with the actions, the hitherto inexplicable actions of the personnel in the German concentration camps, including the scientists and physicians who made these frightful and atrocious experiments on the prisoners, actions which normal human beings, especially physicians and scientists, could not possibly carry out.

But this is also of equally great significance in connection with the actions of the persons who undoubtedly gave the orders and directions for the atrocities in the concentration camps and who gave the orders for shooting prisoners of war and lynchings and other such things, up to the Führer himself.

I recall that the witness Field Marshal Milch testified here that he had the impression that the Führer was not normal mentally during the last years, and a number of my comrades here have told me, independently of each other and without having any knowledge of what I am saying here now, that during the last years the Führer's eyes and facial expression had something cruel in them, and even had a tendency towards madness. I can name the comrades in question as witnesses.

I said before that a certain incident in England caused me to think of the reports of the earlier trials. The reason was that the people around me during my imprisonment acted towards me in a peculiar and incomprehensible way, in a way which led me to conclude that these people somehow were acting in an abnormal state of mind. Some of them—these persons and people around me were changed from time to time. Some of the new ones who came to me in place of those who had been changed had strange eyes. They were glassy and like eyes in a dream. This symptom, however, lasted only a few days and then they made a completely normal impression. They could no longer be distinguished from normal human beings. Not only I alone noticed these strange eyes, but also the physician who attended me at the time, Dr. Johnston, a British Army doctor, a Scotsman.

In the spring of 1942 I had a visitor, a visitor who quite obviously tried to provoke me and acted towards me in a strange way. This visitor also had these strange eyes. Afterwards, Dr. Johnston asked me what I thought of this visitor. He told me—I told him I had the impression that for some reason or other he was not completely normal mentally, whereupon Dr. Johnston did not protest, as I had expected, but agreed with me and asked me whether I had not noticed those strange eyes, these eyes with a dreamy look. Dr. Johnston did not suspect that he himself had exactly the same eyes when he came to me.

The essential point, however, is that in one of the reports of the time, which must still be in the press files on the proceedings—this was in Paris, about the Moscow trial—it said that the defendants had had strange eyes. They had had glazed and dreamy eyes! I have already said that I am convinced that the governments here concerned knew nothing of these happenings. Therefore it would not be in the interest of the British Government either if my statements about what I experienced during my imprisonment were denied publicity in any way, for that would give the impression that something was actually supposed to be concealed here, and that the British Government had actually had a finger in the pie.

On the contrary, however, I am convinced that both the Churchill Government and the present Government gave instructions that I was to be treated fairly and according to the rules of the Geneva Convention. I am conscious of the fact that what I have to say about the treatment which I received will at first glance appear incredible. Fortunately for me, however, prison guards at a very much earlier time had already treated their prisoners in a way which at first appeared absolutely incredible when the first rumors about it reached the outside world. These rumors were to the effect that prisoners had been deliberately allowed to starve to death, that ground glass, among other things, had been put in the meager food which had been given them, that the physicians who attended the prisoners who had been taken sick in this way had added harmful substances to their medicine, which increased their sufferings and at the same time increased the number of victims. As a matter of fact, all of these rumors afterwards proved to be true. It is a historical fact that a monument was erected for 26,370 Boer women and children who died in British concentration camps, and who for the most part died of hunger. Many Englishmen at that time, among others, Lloyd George, protested strongly against these happenings in British concentration camps, and likewise an English eye witness, Miss Emily Hopfords.

However, at that time the world was confronted with an insoluble riddle, the same riddle which confronts it today with regard to the happenings in the German concentration camps.

At that time the English people were confronted with an incomprehensible riddle, the same riddle which today confronts the German people with regard to the happenings in the German concentration camps. Indeed, at that time, the British Government itself was confronted with a riddle regarding the happenings in the South African concentration camps, with the same riddle which today confronts the members of the Reich Cabinet and the other defendants, here and in other trials, regarding the happenings in the German concentration camps.

Obviously, it would have been of the utmost importance if I had stated under oath what I have to say about the happenings during my own imprisonment in England. However, it was impossible for me to persuade my counsel to declare himself willing to put the proper questions to me. It was likewise impossible for me to get another counsel to agree to put these questions to me. But it is of the utmost importance that what I am saying be said under oath. Therefore I now declare once more: I swear by God the Almighty and Omniscient, that I will speak the pure truth, that I shall leave out nothing and add nothing. I ask the High Tribunal, therefore, to consider everything which I shall say from now on as under oath. Concerning my oath, I should also like to say that I am not a church-goer; I have no spiritual relationship with the Church, but I am a deeply religious person. I am convinced that my belief in God is stronger than that of most other people. I ask the High Tribunal to give all the more weight to everything which I declare under oath, expressly calling God as my witness.

In the spring of 1942...

THE PRESIDENT *[Interposing]*: I must draw the attention of the Defendant Hess to the fact that he has already spoken for 20 minutes, and the Tribunal has indicated to the defendants that it cannot allow them to continue to make statements of great length at this stage of the proceedings.

We have to hear all the defendants. The Tribunal, therefore, hopes that the Defendant Hess will conclude his speech.

HESS: Mr. President, may I point out that I was taking into account the fact that I am the only defendant who, up to now, has not been able to make a statement here. For what I have to say here, I could only have said as a witness if the proper questions had been put to me. But as I have already stated...

THE PRESIDENT: I do not propose to argue with the defendants. The Tribunal has made its order that the defendants shall only make short statements. The Defendant Hess had full opportunity to go into the witness box and give his evidence upon oath. He chose not to do so. He is now making a statement, and he will be treated like the other defendants and will be confined to a short statement.

HESS: Therefore, Mr. President, I shall forego making the statements which I had wanted to make in connection with the things I have just said. I ask you to listen to only a few more concluding words, which are of a more general nature and have nothing to do with the things that I have just stated.

The statements which my counsel made in my name before the High Tribunal I permitted to be made for the sake of the future judgment of my people and of history. That is the only thing which matters to me. I do not defend myself against accusers to whom I deny the right to bring charges against me and my fellow-country-men. I will not discuss accusations which concern things which are purely German matters and therefore of no concern to foreigners. I raise no protest against statements which are aimed at attacking my honor, the honor of the German people. I consider such slanderous attacks by the enemy as a proof of honor.

I was permitted to work for many years of my life under the greatest son whom my people has brought forth in its thousand-year history. Even if I could, I would not want to erase this period of time from my existence. I am happy to know that I have done my duty to my people, my duty as a German, as a National Socialist, as a loyal follower of my Führer. I do not regret anything.

If I were to begin all over again, I would act just as I have acted, even if I knew that in the end I should met a fiery death at the stake. No matter what human beings may do, I shall some day stand before the judgment seat of the Eternal. I shall answer to Him, and I know He will judge me innocent.

Appendix 3. Hess's Preface to Rees et al. (eds.), The Case of Rudolf Hess

COPY

RUDOLF HESS
NUERNBERG
GEFAENGNIS DER
SOG. KRIEGSVER-
BRECHER

NUERNBERG, DEN 27. 9. 46

HERRN
BRIGADIER DR. REES
LONDON

SEHR GEEHRTER HERR DR. REES,

HERR DR. GILBERT GAB
MIR KENNTNIS VON IHREM WUNSCH NACH EINER BESTAETIGUNG VON
MIR, WONACH ICH ES GERN SEHEN WUERDE, WENN DIE AERZTE, DIE
MICH IN ENGLAND UND SPAETER IN NUERNBERG BETREUTEN, IHRE
MICH BETREFFENDEN BERICHTE UND KRANKENGESCHICHTEN ZU WIS-
SENSCHAFTLICHEN ZWECKEN VOLL VEROEFFENTLICHTEN.
ICH TEILE IHNEN DAHER MIT, DASS ICH EINE SOLCHE VER-
OEFFENTLICHUNG SEHR BEGRUESSEN WUERDE. NICHT ABER WEIL
ICH ETWA DES GLAUBENS WAERE, DASS DADURCH DIE OEFFENT -
LICHKEIT RICHTIGER INFORMIERT WUERDE ALS BISHER, WIE HERR
DR. GILBERT MEINTE. SONDERN ICH WUERDE SIE DESHALB BEGRUES-
SEN, WEIL SIE EINMAL ALS ERGAENZENDER BEWEIS DAFUER ANGE-
SEHEN WERDEN WIRD, DASS AUF EINE BISHER NICHT BEKANNTE
WEISE MENSCHEN IN EINEN ZUSTAND VERSETZT WERDEN KOENNEN,
DER AEHNLICH DEM IST, DER DURCH EINE NACHWIRKENDE HYPNOSE
/„POSTHYPNOTHIC SUGGESTION"/ ERREICHT WERDEN KANN — EIN
ZUSTAND, IN DEM DIE BETREFFENDEN PERSONEN UNTER AUSSCHAL-
TUNG DES EIGENEN WILLENS ALLES TUN, WAS IHNEN SUGGERIERT
WURDE, VERMUTLICH OHNE DASS SIE SICH SELBST DESSEN BEWUSST
SIND.
FUER DEN VORLIEGENDEN FALL WUERDE DER BEWEIS ERBRACHT
WERDEN, DASS SELBST EHRENHAFTE MAENNER, AERZTE UND FACH-
LEUTE VON ZUM TEIL HOHEM ANSEHEN, DURCH DEN AUSGEUEBTEN
GEISTESZWANG DAZU GEBRACHT WURDEN, SCHWERSTE VERBRECHEN
ZU BEGEHEN UND ZUGLEICH URTEILE ABZUGEBEN, DIE DER WAHR-
HEIT WIDERSPRECHEN, DAMIT DIE VERBRECHEN VERTUSCHT WERDEN.
DIE EINZIGE BEDINGUNG FUER DAS ERTEILEN MEINES EIN -
VERSTAENDNISSES ZU DER BEABSICHTIGTEN VEROEFFENTLICHUNG
IST, DASS DIESER BRIEF MIT ABGEDRUCKT WIRD, UND ZWAR IM
VOLLEN WORTLAUT.

HOCHACHTUNGSVOLL

Rudolf Heß

TRANSLATION

RUDOLF HESS
NUREMBERG   NUREMBERG
PRISON OF THE   27TH SEPTEMBER, 1946.
SO-CALLED
WAR CRIMINALS

BRIGADIER DR. R E E S
L O N D O N

DEAR DR. REES,

DR. GILBERT BROUGHT TO MY NOTICE YOUR WISH FOR A CONFIRMATION FROM ME THAT I SHOULD CONSIDER IT FAVOURABLY IF THE PHYSICIANS WHO HAD ME UNDER THEIR CARE IN ENGLAND AND LATER IN NUREMBERG PUBLISHED THEIR REPORTS AND CASE HISTORIES CONCERNING MYSELF FOR SCIENTIFIC PURPOSES.

I AM THEREFORE INFORMING YOU THAT I SHOULD WELCOME SUCH A PUBLICATION VERY MUCH. THIS IS NOT BECAUSE I PERHAPS HOLD THE BELIEF THAT THE PUBLIC WOULD THEREBY BE INFORMED MORE CORRECTLY THAN HITHERTO, AS DR. GILBERT THOUGHT. BUT I WOULD WELCOME IT BECAUSE ONE DAY IT WILL BE REGARDED AS SUPPLEMENTARY PROOF OF THE FACT THAT IN SOME HITHERTO UNKNOWN MANNER PEOPLE CAN BE PUT INTO A CONDITION WHICH RESEMBLES THAT WHICH CAN BE ATTAINED THROUGH A HYPNOSIS LEAVING ITS AFTER-EFFECTS("POST-HYPNOTIC SUGGESTION")—A CONDITION IN WHICH THE PERSONS CONCERNED DO EVERYTHING THAT HAS BEEN SUGGESTED TO THEM, UNDER THE ELIMINATION OF THEIR OWN WILL, PRESUMABLY WITHOUT THEIR BEING CONSCIOUS OF IT.

FOR THE PRESENT CASE PROOF WOULD BE SUPPLIED THAT EVEN HONOURABLE MEN, PHYSICIANS AND EXPERTS, PARTLY OF HIGH REPUTE, THROUGH THE COMPULSION EXERCISED ON THEIR MINDS, WERE BROUGHT TO COMMIT THE GRAVEST CRIMES AND AT THE SAME TIME TO DELIVER JUDGMENTS WHICH CONTRADICT THE TRUTH, IN ORDER THAT THE CRIMES SHOULD BE HUSHED UP.

THE ONLY CONDITION FOR GIVING MY CONSENT TO THE INTENDED PUBLICATION IS THAT THIS LETTER IS PUBLISHED WITH IT, AND THAT FULLY AND LITERALLY.

RESPECTFULLY

(sgd) RUDOLF HESS.

A*

Notes

These notes list the sources that are directly referred to in the text. An accompanying website provides a larger sample of wartime and post-war papers, logs, letters, etc. assembled in the course of this research. See http://www.bbk.ac.uk/ thepursuitofthenazimind.

The following abbreviations are used to refer to frequently cited books, papers and archives:

HD   Henry Dicks, Papers, Wellcome Library, London. [Note this collection had not yet been catalogued at the time the present book was written, so references are restricted to the name of the item, rather than to the subsequent, more precise Wellcome Library classification]

HH   Ian Kershaw, *Hitler: 1889-1936: Hubris* (London, 1998)

HN   Ian Kershaw, *Hitler: 1936-1945: Nemesis* (London, 2000)

IMT   International Military Tribunal, Nuremberg: *Proceedings*, 42 vols. (Nuremberg, 1947)

MH   Walter Langer, *The Mind of Adolf Hitler* (New York, 1972)

NA   National Archives [NARA], College Park, Maryland

RH   John Rawlings Rees *et al.*, *The Case of Rudolf Hess: A Problem in Diagnosis and Forensic Psychiatry, by the Physicians in the Services who have been concerned with him from 1941–1946* (London, 1947)

RPL   Roosevelt Presidential Library, Hyde Park, New York

SB   Walter Langer *et al.*, Source Book for his Report on Adolf Hitler, Office of Strategic Services, NA

SE   The Standard Edition of the Complete Works of Sigmund Freud, 24 vols., ed. James Strachey *et al.* The Hogarth Press and the Institute of Psychoanalysis (London, 1953–74)

TIU   'Tensions Affecting International Understanding'. Archives of the multi-authored research project, colloquia etc., UNESCO, Paris

WL   Archives in the Wellcome Library for the History of Medicine, London

CHAPTER I

1. Dicks began as a major and was promoted to lieutenant-colonel during the war.

2. There are exceptions; see, for instance, Peter Loewenberg's useful sketch of the history of the genre, 'Psychohistorical Perspectives on Modern German History', *Journal of Modern History*, 47 (1975), 229–79 and his account of the personal circumstances of the Langer family in *Decoding the Past: The Psychohistorical Approach* (New York, 1983). See also his review essay on Walter Langer's *The Mind of Adolf Hitler*, in *Central European History*, 7 (1974), 262–75.

3. Important work in this field includes Pearl King and Riccardo Steiner (eds.), *The Freud–Klein Controversies, 1941–5* (London, 1991); Nathan Hale, *The Rise and Crisis of Psychoanalysis in the United States, 1917–1985* (New York, 1995); Riccardo Steiner, *'It is a New Kind of Diaspora': Explorations in the Sociopolitical and Cultural Context of Psychoanalysis* and *Tradition, Change, Creativity: Repercussions of the New Diaspora on Aspects of British Psychoanalysis* (both London, 2000); Tom Harrison, *Bion, Rickman, Foulkes, and the Northfield Experiments: Advancing on a Different Front* (London, 2000); Stephen Frosh, *Hate and the 'Jewish Science': Anti-Semitism, Nazism and Psychoanalysis* (Basingstoke, 2005).

4. Perry Anderson, 'Components of the National Culture', *New Left Review*, 50 (1968), 3–57, at p. 39. Cultural theorists now routinely regard applied psychoanalysis in history as naive because it tends to 'jump' from the treatment of individuals to analysis of the social order, as though they are one and the same thing. Slavoj Žižek cautions against such a misuse of psychoanalysis, for example, in *The Parallax View* (Cambridge, Mass., 1999), 6.

5. See Peter Mandler, *Return from the Natives: How Margaret Mead Won the Second World War and Lost The Cold War* (New Haven, 2013); id., 'One World, Many Cultures: Margaret Mead and the Limits to Cold War Anthropology', *History Workshop Journal*, 86 (2009), 149–72.

6. The underline is in the original text. See Henry Murray, 'Analysis of the Personality of Adolph Hitler with predictions of his future behaviour and suggestions for dealing with him now and after Germany's surrender', OSS report, October 1943, Foreword. This text is available *inter alia* at RPL or online at http://library.law school.cornell.edu/WhatWeHave/SpecialCollections/Donovan/Hitler/Hitler-TOC.cfm. Cf. Callon Humphreys, *Mind of a Tyrant: A Psychological Study of the Character of Hitler* (London, 1940); N. Gangulee (ed.), *The Mind and Face of Nazi Germany* (London, 1941); Walter Langer, *The Mind of Adolf Hitler* (New York, 1972); Florence R Miale, *The Nuremberg Mind: The Psychology of the Nazi Leaders* (New York, 1975); Eric Zillmer, *The Quest for the Nazi Personality: A Psychological Investigation of Nazi War Criminals* (Hillside, NJ, 1995).

7. For a brilliant reading of Freud's 'Group Psychology' and its significance for the analysis of fascism, see Theodor Adorno, 'Freudian Theory and the Pattern of Fascist Propaganda', (1951), reprinted in *The Culture Industry: Selected Essays on Mass Culture*, ed. J. M. Bernstein (London, 1991), 118–37.

8. Extant work that is especially relevant to the themes of the present inquiry includes Denise Riley, *War in the Nursery: Theories of the Child and Mother* (London, 1983); Eli Zaretsky, *Secrets of the Soul: A Social and Cultural History of Psychoanalysis* (New York, 2004); Mark Edmundson, The *Death of Sigmund Freud: Fascism, Psychoanalysis and the Rise of Fundamentalism* (London, 2007); Lyndsey Stonebridge, *The Writing of Anxiety: Imagining Wartime in Mid-Century British Culture* (London, 2007).

9. For a sceptical view of psychoanalytical influence in post-war mental health, see Edgar Jones, 'War and the Practice of Psychotherapy: The UK Experience 1939–1960', *Medical History*, 48 (2004), 493–510. Cf. Nafsika Thalassis, 'Treating and Preventing Trauma: British Military Psychiatry in the Second World War', Ph.D. thesis, University of Salford (2004); id., 'The Use of Intelligence Testing in the Recruitment of Other Ranks in the Armed Forces during the Second World War', *History and Philosophy of Psychology*, 5 (2003), 17–29. On the role of British analysts in the war effort, Pearl King, 'Activities of British Psychoanalysts during the Second World War and the Influence of their Inter-disciplinary Collaboration on the Development of Psychoanalysis in Great Britain', *International Review of Psychoanalysis*, 16 (1989), 15–33.

10. Jane Caplan, 'The Historiography of National Socialism', in Michael Bentley (ed.), *Companion to Historiography* (London, 1997), ch. 21, p. 549.

11. Erich Fromm, *The Anatomy of Human Destructiveness* (New York, 1973), chs. 12 and 13. Fromm writes of Hitler's 'Necrophilous character' and declares that the Nazis' 'passion to destroy' was their 'dominant' passion; ibid. 347–8.

12. Caplan, 'The Historiography', 551.

13. Klaus Theweleit, *Male Fantasies*, 2 vols. (Cambridge, 1987 and 1989).

14. Thus Lacan reviewing (in 1958) the psychiatrist Jean Delay's account of André Gide's youth, praised him for 'not ... [running] the risk of resembling what the analytic world calls a work of "applied psychoanalysis". Delay immediately rejects what this absurd qualification translates by way of confusion on the part of analysts. Psychoanalysis is applied, strictly speaking, only as a treatment and thus to a subject who speaks and hears.' *Écrits*, tr. Bruce Fink (New York, 2006), 629–30. This is not to deny that certain French psychoanalytic (and philosophical) reflections on the Nazi mind did emerge, but to acknowledge they are beyond the range of this book, were especially vulnerable to intellectual criticism in the era of structuralism and post-structuralism, and also to suggest that they were not deployed in the Allied war effort of the 1940s in the manner described here. Important French intellectual contributions to postwar analysis of the 'mind' of colonialism and post-colonialism also lie beyond the scope of this study. For the influence of Sartre (especially of his essay on the anti-Semite and the Jew, first published in *Les Temps Modernes* in 1945), and for the role of the psychiatrist and revolutionary, Frantz Fanon (born in Martinique in 1925), in pioneering a new field of psycho-social analysis in the 1950s and after, see the fine recent study by Derek Hook, *A Critical Psychology of the Postcolonial: The Mind of Apartheid* (London, 2012).

15. See e.g. Arthur M. Schlesinger, Jr., *The Vital Center: The Politics of Freedom* (New York, 1992 [1949]).

16. King and Steiner (eds.), *The Freud–Klein Controversies*.

17. See Eric Trist's vivid account of the Maudsley Hospital's wartime psychiatric work (in a centre provided temporarily at Mill Hill School in North London) and the nature of the rivalries and enmities that were stirred up by the development of the Tavistock approach, in his memoir 'Guilty of Enthusiasm', in Arthur G. Bedeian (ed.), *Management Laureates: A Collection of Autobiographical Essays* (Greenwich, Conn., 1993), vol. 3, ch. 6, pp. 193–221, at p. 202.

18. See e.g. Bertram D. Lewin, 'Interviews with German Prisoners of War', Lewin Papers, Library of Congress, box 8, folder 7.

19. Trist, 'Guilty of Enthusiasm', 202.

20. Rickman's reports are included in Pearl King, *No Ordinary Psychoanalyst: The Exceptional Contributions of John Rickman* (London, 2003); for an example of such briefings for US intelligence, see Paul Federn Papers, Library of Congress, box 10, folder 6.

21. I borrow the terms from Daniel Todes, *Pavlov's Physiology Factory: Experiment, Interpretation, Laboratory Enterprise* (Baltimore, 2002), 104, 106.

22. Paul Linebarger, *Psychological Warfare* (Washington, DC, 1948), 26.

23. By 1935, Freud was pleased to note further expansion, with the formation of societies in Scandinavia, as well as in France, Palestine, India, South Africa and Japan. Postscript [1935] to 'An Autobiographical Study', SE vol. 20, p. 73.

24. The exact figure given for 1924 was 263 members. Karl Abraham and Ernest Jones also provided an indication of the geographical reach of the movement in a report that they submitted on the Salzburg Congress in 1924. At this time the British Society had 49 members; the Vienna Society 42; the Swiss Society 40; the American Society 31 (in addition the separate New York Society numbered 26); Berlin had 27 members; the Dutch Society 19; the Indian Society 16 and the Hungarian Society 13. The authors announced they were unable to verify the numbers in the recently created and at that stage, they believed, flourishing Russian Psychoanalytical Society. 'Report of the Eighth International Psycho-Analytical Congress', *Bulletin of the International Psycho-Analytical Association*, 5 (1924), 391-408, at p. 402. For the worldwide spread of psychoanalysis, see Zaretksy, *Secrets of the Soul*, and Forrester, *The Freudian Century* (forthcoming). For Latin American developments (which remain entirely beyond the scope of the present study), see e.g. Mariano Ben Plotkin, *Freud on the Pampas: The Emergence and Development of a Psychoanalytic Culture in Argentina* (Stanford, 2001).

25. Geoffrey Cocks, *Psychotherapy in the Third Reich: The Göring Institute* (New York, 1985); James E. Goggin, *Death of a 'Jewish Science': Psychoanalysis in the Third Reich* (West Lafayette, Ind., 2000); Frosh, *Hate and the 'Jewish Science'*. For a suggestive essay on French psychoanalysis and collaboration with the Nazis, see Elisabeth Roudinesco, 'Georges Mauco 1899–1988: un psychanalyste au service

de Vichy. De l'antisémitisme à la psychopédagogie', *L'Infini* (autumn 1995), 73–84.

26. Karen Brecht *et al.* (eds.), *Here Life Goes on in a Most Peculiar Way: Psychoanalysis Before and After 1933* (Hamburg, 1995).

27. Matthew Thomson, 'Mental Hygiene as an International Movement', in Paul Weindling (ed.), *International Health Organisations and Movements, 1918–1939* (Cambridge, 1995), 283–304.

28. I draw here on John Cornwell's account in *Hitler's Scientists: Science, War and the Devil's Pact* (London, 2003), esp. 159–60. The Gestalt School was also attacked for harbouring Jewish members and for its supposed soulless materialism. For the uses that were made of psychiatry, psychology, and psychotherapy in the German armed forces, and for the history of investigations undertaken inside the Third Reich on the mental health of the civilian population, see Geoffrey Cocks, *The State of Health: Illness in Nazi Germany* (Oxford, 2012), esp. pp. 210–18.

29. For the details, Cocks, *Psychotherapy*; cf. Zaretsky, *Secrets of the Soul*.

30. The Jungian analyst Andrew Samuels has addressed this past directly in 'National Psychology, National Socialism, and Analytical Psychology: Reflections on Jung and Anti-Semitism', part 1, *Journal of Analytical Psychology*, 37 (1992), 3–28; part 2, ibid. 127–48. For the background to Jung and his accommodations with the Third Reich in the 1930s, see Sonu Shamdasani, *C. G. Jung and the Making of Modern Psychology: The Dream of a Science* (Cambridge, 2003). On the German psychoanalytic past, see Brecht *et al.*, *Here Life Goes on in a Most Peculiar Way*.

31. In this book I capitalize 'Fascism' to indicate the model and movement that originated in Italy and was quickly matched, and sometimes copied, elsewhere, and use 'fascism' to refer to the generic (non-geographically specific) political term. By Nazism, I indicate the specific ideology that emerged in Germany after 1918. There were, of course, important differences between Fascism and Nazism. Several excellent recent surveys by Roger Griffin explore the affinities, differences, and developments of the concepts and movements. Other helpful contemporary authors on these concepts and ideologies include Roger Eatwell, Michael Mann, Kevin Passmore, and Enzo Traverso.

32. Daniel Pick, *Faces of Degeneration: A European Disorder, c. 1848–c. 1918* (Cambridge, 1989); Richard Overy, *The Morbid Age: Britain and the Crisis of Civilization, 1919–1939* (London, 2009).

33. Sigmund Freud, 'Obsessive Actions and Religious Practices', SE vol. 9, pp. 115–28, at p. 123.

34. The reasons for choosing the term 'superego' instead of 'Over I', or even 'Over ego' are set out by Strachey in the editorial introduction to *The Ego and the Id* (SE vol. 19, pp. 6–7). 'Ego' was of long-established philosophical usage in English, albeit (as later critics of the translation pointed out), this term lost the more colloquial immediacy of Freud's original (literally rendered as 'Over I'). 'Over ego' might have been an alternative.

35. Ernest Jones, letter to Freud (2 July 1923), in *The Complete Correspondence of Sigmund Freud and Ernest Jones 1908–1939*, ed. Andrew Paskauskas (Cambridge, Mass., 1993), 524.

36. Ernest Jones, 'The Origin and Structure of the Super-Ego', *International Journal of Psycho-Analysis*, 7 (1926), 303–11.

37. Melanie Klein, *The Psycho-Analysis of Children* (London, 1932), 40.

38. Melanie Klein, *Narrative of a Child Analysis* (London, 1961).

39. See Chapters 3 and 4.

40. For the broader context of this forced emigration of doctors and psychiatrists from Nazi Germany, see the collection of papers, 'Medical Refugees in Britain and the Wider World, 1930–1960', ed. Paul Weindling, *Social History of Medicine*, 22 (2009), 451–587.

41. For the context and consequences, see Steiner, 'It is a New Kind of Diaspora'; Zarestsky, *Secrets of the Soul*; George Makari, *Revolution in Mind: The Creation of Psychoanalysis* (New York, 2008).

42. The early American reception of Klein is well described by Nellie Thompson (New York Psychoanalytical Society) in an as-yet unpublished paper that was presented (*inter alia*) at the British Psychoanalytical Society in 2010.

43. Heinz Hartmann, 'Psychoanalysis and the Concept of Health', *International Journal of Psycho-Analysis*, 20 (1939), 308–21.

44. Robert Wallerstein, *Lay Analysis: Life Inside the Controversy* (Hillsdale, NJ, 1998).

CHAPTER 2

1. After Dicks's retirement from the NHS he moved his private practice, seeing both individuals and couples for treatment in his sitting-room in Hampstead.

2. Information supplied by Adrian Dicks, Henry's younger son (personal communications, 4 and 5 Nov. 2010) and by the psychoanalyst Rob Hale, a schoolfriend of Adrian Dicks, who also became close to Henry Dicks in his later years (4 Nov. 2010). It is quite possible, however, that Dicks did have analysis in the interwar period but did not write about this publicly or in letters. Like Wilfred Bion and various Cambridge academics, Dicks may, for instance, have had some treatment with J. A. Hadfield (about whose work he later wrote respectfully), but this is by no means certain.

3. Personal communication: Adrian Dicks, 4 Nov. 2010.

4. Dicks was initially sent to a German-language Gymnasium in Riga. However, his parents feared (correctly as it turned out) that the German army might invade the Baltic area. They decided that St Petersburg would be a safer location for their son. His parents and two aunts remained behind and found themselves interned by the Germans. In St Petersburg Henry came into contact at school with the children of various high-ranking Russian officials and lodged

with the family of one of his teachers. Personal communications: Adrian Dicks, 5 July 2011; Anthony Dicks, 22 July 2011.

5. Dicks was prominent in the campaign against abuses of psychiatry in the Soviet Union during the 1970s. See *Abuses of Psychiatry for Political Repression in the Soviet Union*, US Senate Committee on the Judiciary [sub-committee] (Washington, DC, 1972, repr. New York, 1973), 44–5. For the context see Malcolm Lader, *Psychiatry on Trial* (Harmondsworth, 1977).

6. Various personal communications from Dicks's children—Gillian Higson-Smith, Adrian Dicks, and Anthony Dicks (Nov.–Dec. 2009).

7. Dicks gained a first in Part I of the Tripos but (as was not uncommon) did not take Part II before he embarked on medical school. My thanks to John Forrester for this information.

8. I draw here on notes that Adrian Dicks compiled for obituaries of his father that appeared in *The Times* and elsewhere. Several biographical sketches are included in HD.

9. Apparently he frequented a continental branch of the Masonic organization that also admitted women. Both Henry Dicks and his wife were members. Personal communication: Anthony Dicks, 22 July 2011.

10. Personal communications: Gillian Higson-Smith, and Lucy Jayne (Henry Dicks's granddaughter), 5 Dec. 2010. On the revival of popular interest in spiritualism and other esoteric beliefs during and after the Great War, see Jay Winter, *Sites of Memory, Sites of Mourning: The Great War in European Cultural History* (Cambridge, 1995).

11. Laura Cameron and John Forrester, 'A Nice Type of the English Scientist: Tansley and Freud', in Daniel Pick and Lyndal Roper (eds.), *Dreams and History: The Interpretation of Dreams from Ancient Greece to Modern Psychoanalysis* (New York, 2004), 199–236.

12. King and Steiner (eds.), *The Freud–Klein Controversies*, 27.

13. Personal Communication: Anthony Dicks, 22 July 2011.

14. Henry Dicks, 'The Proper Study of Mankind', *British Journal of Psychiatry*, 113 (1967), 1333–44. Here he makes clear his misgivings about the cliquishness of psychoanalysis, its preoccupation with sub-specialist 'enclaves' (such as those which emerged within the British Psychoanalytical Society), laments the failure of psychologists and psychiatrists to 'cross-fertilise', and proposes an ecumenical approach to patient treatment in general.

15. On the background to this work, see Trist, *Management Laureates.*

16. Personal communications: Gillian Higson-Smith and Adrian Dicks, 5 Nov. and 5 Dec. 2010.

17. *MH* 6.

18. Sanford Gifford, 'Rediscovery of Walter Langer', unpublished paper, 1999; Boston Psychoanalytic Society archives.

19. Quoted in Gifford, 'Rediscovery'.

20. Personal communication: Leonard Langer, 22 July 2008.

21. Interview transcript, Dr Sanford Gifford with Mrs Juanita Franks, 22 May 1999, in the archives of the Boston Psychoanalytic Society. Langer's papers are at the same location.

22. Press clippings and other items relating to the fire are contained in the Langer archives at the Boston Psychoanalytic Society. The Oral History Collection (at the same location) contains Sanford Gifford's interviews with Walter Langer and others, as well as material donated by Leonard Langer. Cf. Gifford, 'Rediscovery', 3.

23. Personal Communication: Leonard Langer, 22 July 2008.

24. Walter C. Langer, 'An Investigation of the Positive Transfer Effects in the Learning of a Sensory-motor Task', *Journal of Psychology*, 3 (1936), 371–9.

25. Gifford, 'Rediscovery'.

26. For the details, see Peter Gay, *Freud: A Life for Our Time* (London, 1998).

27. Walter C. Langer and Sanford Gifford, 'An American Analyst during the Anschluss 1936–1938,' *Journal of the History of the Behavioral Sciences*, 14 (1978), 37–54; cf. Gifford, 'Rediscovery'.

28. *MH*, p. vi.

29. Gifford, 'Rediscovery'.

30. The analyst's ability to establish boundaries and remain reticent about his or her own personal circumstances, tastes, or opinions is regarded as crucial; such 'abstinence' by the analyst can never perhaps be complete, but in so far as it can be maintained it facilitates the emergence and exploration of the patient's transference. The latter term refers to the patient's host of fantasies and feelings, derived from the patient's own lived history and myriad modes of relating, that come to be invested in the analyst. According to this theory, transference occurs outside the consulting-room too, but it is the psychoanalytic setting that enables it to be investigated most acutely, and for a therapeutic purpose.

31. Elizabeth Young-Bruehl, *Anna Freud: A Biography* (New York, 1988), 244. The connection with Langer is not mentioned in Michael John Burlingham, *The Last Tiffany: A Biography of Dorothy Tiffany Burlingham* (New York, 1989).

32. *In and Out of the Ivory Tower: The Autobiography of William L. Langer* (New York, 1977).

33. Formally speaking, Langer's election to the Boston Psychoanalytic Society did not take place until 1949, his progress having been slowed, presumably, by his several other wartime occupations.

34. Anthony Cave Brown, *The Last Hero: Wild Bill Donovan* (London, 1992).

35. *MH*, Introduction. Cf. William Langer's observation: 'Still, I marvel at Donovan's readiness to accept psychoanalysis as a potential contributor to the solution of current problems.' *MH*, p. v.

36. *MH*, pp. vi and 5.

37. Smith, *The Shadow Warriors: OSS and the Origins of the CIA* (London, 1983), 276.

38. See OSS, RG 226, box 431, Personnel Files, 'Walter Langer'. NA.

39. On Hitler's childhood and its subsequent representation, see Erik Erikson's classic essay 'The Legend of Hitler's Childhood', in his *Childhood and Society* (London, 1995 [1963]), 294–323. For the best and most up-to-date general account, see *HH*.

40. In 1946 Rees *et al.* remarked that Hess's brother Alfred was at that time 'an accountant in industry', one of his sisters had married an operatic singer, and the other brother was a colonel in the German Army. *RH*, 8.

41. Padfield, *Hess: Flight for the Führer* (London, 1991), 3.

42. Quoted in ibid. 3.

43. Quoted in ibid. 7.

44. For the details, *RH* 1–20; Roger Manvell and Heinrich Fraenkel, *Hess: A Biography* (London, 1971); Padfield, *Hess*; Guido Knopp, *Hitler's Henchmen* (Sutton, 2000).

45. Quoted in Wolf Rüdiger Hess, *My Father, Rudolf Hess* (London, 1986; translated from the German edition of 1984), 30. Caution is called for here: the original provenance of these remarks is not made clear by the (far from disinterested) author of this text. Some other depressed soldiers, such as Karl von Schirach (older brother of Baldur von Schirach who was later to become the Hitler Youth leader), had indeed shot themselves after the German defeat in 1918. Christian Goeschel, *Suicide in Nazi Germany* (Oxford, 2009), 11. On Hess's feelings of humiliation in 1918, see also Padfield, *Hess*, 11.

46. Padfield, *Hess*, 13; cf. James Douglas-Hamilton, 'Hess and the Haushofers', in David Stafford (ed.), *Flight from Reality: Rudolf Hess and his Mission to Scotland 1941* (London, 2002), ch. 4, p. 79.

47. *RH* 56.

48. *HH* 158–9.

49. Quoted in Konrad Heiden, 'Hitler's Better Half', *Foreign Affairs*, 20 (1941), 73–86, at p. 77.

50. Padfield, *Hess*, 22.

51. Ilse Hess, claimed later that Hess had not been the typist of *Mein Kampf*. *HH* 675, nn. 100 and 103. This was evidently not because she was ashamed that he would have participated in this ideological work; she (like her son) remained staunchly loyal to and publicly unrepentant about Hess and his cause.

52. Heiden, 'Hitler's Better Half', 79.

53. Padfield, *Hess*, 73.

54. Quoted in Wolf Rüdiger Hess, *My Father Rudolf Hess*, 35. This letter is also quoted in Padfield, *Hess*, 33–4.

55. Padfield, *Hess*, 99.

56. *MH* 30.

57. *SB* 469. The OSS Hitler Source Book is also published in cd-rom format, and is easily accessed via the internet.

58. Dan Stone, 'The *Mein Kampf* Ramp: Emily Overend Lorrimer and Hitler Translations in Britain', *German History*, 26 (2008), 504–19, at p. 513.

59. *Rudolf Hess, Germany and Peace: A Soldier's Message* (Berlin n.d. [1934?]), translator's introduction, p. 2.
60. OSS, interview with Karl Haushofer, 27 Sept. 1945, NA, document XL22853. As the OSS report made plain, Haushofer's testimony could not be relied upon; he was desperate to exculpate himself and played down his links with and sympathies for Hitler, claiming in the interview that it was only through Hess that he had any influence on Hitler's thought at all.
61. Manvell and Fraenkel, *Hess*, 23.
62. Konrad Heiden, 'Hitler's Better Half', 82.
63. *HH* 538.
64. Quoted in Wulf Schwarzwäller, *Rudolf Hess: The Deputy*, translated from the German (London, 1988), 88.
65. The potential for satirizing Riefenstahl's depiction of Hitler's rapport with the crowd had struck Charlie Chaplin when he viewed the film in America before the war; *The Triumph* was one catalyst for Chaplin's *The Great Dictator* (1940). Riefenstahl's production was also the target of mockery and reverse propaganda in Britain, re-edited, for instance, in 'Hitler Assumes Command', a 'short' released by Movietone News in 1941, where the Führer and the goose-stepping soldiers dance to the tune of 'Doing the Lambeth Walk'.
66. Anna von der Goltz, *Hindenburg: Power, Myth, and the Rise of the Nazis* (Oxford, 2009).
67. William Shirer, *Berlin Diary* (London, 1970 [1941]), 22, 23 and 28. For excerpts from Shirer and a host of other observations of the political situation in Germany by visiting writers, see Oliver Lubrich (ed.), *Travels in the Reich, 1933–1945* (Chicago, 2010).
68. Shirer, *Berlin Diary*, 9.
69. The 'degenerate' and 'perverse' Nazism of Röhm and the SA was supposedly purged through these killings in 1934, orchestrated by Hitler, with active encouragement and a considerable direct contribution from Hess. The latter took an active part and was said to have pleaded with Hitler to be allowed to kill Röhm. Hitler's ruthless actions were defended publicly by his lieutenants as essential steps to restore order: he had supposedly stemmed abuses of power, staunched corruption, and dealt with the many jumped-up little leaders who threatened anarchy. *HH* 511–15.
70. *RH* 11 and 207. The subject was revived periodically after the war. Insinuations about Hess's supposed homosexuality were but a final Soviet insult: so claimed Hess's son Wolf, leading an indignant correspondent to the *New York Times* in 1991 to fire off this retort under a heading of 'Hess, Homosexuality and the Third Reich': 'The sexual orientation of Rudolf Hess should not affect the judgment of historians on him; but to interpret the disclosure as "humiliation" is preposterous, a smear against homosexuality.' *New York Times*, letters page (21 June 1991). For the complexity of social and political attitudes to sexuality, and especially towards same-sex relationships, in the Third Reich, see Dagmar

Herzog, *Sex after Fascism: Memory and Morality in Twentieth-Century Germany* (Princeton, 2005); id. (ed.), *Sexuality and German Fascism* (New York, 2005), esp. chs. 4 and 9.

71. For the script, see http://www.geocities.com/emruf4/triumph.html.

72. Konrad Heiden, *Der Fuehrer: Hitler's Rise to Power*, trans. Ralph Manheim, preface by Alan Bullock (London, 1967 [1944]), 185.

73. See ibid., Bullock's preface.

74. Ibid. 117–18.

75. Ibid. 285. For the mythic figure, see Daniel Pick, *Svengali's Web: The Alien Enchanter in Modern Culture* (London, 2000).

76. Konrad Heiden, 'Hitler's Better Half', 73.

77. Heiden, *Der Fuehrer*, 286.

78. Ibid., respectively, pp. 286 and 225.

79. Sebastian Haffner, *Germany: Jekyll and Hyde*, translated from the German (London, 1940).

80. By 1940–1 Hess was not part of the inner circle of decision-makers; see Peter Longerich, 'Hitler's Deputy: The Role of Hess in the Nazi Regime', in Stafford (ed.), *Flight from Reality*, ch. 6.

81. Abraham G. Duker/Irving Dwork Papers. OSS Research and Analysis Branch—Jewish Desk, Record Group 200, Box 14, folder 155, entitled 'Rudolf Hess', report, p. 3. NA.

82. *RH* 16.

CHAPTER 3

1. *HN* 369.

2. *HN* 421.

3. Martin Gilbert (ed.), *The Churchill War Papers*, vol. 3: *The Ever-Widening War, 1941* (London, 2000), 1142.

4. 'I accordingly forwarded my observations with such a request on May 23rd and again on May 24th [1941]' (the words of the attending officer, Dr Graham). *RH* 19.

5. Lynn Picknett, Clive Prince, and Stephen Prior, *Double Standards: The Rudolf Hess Cover Up* (London, 2001), offer a compilation of many of the original reports, as well as wilder claims and conspiracy theories, in their own sometimes overblown account. Certain writers have also evidently used the Hess case to pursue a sinister political agenda; not content with decrying British maltreatment, they present the Nazi prisoner as akin to a martyr; see e.g. David Irving, *Hess: The Missing Years, 1941–1945* (London, 1987). Irving's work cannot be relied upon by historians for the reasons described in D. D. Guttenplan, *The Holocaust on Trial: History, Justice and the David Irving Libel Case* (London, 2001) and Richard Evans, *Telling Lies about Hitler: The Holocaust, History and the David Irving Trial* (London, 2002). On the evidence regarding

MI5 intercepts of Albrecht Haushofer's letters in November 1940, see *HN* 940, n. 223.

6. Hugh Trevor-Roper, 'Rudolf Hess: The Incorrigible Intruder', in Stafford (ed.), *Flight from Reality*, 153.

7. Warren F. Kimbell, *Churchill and Roosevelt: The Complete Correspondence* (Princeton, 1984), i. 186–8. Cf. the letters from John F. Coar and Ambassador William Dodd, President's personal file (PPF3716) and also files relating to William Dodd (OF523), RPL. Cf. *HN* 369 and 436. See also John Erickson, 'Rudolf Hess: A Post-Soviet Postscript', in Stafford (ed.), *Flight from Reality*, ch. 3.

8. The extensive debates that ensued, and the reasons for the British government's reluctance to parade Hess (or even to broadcast his voice) in public, are well described by Jo Fox; see 'Propaganda and the Flight of Rudolf Hess, 1941–1945', *Journal of Modern History*, 83 (2011), 78–110.

9. *HN* 436. Cf. *The Goebbels Diary*, trans. and ed. Fred Taylor (London, 1982), entry for 16 May 1941, p. 368. The German and British propaganda responses to Hess's flight are compared in Fox, 'Propaganda'.

10. Ivone Kirkpatrick, *The Inner Circle: Memoirs of Ivone Kirkpatrick* (London, 1959), 171.

11. *HN* 369.

12. Mark Mazower, *Hitler's Empire: Nazi Rule in Occupied Europe* (London, 2008), 223.

13. *RH* ch. 1.

14. Hess's title (*Stellvertreter*) is easily misconstrued. It indicated that he was the deputy to the Führer within the Party. Deputy Führer (as he is sometimes still described) might incorrectly imply that he was Hitler's overall second-in-command in Germany.

15. Norman Cohn, interview with the author, 11 July 2006. For diverse memories of Hess and the impact of the first news of his flight in 1941, contributed by members of the public, see http://www.bbc.co.uk/ww2peopleswar/.

16. Peter Fleming, *The Flying Visit* (London, 1940). Cf. Fox, 'Propaganda'.

17. For public records on Hess, and a discussion of the remaining closed files, see Roy Nesbit, 'Hess and Public Records', in Stafford (ed.), *Flight From Reality*, ch. 8.

18. Suggestions that British Intelligence and/or Hitler had been briefed about Hess's flight in advance are doubtful for reasons that Ian Kershaw sets out in *HN* 370-81.

19. See e.g. *HN* 376.

20. Anthony Cave Brown, *The Secret Servant: The Life of Sir Stuart Menzies, Churchill's Spymaster* (London, 1988), 346.

21. *HH* ch. 13, and *HN* 10, 93, and 249.

22. For historical assessments and challenges to some of the wilder conspiratorial hypotheses, see Stafford (ed.), *Flight from Reality*. For the context, see *HN* 370–81; Richard Evans, *The Third Reich at War: 1939–1945* (London, 2008), 167–70.

23. See Chapter 5.

24. *HN* 371.
25. *HN* 372.
26. *HN* 370–2.
27. Manvell and Fraenkel, *Hess*, 131.
28. *The Goebbels Diary*, entry for 16 May 1941, p. 367. These arrests mostly took place in early June 1941. Manvell and Fraenkel, *Hess*, 131.
29. *HN* 372.
30. Manvell and Fraenkel, *Hess*, 132.
31. Joachim Fest, *Hitler*, translated from the German (London, 1974), 728.
32. *HN* 504.
33. *HN* 372–3, 375, 436 and 786; *RH* 2. Evans, *The Third Reich at War*, 161–70.
34. Gilbert (ed.), *Churchill War Papers*, vol. 3 [containing Hansard Report, 13 May 1941], pp. 655–6.
35. *The Diaries of Sir Robert Bruce Lockhart*, 2 vols. (London, 1980), vol. 2 (entry for 13 May 1941), p. 99.
36. *The Goebbels Diary*, entries for 13 and 14 May 1941, pp. 361–3. Cf. *HN* 373–4.
37. *HN* 373.
38. *HN* 374; *The Goebbels Diary*, entry for 16 May 1941, p. 369.
39. *The Goebbels Diary*, entries for 16 and 17 May 1941, pp. 367–9.
40. *HN* 374.
41. *HN* 379.
42. IMT, vol. 7, p. 138; vol. 10, p. 37 and vol. 13, p. 626. Records of Karl Haushofer's interrogations at Nuremberg are available at NA. See Interrogation Records Prepared for War Crimes Proceedings at Nuremberg 1945–47. Microfilm Publication M1270, roll 6 (frame 10) and roll 24 (frame 10); reports of 22 Sept. and 5 Oct. 1945. Colonel H. A. Brundage conducted the interrogation here on behalf of the American prosecutor at the IMT. Haushofer acknowledged his own intimacy with Hess, and stressed his friend's good character, 'heart', and infatuation with Hitler whilst pouring scorn on Hess's intelligence. He pointedly added that, in his view, Hess had much less influence over Hitler than was commonly supposed. For Haushofer's reliability as a witness see Ch. 2, n. 60.
43. Quoted in *HN* 371 and 375.
44. Gilbert (ed.), *Churchill War Papers*, iii. 648.
45. *HN* 375.
46. For Kirkpatrick's account, see *The Inner Circle*.
47. *Diaries of Sir Robert Bruce Lockhart*, vol. 2 (entry for 13 May 1941), p. 99.
48. Later Ivone Kirkpatrick played a significant role in the creation of British facilities for the re-education of German army and civilian personnel. See Richard Mayne, *In Victory, Magnanimity in Peace, Goodwill: A History of Wilton Park* (London, 2003), 24. After 1945 he served for a year in the Foreign Office's German section and from 1950 to 1953 he was High Commissioner in Bonn. He published his account of the Hess affair in 1959. See *The Inner Circle*.

49. Kirkpatrick, *The Inner Circle*, p. 171.
50. Martin Gilbert, *Winston S. Churchill*, vol. 6: *Finest Hour 1939–41* (London, 1989 [1983]), 1087. The shorthand 'C' derived from the initial of the first chief of the secret intelligence service, Captain Sir Mansfield Smith Cumming.
51. Ibid. 1087.
52. *RH* 18; cf. Manvell and Fraenkel, *Hess*.
53. Gilbert (ed.), *The Churchill War Papers*, iii. 656. On Hamilton's fervent (and apparently justified) denials of complicity with Hess or Haushofer, see *HN* 379.
54. Knopp, *Hitler's Henchmen*, 187.
55. *RH* 27 and 39.
56. Padfield, *Hess*, 242.
57. Note the descriptions in *The Diaries of Sir Robert Bruce Lockhart*, vol. 2 (entry for 28 May 1941), p. 101. Cf. Padfield, *Hess*; Picknett *et al.*, *Double Standards*. An inquiry by Stephen McGinty (*Camp Z: The Secret Life of Rudolf Hess* (London, 2011)) contains interesting material about the Nazi prisoner's dealings with MI6, as well as with Dicks, Simon, and Beaverbrook (among others). The book draws on *The Case of Rudolf Hess* and PRO records, amongst others, and provides extensive transcripts of the prisoner's interviews with Lord Beaverbrook and Lord Simon.
58. Churchill, letter of 5 July 1941, to Admiral Pound, in Gilbert (ed.), *Churchill War Papers*, iii. 899.
59. *The Diaries of Sir Robert Bruce Lockhart*, vol. 2 (entry for 13 Sept. 1943), p. 262. On the wiring of Mytchett Place in order to record Hess's conversations, see Padfield, *Hess*, 240, 243.
60. See McGinty, *Camp Z*.
61. David Stafford, *Churchill and Secret Service* (London, 1997), 257. The bugging by the secret services of Heisenberg and the other captured scientists is described in Jeremy Bernstein, *Hitler's Uranium Club: The Secret Recordings at Farm Hall* (Woodbury, NY, 1996).
62. In 1939 the British government established the Combined Services Detailed Interrogation Centre in order to gather intelligence from German POWs. Facilities were developed to monitor and analyse the conversations of prisoners, notably at Trent Park in North London and Latimer House in Buckinghamshire. Some of the generals housed at Trent Park were subsequently transferred to the United States for questioning at the army camp at Clinton, Mississippi. See Sönke Neitzel, *Tapping Hitler's Generals: Transcripts of Secret Conversations, 1942–1945,* introduced by Ian Kershaw (Barnsley, 2007), 17–19.
63. The consular official 'must have felt very strange at being suddenly precipitated into this dramatic episode'. *RH* 39.
64. *RH* 41.
65. Padfield, *Hess*, 134.
66. *RH* 41.

67. *The Diaries of Sir Robert Bruce Lockhart*, vol. 2 (entry for 28 May 1941), p. 101.
68. Gilbert (ed.), *Churchill War Papers*, iii. 677–8.
69. Ibid. Cf. Fox, 'Propaganda'.
70. Gilbert (ed.), *Churchill War Papers*, vi. 1087.
71. Stafford (ed.), *Flight from Reality*, ch. 3.
72. *RH* 27.
73. Ibid.
74. '[Hess's] health and comfort should be assured'. Gilbert (ed.), *Churchill War Papers*, iii. 657.
75. *RH* 121.
76. For details of conditions at Mytchett Place, see *RH* 27.
77. *RH* 26.
78. See *RH*, introduction and p. 208.
79. See Appendix 3.
80. *RH*. Cf. correspondence from Dr G. Ridoch and Dr J. R. Rees, 19 Nov. 1945, to British War Crimes Executive; clinical notes on Rudolf Hess, by Dr J. R. Rees, 1941–1945; letter on Hess, from A. J. Riley, 15 Jan. 1946, Contemporary Medical Collection (PP/CMW/G.3/2). WL. According to the penultimate prison director at Spandau, Hess had received as many as 35 visits from Rees during the war; Eugene K. Bird, *The Loneliest Man in the World: The Inside Story of the 30-year Imprisonment of Rudolf Hess* (London, 1974), 24. Hess recalled Rees as a man who had treated him well, but who had peculiarly glassy and dreamy eyes. These were symptoms, he suspected, of mesmerism; *RH* 100.
81. *RH* 213; psychiatric diagnoses, ranging from 'mildly psychopathic' to traces of schizophrenia, seasoned the wartime reports.
82. *RH* 37.
83. *RH* 25.
84. *RH* 8.
85. *RH* 12.
86. Roger Proctor, *The Nazi War on Cancer* (Princeton, 1999).
87. *RH* 12.
88. See *RH* and the handwritten medical reports concerning Hess, held in Record Group 260, Records of US Occupied HQ, World War II, Office of Military Government, Chief of Counsel for War Crimes, General Records, 1944–46, box 113, Folder entitled 'Medical Reports concerning Rudolf Hess' for instance, June-November 1941, notebook 7. NA.
89. Sigmund Freud, 'Hysterical Phantasies and their Relation to Bisexuality' (1908), SE, vol. 9.
90. *RH* 25.
91. *RH* 14.
92. See Appendix 3.
93. *RH* 62.
94. *RH* 17.

95. Quoted in *RH* 16.
96. *RH* 20.
97. *RH* 20–1.

CHAPTER 4

1. Dicks, *Fifty Years of the Tavistock Clinic* (London, 1970), 109.
2. *RH* 27.
3. See Appendix 1.
4. Charles and Alice Dicks, who resided first in Pernau and then in London, travelled frequently between the two countries. Personal communication: Anthony Dicks, 22 July 2011.
5. Not all of the British or American army psychiatrists and psychologists who were involved in analysing Nazi attitudes during and after the war did understand German, and certainly not with the facility of Dicks. Some, for instance at the Nuremberg trial, required the assistance of translators. The fact that the American psychologist Gustave Gilbert spoke fluent German (unlike, say, the army psychiatrist Major Kelley whom Gilbert initially served in the role of translator) placed him at a considerable advantage when interviewing and assessing the prisoners.
6. The reference to 'Dr Dix' is contained in a statement that Hess wrote at Maindiff Court in 1941 (see *RH* 100, 126). The pronunciation of the two names would have been the same. It would be fanciful, no doubt, to claim on this evidence alone that he could have unconsciously conflated Dicks with some other specific figure. 'Dix' was not an uncommon name—witness the German Expressionist painter Otto Dix (loathed by the Nazis) or the German lawyer Dr Rudolf Dix, who later on at Nuremberg represented one of the accused men, Hjalmar Schacht (see IMT vol. 2).
7. *RH* 115, 127.
8. *RH* 34.
9. *RH* 53.
10. *RH* 69–71.
11. *RH* 35. Cf. pp. 17, 43, 54, 60, and 211.
12. On the American Jewish Committee and its funding of studies of anti-Semitism, see Martin Jay, *The Dialectical Imagination* (California, 1996), 221.
13. http://www.nizkor.org/hweb/people/e/eichmann-adolf/transcripts/, vol. 3, session 56 (29 May 1961).
14. Dicks vividly recalls the episode in an interview for the 1970 BBC television documentary, *The Strange Case of Rudolf Hess*. A number of other doctors who worked on the case also participated in this programme, which was scripted by Correlli Barnett and directed by Harry Hastings.
15. *RH* 50.
16. *RH* 55.

17. *RH* 4–5, 55. Cf. Record Group 260, US Occupied HQ, World War II, Office of Military Government, Chief of Counsel for War Crimes, General Records, 1944–46, box 113, Folder entitled 'Medical Reports concerning Rudolf Hess'. NA.

18. *RH* 50–1.

19. *RH* 51.

20. *RH* 48–9, 56, 99, 103, 118, 120, and 128.

21. *RH* 60.

22. *RH* 50.

23. *RH* 60.

24. *RH* 20. This view of British brutality against the Boers (among others) was in line with German propaganda images of the time; see Gerwin Strobl, *The Germanic Isle: Nazi Perceptions of Britain* (Cambridge, 2000), 190.

25. *RH* 127.

26. Ibid.

27. *RH* 52.

28. At a meeting in 1943 Beaverbrook apparently voiced to a colleague his misgivings about the state of Hess's mind at the time of his meeting with the prisoner in September 1941; he suspected he had been doped by the intelligence service in order to make him talk; the description is provided in *The Diaries of Sir Robert Bruce Lockhart* (4 Sept. 1943), ii. 254–6.

29. *RH* 51.

30. *RH* 128.

31. For examples see Daniel Pick, *War Machine: The Rationalisation of Slaughter in the Modern Age* (New Haven, 1993), ch. 9.

32. The diversity of responses and the shifting nature of generational attitudes to the Third Reich are well described in A. Dirk Moses, *German Intellectuals and the Nazi Past* (Cambridge, 2007). For an illuminating study of diverse attitudes to war and death in modern Germany, see Alon Confino, Paul Betts, and Dirk Schumann (eds.), *Between Mass Death and Individual Loss: The Place of the Dead in Twentieth-Century Germany* (New York, 2008).

33. *RH* 204.

34. *RH* 38.

35. *RH* 50.

36. *RH* 37.

37. *RH* 51–2.

38. *RH* 62.

39. *RH* ch. 6.

40. *RH* 63.

41. *RH* 64.

42. See Chapter 8.

43. *RH* 63.

44. Henry Dicks, clinical notebook on Rudolf Hess, entries for June and July 1941. HD.

45. *RH* 5–6.
46. This temporary shift in Hess's behaviour and communications is described in *RH* and also in the BBC television documentary to which Dicks *et al.* contributed, *The Strange Case of Rudolf Hess*.
47. *RH* 112.
48. Henry Dicks, *Fifty Years of the Tavistock Clinic* (London, 1970), 110.
49. Dicks's wartime reports on the Wehrmacht, German deserters, morale, and the 'national problem' of National Socialism can be consulted in HD, and are also accessible in the National Archives; Public Record Office, London, at WO/241/1, WO/241/2, and WO/241/6.
50. The report, dated 30 August 1943, was prepared under the auspices of the Directorate of Army Psychiatry. HD.
51. *RH* 69.
52. *RH* 77.
53. *RH* 205.
54. *RH* 13.
55. Henry Dicks, Clinical Notebook, entries for February 1944. HD.
56. Henry Dicks, 'Analysis under Hypnotics', paper delivered in London, 9 May 1940, in a series entitled 'Individual Psychological Medical Pamphlets', no. 23, ed. H. C. Squires.
57. *RH* 87–9. Cf. Dicks's clinical notes on Hess, dated 7 May 1944, in HD.
58. Alison Winter, 'The Making of "truth serum"', *Bulletin of the History of Medicine*, 79 (2005), 500–33.
59. José Brunner, '"Oh Those Crazy Cards Again": A History of the Debate on the Nazi Rorschachs, 1946–2001', *Political Psychology*, 22 (2001), 233–61.
60. On OSS experiments with toxins that might induce stomach problems, hairloss, itching, as well as (ironically in light of the Hess case) amnesia, see John Marks, *The Search for the 'Manchurian Candidate': The CIA and Mind Control* (London, 1979), ch. 1.
61. *RH* 82–8.
62. *RH* 88. Cf. Clinical Notebook March 1944. HD.
63. Clinical Notebook, entry for 7 March 1944. HD.
64. *RH* 115.
65. *RH* 106.
66. *RH* 129.
67. *RH* 116.
68. *RH* 110 and 128.
69. *RH* 79.
70. *RH* 71.
71. Ibid.
72. *RH* 72.
73. *RH* 32.
74. Ibid.

75. Dicks's handwritten report (12–13 Feb. 1945) on his visit to Maindiff Court. HD.
76. Pick, *Faces of Degeneration*; Sander L. Gilman and J. Edward Chamberlin, *Degeneration: The Dark Side of Progress* (New York, 1985).
77. *RH* 28–9.
78. *RH* p. xii.
79. Hitler perused architectural plans avidly and visited the models for the reconstruction of his hometown Linz frequently, sometimes twice a day, in 1945; *HH* 15, and *HN* 778.
80. *RH* 36.
81. *RH* 35.
82. My summary condenses views expressed by Rees and Dicks, respectively in the introduction and in ch. 5 of *RH*. See esp. pp. 8, 13, 53–8.
83. Langer, *MH*. Cf. *RH* 203.
84. *RH* ch. 16.
85. Robert Gellately (ed.), *The Nuremberg Interviews Conducted by Leon Goldensohn* (London, 2006), p. xix.

CHAPTER 5

1. Adorno argued that 'What distinguishes [Freud] from Le Bon is … the absence of the traditional contempt for the masses'. Adorno, 'Freudian Theory and the Pattern of Fascist Propaganda', 121.
2. Ernst Simmel, 'National Socialism and Public Health', first published in *Der Sozialistiche Arzt* [The Socialist Physician], 1932, trans. in *Los Angeles Psychoanalytic Bulletin* (1989), 17–27; quotations at pp. 25–6.
3. Zaretsky, *Secrets of the Soul*, 222–3.
4. Freud, *Group Psychology*, SE, vol. 18.
5. Zaretsky, *Secrets of the Soul*, 220. For the history of Reich's troubled career, Myron Sharaf, *Fury on Earth: A Biography of Wilhelm Reich* (New York, 1983).
6. *Totem and Taboo*, SE, vol. 13, p. 144. For the history of discourse on Nazism and homosexuality, see Herzog (ed.), *Sexuality and German Fascism*.
7. Glenda Sluga, *Nation, Psychology, and International Politics, 1870–1919* (Basingstoke, 2006).
8. Robert Nye, *Crime, Madness and Politics in Modern France: The Medical Concept of National Decline* (Princeton, 1984); Jaap Van Ginneken, *Crowds, Psychology and Politics, 1871–99* (Cambridge, 1992).
9. John Burrow, *The Crisis of Reason: European Thought, 1848–1914* (New Haven, 2000).
10. For the economist's reading of Freud, especially in the 1920s, see Robert Skidelsky, *John Maynard Keynes, 1883–1946* (London, 2003), 46, 346, 372.
11. John Maynard Keynes, *The Economic Consequences of the Peace* (London, 1971 [1919]), 1–2. See Keynes's references to 'the unconscious recesses of [society's] being', p. 12; cf. pp. 142, 144–6, 158, 170, 188.

12. Paul Fussell, *The Great War and Modern Memory* (Oxford, 1975); Modris Eksteins, *Rites of Spring: The Great War and the Birth of the Modern Age* (London, 1989); Samuel Hynes, *A War Imagined: the First World War and English Culture* (London, 1990).

13. Ernest Jones, *Sigmund Freud: Life and Work*, 3 vols. (London, 1955), ii. 192.

14. Fussell, *The Great War.* Cf. Burrow, *The Crisis of Reason*; Winter, *Sites of Memory, Sites of Mourning*; Pick, *War Machine.*

15. Thomson, 'Mental Hygiene', 291.

16. Ibid.

17. Ibid.

18. Benjamin L. Alpers, *Dictators, Democracy, and American Public Culture: Envisioning the Totalitarian Enemy 1920s–1950s* (Chapel Hill, NC, 2003).

19. See Brett Gray, *Nervous Liberals: Propaganda Anxieties from World War I to the Cold War* (New York, 1999), esp. ch. 2.

20. Harold Lasswell, 'The Psychology of Hitlerism', *Political Quarterly*, 4 (1933), 373–84, at p. 373. On Lasswell's Freudianism, see Dwaine Marvick, 'The World of Harold D. Lasswell: His Approach, Concerns and Influence', *Political Behavior*, 2 (1980), 219–29.

21. *MH* 29.

22. Alpers, *Dictators*, 15.

23. Dorothy Thompson, *The New Russia* (New York, 1928), 22.

24. *Headway*, 15 (May 1933), 15.

25. *Headway*, 15 (Feb. 1933), 32–3; 15 (Sept. 1933), 173. For a critical response, ibid. (Oct. 1933), 204.

26. Vivian Ogilvie, 'Nazi Tactics and Mass Psychology', *Headway*, 15 (Aug. 1933), 153.

27. In the autumn of 1933 Baldwin confided to one of his colleagues that he believed 'the world is stark mad. I have no idea what the matter is with it but it's all wrong and at times I am sick to death of being an asylum attendant.' He added: 'I think we are the sanest but the disease is catching.' In April 1936 (by then Prime Minister again), he went further: '[w]ith two lunatics like Mussolini and Hitler you can never be sure of anything. But I am determined to keep the country out of the war.' Thomas Jones, *A Diary with Letters 1931–1950* (London, 1954), 191 and 391.

28. Quoted in Zaretsky, *Secrets of the Soul*, 264.

29. David Reynolds, *From Munich to Pearl Harbor: Roosevelt's America and the Origins of the Second World War* (Chicago, 2001), 43.

30. Ibid.

31. Sigmund Freud and William C. Bullitt, *Thomas Woodrow Wilson: A Psychological Study* (London, 1967).

32. Orville H. Bullitt (ed.), *For the President: Personal and Secret Correspondence between Franklin D. Roosevelt and William C. Bullitt* (Boston, 1972), p. vii.

33. Ibid. (letters of 7 Apr. 1935, 10 May 1937, and 19 Apr. 1939), pp. 103, 214, and 344.

34. Bullitt and Hanfstaengl met, for instance, in Berlin in 1934; ibid. 62.

35. William C. Bullitt, *Report to the American People* (Boston, 1940).

36. *For the President* (letter from Bullitt to Roosevelt, 4 Nov. 1937), p. 230.

37. See Michaela Hoenicke Moore, *Know your Enemy: The American Debate on Nazism, 1933–1945* (Cambridge, 2010), 81–2.

38. Lloyd George called Hitler 'a remarkable man', and claimed he was a solid character, unlike the excitable Mussolini. Jones, *A Diary*, 245. Jones also refers to the historian Arnold J. Toynbee's view of the German leader in 1936: 'He is convinced of [Hitler's] sincerity in desiring peace in Europe and a close friendship with England.' Ibid. 181.

39. Quoted in Keith Jeffery, *MI6: The History of the Secret Intelligence Service, 1909–1949* (London, 2010), 309. Emphasis added.

40. Richard Overy, *Goering: The 'Iron Man'* (London, 1984), 7; Robert Manvell and Heinrich Fraenkel, *Goering* (London, 2005), 61.

41. Federico Finchelstein, *Transatlantic Fascism: Ideology, Violence, and the Sacred in Argentina and Italy, 1919–1945* (Durham, NC, 2010), 15.

42. Orwell wondered what Hess was doing here, and suggested that if a possibility existed to miss the propaganda opportunity that this eventuality presented, the British government would surely take it. *The Collected Essays of George Orwell*, vol. 2 [1940–1943] (Harmondsworth, 1970), 147, 454.

43. George Orwell, 'Wells, Hitler and the World State', *Critical Essays* (London, 1954), 92–8, at p. 98. Also in *Collected Essays*, ii. 166–71.

44. George Orwell, 'Antisemitism in Britain', *Contemporary Jewish Record* (Apr. 1945), reprinted in *The Collected Essays, Journalism and Letters of George Orwell*, ed. Sonia Orwell and Ian Angus (London, 1968), iii. 332–41. Cf. John Newsinger, 'Orwell, Antisemitism and the Holocaust', in John Rodden (ed.), *The Cambridge Companion to Orwell* (Cambridge, 2007), ch. 9.

45. Alpers, *Dictators*. The failure of so many theories of 'totalitarianism' to elucidate the profound differences between the nature of the Soviet and Nazi systems are well summarized by Ian Kershaw in 'Hitler and the Uniqueness of Nazism', part of the special issue, 'Understanding Nazi Germany', *Journal of Contemporary History*, 39 (2004), 239–54. Cf. Caplan, 'The Historiography', 555.

46. Henry Dicks, 'Anatomy of Totalitarianism', in HD, box 1, folder entitled 'Writings and Proposals based on Wartime Work'.

47. *Abuses of Psychiatry for Political Repression in the Soviet Union*, 44–5.

48. Dorothy Thompson, *Let the Record Speak* (London, 1939), 217, 251, 335.

49. See Alpers, *Dictators, passim*, for examples.

50. Ibid. 40.

51. Peter Drucker, *The End of Economic Man: A Study of the New Totalitarianism* (London, 1939), 22. See also pp. 4–9.

52. See folder entitled 'Germany, conference on, 1944', Papers of Talcott Parsons, Pusey Library, Harvard University [reference HUG (FP), 15.2].

53. Uta Gerhardt (ed. and intr.), *Talcott Parsons on National Socialism* (New York, 1993), 48–9. Jennifer Fay, 'Germany is a Boy in Trouble', *Cultural Critique*, 64 (2006), 196–234.

54. There are more than passing echoes of those wartime psychiatric approaches in various much later 'diagnostic' accounts; see e.g. Paul Matussek *et al.*, *Affirming Psychosis: The Mass Appeal of Adolf Hitler* (Frankfurt, 2007); Norbert Bromberg and Verna Volz Small, *Hitler's Psychopathology* (New York, 1983). The latter work diagnoses the Führer as a narcissistic borderline personality type.

55. Kurt Krueger, *Inside Hitler* (New York, 1941), 58–9.

56. Ibid. 65.

57. Ibid. 277.

58. Quoted in *HN* 803.

59. As listed in the index to Krueger, *Inside Hitler*.

60. Leo Hamalian, 'Nobody Knows My Names: Samuel Roth and the Underside of Modern Letters', *Journal of Modern Literature*, 3 (1974), 889–921, at p. 913.

61. Roth emigrated to North America and pursued a colourful and controversial clandestine career during the inter-war period. He once ran a bookshop in Greenwich Village, and wrote poetry and erotic stories (some called them pornography). In his spare time he produced a series of literary impersonations as well as pirated (and bowdlerized) editions of extant works, including *Ulysses*. Even in its doctored form, his American serialization of James Joyce's work in 1927 may have shocked some unsuspecting readers, but those most dismayed by this freelance venture were apparently the original author, his friends, and admirers. Ibid. 893.

62. Ibid.

63. See Siegfried Kracauer, *From Caligari to Hitler: A Psychological History of the German Film* [1947], revised and extended edition (Princeton, 2004). Cf. Claudia Schmölders, *Hitler's Face: The Biography of an Image* (Philadelphia, 2006).

64. For this comment by Lang and other subsequent descriptions of the film by the director as an ironic commentary on Nazism, see 'Fritz Lang on *Das Testament des Dr. Mabuse*: A Scrapbook', in the viewing notes that accompany the DVD, *The Testament of Dr Mabuse*, Masters of Cinema Series (2009), pp. 25, 28.

CHAPTER 6

1. See F. H. Hinsley and Alan Stripp (eds.), *Codebreakers: The Inside Story of Bletchley Park* (Oxford, 1993), 24, 51.

2. See Telford Taylor, 'Anglo-American Signals Intelligence Co-Operation', in ibid., ch. 8.

3. Richard Rhodes, *The Making of the Atomic Bomb* (New York, 1986).

4. Joseph Bendersky, 'Psychohistory before Hitler: Early Military Analyses of German National Psychology', *Journal of the History of the Behavioral Sciences*, 24 (1988), 166–82.

5. David C. Engerman, *Know Your Enemy: The Rise and Fall of America's Soviet Experts* (New York, 2009).

6. Cora Sol Goldstein, *Capturing the German Eye: American Visual Propaganda in Occupied Germany* (Chicago, 2009), 5–6.

7. For the background, see Louise Hoffman, 'American Psychologists and Wartime Research on Germany, 1941–1945', *American Psychologist*, 47 (1992), 264–73, and 'Psychoanalytical Interpretations of Adolf Hitler and Nazism, 1933–1945: A Prelude to Psychohistory', *Psychohistory Review*, 47 (1975), 229–79. A number of FDR's political opponents attacked his entire administration for including too many Jews; see Peter Novick, *The Holocaust in American Life* (New York, 2000), p. 33.

8. Dicks, *Fifty Years*, ch. 6. Cf. Eric Trist and Hugh Murray (eds.), *The Social Engagement of Social Science: A Tavistock Anthology*, vol. 1: *The Socio-Psychological Perspective* (Philadelphia, 1990), especially section one: 'A New Social Psychiatry: A World War II Legacy.'

9. Many years later, Dicks wrote an appreciative review of Langer's book on Hitler for the *New Statesman*. A draft copy of the review, dated February 1973, is contained in HD.

10. Christopher Andrew, *For the President's Eyes: Secret Intelligence and the American Presidency, from Washington to Bush* (London, 1995), 96.

11. *MH* 6.

12. Ernst Kris and Hans Speier, in association with Sidney Axelrad, Hans Herma, Janice Loeb *et al.*, *German Radio Propaganda: Report on Home Broadcasts during the War* (London, 1944).

13. Personal communication: Leonard Langer, 22 July 2008.

14. Letter from William Langer to Donovan (14 Nov. 1942): RB 226, OSS A1, entry 146, Box 129. Folder 'Walter C. Langer'. NA.

15. Material relating to the finance of his project is included in RB 226 OSS A-1, Entry 169A. RB 226 OSS A-1, Entry 146, box 129. NA.

16. See, for instance, in the BBC archives (at Reading), files on Germany, broadcasting, propaganda, etc. E1/742, E 1/743/1, E 1/743/2; New York Psychoanalytic Society archives, report (anonymous) on the work of the Joint Committee on Post-war Planning, held at Columbia University, May and June 1944; Richard Brickner and L. Vosburgh Lyons, 'A Neuropsychiatric View of German Culture and the Treatment of Germany'; *Journal of Nervous and Mental Disease* (Sept. 1943); 'Health and Human Relations in Germany', publication for the Macey Foundation (held in New York Psychoanalytic Society archives). See also in HD, the feature article, 'A Study in German Mentality', *British Zone Review* (14 Sept. 1946), 1–2; David Levy Papers, Cornell Medical School, Oskar Diethelm Library, New York, box 34, folders 4001, 13001, 15001, 16001, 19001. See also Jessica Reinisch, *Public Health in Germany under Allied Occupation, 1943–1949* (Rochester, NY, in press).

17. Roosevelt announced the policy of unconditional surrender at the Casablanca Conference in January 1943. Moore, *Know your Enemy*, 131.

18. William Langer, foreword, *MH*. Despite this surge of support, some opinion polls indicated that 30% of Americans still hoped for a negotiated peace with Germany after Pearl Harbor. Levels of public approval and disapproval for the war against Germany and Japan were carefully and sometimes anxiously monitored by key advisers to the president thereafter. Moore, *Know your Enemy*, 105–6.

19. Richard Harris Smith, *OSS: The Secret History of America's First Intelligence Agency* (Guildford, 2005), 1–3.

20. Andrew, *For the President's Eyes*, 85. Cf. Smith, *OSS*, 1–3.

21. Andrew, *For the President's Eyes*, 85.

22. Smith, *OSS*, 13.

23. Christopher Andrew, *The Defence of the Realm: The Authorized History of MI5* (London, 2009), 368.

24. Ibid.

25. Herbert Marcuse, *Technology, War and Fascism: Collected Papers of Herbert Marcuse*, ed. Douglas Kellner (London, 1998), e.g. 25 and 231 ff. Cf. Jay, *The Dialectical Imagination*, 80.

26. Barry M. Katz, *Foreign Intelligence: Research and Analysis in the Office of Strategic Services, 1942–1945* (Cambridge, Mass., 1989), 11.

27. Marcuse, *Technology, War and Fascism*, passim.

28. Katz, *Foreign Intelligence*, 44.

29. Ibid. 39.

30. Ibid. 34–5.

31. Jay, *The Dialectical Imagination*, 172.

32. Smith, *OSS*, 218–19.

33. Ibid. 3.

34. http://www.psywar.org/malingering.php. This site (accessed 19 July 2011) contains research by Lee Richards (dated 2004) entitled 'Black Propaganda: British Covert Propaganda against the Third Reich'. A notable case was the work of a Canadian doctor and army officer John T. MacCurdy, a lecturer in psychopathology at Cambridge, who worked for the PWE during the war and devised a number of ploys and techniques for undermining enemy morale. See Richards, 'Black Propaganda', and John Forrester, '1919: Psychology and Psychoanalysis, Cambridge and London—Myers, Jones and MacCurdy', *Psychoanalysis and History*, 10 (2008), 37–94.

35. Corey Ford, *Donovan of OSS* (London, 1970), 135. Many other experiments were conducted at the OSS on the manipulation of the minds of soldiers and the possibility of loosening tongues in interviews through drug treatment. Walter Langer was evidently an enthusiastic participant in this type of work. Note that a letter from Langer to Donovan (1 January 1943) refers to his discussions with Stanley Lovell (among others), and the possibility of manipulating the psyche through marijuana. Langer also suggests ways of disguising the real purpose of such inquiries. Previous research, he claimed, had been confined to

'therapeutic uses' and 'physiological effects'. See 'Research on the Psychological Effects Produced by Synthetic Marijuana', RG 226, A1 Entry 146, Box 129, Folder 1863. NA. I am grateful to Knuth Müller for drawing this document to my attention.

36. *Childhood and Society*, 296–7.

37. Lovell recorded various far-fetched tricks that were tried at the OSS. Some of these, he claimed, produced good results; others, he acknowledged, had mis-fired. An entire chapter of his book, *Of Spies and Stratagems*, records such aborted schemes.

38. Marks, *The Search for the 'Manchurian Candidate'*, ch. 1, p. 16.

39. Stanley Platt Lovell, *Of Spies and Stratagems* (Englewood Cliffs, NJ, 1963), 19.

40. For the legend of Hitler's monorchism and the psychobiographical speculation surrounding it, see *HH* 45 and 617–18, n 137. Kershaw also sets out the reasons the story is in fact so doubtful. Note the continuing return of the topic of Hitler's monorchism in the popular media; e.g. (following the publication of new material by an army doctor from the First World War who claimed he treated Hitler for his serious groin injuries), Andrew Roberts, 'Did Hitler really only have one testicle?', *Daily Mail*, 20 Nov. 2008.

41. Lovell, *Of Spies and Stratagems*, 84.

42. Ibid. 25, 62, 82, 84, 87, and 89.

43. See e.g. Henry Murray and Morris Stein, 'Notes on the Selection of Combat Officers', *Psychosomatic Medicine*, 5 (1943), 386–91; Henry Murray and D.W. Mackinnon, 'Assessment of OSS Personnel', *Journal of Consulting Psychology*, 10 (1946), 76–80. Murray brought several other staff from the Harvard Psychological Clinic to work with him at the OSS, including Nevitt Sanford (who later collaborated with Adorno on *The Authoritarian Personality*) and Eliot Jaques (who became a psychoanalyst and a close associate of Melanie Klein after he moved to London); Claire Douglas, *Translate this Darkness: The Life of Christiana Morgan, the Veiled Woman in Jung's Circle* (New York, 1993), 233.

44. Quoted in Smith, *OSS*, and p. 5. Cf. the material on the OSS and the copy of the Alger Hiss trial transcript contained in the file marked 'Hiss', Murray Papers, HUGFP 97.45.4, boxes 1 and 2; accession 13755; Pusey Library, Harvard. The Hiss trial transcript also includes an interchange with Murray regarding his OSS Hitler study, which he claims took a month to write, and which, he pointedly added, he produced alone; see trial transcript, p. 2853. See also the correspondence with William Langer contained in this same collection in the folder entitled 'Hitler Study: Other Works and Langer Controversy'.

45. Hugh Murray, 'The Transformation of Selection Procedures: The War Office Selection Boards'. This was one of a series of unpublished papers from the Tavistock Institute now available online at http://www.moderntimesworkplace.com/archives/ericsess/sessvol1/Murrayp45.opd.pdf. Among the other staff involved in wartime officer selection experiments were Eric Trist and 'Tommy'

Wilson (both important figures at the Tavistock Clinic) and the psychoanalysts Tom Main and Harold Bridger.

46. Andrew Scull, 'The Mental Health Sector and the Social Sciences in Post-World War II USA. Part 1: Total War and its Aftermath', *History of Psychiatry*, 22 (2011), 3–19, at pp. 8–9.

47. Ibid. 6.

48. According to one calculation, 250 men in every thousand based in American army combat units in the European theatre of war were sent for mental health assessment or psychiatric hospitalization during 1944; ibid. 6–7.

49. Ford, *Donovan of OSS*, 132 and 137; see also Marks, *The Search for the 'Manchurian Candidate'*, 17.

50. OSS 'alumni' such as Norman O. Brown, H. Stuart Hughes, and Karl Schorske produced a number of the key works on psychoanalysis, culture, and history that marked the post-war period.

51. Graham Richards, 'Putting Britain on the Couch: The Popularisation of Psychoanalysis in Britain 1918–1940', *Science in Context*, 13 (2000), 183–230, esp. pp. 199-202.

52. Edward Bernays was doubly related to Freud: the son of Freud's sister Anna and of his wife's brother Eli.

53. To treat Goebbels as a dark 'genius' of propaganda (as even some of his opponents have done) was, so Adorno suggested, to inflate his talent and to 'buy in' to a self-serving Nazi legend. See Adorno, 'Freudian Theory and the Pattern of Fascist Propaganda'.

54. Sinclair Lewis, *It Can't Happen Here* (New York, 1935), 426. Cf. the more recent 'counterfactual' experiment in this genre, Philip Roth, *The Plot against America* (Boston, 2004).

55. Eric Caplan, *Mind Games: American Culture and the Birth of Psychotherapy* (Berkeley, 1998); Zaretsky, *Secrets of the Soul*.

56. Hitler speech (August 1939), Donovan Papers, Nuremberg Trial Collection, vol. XC, section 8.001, Cornell Law School Library [index online at http://library2. lawschool.cornell.edu/Donovan]. These archives at Cornell also contain extensive documents covering interviews with and profiles of the Nazi leadership during the Nuremberg trials.

57. Ibid., vol. IV, section 8.06 which contains the OSS translation of this speech. http://library2.lawschool.cornell.edu/donovan/pdf/Batch_2_pdfs/Vol_IV_8_06.pdf.

58. Despite the copious secondary literature on the culture and thought of the Third Reich, a dedicated study by a historian of modern Germany, tracking the precise psychological models, theories, and metaphors of mind that were embedded in the writings of Hitler and of his associates, remains to be written.

59. Katz, *Foreign Intelligence*, 34–5.

60. Ibid. 14.

61. For an overview of the IMT-related material in Donovan's papers, see http://library.lawschool.cornell.edu/WhatWeHave/SpecialCollections/Donovan/Highlights.cfm

62. Lawrence Douglas, *The Memory of Judgment: Making Law and History in the Trials of the Holocaust* (New Haven, 2001), 17.

63. Jackson Papers, Library of Congress, box 95; letter from Donovan, 15 June 1945; from Alvan Barach, Carl Binger, Richard Brickner, Frank Fremont-Smith, Adolf Meyer, John Millet, Tracy Putnam, and George Stephenson, 11 June 1945; from Millet, 16 Aug. 1945.

64. Paul Weindling, *John W. Thompson: Psychiatrist in the Shadow of the Holocaust* (New York, 2010), ch. 12. See also Paul Weindling, *Nazi Medicine and the Nuremberg Trials: From Medical War Crimes to Informed Consent* (London, 2004), 130.

65. Weindling, *Nazi Medicine and the Nuremberg Trials*, 130.

66. Smith, *OSS*, 8.

67. Ford, *Donovan of OSS*, 316.

CHAPTER 7

1. *MH*, Introduction.

2. Letters from Langer to Toland, 25 Mar.–24 May 1972, in John Toland Papers: Adolf Hitler (Walter Langer), box 47. RPL.

3. See e.g. *HH* and *HN*.

4. *MH* 29.

5. Ibid.

6. Ibid.

7. *MH* 33.

8. On different views of Hitler's 'sincerity' (notably by Alan Bullock and Hugh Trevor-Roper), see Ron Rosenbaum, *Explaining Hitler: The Search for the Origins of His Evil* (New York, 1998).

9. SB 317.

10. Criticism of Freud's 1910 paper on Leonardo took shape in the 1920s. One feature that critics returned to frequently was Freud's gaffe in relying on a German version of the artist's notebook that erroneously offered 'vulture' (a creature whose meanings Freud proceeded to explore) rather than 'kite', in the translation of the original Italian term, *nibbio*. 'Leonardo DaVinci and a Memory of his Childhood', SE vol. 11; Gay, *Freud*, 268–74, esp. p. 273.

11. Murray's role in the establishment of the Boston Psychoanalytic Society, training analysis with Franz Alexander, and intellectual debts to his lover and 'muse' Christiana Morgan, are described in Douglas, *Translate this Darkness*, esp. pp. 188–93.

12. Henry Murray, *Explorations in Personality: A Clinical and Experimental Study of Fifty Men of College Age by the Workers of Harvard Psychological Clinic* (New York, 1938).

13. On Henry Murray's influence on the pioneering British psychologist Eric Trist, as he worked on new techniques of officer selection during the war, see Trist, 'Guilty of Enthusiasm', 203. Trist claims: 'At that time I had the only copy of Henry A. Murray's [*Thematic Apperception Tests*] in Britain and I kept it longer than I should out of the Cambridge [University] library.' Ibid. 202.

14. For details of the invitation that was extended by Langer to Kris and Lewin, as well as to other colleagues, including Lawrence Kubie and John Millet, see Ernst Kris Papers, Library of Congress, box 9, folder 14, letters dated 10 Sept. and 21 Oct. 1941. For other first-hand accounts and diagnoses of Hess's mental state at the IMT, see Hilary Gaskin, *Eyewitnesses at Nuremberg* (London, 1990).

15. Walter Langer to Toland (25 Mar. 1972), Toland Papers, box 47, folder marked 'Adolf Hitler, Psychological (Langer Walter)'. RPL.

16. Letters from Walter Langer to Toland, 25 Mar. 1972, 17 Apr. 1972 and 24 May 1972; letter from Murray to Toland, 18 Apr. 1972. Toland Papers, box 47, folder marked 'Adolf Hitler, Psychological (Langer Walter)'. RPL. For Murray's very different perception of this dispute, see Forrest G. Robinson, *Love's Story Told: A Life of Henry Murray*, (Cambridge, Mass., 1992), pp. 275–79.

17. *MH* 13.

18. SB 191 and 365.

19. See the translation of the prison report (8 Jan. 1924) on Hitler's mental state in SB. It noted the view that Hitler might have been insane in mounting the Putsch, but suggested that, if so, he had quickly recovered his lucidity. He may have suffered a temporary depression, but it was said this was not as a result of mental illness. The report concluded that there was nothing to suggest any impairment to his free will. This account, together with associated documents, is also located in the Toland Papers, 'Adolf Hitler (Walter Langer)', Box 47. RPL.

20. For an account of the collusion and soft-pedalling by the authorities after the Putsch, *HH* 213–18.

21. SB 496–9.

22. SB 503.

23. SB 305.

24. SB 430.

25. Personal communication: Leonard Langer, 22 July 2008.

26. *MH*, Introduction.

27. SB 432.

28. SB 432–3.

29. For the background, Rosenbaum, *Explaining Hitler*, ch. 2.

30. 'Putzi' Hanfstaengl, *The Unknown Hitler: Notes from the Young Nazi Party 1921–1936*, introduced by Richard. J. Evans (London, 2005).

31. Brown, *The Last Hero*, 211.

32. PSF. John F. Carter. Box 99, May 1943–May 1944, folder, June–July 1943 (Letter from Field to Grace Tully, 4 Mar. 1944). RPL.

33. Ibid. (Memo, 10 June 1943). Hanfstaengl's comments on Goebbels, Hans Frank, and other leading Nazis are also on file here. White House briefing material on

Hitler's personality and especially on the evidence of Dr Hermann Rauschning
are to be found in the President's Personal Files, 5765–5804, folder 5780, headed
'Hitler, Adolf, 1938–1941'. For discussion of the Hess affair and the prisoner's
mental state, see the President's Secretary's File, Diplomatic Correspondence,
Great Britain: 1943, Box 36. RPL.

34. PSF. John F. Carter. Box 99, May 1943–May 1944, folder, June–July 1943
(Report, 21 July 1943). RPL.

35. Ibid., folder dated October 1943, headed 'Hitler, Analysis of Personality'. This
contains Murray's text and Carter's letter, headed 'Report on Psychiatric analysis of Adolph Hitler'. Carter noted that the documents were received from
Arthur Upham Pope and costs were paid by the OSS.

36. Ibid., folder: President's Secretary's File (August–December 1943), Carter, letter
to Grace Tully, for the President, 11 Sept. 1943, headed 'Memorandum on Hitler
speech'.

37. Ibid., folder for Aug.–Dec. 1943; Hanfstaengl's report on Hitler's Speech
(pp. 7–8) and covering letter from Carter, dated 11 Nov. 1943. RPL.

38. Ibid., 16-page report and covering letter, dated 14 Dec. 1943, p. 13. This document contains Pope's interview with Hanfstaengl the previous month.

39. Ibid., p. 9.

40. Ibid., p. 5.

41. HH 188.

42. MH 171.

43. MH 171–2.

44. MH 155.

45. In the late nineteenth century specialist commentators on the subject, such as
Gustave Le Bon, Gabriel Tarde, and Scipio Sighele, had regularly compared the
nature of crowds and femininity. See Susanna Barrows, Distorting Mirrors: Visions
of the Crowd in Late Nineteenth-Century France (New Haven, 1991); Pick, Faces of
Degeneration, chs. 3 and 5. In Mein Kampf Hitler had also expressed similar
assumptions. Cf. the covering letter by William Langer, 25 May 1942, together
with report on Hitler by Walter Langer, dated 26 April, 1942, pp. 5, 28, 30, 32;
in Toland Papers, Adolf Hitler (Walter Langer), box 52, RPL. Cf. MH 91–2.

46. SB 475.

47. SB 483. On Roth see Chapter 5, nn. 60–1.

48. On assumptions of interiority within modern psychology at large, see Nikolas
Rose, Governing the Soul: The Shaping of the Private Self (London, 1990) and
Charles Taylor, Sources of the Self: The Making of the Modern Identity (Cambridge,
Mass., 1989).

49. Murray, 'Hitler, Analysis of Personality', 5.

50. Ibid. 6.

51. e.g. ibid. 16 and 26.

52. Moore, Know your Enemy, 219.

53. Ibid., Foreword.

54. *MH* 47.
55. *MH* 30.
56. *MH* 35.
57. *MH*, Introduction.
58. Toland Papers, 'Adolf Hitler (Walter Langer)', box 52. RPL.
59. *HH* 352, and 705, n. 227.
60. *HH* 353.
61. *HH* 354.
62. Rosenbaum, *Explaining Hitler*, p. i.
63. *HH* 617-18, n. 137; Cf. Rosenbaum, *Explaining Hitler*, e.g. p. xxx.
64. Rosenbaum, *Explaining Hitler*, p. xii. On speculations about the Russian removal of Hitler's organs to Moscow, and Bullock's ironic commentary, ibid. 81.
65. *MH* 100.
66. *MH* 112.
67. *MH* 184.
68. *MH* 170.
69. Sebastian Haffner, *Germany: Jekyll and Hyde* (London, 1940), 24.
70. 'Who are the War Criminals?', *Tribune*, 22 Oct. 1943, reprinted in Orwell, *The Collected Essays* (Harmondsworth, 1970), vol. 2 [1940–43], p. 369.
71. *MH* 212.
72. SB 13.
73. *HN* 755. Another contemporary observer to consider the prospects of suicide within—and indeed the suicide of—the regime was William Shirer, who said as much in his *Berlin Diary*.
74. Christian Goeschel, *Suicide in Nazi Germany* (Oxford, 2009).
75. *HN* 836.
76. *MH*, Introduction.
77. William Langer, foreword to *MH*. Cf. the wartime intelligence analyst Daniel Lerner's view that Churchill had shown little sympathy for or grasp of the more intricate psychological ploys considered by officials within the Supreme Headquarters Allied Expeditionary Force (SHAEF): Daniel Lerner, *Psychological Warfare against Nazi Germany: The Sykewar Campaign, D-Day to VE-Day* (Cambridge, Mass., 1971 [1949]), p. xiv.
78. See n. 35 above.
79. William Langer, 'The Next Assignment', *American Historical Review*, 63 (1958), 283–304.
80. *MH* 23.
81. Neither Langer's papers at the Boston Psychoanalytic Society, nor Kris and Lewin's at the Library of Congress, nor Murray's at Harvard University Library reveal the details of these exchanges between the collaborators.
82. A doctoral thesis by Knuth Müller ('Im Auftrag der Firma: Begegnungen der psychoanalytischen Gemeinschaft mit US-amerikanischen Geheimdienstnetzwerken seit 1940') Free University, Berlin, 2012) throws more light on the extent of such post-war collaborations.

CHAPTER 8

1. I quote here from <http://www.memorium-nuremberg.de/download/Memorium_Broschuere_en.pdf>, p. 2.
2. IMT vol. 2, p. 30.
3. Tony Judt, *Postwar: A History of Europe since 1945* (London, 1995), 53. For Judt's evaluation of the successes and failures of this judicial process and other measures aimed at denazification in post-war Germany, see esp. pp. 52–61.
4. The Japanese war crimes trials followed the Nuremberg model; defendants were examined by an International Military Tribunal for the Far East, as established by General Douglas MacArthur. Seven defendants were sentenced to hang; sixteen others were given life imprisonment.
5. Rebecca West, 'Greenhouse with Cyclamens 1' [1946], in *A Train of Powder: Six Reports on the Problems of Guilt and Punishment in our Time* (New York, 1955), 47.
6. Rebecca West, *Black Lamb and Grey Falcon: A Journey through Yugoslavia* (Edinburgh, 2006 [1941]), 481, 1108.
7. See document 17, in Richard Overy, *Interrogations* (London, 2001), 404. (Note that different published versions of *Interrogations* have distinct subtitles: the original version, *The Nazi Elite in Allied Hands*, was changed to *Inside the Minds of the Nazi Elite*.)
8. Document 17, in Overy, *Interrogations*, 404.
9. IMT vol. 2, pp. 21, 23. For the medical reports, defence appeals, and court decisions regarding the fitness of Krupp von Bohlen, Streicher, and Hess, see vol. 1, pp. 118–70 and vol. 2, pp. 1–21. On the question of Hess's amnesia, cf. vol. 2, pp. 478 ff.
10. Shirer, *Berlin Diary*, p. 23.
11. IMT vol. 2, p. 73.
12. *A Train of Powder*, 5.
13. On public fascination with Hess's gesticulations, antics and disconcerting grin, see Ann Tusa and John Tusa, *The Nuremberg Trial* (London, 1983); Michael R. Marrus, *The Nuremberg War Crimes Trial 1945–46* (Toronto, 1997), 132.
14. West, *Train of Powder*, 5.
15. Ibid.
16. See Appendix 2. Hess's attitude of derision towards the court is well described by Airey Neave (who attended the prisoner in his cell to let him know of the charges he would face) in a contribution to the aforementioned BBC television documentary, *The Strange Case of Rudolf Hess*.
17. Airey Neave, *Nuremberg* (London, 1978), 51.
18. Ibid. 88.
19. Ibid. 87.
20. Record Group 260, 'Records of United States Occupation Headquarters, World War II, Office of Military Government for Germany (U.S.)]', Office of Chief of Counsel for War Crimes, General Records, 1944–1946. Box 113. NA.

A microfiche copy of the orderlies' notebooks is also available at the Army Medical Services Museum, Aldershot.

21. *RH.*

22. *RH* 141. See also Lord Moran's papers, in the Contemporary Medicine Collection, WL. These detail various practical aspects of Moran's work on the case and reveal that the doctor was paid £262 and 10 shillings in fees; PP/CMW/G3/2.

23. A notable example was the French psychoanalyst Jacques Lacan; it appears that he followed developments at the IMT in some detail, took note of Jean Delay's reports on Hess, and wanted to visit the trial to study this prisoner himself. Personal communication: Elisabeth Roudinesco, 14 July 2011. Cf. Roudinesco, *Lacan, envers et contre tout* (Paris, 2011), 166. Perhaps the Nuremberg trial may have been one of the points of departure for Lacan's subsequent explorations of *jouissance* and the death drive in *The Ethics of Psychoanalysis* [1959–60], in *Seminars, Book 7* (New York, 1992) and 'Kant avec Sade' [1963], in Jacques Lacan, *Écrits*, 645–68.

24. Delay was an enthusiastic researcher on cerebral waves, who had spearheaded the introduction of ECT to France, following the pioneering work of Cerletti in Italy.

25. *RH* 214–15.

26. Summary drawn from *RH*, and IMT vol. 2, pp. 478–96.

27. *RH* 170.

28. *RH* 171.

29. Nolan C. Lewis Papers, Library of Congress, Subject Files, Box 10, 'Translation of document written by Rudolf Hess', p. 33. The box also contains clinical notes on Hess, 1941–1945 by Rees, reports of British observations and findings, IMT memos, records of the examination of the prisoner, handwritten notes, and psychiatric comments on the case, as well as some transcribed passages from the trial.

30. Robert Jay Lifton, *The Nazi Doctors: Medical Killing and the Psychology of Genocide* (New York, 1986).

31. *RH* 133–4.

32. *RH* 139–41.

33. *RH* 161.

34. *RH* 141–2.

35. *RH* 134.

36. Ibid.

37. *RH* 142.

38. Ibid.

39. Quoted in Neave, *Nuremberg*, 30.

40. *RH* 131–2. Alfred Steer, administrative head of the language division at the IMT, wrote of Hess's reaction to such film material: 'when these things came

on the screen there was a triumphant leer on Hess's face. Nuts, completely nuts.'
Quoted in Gaskin, *Eyewitnesses at Nuremberg*, 86.

41. *RH* ch. 16.
42. *RH* 186–7.
43. *RH* 185.
44. IMT vol. 2, pp. 478 ff.
45. *RH* 150.
46. *RH* 157–9.
47. *RH* 159.
48. *RH* 157–9; IMT vol., 2, pp. 478-496. The footage of Jackson pleading this case can be found via Youtube.
49. IMT vol. 2, p. 496.
50. *RH* 135, 176–9.
51. *RH* 183.
52. Ibid.
53. *RH* 173.
54. Goldensohn, *The Nuremberg Interviews*, 124.
55. Ibid.
56. *RH* 184.
57. Goldensohn, *The Nuremberg Interviews*, 212.
58. Ibid. 192.
59. *RH* 177–9.
60. *RH* 167.
61. *RH* 176.
62. *RH* 177, 179.
63. *RH* 181.
64. *RH* 183.
65. *RH* 182.
66. *RH* 191.
67. IMT vol. 22, p. 370.
68. IMT vol. 22, p. 530.
69. West, *Train of Powder*, 47.

CHAPTER 9

1. Moore, *Know your Enemy*, 237.
2. Although Murray Bernays' surname was originally Cohen, he adopted and kept the surname of his wife Hella, the daughter of Freud's sister and of Martha Freud's brother. The couple married and divorced in the 1920s. Murray was thus also the brother-in-law of Edward L. Bernays. See Murray Bernays' obituary, *New York Times* (22 Sept. 1970), 48. For a review of the history of the concept of conspiracy and its use in American jurisprudence, see Marie Siesseger 'Conspiracy Theory: The Use of Conspiracy Theory in

Times of National Crisis', *William and Mary Law Review*, 46 (2004), 1177–218.

3. Judt, *Postwar*, 56; Mark Mazower, *Dark Continent: Europe's Twentieth Century* (New York, 1998), 214.

4. For the background, Robert Cryer *et al.*, *An Introduction to International Criminal Law and Procedure* (Cambridge, 2007), 109–10; James Willis, *Prologue to Nuremberg: The Politics and Diplomacy of Punishing War Criminals of the First World War* (Westport, Conn., 1982). For an earlier verdict, by a British lawyer, on the failings and fiascos of the Leipzig trials held in the early 1920s, in lieu of an international tribunal, see Claud Mullins, *The Leipzig Trials: An Account of the War Criminal Trial and a Study of German Mentality* (London, 1921). Mullins concluded that whilst all sides committed crimes in the war, only Germany 'makes a system of atrocities'. He claimed that there is such a thing as a 'German mentality' and pointed to sadism and the constitutional factor of 'degeneracy' (pp. 83, 197, 229).

5. The reasons are summarized in Marrus, *The Nuremberg War Crimes Trial*, 3–7.

6. For a summary of possible precursors, see Robert Woetzel, *The Nuremberg Trials in International Law with a Postlude on the Eichmann Case* (London, 1962), ch. 2. See also the discussion in Cryer *et al.*, *An Introduction to International Criminal Law, passim*.

7. Norbert Ehrenfreund, *The Nuremberg Legacy: How the Nazi War Crimes Trials Changed the Course of History* (London, 2007), 13.

8. For the background and influence of Lemkin, see Mark Mazower, *No Enchanted Palace: The End of Empire and the Ideological Origins of the United Nations* (Princeton, 2009).

9. Overy, *Interrogations*, 47.

10. Francis B. Sayre, 'Criminal Conspiracy', *Harvard Law Review*, 35 (1921–2), 393–427, at p. 427; cf. Woetzel, *The Nuremberg Trials in International Law*, 200.

11. Sayre, 'Criminal Conspiracy', 408–9.

12. Cordell Hull, Henry Stimson, and James Forrestal, five-page memorandum to the President, Nov. 1944; cf. the further eleven-page memorandum by Hull and Stimson, 24 Nov. 1944, and the letter from John McCloy to Harry Hopkins and from John McCloy to Francis Biddle, 4 Dec. 1944, War Crimes File, Rosenman Papers, Harry S. Truman Presidential Library. These documents are at http://www.trumanlibrary.org/whistlestop/study_collections/Nuremberg (see under Documents, Nov.–Dec. 1944).

13. Ehrenfreund, *The Nuremberg Legacy*, 39.

14. Quoted in Marrus, *The Nuremberg War Crimes Trial*, 77–8.

15. Ibid. 91.

16. Neil Gregor, *Haunted City: Nuremberg and the Nazi Past* (New Haven, 2008).

17. Goldensohn, *The Nuremberg Interviews*, p. xx. For the views of Kelley and his colleagues as to the psychological value of the Nuremberg prisoner studies, see Eric A. Zillmer *et al.*, *The Quest for the Nazi Personality: A Psychological Investigation of Nazi War Criminals* (Hillsdale, NJ, 1995).

18. Marrus, *The Nuremberg War Crimes Trials*, 93.

19. Goldensohn, *The Nuremberg Interviews*, 29.

20. Cf. *HN* 838–9.

21. Gitta Sereny, *Albert Speer: His Battle with Truth* (New York 1995), 169. For further examples of the claim that Hitler could sweep away, in hypnotic fashion, all critical faculties, see *HH* 186.

22. Overy, *Goering*, 13.

23. Jackson Papers, box 95, memo from Jackson to Bernays, 23 June 1945.

24. On the extreme violence and arbitrary terror that prevailed at Dachau, Buchenwald, and other camps in the 1930s, see Nicholas Wachsmann, *Hitler's Prisons: Legal Terror in Nazi Germany* (New Haven, 2004), 170. For discussions of differences between 'ordinary' penal institutions and the camp system in Nazi Germany and the variability of treatment according to the classification given to prisoners and inmates, see ibid. 256.

25. Nina Sutton, *Bruno Bettelheim: The Other Side of Madness* (London, 1995). The connections between his own painful early life, sufferings in and departure from Nazi Germany, uses and abuses of psychoanalysis, and exploitations of and violent rages against children and staff during his many years (1944–73) as director of a school for severely disturbed children are described in Sutton's biography. Cf. David James Fisher, *Bettelheim: Living and Dying* (New York, 2008).

26. Fisher, *Bettelheim*, 6.

27. See Nicholas Wachsmann, *The Camps: A History of the Nazi Concentration Camps* (New York, forthcoming 2012).

28. Bruno Bettelheim, 'Individual and Mass Behavior in Extreme Situations', *Journal of Abnormal and Social Psychology*, 38 (1943), 417–52, at p. 448.

29. Ibid. 418–19. Italics in the original.

30. Ibid.; cf. Weindling, *Nazi Medicine*, 129–30. The psychoanalyst Edith Jacobson (also a prisoner of the Nazis during the 1930s before she made her escape and reached the United States) produced studies that bear comparison with Bettelheim's. Jacobson focused more upon feelings of guilt and depression in the inmates. See 'Observations on the Psychological Effects of Imprisonment on Female Political Prisoners', in Kurt Eissler (ed.), *Searchlight on Delinquency* (New York, 1949), pp. 341-368, and 'Depersonalization', *Journal of the American Psychoanalytical Association* (1959), vol. 7, pp. 581–610. Here Jacobson writes, '[d]epersonalization thus appears to be the pathological result of a conflict within the ego, between the part that has accepted and the part that attempts to undo identification with a degraded object image; in this case, with the image of the infantile, pregenital, sadomasochistic, castrated criminal.'

31. Bettelheim's article influenced Hanna Arendt as she prepared *The Origins of Totalitarianism* (1951), and Stanley Elkins as he developed his ground-breaking thesis on the psychology of slavery (published in book-form as *Slavery: A Problem in American Institutional and Intellectual Life* in 1959). As the historian

of psychoanalysis Eli Zaretksy concludes, Bettelheim's contribution 'attained iconic status'. Zaretsky, *Secrets of the Soul*, p. 283.

32. Weindling, *Nazi Medicine and the Nuremberg Trials*, 129–30.

33. Weindling, *John W. Thompson*, ch. 12.

34. For the vehement arguments of critics (notably the director of the documentary *Shoah*, Claude Lanzmann) against psychological explorations of Nazism, see Rosenbaum, 'Claude Lanzmann and the War against the Question Why', *Explaining Hitler*, ch. 14.

35. Rudolf Hess interrogation by Colonel John Amen, 9 Oct. 1945, ARC Identifier: 2674938, Record Group 242, Motion Picture, Sound and Video Record Section. NA.

36. Overy, *Interrogations*, p. xix.

37. The émigré academic and wartime adviser to the American government Hans Speier, for example, sent reports on German popular attitudes, Hitler's mental state in the last stage of the war, and the particular pathologies of members of the German government. Speier Papers, New York State University Library at Albany; e.g. box 13, folder 62, 'Allied Forces Psychological Warfare Section, Report on Hitler, 1945'.

38. West, *Train of Powder*, 69.

39. Ibid.

40. Quoted in Douglas, *The Memory*, 25–6. See also Neave, *Nuremberg*, 87–8.

41. *Proceedings of the International Congress on Mental Health*, ed. J. C. Flügel, 4 vols. (London, 1948), iii. 63.

42. Dicks wrote that 'our expectations on super-ego grounds, that the delinquent gang or the aggressive Nazis "ought" to feel guilty is a confusion, based on the Judeo-Protestant achievement of intra-punitive and reparative guilt only found in a minority of mankind of which Dr. Mead has spoken. . . . Only when deep guilt is lightened to make it tolerable can it express itself as a predominantly love-impaired restitution—making personal sense of moral responsibility, that is of guilt feeling in the commonly accepted sense.' Ibid. 86; cf. Mead, ibid. 63.

43. Gilbert, *Nuremberg Diary*, New York, 1947 (back cover).

44. Goldensohn, *The Nuremberg Interviews*, 105–6, 131.

45. Ibid. 115.

46. Ibid. 447.

47. Ibid. 71.

48. Ibid. 73.

49. Rosenbaum, *Explaining Hitler*, 26–7.

50. Goldensohn, *The Nuremberg Interviews*, 39; Weindling, *The Medical Trial*, 128.

51. Goldensohn, *The Nuremberg Interviews*, 39. Cf. Rosenbaum, *Explaining Hitler*, 26–7.

52. Goldensohn, *The Nuremberg Interviews*, 437.

53. Ibid. 87, 88.

54. Ibid.

55. The exchanges between Hoess and Kaltenbrunner's lawyer, Dr Kurt Kauffmann, at the IMT at Nuremberg can be downloaded at http://law2.umkc.edu/faculty/projects/ftrials/nuremberg/hoesstest.html.
56. West, *Train of Powder*, 69.
57. Ibid. 69–70.
58. Ibid. 70.
59. Ibid. 72.

CHAPTER 10

1. Churchill famously referred to the 'Iron Curtain' that divided Europe in a speech delivered at Fulton, Missouri, in March 1946.
2. The epigraph that was included in the 4 volumes of the conference proceedings stated that wars begin in the minds of men. It was drawn from the UNESCO constitution.
3. John Millet, 'The International Congress on Mental Health', *Bulletin of the American Psychoanalytic Association*, 46 (1948), 12–16, at p. 12.
4. Ibid. 13.
5. Another organization, launched at this congress, also typified the spirit of the time: the World Federation for Mental Health.
6. Rees, in *Proceedings of the International Congress on Mental Health* (London, 1948), vol. 3, p. 31.
7. Ibid. 83–7.
8. Ibid. 85.
9. Ibid. 83.
10. *Proceedings of the International Congress on Mental Health*, vol. 2, pp. 61–2.
11. For the background, see Daniel Kevles, *In the Name of Eugenics: Genetics and Human Heredity* (New York, 1985).
12. See e.g. Riley, *War in the Nursery* and Stonebridge, *The Writing of Anxiety*. Winnicott's radio talks were published in pamphlet form in 1950, and were subsequently included in *The Child and the Family: First Relationships* (London, 1957). Comparable, popularizing work on best practice in the United States was provided by Benjamin Spock; see, for instance, from the same period, *The Commonsense Book of Baby and Child Care* (New York, 1946); *Avoiding Behavior Problems* (New York, 1947).
13. Huxley's disquiet is evident in a letter he wrote to a colleague at the organization in Paris on 17 January 1950: 'I think it most unsatisfactory, and indeed unscientific in making sweeping but unproved assertions as to racial differences being entirely due to environmental and social factors'; the proper attitude was 'to point out the great role which such factors undoubtedly do play', to show the position of the 'uncritical racialist' to be untenable, 'but also to emphasize that there is a presumption that the major racial types of man will have genetic differences in mental and temperamental character as well as in physical char-

acter, and to stress the need for further research into this important but difficult subject.' File 327.5: 301.18 A 53, pt. 2, from 1/XI/49; TIU.

14. 'Social Conflict and the Challenge to Psychology', paper read before the medical section of the British Psychological Society, 17 Dec. 1947, published in the *British Journal of Medical Psychology*, 21 (1947–8), repr. in Roger Money-Kyrle, *Collected Papers* (Strath Tay, 1978), ch. 12. Italics added. Money-Kyrle used the common 'ph' spelling of fantasy in psychoanalytic discussions, in order to indicate the *unconscious* nature of this mental activity.

15. Millet, 'The International Congress', 15.

16. Millet, 'Notes and News', *Psychoanalytic Review*, 28 (1941), 555–6.

17. Millet, 'The International Congress', 16.

18. Ibid.

19. Ibid.

20. See Harold G. Moulton [President of the Brookings Institute], Preface to Charles A. H. Thomson, *Overseas Information Service of the United States Government* (Washington, DC, 1948).

21. Ibid. 1.

22. Jones's essay on this subject is included in S. D. Schmalhausen (ed.), *Our Neurotic Age: A Consultation* (New York, 1932).

23. Brock Chisholm, *Prescription for Survival* (New York, 1957), 44 and 63. On Chisholm's enduring interest in the relevance of both psychoanalysis and psychiatry to problems of international health, see Irving Allan, *Brock Chisholm: Doctor to the World* (Markham, Ont., 1998), 30, 72, 81, 101, 115, 120.

24. Lewin set out his views of social psychological differences between Germany and the United States in a paper in the journal *Culture and Personality* in 1936. It was reprinted in his *Resolving Social Conflicts: Selected Papers on Group Dynamics* (New York, 1948), ch. 1.

25. Lewin, *Resolving Social Conflict*, ch. 5, p. 80.

26. Ibid. 83.

27. Stephen Mennell, *Norbert Elias: An Introduction* (Dublin, 1989), 31. Thirty years after the first appearance of *The Civilizing Process*, Elias revisited his work and in a new preface stood by his claim that, for the most part, aggression, cruelty, and sadism had become the exception rather than the norm in modern times. Acts of wanton destructiveness were as nothing today, he claimed, compared to the violence inflicted by warriors in much earlier periods. He also argued, however, that his approach did not assume the necessity of moral advance, and thus he allowed for Nazi and other modern barbarisms.

28. The post-war edition of his history of manners was dedicated to the memory of his parents, Hermann Elias, d. Breslau 1940, and Sophie Elias, d. Auschwitz 1941.

29. Norbert Elias, *The Germans: Power Struggles and the Development of Habitus in the Nineteenth and Twentieth Centuries* (Cambridge, 1996).

30. Norbert Elias, *The Civilizing Process: The History of Manners* (Oxford, 1978), 307 n. Cf. Mennell, *Elias*, 249.

31. Foulkes Papers, esp. PP/SHF/A5; PP SHF/C3 (1–9); PP/SHF/F/2/39. WL.

32. Mennell, *Elias*, 31–8.

33. Elias, *History of Manners*, 260.

34. For Bowlby and attachment theory, see Riley, *War in the Nursery*; Jeremy Holmes, *John Bowlby and Attachment Theory* (London, 1993).

35. Freud, 'Group Psychology and its Relation to the Ego', SE vol. 18, p. 69.

36. The debate as such was not new. Questions as to whether the personal experience of liberty and the degree of 'civilization' achieved at any given time increased or decreased the incidence of insanity had frequently been explored by psychiatrists and other commentators during the previous century. In the early decades of the nineteenth century, for instance, some had argued that too much economic and political liberty actually exacerbated the degree of madness in society. See Michel Foucault, *History of Madness*, ed. Jean Khalfa (London, 2006), 366.

37. On Popper's connections with the Freud family in Vienna and hostility to psychoanalysis, see Malachi Haim Hacohen, *Karl Popper—The Formative Years, 1902–1945: Politics and Philosophy in Interwar Vienna* (Cambridge, 2000), 16, 93–4, and 144. The (Jewish) Poppers spent some summer vacations with members of the Freud family, something Hayek said would have been unthinkable for his family. See ibid. 33 n.

38. Michael Ignatieff, *Isaiah Berlin* (London, 1998), 91–2.

39. A. F. Hayek, *The Road to Serfdom* (London, 1944). Cf. Jeremy Shearmur, 'Hayek's Politics', in Edward Feser (ed.), *The Cambridge Companion to Hayek* (Cambridge, 2006), ch. 8. On the relationship of Hayek and Popper, and their respective contributions to post-war European liberalism, see Hacohen, *Karl Popper*, 495–510.

40. For the earlier argument, see Michael Freeden, *The New Liberalism: An Ideology of Social Reform* (Oxford, 1978).

41. Schlesinger, *The Vital Center*, 53. Cf. Alpers, *Dictators*, 108.

42. Erikson's *Childhood and Society* sought to compare and contrast upbringing and values in Nazi Germany, the Soviet Union, and modern America.

43. For several examples of admiring inter-war commentators extolling the model 'sanity' of the Soviet mode of organizing life and resources, and berating the insanity of other political systems, see the contributions to Schmalhausen (ed.), *Our Neurotic Age*.

44. Dicks's contributions to denazification planning and procedure are described by Reinisch in *Public Health*, chs. 2 and 5.

45. Roger Money-Kyrle, 'Some Aspects of State and Character in Germany' (1951), in *Collected Papers*, ch. 14. He describes here how he continued for approximately five months the work that Dicks and others pioneered at the GPRB in 1946. See also Money-Kyrle's report, 'The German Situation, 1945–47', in folder

marked 'Memos on German Situation', Money-Kyrle Papers, PP/RMK/D.3/2, WL. Cf. Fromm, *The Sane Society* (London, 1956); Roger Money-Kyrle, *Man's Picture of his World: A Psychoanalytical Study* (London, 1961).

46. Money-Kyrle, *Collected Papers*, 137 n. In this particular *mea culpa*, he expressed puzzlement at the 'mild note' he had struck in a BBC radio broadcast that he made on the causes of war in 1934. He mused over his previous failure to take in the full monstrosity of political events that were already before his eyes. As to whether that optimism reflected his fear of making things worse, lingering uncertainty about Hitler, or anxiety about becoming unpopular at home (when 'except for Churchill and his supporters, everyone seemed all for peace'), Money-Kyrle acknowledged, 'I do not know'.

47. Harrison, *Bion, Rickman, Foulkes*. The work was signalled at an early stage by Bion and Rickman in their joint communiqué, 'Intra-group Tensions in Therapy: Their Study as the Task of the Group', *Lancet*, 2 (1943), 678–81. See also Bion, 'Group Dynamics: A Review', *International Journal of Psycho-Analysis*, 33 (1952), 235–47.

48. Commenting on Bion's work, Dicks remarked: 'I bear personal witness, as a one-time member of such a group, to the correctness of Bion's observation... In minutiae, working with small groups, Bion has observed the genesis of acute hostility shared by all members of the group against himself as the leader figure when he failed to live up to the phantasies of parental omnipotent goodness that they cherished.' *Proceedings of the International Congress on Mental Health*, vol. 3, p. 86.

49. Harrison, *Bion, Rickman, Foulkes*.

50. 'Varieties of Group Formation', in Money-Kyrle, *Collected Papers*, ch. 13, p. 227.

51. Bion, 'Group Dynamics'.

52. Money-Kyrle, 'State and Character in Germany', 236–7.

53. Orwell (writing in the *Observer*, 25 Mar. 1945). Quoted in Reinisch, *Public Heath*, ch. 5.

54. Reinisch, *Public Health*, ch. 5.

55. The present inquiry focuses upon British and American material. Approaches to denazification and re-education differed significantly across the zones of the four Allied powers. See e.g. Judt, *Postwar*, part 1; Norbert Frei, *Adenauer's Germany and the Nazi Past: The Politics of Amnesty and Integration* (New York, 1997); James Tent, *Mission on the Rhine: Re-education and Denazification in American-Occupied Germany* (Chicago, 1982); Riccarda Torriani, 'Nazis into Germans: Re-education and Democratisation in the British and French Occupation Zones, 1945–1949', Ph.D. thesis, Cambridge University (2005).

56. Letter (August 1945), David Levy to Mr. Cleveland (at the OSS). This describes Levy's travel plans to Europe, and his wish to meet Dicks in London before going on to Bad Homberg. See also letters from Levy to Dicks (August and September 1945); David Levy Papers, Cornell Medical School, Oskar Diethelm Library, New York, Box 34. For Dicks's work in occupied Germany, in collaboration with Wing

Commander O. A. Oeser, Colonel 'Dick' Rendel and others, see Dicks, *Fifty Years*, 110. Dicks's proposals for screening operations in Germany had been set out in various official memoranda, e.g. on 9 June 1945; see FO 1032/1464, at the PRO.

57. Money-Kyrle, 'State and Character in Germany', 234.

58. Levy Papers, box 34 (report of 11 Oct. 1945); see also the documents included in <http://www.bbk.ac.uk/thepursuitofthenazimind>. For Oeser's approach to social psychology and social democratic orientation, see Trist, 'Guilty of Enthusiasm', 200. For Oeser's role at Bletchley, see Hinsley and Stripp (eds.), *Codebreakers*, 24.

59. Money-Kyrle, 'State and Character in Germany', p. 235.

60. For an account of twentieth-century 'human engineering' that places the accent almost entirely upon sinister surveillance, profiling, and screening, and that ranges across behaviourism, cybernetics, psychoanalysis, and experimental psychology, see Rebecca Lemov, *World as Laboratory: Experiments with Mice, Mazes and Men* (New York, 2006).

61. Mayne, *In Victory*, 42. Cf. Arthur L. Smith, *The War for the German Mind: Re-Educating Hitler's Soldiers* (Oxford, 1996).

62. Mayne, *In Victory*, 131.

63. Ibid. 35.

64. Ibid.

65. Ibid. 72.

66. See e.g. Brecht *et al.*, *Here Life Goes on in a Most Peculiar Way*. Cf. Cocks, *Psychotherapy in the Third Reich*. See also Helmut Thomä, 'Some Remarks on Psychoanalysis in Germany, Past and Present', *International Journal of Psycho-Analysis*, 50 (1969), 683–92; Käthe Dräger and Jeanette Friedeberg, 'Psychoanalysis in Hitler's Germany: 1933–1949', *American Imago*, 29 (1972), 99–214; Karen Brecht, 'Adaptation and Resistance: Reparation and the Return of the Repressed', *Psychoanalysis and Contemporary Thought*, 11 (1988), 233–47. On German film and the Third Reich, see esp. Eric Santner, *Stranded Objects* (Ithaca, NY, 1990). A useful introduction to post-war German literary responses to the Third Reich is provided in *The Cambridge Companion to the Modern German Novel*, edited by Graham Bartram (Cambridge, 2004); see esp. ch. 12.

67. Evans, *The Third Reich at War*, ch. 7, pp. 738–64.

68. Briefing note, 22 June 1947, 327.5: 301.18 A 53, pt. 2 (1/XI/49), TIU.

69. Henry Dicks, 'Personality Traits and National Socialist Ideology', *Human Relations*, 3 (1950), 111–54; 'Observations on Contemporary Russian Behaviour', *Human Relations*, 5 (1952), 111–75; V. S. de Reuck and Julie Knight (eds.), 'Intra-Personal Conflict and the Authoritarian Character', *Ciba Foundation Symposium on Conflict in Society* (1966), 82–106.

70. Files at 327.5: 301.18 A 53, pt. 2; 327.6:37 A 074; 237.6:37 A 074 (44) 47. TIU.

71. On Dicks's proposals regarding cultural attitudes and the social role of women in post-war Germany, file 27.5:301.18 A 53 (Community Issues), TIU. Also see letters from the Office of the War Cabinet to Dicks and Ronald Hargreaves, 5

and 10 March 1945, in HD. For accounts by historians of women's lives in Fascist Italy and Nazi Germany , see e.g. Victoria De Grazia, *How Fascism Ruled Women: Italy, 1922–1945* (Berkeley, 1992), and Claudia Koonz, *Mothers in the Fatherland: Women, the Family, and Nazi Politics* (New York, 1987).

72. Quoted in Lerner, *Psychological Warfare*, 160 n. 43.

73. Ibid. Dicks claimed there had been what he called a notable loss of restraint in a substantial portion of German girls, aged roughly 18–30, 'whose normal relations with men have been upset by the war'. He added: 'There is evidence that many German girls have, to an even greater extent than in other countries, lost all moral hold and can be described as "sex mad".'

74. File 327.5:301.18 A 53; file box on community issues; TIU.

75. Ibid.

76. Ibid. Segerstedt was at pains to remind his colleagues that 'the very first relation between child and parents (or substitutive figures) is of fundamental importance'. Letter of 26 Jan. 1949, ibid.

77. File 237.6:37 A 074 (44) 47—teaching meeting 1947; TIU.

78. Dicks was deemed especially suitable thanks to his long-standing interest in the relation of personality and culture. Telegrams between M. Guiton (for UNESCO) and B. Morris (Tavistock Clinic), 18 June 1947 are located in 'Education for International Understanding', file 327.6:37 A 074 (44) 47, pt. xi, 1 June–31 July 1947; TIU.

79. Education for International Understanding, seminar, file 327.6:37 A. 074 (44) 47, folder 12, 1–31 Aug. 1947; TIU.

80. File 327.5:301.18 A 53; file box on community issues; TIU.

81. Correspondence of Dr Robert C. Angell, acting head, social sciences dept., UNESCO, to the director of community studies, 17/11/1949; file 327.5: 301.18 A 53, pt. 2, from 1/XI/49; TIU.

82. P. W. Martin, letter of 11 Apr. 1948; 327.5, part 3 from 1 Apr. to 30 June 1948; TIU.

83. 'Minutes of Tensions sub-committee, 18 Oct. 1949; file 327.5, pt. 5 (1 Jan. 1949–31 Dec. 1949); TIU.

84. Letters, 29 May–6 June 1947, between Howard E Wilson and Anna Freud; 237.6:37 A 074 (44) 47 and 327.6:37 A 074 (44) 47, pt. 9, 'proposal to lecturers'. Also see the correspondence between P. W. Martin and Anna Freud, 11 and 21 Apr. 1948, in file 327.5, pt. 3, TIU. Among other guests to decline this somewhat last-minute invitation to attend the summer school was Eleanor Roosevelt; letter of 30 July 1947, ibid.

85. File 327.5, Pt. 3 (1 Apr. to 30 June, 1948); TIU.

86. Anna Freud, 'Instinctual Drives and their bearing on Human Behavior' (Lecture, UNESCO, 1948), first published 1953, repr. in her *Indications for Child Analysis and Other Papers 1945–1956* (London, 1969), ch. 23, pp. 498–527, at p. 525.

87. Undated memo (presumably 1948); 327.5:301.18 A 53; file box on Community Issues; TIU.

88. File 327.5:301.18 A 53; file box on community issues; TIU.

89. See the remarks of Harry Stack Sullivan, (13 Jan. 1949); file 327.5:301.18 A 53; file box on community issues; TIU.

90. Report by Gerhart Saenger and Samuel H. Flowerman [the latter was the editor, with Horkheimer of the 'Studies in Prejudice' Series in which Adorno *et al.'s The Authoritarian Personality* was published: see Ch. 11, n. 12], file 327.5:301.18 A 53; file box on community issues; TIU.

91. File 327.5:301.18 A 53; file box on community issues; TIU.

CHAPTER 11

1. Richard Evans, *The Third Reich at War*; Richard Bessel, *Germany 1945: From War to Peace* (London, 2009); Ian Kershaw, *The End: Hitler's Germany, 1944–45* (London, 2011); Nicholas Stargardt, *The German War* (forthcoming).

2. The most fêted contemporary critic to rehabilitate psychoanalysis (in the terms of Lacanian theory, rather than British object relations or American ego psychology) and, simultaneously, to seek to eschew the 'psychologism' of the past is Slavoj Žižek. See e.g. *Did Somebody Say Totalitarianism?* (London, 2001) and *The Parallax View*. For a useful summary of work in contemporary psychosocial studies that seeks to move out of this deadlock, and to integrate psychoanalytic thought and discourse analysis, see Hook, *A Critical Psychology of the Postcolonial*.

3. Émile Durkheim, *Les Règles de méthode sociologique* (Paris, 1895), 128.

4. Hugh Trevor-Roper, *The Last Days of Hitler* (London, 1947).

5. Adorno, 'Freudian Theory and the Pattern of Fascist Propaganda', 136–8.

6. 'Revenge is Sour', *Tribune*, 26 Oct. 1945, repr. in *The Collected Essays, Journalism and Letters of George Orwell*, iv. 3–6, at p. 4.

7. The possibility of an eruption of insanity, crippling, fear and murderousness where it does not 'officially' belong can also be seen in the depiction of the American razor-wielding somnambulistic hero of Hitchcock's *Spellbound* in 1945: it is the attractive and upright discharged World War II soldier (part of the Allied army that heads north towards Rome after the successful invasion of Sicily) and new mental asylum director, played by Gregory Peck, who is shown to be almost as dangerous—in his illness—as the true villain of the story (the old and seemingly urbane medical colleague whose role he takes over). In the proselytizing terms of the film, psychoanalysis constitutes something verging on a miracle cure for mental illness, even within hours and days, but perhaps this was not supposed to be taken too seriously.

8. For British representations of Germany in politics and popular culture, see John Ramsden, *Don't Mention the War: The British and the Germans since 1890* (London, 2006). See also the feature on Anglo-American perceptions in *German History*, 26: 4 (2008). So familiar was the rhetorical trope that equated German with Nazi, or at least anti-democrat, that Arthur Miller, in an autobiographical memoir of the 1980s, could half-facetiously use 'German' to describe the authoritar-

ian psychology of his grandfather. The latter had railed against opponents of the great FDR and 'considered elections insulting to those in power, *such was the German streak in him*'. Miller also reprised the psychiatric view of the Nazi regime when summarizing his own views (and those of what he called the American 'radical mind-set of the thirties'): Germany had fallen into the hands of a government of 'perverts, hoodlums, and the raving mad'. Arthur Miller, *Timebends: A Life* (London, 1987), 6, 84–5. Emphasis added.

9. Alpers, *Dictators*, 286.

10. Jay, *The Dialectical Imagination*, 231–3.

11. Rolf Wiggershaus, *The Frankfurt School: Its History, Theories and Political Significance* (Cambridge, 1994), 396.

12. Theodor Adorno, Else Frenkel-Brunswick, Daniel J. Levinson, and R. Nevitt Sanford, *The Authoritarian Personality* (New York, 1950).

13. Quoted in Jay, *The Dialectical Imagination*, 240.

14. For the context of Adorno's study, see ibid., chs. 4 and 5.

15. Adorno *et al.*, *The Authoritarian Personality*, p. v. The idea here that the Jews are the containers for massive projections by the anti-Semite can be compared with Sartre's reflections on the Jewish question, published after the liberation of France as *The Anti-Semite and Jew*. For Sartre's argument and ambivalent attitude to Judaism, see the account by Susan Rubin Soleiman in *The Jew in the Text: Modernity and the Construction of Identity*, ed. Linda Nochlin and Tamar Garb (London, 1995), ch. 11; cf. Jay, *The Dialectical Imagination*, 240.

16. See the foreword to 'Studies in Prejudice', in Adorno *et al.*, *The Authoritarian Personality*. Other contributors to the series included Bettelheim, Leo Lowenthal, and Marie Jahoda. See Jay *The Dialectical Imagination*, 235.

17. *Childhood and Society*, 294.

18. Caplan, 'The Historiography', 559.

19. Jay, *The Dialectical Imagination*, 242.

20. Adorno *et al.*, *The Authoritarian Personality*, 921.

21. Erich Fromm, brought up in an orthodox family, was an exception in this regard, as, to some extent, were those other associated intellectuals of the Frankfurt School, Walter Benjamin and Leo Lowenthal. See Jay, *The Dialectical Imagination*, 33.

22. Personal communication to the author.

23. See Lerner, *Psychological Warfare*. See also Alfred H. Paddock Jr., *US Army Special Warfare* (Lawrence, Kan., 2002).

24. See Müller, 'On Behalf of the Agency'. Some of the CIA manuals on counter-intelligence interrogation techniques, notably those produced in 1963, are now in the public domain. For these and other intelligence manuals, see 'The National Security Archive', online at: http://www.gwu.edu/~nsarchiv/NSAEBB/NSAEBB122/#kubark.

25. For recent representations of 'extremists', 'suicide bombers', and 'terrorists' as insane, psychopathic or otherwise abnormal individuals, see e.g. Robert S.

Robins, *Political Paranoia: The Psychopolitics of Hatred* (New Haven, 1997); Jerrold Post (ed.), *The Psychological Assessment of Political Leaders: With Profiles of Saddam Hussein and Bill Clinton* (Ann Arbor, Mich., 2003); id., *Leaders and their Followers in a Dangerous World: The Psychology of Political Behavior* (Ithaca, NY, 2006); id., *The Mind of the Terrorist: The Psychology of Terrorism from the IRA to al-Quaeda* (Basingstoke, 2007).

26. Engerman, *Know your Enemy*; Mandler, *Return from the Natives*.

27. Dicks was singled out in the later 1940s as one of the most significant and sophisticated contributors to the field of propaganda and intelligence. See, for instance, Lerner, *Psychological Warfare*, 93 n. 9, On OSS psychological warfare, and post-war developments in psychological techniques, see also Paddock, *US Army Special Warfare*.

28. Linebarger, *Psychological Warfare*, 26. Emphasis added.

29. Ibid.

30. Ibid. 30.

31. Ibid. 145.

32. Lerner, *Psychological Warfare*, 23.

33. Ibid. 97.

34. Ibid. 110–11.

35. Ibid. 112, 121–4.

36. Kershaw, 'Hitler and the Uniqueness of Nazism', esp. p. 243. See also Richard Evans's introduction to the special issue, 'Understanding Nazi Germany', *Journal of Contemporary History*, 39 (2004), 163–7; Kershaw, preface and introduction, *HH*; Caplan, 'The Historiography', 545–90; Michael Pomper, 'Historians and Individual Agency', *History and Theory*, 35 (1996), 281–308.

37. 'In conclusion I would suggest that the people who are most subject to the wiles of Nazi propaganda are those who have neither securely established their own manhood and independence of the Father nor have been able to combine the instincts of sexuality and love in their attitude towards the Mother or other women. This is the psychological position of the homosexual.' Ernest Jones, 'The Psychology of Quislingism', *International Journal of Psycho-Analysis*, 22 (1941), 1–6.

38. Astor went on to promote a visiting professorial post for a psychoanalyst at University College London and became a trustee of the Anna Freud Centre in Hampstead. In his editorial policy at the *Observer* Astor sought to promote work that acknowledged, as his biographer puts it, 'the twin forces of the "conscious" and "unconscious" in man'. Richard Cockett, *David Astor and the 'Observer'* (London, 1991), 1, 168–9.

39. These quotations from Cohn are drawn from the transcript of an unpublished interview of Cohn by the present author in July 2006.

40. Henry Dicks, *Licensed Mass Murder: A Socio-Psychological Study of Some SS Killers* (London, 1972), 18.

41. Frequent differences of view emerged on this point at the Columbus Trust seminars regarding the value of psychology compared with history, sociology,

and so forth. See the various debates about method recorded in the minutes of the meetings of the research group that was convened by Astor and Cohn; papers of the late David Astor (boxes 9 and 10), private collection.

42. See e.g. Sally Alexander, *Becoming a Woman and Other Essays in Nineteenth and Twentieth-Century Feminist History* (London, 1994).

43. As Quentin Skinner observes: 'It would be a quixotic form of self-denying ordinance to insist that our language of explanation must at this juncture match whatever language the people in question applied or could have applied to themselves. If we wish to furnish what we take to be the most powerful explanations available to us, we are bound to employ what we believe to be the best available explanatory theories and the concepts embodied in them.' *Visions of Politics*, vol. 1: *Regarding Method* (Cambridge, 2002), 51.

44. Deborah E. Lipstadt, *Denying the Holocaust: The Growing Assault on Truth and Memory* (New York, 1993).

45. Ibid. 2.

46. See the excellent survey by Caplan, 'The Historiography'. On the question of structure and agency, see esp. p. 569.

47. See Erving Goffman, *Asylums: Essays on the Social Situation of Mental Patients and Other Inmates* (New York, 1961), 35, 40, 60–1, 63, 64, 66, etc. Goffman used the extreme 'mortification' of the victim in the camps as the example par excellence of the psychological impact of total institutions. See ibid. 35.

48. Ibid. 168; cf. *The Goffman Reader*, ed. Charles Lemert and Ann Branaman (Oxford, 1997), p. xiii.

49. Hannah Arendt, *Eichmann in Jerusalem: A Report on the Banality of Evil* (New York, 1977).

50. See e.g. Jacques Barzun, *Clio and the Doctors: Psycho-history, Quanto-history & History* (Chicago, 1974); David Stannard, *Shrinking History: On Freud and the Failure of Psychohistory* (Oxford, 1980). For a defence of Freud's methodological relevance, see Peter Gay, *Freud for Historians* (New York, 1985). The history of the genre is considered by Loewenberg in 'Psychohistorical Perspectives on Modern German History'. Cf. Rudolph Binion, 'Foam on the Hitler Wave', *Journal of Modern History*, 46 (1974), 522–8. Even some of those sympathetic to the application of psychoanalysis observed '[the] inherent evidentiary problems of psychohistory: the difficulty of gathering data on childhood; the resultant danger of circular reasoning in hypothesising antecedents from adult words and actions; the absence of personal contact enjoyed by the psychoanalyst; the misuses of subjectivity; the danger of reductionism; the question of whether psychoanalytic theory is valid for other times and places (and indeed, whether the application of any contemporary model can illuminate the special "mentalities" of earlier periods)'. Geoffrey Cocks and Travis L. Crosby (eds.), *Psycho/History: Readings in the Method of Psychology, Psychoanalysis and History* (New Haven, 1987), p. x. The weaknesses of the clinical approach had in fact been amply set out much earlier, in a coruscating article by an astute sociologist. See Theodore

Abel, 'Is a Psychiatric Interpretation of the German Enigma Necessary?', *American Sociological Review*, 10 (1945), 457–64, at p. 464. Cf. his earlier study, *Why Hitler Came to Power* (Cambridge, Mass., 1938).

51. Peter Loewenberg, 'The Unsuccessful Adolescence of Heinrich Himmler', *American Historical Review*, 76 (1971), 612–41, esp. pp. 616 and 627.

52. Fest's depiction bears comparison with Langer's (see *MH*, part 5). The claims that had been made to Langer about the perverse sexual relationship of Hitler and Raubal were in turn based on Raubal's supposed revelation of such behaviour to Otto Strasser. The picture has often been echoed since, as, for example, recently in *The Castle in the Forest* by Norman Mailer (Waterville, Maine, 2007). Here a character insists of Hitler and his niece: 'They had the most perverse relations' (p. 686).

53. Fest, *Hitler*, 5, 321–4.

54. Quoted in both the original German of Maser's account and in English translation, by Peter Loewenberg in his review essay, *The Mind*, p. 270. Langer, by contrast, Loewenberg suggests, inferred that Hitler 'must have had a sexual abnormality from his "super-masculinity", by which the psychoanalyst means it is too much, it is exaggerated in the nature of a caricature and defensive of underlying passive and castrative fantasies' (ibid.).

55. Norman Stone, *Hitler* (London, 1980), 4–6, 14, 20–1, 55, 61–2, 69, 156, 165.

56. Andrew Roberts, *Hitler and Churchill: Secrets of Leadership* (London, 2003), 60.

57. Ibid. 155.

58. Richard Overy, *The Dictators: Hitler's Germany and Stalin's Russia* (London, 2004), 5.

59. *HH* 354.

60. *HH* 21.

61. *HH* 23.

62. *HH* 26.

63. *HH* 81.

64. *HH* 45.

65. *HN* 605.

66. *HN* 636.

67. Quoted in *HN* 470.

68. *HN* 489.

69. George Steiner, *The Portage to St Cristobal of A.H.* [first published in *Kenyon Review*, 1979] (London, 1981), 122.

70. Ibid. 124.

71. Susanne Kappeler, *The Pornography of Representation* (Cambridge, 1986).

72. Klaus Theweleit, 'German Reactions to *Les Bienveillants*', *New German Critique*, 106 (2009), 21–34, at pp. 27 and 33.

73. *The Night Porter* (1974) is centred on the complex emotional connections and sadomasochistic sexual transactions of a one-time SS officer (working, postwar, incognito as a furtive hotel porter who prefers to avoid daylight) and a

Jewish woman who recognizes him, and who had once been an inmate of a camp where he worked. She had survived at his mercy, but as a cruelly tormented sexual victim, forced to dress up in an SS uniform and 'entertain' the officers. Directed by Liliana Cavani, the film starred Dirk Bogarde and Charlotte Rampling.

74. Douglas, *The Memory*, 142–4. Cf. José Brunner, 'Eichmann's Mind: Psychological, Philosophical, and Legal Perspectives', *Theoretical Inquiries in Law*, 1 (2000), art. 7. This illuminating article also includes a discussion of alternative interpretations of the case encompassed neither by talk of Eichmann's banality nor his demonic character; instead, the question was how he presented himself in this particular 'banal' way, as a conscious or unconscious subterfuge. Brunner also makes astute use of Eichmann's recently released prison memoir.

75. The idea of the machine-like mentality of Germans, or more specifically of Prussians, was not uncommon in French and English cultural commentary in the decades after the Franco-Prussian War (1870) and again in and around the First World War. Pick, *War Machine*.

76. For the trial transcripts, see http://www.nizkor.org/hweb/people/e/ eichmann-adolf/transcripts/ Gilbert's testimony is in sessions 56 and 57. Cf. Douglas, *The Memory*, 144.

77. Soon after, Gilbert produced a report for Yad Vashem on 'The Mentality of Murderous Robots'. Douglas, *The Memory*, 143–4.

78. That Arendt was not in fact present throughout the trial had consequences for her interpretation of it that are considered critically in David Cesarani, *Eichmann: His Life and Crimes* (London, 2004). See esp. p. 344. This book also describes earlier debates about Arendt's approach to the trial in the context of her criticisms of Zionism and other aspects of her reputation and legacy; ibid. 343–9. Cf. Cesarani (ed.), *After Eichmann: Collective Memory and the Holocaust since 1961* (London, 2005).

79. Douglas, *The Memory*, 3. Douglas also conveys well the particular significance of the trial for Israeli national identity in the 1960s.

80. The poetic licence (to put it generously) that Arendt took here, regarding the supposedly dozen or so psychiatric reports produced that averred that Eichmann was normal, is described in Cesarani, *Eichmann*, 348.

81. Arendt, *Eichmann in Jerusalem*, 25–6.

82. Thomas Blass, *The Man Who Shocked the World: The Life and Legacy of Stanley Milgram* (New York, 2004), p. xxi.

83. Stanley Milgram, *Obedience to Authority: An Experimental View* (London, 1974), 123 183, 194.

84. Blass, *Milgram*, 217–18.

85. Kirsten Fremaglich, *American Dreams and Nazi Nightmares: Early Holocaust Consciousness and Liberal America, 1957–1965* (Walthan, Mass., 2007).

86. An online account of Philip Lombardo's experiment can be found at http:// www.prisonexp.org/. A recent book by Lombardo links that earlier work to the

more recent widely discussed events such as the behaviour of American guards at Abu Ghraib in Iraq: *The Lucifer Effect: Understanding How Good People Turn Evil* (New York, 2007). Cf. Fermaglich, *American Dreams and Nazi Nightmares.*

87. On Kurt Lewin's influence, see Eric Trist, 'Guilty of Enthusiasm', 196, 198.

88. See Philippe Sands, *Lawless World: America and the Making and Breaking of Global Rules* (London, 2005) and *Torture Team: Deception, Cruelty and the Compromise of the Law* (London, 2008).

89. *Childhood and Society*, 294.

90. Fromm, *The Anatomy*, 323.

91. Hans Askenasy, *Are We All Nazis?* (Secaucus, NJ, 1978).

92. Douglas, *The Memory*, 209.

93. Ibid.

94. Ibid. 208.

95. For this argument, see Phillip Cole, *The Myth of Evil* (Edinburgh, 2006);

96. Primo Levi's remarks (from *If this is a Man*) are quoted and discussed in Lyndsey Stonebridge, 'Theories of Trauma', in Marina Mackay (ed.), *The Cambridge Companion to The Literature of World War II* (Cambridge, 2009), ch. 14, pp. 194–206, at pp. 200–1. Cf. Levi's insistence that many of the guards he encountered 'were average human beings, averagely intelligent, averagely wicked: save for exceptions, they were not monsters, they had faces'; quoted in Cole, *The Myth of Evil*, 179.

97. Alexander Mitscherlich and Margarete Mitscherlich, *Die Unfähigkeit zu trauern* (tr. as *The Inability to Mourn: Principles of Collective Behavior* (New York, 1975)) was first published in 1967. For the context, see Geoffrey Cocks, 'Repressing, Remembering, Working Through: German Psychiatry, Psychotherapy, Psychoanalysis and the "Missed Resistance" in the Third Reich', *Journal of Modern History*, 64 (1992) (supplement), 204–16. On Alexander Mitscherlich's political ambiguities and later interventions on the German relationship to the Nazi past, see Timo Hoyer, *Im Getummel der Welt: Alexander Mitscherlich—Ein Portrat* (Göttingen, 2008); Martin Dehli, 'Shaping History: Alexander Mitscherlich and German Psychoanalysis after 1945', *Psychoanalysis and History*, 11 (2009), 55–73; Karen Brecht, 'In the Aftermath of Nazi Germany, Alexander Mitscherlich and Psychoanalysis—Legend and Legacy', *American Imago*, 52 (1995), 291–312.

98. To take two examples of many, see the discussion of the Mitscherlichs in Santner, *Stranded Objects* (Ithaca, NY, 1990) and Gavriel D. Rosenfeld, *Munich and Memory: Architecture, Monuments and the Legacy of the Third Reich* (Los Angeles, 2000). This model has also been taken up in contemporary debates on national identity, multiculturalism, and racial discourse outside the German context. The sociologist Paul Gilroy, for example, has redeployed the Mitscherlichs' idea of a failed or incomplete mourning in his analysis of the psycho-social aftermaths of empire and imperialism in Britain. See Gilroy, *After Empire: Melancholia or Convivial Culture* (London, 2004), esp. pp. 107–8.

99. See Ilse Grubrich-Simitis, 'Extreme Traumatization as Cumulative Trauma— Psychoanalytic Investigations of the Effects of Concentration Camp Experiences

on Survivors and their Children', *Psychoanalytic Study of the Child*, 36 (1981), 415–50. See also Dominick LaCapra, *Representing the Holocaust, History, Theory, Trauma* (Ithaca, NY, 1994), and *History and Memory after Auschwitz* (Ithaca, NY, 1998).

100. When news finally broke in 1925, it led, as the historian Andrew Scull has shown, to the exposure of many '[s]tories of patients being beaten, kicked and dragged screaming into the operating room, of trolleys filled and not a few corpses streaming in the opposite direction', arousing 'the archetypal fears of the horrors of the madhouse that always linger just below the surface in our collective unconscious'. Andrew Scull, *Madhouse: A Tragic Tale of Megalomania and Modern Medicine* (New Haven, 2005), 2.

101. Phyllis Greenacre, 'The Impostor', *Psychoanalytic Quarterly*, 27 (1958), 358–82, quotations from pp. 358–62.

102. Personal communication to the author.

103. Eric Brenman, 'Cruelty and Narrow-Mindedness' [1970] in Roy Schafer (ed.), *The Contemporary Kleinians of London* (Madison, Wisc., 1997), 174–94, at p. 177.

104. Ibid. 179.

105. Robin Anderson, 'Putting the Boot In: Violent Defences against Depressive Anxiety', in David Bell (ed.), *Reason and Passion: A Celebration of the Work of Hanna Segal* (London, 1997), 75–88, at p. 77.

106. Otto Kernberg, 'The Psychopathology of Hatred', *Journal of the American Psychoanalytic Association*, 39 (1991), 209–38.

107. For a summary and bibliography, see 'Pathological Organisations', in Elizabeth Bott Spillius *et al.* (eds.), *The New Dictionary of Kleinian Thought* (Hove, 2011). See also Steiner, *Psychic Retreats: Pathological Organizations in Psychotic, Neurotic and Borderline Patients* (London, 1993) and *Seeing and Being Seen: Emerging from a Psychic Retreat* (Hove, 2011).

108. Herbert Rosenfeld, 'A Psychoanalytical Approach to the Treatment of Psychosis', in *Impasse and Interpretation* (London, 1987), ch. 1, pp. 4–9.

109. Spillius *et al.* (eds.), *The New Dictionary*, 146. Cf. Edna O'Shaughnessy, 'Relating to the Superego', *International Journal of Psycho-Analysis*, 80 (1999), 861–70.

110. See e.g. Douglas Kirsner, *Unfree Associations: Inside Psychoanalytic Institutes* (London, 2000).

111. Sherry Turkle, *Psychoanalytic Politics: Freud's French Revolution* (New York, 1978); Elisabeth Roudinesco, *Lacan and Co.: A History of Psychoanalysis in France 1925–1985* (London 1990) and *Jacques Lacan*.

112. *Moses and Monotheism: Three Essays*, SE vol. 23, p. 109.

CHAPTER 12

1. See Dicks, handwritten corrections (pointing out inaccuracies in the summary of his views), on letter from BBC director, Harry Hastings, 7 July 1970. HD.

2. For more on the project see Chapters 3 and 11 above. Other landmark publications to appear in the series included *The Aryan Myth* by Leon Poliakov and

Cohn's own study of racial conspiracy literature, including the notorious 'Protocols of the Elders of Zion', *Warrant for Genocide*. Cohn's book aroused the ire of Hannah Arendt: she roundly criticized it for assuming, in her view erroneously, that modern racial anti-Semitism could be understood as part of a continuum of attitudes since the Middle Ages. See Arendt's foreword to the new edition of *The Origins of Totalitarianism* (New York, 1968), p. xi.

3. *Licensed Mass Murder: A Socio-Psychological Study of Some SS Killers* (London, 1972), 17.

4. Ibid. 96.

5. Ibid. 106.

6. Ibid. 107.

7. Cohn, interview with the present author, 15 July 2006.

8. Michael Briant, 'Psychoanalysis and Society', *Outwrite: Journal of the Cambridge Society for Psychotherapy*, 6 (Dec. 2003), 7–12, at p. 7.

9. These quotations were contained in publicity leaflets produced by Basic Books to promote Langer's study. A copy of the promotional material is in Walter Langer's Papers (file on *The Mind of Adolf Hitler*), Boston Psychoanalytic Society.

10. Letter, Walter Langer to Dr John A. Abbott, 19 July 1972, in Henry A. Murray, archives, HUGFP 97.45.4 Pusey Library, Harvard, box 1, in the folder entitled 'Walter Langer's study of Hitler'.

11. For an example of Trevor-Roper's own forays into the genre, see e.g. his essay 'Thomas Carlyle's Historical Philosophy', *Times Literary Supplement*, 26 June 1981, pp. 731–4.

12. It is perhaps not without irony that this rather withering reviewer of the naive Langer was himself taken in a few years later by a hoaxer, when he authenticated the so-called 'Hitler Diaries' in 1983 (he was not by any means the only person, however, to be duped by the forgery).

13. Langer's Hitler, was, according to Trevor-Roper, really just a fanciful invention, or at least a 'grotesque exaggeration'. Hugh Trevor-Roper, 'Re-inventing Hitler', *Sunday Times*, 18 Feb. 1973, p. 35. Cf. Michael Shepherd, 'Clio and Psyche: The Lessons of Psychohistory', *Journal of the Royal Society of Medicine*, 71 (1978), 406–12.

14. Elias, *The Germans*, 430.

15. From the blurb on the inside-cover of *Camp Z*.

16. I borrow the term 'aura' here from Walter Benjamin, who meant the intense and melancholy power of fascination that something may possess at the moment of its disappearance; in the present context one might say prolonged twilight existence rather than disappearance.

17. See, for instance, the copious files of letters appealing for Hess's release; National Archives, PRO, London, FO 1042/249–252.

18. See folder entitled 'Hess's remains', Sept.–Dec. 1982, Hess File Group 50, RG 84, box 2. NA.

19. 'Top Nazi Rudolf Hess exhumed from "Pilgrimage" Grave', BBC News Report (21 July 2011) at http://www.bbc.co.uk/news/world-europe-14232768.

20. 'Hess's remains', Sept.–Dec. 1982, Hess File Group 50, RG 84, box 2; memorandum, 11 July 1975, RG 84 box 1; folder, 'Theft of Hess items', especially the letter from the US Army Dept., 15 Sept. 1986, RG 84, box 10. NA.

21. Memorandum, 11 July 1975, Hess File Group 50, RG 84, box 1. NA.

22. For instance, the collection of letters, reports and documents from the 1980s, in RG 84. Box 2, 'entitled Hess remains'. NA.

23. At the bus stop by the main gate to the site in December 2010 an advertisement promised beer 'for a new generation'; at the Kaiser supermarket that then occupied part of the site (following the withdrawal of the British army from this location in the 1990s) a promotional campaign heralded 'every week a new world'.

24. For the context of this architectural work, Rosenfeld, *Munich*, pp. 312–13.

25. J. Laplanche and J.-B. Pontalis, *The Language of Psychoanalysis* (London, 1973), 488.

26. 'Constructions in Psycho-Analysis', SE vol. 19, pp. 378–9.

27. 'It may indeed be questioned whether we have any memories at all *from* our childhood: memories *relating to* our childhood may be all that we possess. Our childhood memories show us our earliest years not as they were but as they appeared at the later periods when the memories were aroused.' 'Screen Memories' (1899), SE vol. 3, pp. 299–322, at p. 322.

28. Ernest Renan, 'What is a Nation?', reprinted in Homi K. Bhabha (ed.), *Nation and Narration* (London, 1990), ch. 2.

29. *Beyond the Pleasure Principle*, SE vol. 18, p. 13.

30. 'Screen Memories', SE vol. 3, p. 307.

31. Daniel Libeskind, *The Space of Encounter* (London, 2001), 30.

32. Arendt, *The Origins of Totalitarianism,* p. ix.

33. Cf. Mazower, *Dark Continent*, p. xii.

34. Ibid.

35. Miller, *Timebends*, 84–5.

Further Reading

What follows is a selection of recent historical studies and some additional, older material that the reader may find especially illuminating in pursuing further the diverse themes and arguments of the present book. The endnotes provide a full list of the primary and secondary sources directly referred to in the present text. In addition, samples of some of the wartime and post-war papers, logs, letters, and so on assembled in the course of this research can be consulted at http://www.bbk.ac.uk/thepursuitofthenazimind.

Theodore Abel, 'Is a Psychiatric Interpretation of the German Enigma Necessary?', *American Sociological Review*, 10 (1945), 457–64.
—— *Why Hitler Came to Power* (Cambridge, Mass., 1938).
Theodor Adorno, 'Freudian Theory and the Pattern of Fascist Propaganda' (1951), repr. in id., *The Culture Industry: Selected Essays on Mass Culture*, ed. J. M. Bernstein (London 1991).
——Else Frenkel-Brunswick, Daniel J. Levinson, and R. Nevitt Sanford, *The Authoritarian Personality* (New York, 1950).
Benjamin L. Alpers, *Dictators, Democracy, and American Public Culture: Envisioning the Totalitarian Enemy 1920s–1950s* (Chapel Hill, NC, 2003).
Hannah Arendt, *The Origins of Totalitarianism* [1951] (New York, 1968).
—— *Eichmann in Jerusalem: A Report on the Banality of Evil* [1963] (New York, 1977).
Hans Askenasy, *Are We All Nazis?* (Secaucus, NJ, 1978).
Joseph Bendersky, 'Psychohistory before Hitler: Early Military Analyses of German National Psychology', *Journal of the History of the Behavioral Sciences*, 24 (1988), 166–82.
Volker R. Berghahn, *America and the Intellectual Cold Wars in Europe: Shepard Stone between Philanthropy, Academy, and Diplomacy* (Princeton, 2001).
Bruno Bettelheim, 'Individual and Mass Behavior in Extreme Situations', *Journal of Abnormal and Social Psychology*, 38 (1943), 417–52.
Rudolph Binion, 'Foam on the Hitler Wave', *Journal of Modern History*, 46 (1974), 522–8.
Wilfred Bion, 'Group Dynamics: A Review', *International Journal of Psycho-Analysis*, 33 (1952), 235–47.
——and John Rickman, 'Intra-group Tensions in Therapy: Their Study as the Task of the Group', *Lancet*, 2 (1943), 678–81.

Thomas Blass, *The Man Who Shocked the World: The Life and Legacy of Stanley Milgram* (New York, 2004).

Julia Borossa and Ivan Ward (eds.), 'Psychoanalysis, Fascism, Fundamentalism', special issue of *Psychoanalysis and History*, 11: 2 (2009).

Karen Brecht *et al.* (eds.), *Here Life Goes on in a Most Peculiar Way: Psychoanalysis Before and After 1933* (Hamburg, 1995).

——'In the Aftermath of Nazi Germany, Alexander Mitscherlich and Psycho-analysis—Legend and Legacy', *American Imago*, 55 (1995), 291–312.

Anthony Cave Brown, *The Last Hero: Wild Bill Donovan* (London, 1992).

José Brunner, 'Eichmann's Mind: Psychological, Philosophical, and Legal Perspectives', *Theoretical Inquiries in Law*, 1 (2000), article 7.

——'"On Those Crazy Cards Again": A History of the Debate on the Nazi Rorschachs, 1946–2001', *Political Psychology*, 22 (2001), 233–61.

John Burrow, *The Crisis of Reason: European Thought, 1848–1914* (New Haven, 2000).

Jane Caplan, 'The Historiography of National Socialism', in Michael Bentley (ed.), *Companion to Historiography* (London, 1997), ch. 21.

David Cesarani, *Eichmann: His Life and Crimes* (London, 2004).

Geoffrey Cocks, *Psychotherapy in the Third Reich: The Göring Institute* (New York, 1985).

——'Repressing, Remembering, Working Through: German Psychiatry, Psychotherapy, Psychoanalysis and the "Missed Resistance" in the Third Reich', *Journal of Modern History*, 64 [supplement] (1992), 204–16.

——and Travis L. Crosby (eds.) *Psycho/History: Readings in the Method of Psychology, Psychoanalysis and History* (New Haven, 1987).

Phillip Cole, *The Myth of Evil* (Edinburgh, 2006).

Martin Dehli, 'Shaping History: Alexander Mitscherlich and German Psychoanalysis after 1945', *Psychoanalysis and History*, 11 (2009), 55–73.

Henry Dicks, 'Personality Traits and National Socialist Ideology', *Human Relations*, 3 (1950), 111–54.

——*Fifty Years of the Tavistock Clinic* (London, 1970).

——*Licensed Mass Murder: A Socio-Psychological Study of Some SS Killers* (London, 1972).

Lawrence Douglas, *The Memory of Judgment: Making Law and History in the Trials of the Holocaust* (New Haven, 2001).

Peter Drucker, *The End of Economic Man: A Study of the New Totalitarianism* (London, 1939).

Roger Eatwell, *Fascism: A History* (London, 1995).

Mark Edmundson, The *Death of Sigmund Freud: Fascism, Psychoanalysis and the Rise of Fundamentalism* (London, 2007).

Norbert Ehrenfreund, *The Nuremberg Legacy: How the Nazi War Crimes Trials Changed the Course of History* (London, 2007).

Richard Evans, *The Third Reich at War: 1939–1945* (London, 2008).

John Forrester and Laura Cameron, *Freud in Cambridge* (forthcoming).

Jo Fox, 'Propaganda and the Flight of Rudolf Hess, 1941–1945', *Journal of Modern History*, 83 (2011), 78–110.

Norbert Frei, *Adenauer's Germany and the Nazi Past: The Politics of Amnesty and Integration* (New York, 1997).

Kirsten Fremaglich, *American Dreams and Nazi Nightmares: Early Holocaust Consciousness and Liberal America, 1957–1965* (Walthan, Mass., 2007).

Erich Fromm, *The Anatomy of Human Destructiveness* (New York, 1973).

Stephen Frosh, *Key Concepts in Psychoanalysis* (London, 2002).

—— *Hate and the 'Jewish Science': Anti-Semitism, Nazism and Psychoanalysis* (Basingstoke, 2005).

Peter Gay, *Freud for Historians* (New York, 1985).

—— *Freud: A Life for Our Time* (London, 1998).

Uta Gerhardt (ed. and intr.), *Talcott Parsons on National Socialism* (New York, 1993).

James E. Goggin, *Death of a 'Jewish Science': Psychoanalysis in the Third Reich* (West Lafayette, Ind., 2000).

Leon Goldensohn, *The Nuremberg Interviews*, edited and introduced by Robert Gellately (London, 2006).

Cora Sol Goldstein, *Capturing the German Eye: American Visual Propaganda in Occupied Germany* (Chicago, 2009).

William Graebner, *The Engineering of Consent: Democracy and Authority in Twentieth-Century America* (Madison, Wisc., 1987).

Brett Gray, *The Nervous Liberals: Propaganda Anxieties from World War I to the Cold War* (New York, 1999).

Neil Gregor, *Haunted City: Nuremberg and the Nazi Past* (New Haven, 2008).

Roger Griffin (ed.), *Fascism* (Oxford, 1995).

—— *Modernism and Fascism: The Sense of a Beginning Under Mussolini and Hitler*, London, 2007.

—— Werner Low, and Andreas Umland (eds.), *Fascism Past and Present, West and East: An International Debate on Concepts and Cases in the Comparative Study of the Extreme Right* (Stuttgart, 2006).

Ilse Grubrich-Simitis, 'Extreme Traumatization as Cumulative Trauma— Psychoanalytic Investigations of the Effects of Concentration Camp Experiences on Survivors and their Children', *Psychoanalytic Study of the Child*, 36 (1981), 415–50.

Nathan Hale, *The Rise and Crisis of Psychoanalysis in the United States, 1917–1985* (New York, 1995).

Tom Harrison, *Bion, Rickman, Foulkes, and the Northfield Experiments: Advancing on a Different Front* (London, 2000).

Dagmar Herzog, *Sex after Fascism: Memory and Morality in Twentieth-Century Germany* (Princeton, 2005).

Louise Hoffman, 'American Psychologists and Wartime Research on Germany, 1941–1945', *American Psychologist*, 42 (1992), 264–73.

Michaela Hönicke Moore, *Know your Enemy: the American Debate on Nazism, 1933–1945* (Cambridge, 2010).

Martin Jay, *The Dialectical Imagination: A History of the Frankfurt School and the Institute of Social Research, 1923–1950* [1973] (Berkeley, 1996).

Keith Jeffery, *MI6: The History of the Secret Intelligence Service, 1909–1949* (London, 2010).

Tony Judt, *Postwar: A History of Europe since 1945* (London, 1995).

Barry M. Katz, *Foreign Intelligence: Research and Analysis in the Office of Strategic Services, 1942–1945* (Cambridge, Mass., 1989).

Ian Kershaw, *Hitler: 1889–1936: Hubris* (London, 1998).

——*Hitler: 1936–1945: Nemesis* (London, 2000).

——'Hitler and the Uniqueness of Nazism', *Journal of Contemporary History*, 39 (2004), 239–54.

——*The End: Hitler's Germany, 1944–45* (London, 2011).

Daniel Kevles, *In the Name of Eugenics: Genetics and Human Heredity* (New York, 1985).

John Maynard Keynes, *The Economic Consequences of the Peace* [1919] (London, 1971).

Pearl King, 'Activities of British Psychoanalysts during the Second World War and the influence of their Inter-disciplinary Collaboration on the Development of Psychoanalysis in Great Britain', *International Review of Psychoanalysis*, 16 (1989), 15–33.

——and Riccardo Steiner (eds.), *The Freud–Klein Controversies, 1941–5* (London, 1991).

Melanie Klein, *The Psycho-Analysis of Children* (London, 1932).

——and Joan Riviere, *Love, Hate and Reparation* [1937] (London, 1967).

Siegfried Kracauer, *From Caligari to Hitler: A Psychological History of the German Film* [1947], revised and extended edition (Princeton, 2004).

Dominick LaCapra, *History and Memory after Auschwitz* (Ithaca, NY, 1998).

——*Representing the Holocaust: History, Theory, Trauma* (Ithaca, NY, 1994).

Walter Langer, *The Mind of Adolf Hitler* (New York, 1972).

——and Sanford Gifford, 'An American Analyst during the *Anschluss* 1936–1938', *Journal of the History of the Behavioral Sciences*, 14 (1978), 37–54.

William Langer, 'The Next Assignment', *American Historical Review*, 63 (1958), 283–304.

——*In and Out of the Ivory Tower: The Autobiography of William L. Langer* (New York, 1977).

Harold Lasswell, 'The Psychology of Hitlerism', *Political Quarterly*, 4 (1933), 373–84.

Rebecca Lemov, *World as Laboratory: Experiments with Mice, Mazes and Men* (New York, 2006).

Daniel Lerner, *Psychological Warfare against Nazi Germany: The Sykewar Campaign, D-Day to VE-Day* [1949] (Cambridge, Mass., 1971).

Kurt Lewin, *Resolving Social Conflicts: Selected Papers on Group Dynamics* (New York, 1948).

Robert Jay Lifton, *The Nazi Doctors: Medical Killing and the Psychology of Genocide* (New York, 1986).

Gilbert, Gustave, *Nuremberg Diary* (New York, 1947).

Meira Likierman, *Melanie Klein: Her Work in Context* (London, 2001).

Paul Linebarger, *Psychological Warfare* (Washington, DC, 1948).

Deborah E. Lipstadt, *Denying the Holocaust: The Growing Assault on Truth and Memory* (New York, 1993).

Peter Loewenberg, 'Psychohistorical Perspectives on Modern German History', *Journal of Modern History*, 47 (1975), 229–79.

Philip Lombardo, *The Lucifer Effect: Understanding How Good People Turn Evil* (New York, 2007).

Oliver Lubrich (ed.), *Travels in the Reich, 1933–1945* (Chicago, 2010).

George Makari, *Revolution in Mind: The Creation of Psychoanalysis* (New York, 2008).

Peter Mandler, 'One World, Many Cultures: Margaret Mead and the Limits to Cold War Anthropology', *History Workshop Journal*, 86 (2009), 149–72.

—— *Return from the Natives: How Margaret Mead Won the Second World War and Lost The Cold War* (forthcoming).

Michael Mann, *Fascists* (Cambridge, 2004).

Herbert Marcuse, *Technology, War and Fascism: Collected Papers of Herbert Marcuse*, ed. Douglas Kellner (London, 1998).

Michael Marrus, *The Nuremberg War Crimes Trial 1945–46* (Toronto, 1997).

Richard Mayne, *In Victory, Magnanimity in Peace, Goodwill: A History of Wilton Park* (London, 2003).

Mark Mazower, *Dark Continent: Europe's Twentieth Century* (New York, 1998).

Isabel Menzies Lyth, *Containing Anxiety in Institutions: Selected Essays* (London, 1988).

Florence R. Miale, *The Nuremberg Mind: The Psychology of the Nazi Leaders* (New York, 1975).

Stanley Milgram, *Obedience to Authority: An Experimental View* (London, 1974).

Alexander Mitscherlich and Margarete Mitscherlich, *The Inability to Mourn: Principles of Collective Behavior* (New York, 1975).

Roger Money-Kyrle, 'Some Aspects of State and Character in Germany' [1951], in *The Collected Papers of Roger Money-Kyrle*, ed. D. Meltzer (Strath Tay, 1978), ch. 14.

Peter Novick, *The Holocaust in American Life* (New York, 2000).

Edna O'Shaughnessy, 'Relating to the Superego', *International Journal of Psycho-Analysis*, 80 (1999), 861–70.

Richard Overy, *Interrogations: The Nazi Elite in Allied Hands* (London, 2001).

—— *The Morbid Age: Britain and the Crisis of Civilization, 1919–1939* (London, 2009).

Peter Padfield, *Hess: Flight for the Führer* (London, 1991).

Kevin Passmore, *Fascism: A Very Short Introduction* (Oxford, 2002).

Stanley Platt Lovell, *Of Spies and Stratagems* (Englewood Cliffs, NJ, 1963).

Proceedings of the International Congress on Mental Health, ed. J. C. Flügel, 4 vols. (London, 1948).

John Rawlings Rees *et al.*, *The Case of Rudolf Hess: A Problem in Diagnosis and Forensic Psychiatry* (London, 1947).

Jessica Reinisch, *Public Health in Germany under Allied Occupation, 1943–1949* (forthcoming).

Graham Richards, 'Putting Britain on the Couch: The Popularisation of Psychoanalysis in Britain 1918–1940', *Science in Context*, 13 (2000), 183–230.

Denise Riley, *War in the Nursery: Theories of the Child and Mother* (London, 1983).

Ron Rosenbaum, *Explaining Hitler: The Search for the Origins of His Evil* (New York, 1998).

Michael Rustin, *The Good Society and the Inner World: Psychoanalysis, Politics and Culture* (London, 1991).

Andrew Samuels, 'National Psychology, National Socialism, and Analytical Psychology: Reflections on Jung and Anti-Semitism', part 1, *Journal of Analytical Psychology*, 37 (1992), 3–28; part 2, ibid. 127–48.

Arthur M. Schlesinger Jr., *The Vital Center: The Politics of Freedom* [1949] (New York, 1992).

Claudia Schmölders, *Hitler's Face: The Biography of an Image* (Philadelphia, 2006).

Gitta Sereny, *Albert Speer: His Battle with Truth* (New York 1995).

Michael Shepherd, 'Clio and Psyche: The Lessons of Psychohistory', *Journal of the Royal Society of Medicine*, 71 (1978), 406–12.

William Shirer, *Berlin Diary* [1941] (London, 1970).

Bradley Smith, *The Shadow Warriors: OSS and the Origins of the CIA* (London, 1983).

Michael Smith, *Michael Foley: The Spy Who Saved 10,000 Jews* (London, 1999).

David Stafford (ed.), *Flight from Reality: Rudolf Hess and his Mission to Scotland 1941* (London, 2002), ch. 4.

Riccardo Steiner, *'It is a New Kind of Diaspora': Explorations in the Sociopolitical and Cultural Context of Psychoanalysis* (London, 2000).

—— *Tradition, Change, Creativity: Repercussions of the New Diaspora on Aspects of British Psychoanalysis* (London, 2000).

Lyndsey Stonebridge, *The Writing of Anxiety: Imagining Wartime in Mid-Century British Culture* (London, 2007).

—— 'Theories of Trauma', in Marina Mackay (ed.), *The Cambridge Companion to The Literature of World War II* (Cambridge, 2009), ch. 14.

James Tent, *Mission on the Rhine: Re-education and Denazification in American-Occupied Germany* (Chicago, 1982).

Klaus Theweleit, *Male Fantasies*, 2 vols. (Cambridge, 1987 and 1989).

—— 'German Reactions to *Les Bienveillants*', *New German Critique*, 106 (2009), 21–34.

Matthew Thomson, 'Mental Hygiene as an International Movement', in Paul Weindling (ed.), *International Health Organisations and Movements, 1918–1939* (Cambridge, 1995), 283–304.

Riccarda Torriani, 'Nazis into Germans: Re-education and Democratisation in the British and French Occupation Zones, 1945–1949', Ph.D. thesis, Cambridge University (2005).

Enzo Traverso, *The Origins of Nazi Violence* (New York, 2003).

Hugh Trevor-Roper, *The Last Days of Hitler* (London, 1947).

Eric Trist, 'Guilty of Enthusiasm', in Arthur G. Bedeian (ed.), *Management Laureates: A Collection of Autobiographical Essays* (Greenwich, Conn., 1993), vol. 3.

—— and Hugh Murray (eds.), *The Social Engagement of Social Science: A Tavistock Anthology*, vol. 1: *The Socio-Psychological Perspective* (Philadelphia, 1990).

Paul Weindling, *Nazi Medicine and the Nuremberg Trials: From Medical War Crimes to Informed Consent* (London, 2004).

Rebecca West, *A Train of Powder: Six Reports on the Problems of Guilt and Punishment in our Time* (New York, 1955).

Rolf Wiggershaus, *The Frankfurt School: Its History, Theories and Political Significance* (Cambridge, 1994).

Robin W. Winks, *Cloak and Gown: Scholars in the Secret War, 1939–1961* (New Haven, 1987).

Donald Winnicott, *The Child and the Family: First Relationships* (London, 1957).

Alison Winter, 'The Making of "truth serum"', *Bulletin of the History of Medicine*, 79 (2005), 500–33.

Robert K. Woetzel, *The Nuremberg Trials in International Law, with a Postlude on the Eichmann Case* (London, 1962).

Eli Zaretsky, *Secrets of the Soul: A Social and Cultural History of Psychoanalysis* (New York, 2004).

Slavoj Žižek, *Did Somebody Say Totalitarianism?* (London, 2001).

Acknowledgements

In writing this book, I have received generous help from many colleagues and friends and crucial institutional support. I am especially grateful to have been offered a research leave award from the Wellcome Trust that enabled me to devote the necessary time to the development and completion of this project. A grant from the International Psychoanalytical Association also facilitated my work and enabled me to undertake a number of the preliminary explorations in archives in Europe and the United States.

Birkbeck College has provided a stimulating intellectual context in which to pursue this inquiry; nearby, the resources of the Wellcome Library and the British Library have been indispensable. Clare Alexander at Aitken Alexander Associates has offered much support and astute advice throughout. Many thanks also to the team at OUP, especially my editor, Luciana O'Flaherty, to Matthew Cotton and Emma Barber for overseeing production, Deborah Protheroe and Julia Engelhardt for picture research, and Jeff New and Andrew Hawkey for their expeditious work on the text.

My interest in Henry Dicks and his wartime work was sparked by material I encountered at the library of the Tavistock Clinic. Don Campbell and Rob Hale, colleagues at the British Psychoanalytical Society, kindly put me in touch with three of Henry Dicks's children. Adrian Dicks, Anthony Dicks, Gillian Higson-Smith, and several other members of the family have been exceptionally generous in responding to questions and furnishing documents. I am also grateful to Richard and Bridget Astor for enabling me to explore relevant papers in the archives of David Astor.

Many thanks to Nadia Atia for her excellent and good-humoured research assistance. I have also received most helpful contributions along the way from Paul Bromley, Shaul Bar-Haim, Robert Woodward Hutchinson, Paul Moore, Hila Prestele, Emmanuela Quagliata, Beatrice Riley, and Margaret Simonds. Stuart Oglethorpe also assisted with the archives and has provided valuable editorial suggestions into the bargain.

Discussions with Sally Alexander, Sanjoy Bhattacharya, Louise Braddock, Michael Briant, the late Norman Cohn, David Cornwell, Geoff Eley Matt ffytche, Simon Garfield, Sander Gilman, Colin Jones, Timo Hoyer, Joel Isaacs, the late Leonard Langer, George Makari, Margarete Mitscherlich, Knuth Müller, Jacqueline Rose, Elisabeth Roudinesco, Sonu Shamdasani, Elizabeth Spillius, and Eli Zaretsky

346   ACKNOWLEDGEMENTS

(among others) have also left their mark on this book, as has the interesting dialogue on Nazism between the psychoanalyst John Steiner and the economist Gabriel Palma at the British Psychoanalytical Society some years ago. At Birkbeck, Orlando Figes, Stephen Frosh, Christian Goeschel, and Jessica Reinisch read the emerging text and offered helpful advice and encouragement in equal measure.

I have badgered many librarians and archivists for information over the years; particularly Jens Boel, Mahmoud Ghander, Lesley Hall, Derek Marrison, Diane Richardson, Stephen Roeper, and Olga Umansky. The former archivist, Polly Rossdale at the British Psychoanalytical Society also provided access to a number of relevant materials. For generous hospitality in Washington, I am indebted to Bill and Gail Gorham. For a warm reception and helpful advice, respectively in Albany, Boston, Berlin, and Frankfurt, my thanks to John Spalek, Claude Brenner, Ludger Hermanns, and Ilse Grubrich-Simitis. Two psychoanalysts and archivists, Sanford Gifford (in Boston) and Nellie Thompson (in New York), have been unflaggingly helpful advisors on primary sources and, in addition, generously commented on work in progress and invited me to present my work.

The debts do not end there. I have been most fortunate to receive thoughtful comments on my evolving manuscript from Jane Caplan, Elizabeth Coates-Thümmel, Richard Evans, Peter Mandler, Maria Margaronis, Richard Overy, Matthew Reisz, and Michael Rustin. OUP's (anonymous) advisers were also helpful. Not by any means for the first time since I began to research and write about cultural history, I have turned for advice to John Forrester, Lyndal Roper, Simon Schaffer, Quentin Skinner, Nick Stargardt, and Gareth Stedman Jones. All have influenced the shape of this book, warned me of pitfalls, and challenged me to make the arguments more ambitious.

This research and writing have not been without their share of dilemmas and problems; the book has also taken much longer than I first envisaged. In light of that, I have been all the more fortunate to receive so much support from my family. Conversations with my stepfather Eric Brenman who was himself a young doctor in the British army and who, later on, knew Dicks slightly at the Tavistock Clinic, added to my interest in wartime psychiatric work and its broader intellectual context. My mother, Irma Brenman Pick, has offered warm encouragement and valuable ideas. Special thanks to Anna and Tasha, not least for their forbearance and humour. Above all I am grateful to Isobel. Formal acknowledgements cannot do much justice to such personal contributions, but I want at least to record the fact that she has helped me think through this research agenda from the start and contributed extensively to the account that is presented here.

This book is dedicated to the memory of my late father, Abe Pick, who had a deep interest in politics, psychoanalysis and social justice, and the complex connections between them.

Index

Illustrations denoted in bold

Abraham, Karl 129, 288 n.24
Adenauer, Konrad 205–6
Adler, Alfred 15, 59
Adorno, Theodor 21, 117, 218–19, 224–8
  inquiry into fascism 226–8
  The Authoritarian Personality
    (1950) 224–7
Alexander, Franz 20, 104
Allied Control Commission 197
Allies, the 3, 10
  bombing campaign 249–50
  intelligence 28, 78, 86, 108–27,
    216, 229
  see also individual entries
alternative medicine 1, 60
Amen, John 155, 174
American Foster Parents' Plan for War
  Children 11
American Historical Association 29, 151
American Imago 263
American Jewish Committee 67, 224
American Psychiatric Association 190
amnesia 48, 75, 77–8, 80, 155, 160, 162,
  206, 218, 226; *see also* Hess, Rudolf
'analytical psychology' 15; *see also* Jung, Carl
Anderson, Perry 3, 286 n.4
Anderson, Robin 254
Andrus, Colonel Burton 173
Anschluss 155
anti-Semitism 14, 42, 47, 66–72, 123, 139,
    145–6, 156, 178, 210, 218, 225, 227, 241
  psychology 47, 214, 226–8
Apartheid 185
aphasia 172
'appeasement' policy, *see* Chamberlain,
  Neville
Arendt, Hannah 173, 234, 238, 244–7,
    268–9, 319 n.31, 332 n.78

Eichmann in Jerusalem (1963) 245–6,
    332 n.78 and n.80
The Origins of Totalitarianism
    (1951) 268, 334 n.2
Armenian genocide 244
Aron, Raymond 210
Aryan ideology 15, 35, 47, 60, 139, 141,
    147, 200, 241, 334 n.2
Askenasy, Hans 250
Astor, David 47, 234–5, 259
Atlee, Clement 54, 83
atomic bomb 109, 250
Auschwitz 179–80, 249, 251, 268
'authoritarian personality' 217, 224,
    259–60
Authoritarian Personality, The (1950) 224–7;
    see also Adorno, Theodor

Bad Oeynhausen 201
Baldwin, Stanley 97–8, 304 n.27
'banality of evil', *see* Arendt, Hannah
Barbie, Klaus 250
Beaverbrook, Max Aitken 54, 72,
    301 n.28
Beer Hall Putsch 18, 35, 135, 312 n.19
Béla Kun 71
Belsen 176
Benjamin, Walter 335 n.16
Berlin 14
Berlin air-lift 206
Berlin, Isaiah 195
Berlin Psychoanalytical Society 15
Bernays, Edward 123, 310 n.52
  Democratic Leadership in Total War
    (1943) 123
  Speak up for Democracy (1940) 123
Bernays, Colonel Murray 166, 168,
    317 n.2

Bethlem Royal Hospital 26
Bettelheim, Bruno 171–3, 224, 319 n.31
Bibring, Edward 30
Biddle, Francis 170
Bin Laden, Osama 229
Bion, Wilfred 27, 121, 186, 197–9,
    203, 255
    Experiences in Groups, and Other Papers
    (1961) 199
Bismarck, Otto von 96
Blavatsky, Madam 26
Bletchley Park 109, 201
'Blitz', the 53, 212
Bloch, Eduard 134
'Bloomsbury group' 196
Blum, Léon 210
Boas, Franz 185
Boehm, Felix 15
Boer War 71
Bollas, Christopher 226
Bolshevism 1, 42, 52, 88, 101
Bonaparte, Napoleon 46
Bormann, Martin 50–1, 155
Boston Psychoanalytic Society 29, 32,
    128, 132, 261
Bowlby, John 121, 184–5, 194, 211, 213
Braun, Eva 150, 240
Brenman, Eric 254
Briant, Michael 261
Brickner, Richard 104
    Is Germany Incurable? (1943) 104, 172
Brill, Abraham 21
    Basic Writings of Sigmund Freud
    (1938) 21
    *Fundamental Conceptions of
    Psychoanalysis* (1921) 21
British Broadcasting Corporation
    (BBC) 112, 186, 259
British Psychoanalytical Society 11–12,
    20, 25, 31, 211
British Union of Fascists 100; *see also*
    Mosley, Oswald
British War Relief Society 11
Browning, Christopher 246
Buchanan Castle 53–4
Buchenwald 171, 210, 318 n.24
Bullitt, William C. 99–100
Bullock, Alan 130
Burlingham, Dorothy 31

Cambridge University 25
Cameron, Ewen 158
Campbell, Gerald 57
capitalism 7, 21, 89, 115, 123, 155, 196
Caplan, Jane 226
Carter, John Franklin 138
Cassell Hospital 28
Central Intelligence Agency (CIA) 110,
    127, 229; *see also* OSS; MID
Cesarani, David 332 n.78
Chamberlain, Neville 56, 97–8, 151
Chaplin, Charlie 47
    The Great Dictator 47
Chisholm, Brock 190
Churchill, Winston 44, 49, 51–5, 111
    Hess in Britain 46–64, 57–8
    Nuremberg Trial 167
    opposition to appeasement 97–8
cinema 41, 220–2
Civil Rights Movement 185
Clark University 21
Clemenceau, Georges 92
Cohn, Norman 47, 234, 259–61
    Europe's Inner Demons 47
    The Pursuit of the Millennium 47
Cold War 9, 182, 189, 206
'collective mental sanity' 182
Columbia University 188
Columbus Trust 47, 234
Colville, John 54–5
Communism 86, 89, 94, 96, 110, 224, 227
concentration camps 19, 161, 171–3,
    179–80, 226, 280, 294 n.65, 318 n.24,
    331 n.73, 333 n.99
'conditioned reflexes', *see* Pavlov, Ivan
'Controversial Discussions' 11
Cornell Law Library 110
Cotton, Henry 253
Coughlin, Father Charles 123
Crichton-Miller, Dr Hugh 24; *see also*
    Tavistock Clinic
criminology 82–3
'crisis of reason' 94
Crossman, Richard 203
Czechoslovakia 98

Dachau 171, 318 n.24
Darwin, Charles 82
death drive 3

degeneration 13, 59, 82, 91, 94, 115, 141, 221, 294 n.69
defences, psychological 16, 18, 19, 66, 74, 75, 132, 172, 176, 182, 194, 241, 255
depression 39, 75, 80, 101, 150, 163, 198, 240, 254, 312, 319 n.30
Delay, Jean 158
democracy 4, 23, 87–8, 96, 124, 182, 188, 192, 196, 206
de-Nazification 9, 199–206, 228
Der Stürmer 68, 156
Deutsch, Helene 20
Dicks, Henry 1, 3, 4, 8, 20, 24–5, 35, 43, 59, 102–3, 111, 176, 183, 197, 201, 207–8, 213, 230, 286 n.1, 290 n.1, 2, 4, 5, 7, 291 n.14, 325 n.73, 328 n.27, 334 n.1
  Clinical Studies in Psychopathology 27
  Licensed Mass Murder: A Socio-Psychological Study of Some SS Killers (1972) 259–61
  treatment of Hess 64–74, **271–7**
dictatorship 95
disarmament 97
Dodd, William 134
Doenitz, Karl 179
Donovan, William Joseph 32, 110–11, 114–16, 126, 129, 308 n.35
  investigation of Hitler 110–16, 134–6
Douglas, Lawrence 245
Dr Mabuse, see Lang, Fritz
Drucker, Peter 103–4
  The End of Economic Man: The Origins of Totalitarianism (1939) 103
Drymen Military Hospital 53
Duke of Hamilton 46, 49, 53–5, 63, 69
Dunkirk 46
Durkheim, Émile 217
Dwork, Charles Irving 42

Eden, Anthony 45, 54, 56, 183
Edward VIII 100
ego, the 17, 18, 83, 90, 171, 184, 225, 256, 289 n.34
Eichmann, Adolf 67, 238, 244, 331 n.74
  trial 170, 173, 234, 244–7
Eisenhower, Dwight D. 173
Eitingon, Max 15

Elias, Norbert, 192–4, 264–5
  The Civilizing Process (1939) 192–3
émigrés 11, 22, 115; *see also* individual entries
enlightenment 7, 193–4
Erikson, Erik 20, 30, 118, 196, 233, 250, 262
Estonia 25
eugenics 95, 185, 243
Evald, Alice 65
Evans, Richard 312 n.30, 329 n.36
Evans-Pritchard, E. E. 215
Evipan 70, 78–9

Fanon, Frantz 288 n.14
fanaticism 38, 101
fantasies 39, 19, 74, 76, 105, 131–9, 144, 174, 179, 227, 235, 238, 240–1, 254
fascism 3, 6, 87–9, 95, 195–6, 208, 289 n.31
  Italian 100, 102
  study of 8, 211, 214–15
  see also Nazism
Fath, Hildegard 160
Febvre, Lucien 211, 215
Federal Bureau of Investigation (FBI) 115
Fenichel, Otto 21
Ferenczi, Sándor 15–16, 129
Fest, Joachim 239
Field, Henry 138
Final Solution 154, 244–5; *see also* genocide; Nuremberg Trial
fin-de-siècle 2, 5, 195
Finer, Herman 210
Fleming, Peter 47
  The Flying Visit (1940) 47
Flügel, John-Carl 183, 211
Foley, Frank 55, 75
Ford, Henry 55
Forrestal, James 169
Foucault, Michel 232, 237, 322 n.36
Foulkes, Siegfried Heinrich 194
France 9, 99, 178, 210, 250, 256
Frank, Hans 171, 177–8
Frankfurt School 7, 21, 90, 115, 117, 224–7
Franklin, John 138
Freikorps 8, 33

Freud, Anna 11, 18–19, 30, 83, 210,
    212–13, 238
The Ego and the Mechanisms of Defence
    (1936), 18.
Freud, Sigmund 2, 6, 10–19, 28, 84, 87,
    122, 177–8, 191–2, 194–5, 267
Beyond the Pleasure Principle (1920)
    17, 268
'Constructions in Psycho-Analysis'
    (1937) 267
flight from Austria 31
Freudian tradition 2, 19–20, 28, 215,
    217, 269–70
*Group Psychology and the Analysis of the
    Ego* (1921) 5, 17, 235
influence in the United States 22
influence on historical
    interpretation 231–58
Moses and Monotheism (1937) 257
'Remembering, Repeating, and
    Working Through' (1914) 267
The Ego and the Id (1923) 17
Three Essays on the Theory of Sexuality
    (1905) 131
Totem and Taboo (1913) 90
under the Nazis 14
'Wednesday meetings' 14
'Freudish', *see* Richard, Graham
Fritzsche, Hans 177, 180
Fromm, Erich 6, 20, 196, 213, 215,
    328 n.21
Escape from Freedom (1941) 9, 48
The Anatomy of Human Destructiveness
    (1973) 6–8, 250

Geneva Conference (1863) 167
Geneva Convention 280
genocide 47, 147, 154, 243–4, 259
George VI 69
German Personnel Research Branch
    (GPRB) 197, 201
German Society for Psychology 15
German Society for Psychotherapy, *see*
    International General Medical
    Society for Psychotherapy
Germany
    Cabinet Council of Germany 37
    commemoration 266–7
    'domestic culture' 72–4

Federal Republic 205–6
impact of WWI 6, 92–4
military tradition 124
occupied 173, 175, 182, 198–201
pathology 96–8
responses to Hitler 10–11, 86–7,
    143–4, 208
stereotypes 220–2, 242–4, 259
working classes 7
Gestapo 51, 103, 168, 250
Ghaddafi, Muammar 229
Gibson Graham, J. 53
Gifford, Sanford 29
Gilbert, Gustave 67–8, 161–4, 170, 174,
    179, 244–5, **284**
Nuremberg Diary (1947) 177
Gilbert, Martin 54; *see also* Churchill,
    Winston
Glover, Edward 27, 211
Goebbels, Joseph 37, 45, 50–2, 84, 118,
    123, 177, 179
suicide 150
see also propaganda
Goeschel, Christian 150
Goethe, Johann Wolfgang von 58
Goffman, Erving 237
The Presentation of Self in Everyday Life
    (1956) 237
Goldensohn, Leon 161, 163, 171, 174, 178–9
Goldhagen, Daniel 236
Hitler's Willing Executioners (1996) 236
Golding, William 222
Lord of the Flies (1954) 222–3
Gorer, Geoffrey 28, 215
Göring, Hermann 57, 101, 150, 154
Nuremberg Trial 162–3, 171, 174,
    177–9
suicide 175–6
Göring Institute in Berlin 14–15
Göring, Matthias Heinrich 14–15
graphology 159
Great Britain 18, 52
army 26
Empire 92
General Strike 86
Hess flight to 44–58
House of Commons 51, 54
intelligence 42, 45, 54, 100, 193
Ministry of Health 76

Ministry of Works 58
Political Warfare Executive 117
Special Operations Executive 117
War Crimes Executive 158
see also individual entries
Great War, *see* World War One
Greenacre, Phyllis 252–3
Greene, Graham 221–2
Griffin, Roger 289 n.31
group psychology 2, 105, 116, 194, 219
group therapy 182, 190, 194, 196, 213
Guha, B. S. 210
guilt 17–18, 60, 66, 74–8, 91, 125, 132,
    149, 159, 164, 167, 176, 182, 199,
    201–2, 225–6, 231, 243, 260

Haffner, Sebastian 149
Hahn, Otto 56
Hampstead War Nurseries 11
Hanfstaengl, Ernst 135, 137–40, 240
Hartmann, Heinz 20, 22
Harvard Educational Review 191
Harvard Law Review 168
Harvard University 29–30, 91, 131,
    168, 194
Haushofer, Karl 35–7, 50, 52, 160, 297
    n.42
Hausner, Gideon 245
Hayek, F. A. 195
    The Road to Serfdom (1944) 195
Headway 97
Hedin, Sven 42
Heiden, Konrad 41–2
Heisenberg, Werner 56
Hess, Rudolf 1, 4, 6, 9, 13, 20, 24, 27, 143,
    218, 259, 263–6
    amnesia 75–80, 155, 160–2, 174
    anti-Semitism 33, 42, 66,
        70–1, 80
    attempted suicide 69–71, 80
    biography 33–8, 60
    characteristics 59, 82
    'Deputy Führer' 46, 296 n.14
    eating habits 67, 77–8, 81, 120, 160–1
    disillusionment 49
    flight 45–57
    hallucination 74
    Hess, Ilse 45, 80
    Hess, Wolf Rüdiger, 36

hypochondria 52, 69–71, 74–80,
    158–61
infatuation with Hitler 34–5,
    38–40, 63
mental state 53–4, 59–60, 67, 75
Nuremberg Trial 153–81,
    278–82, **284**
paranoia 63, 67–8, 74, 78–80, 120
Reich Minister without Portfolio 37
self-medication 60
sexuality 40–1, 61, 74, 77, 294 n.70
Himmler, Heinrich 150, 177, 179–80,
    238, 241
Hindenberg, Paul von 38
Hiss, Alger 120
historiography 7, 37, 73, 93, 116–17, 147,
    216, 226, 231–5
Hitchcock, Alfred 221, 327 n.7
Hitler, Adolf 2, 3, 6, 8–9, 128–52, 170–1,
    177–8, 218–19, 279, 308–9 n.40
    'alter ego' 41
    analysis of 4, 8, 83, 99–100, 105,
        118–52, 239–41
    anti-Semitism 145–7
    bomb plot (1944) 216
    'cult of the Führer' 4, 10–1, 39–41,
        170–1, 178–9, 216–18, 252
    fantasies 105, 128–52
    Hess flight 46–8, 84, 162
    'Hitlerism' 96
    influence on German policy 36
    'madness' 100–1, 105, 221
    Mein Kampf 36, 42, 98, 118–19, 124,
        135, 142, 206, 293 n.51
    mental health 24
    'Messiah complex' 143, 147
    psychological deterioration 138–9
    sexuality 118–19, 131–40, 146–7,
        148–9, 177–8, 239–41, 330 nn.52, 54
    speeches 10
    upbringing 134–6, 145
Hobson, J. A. 91
Hoess, Rudolf 179–80
Hohenlohe, Stephanie von 136
Holocaust 226, 243–6, 262, 267
    Holocaust denial 236
    see also Final Solution; genocide
Hoover, Herbert 114
Hoover, J. Edgar 110, 115

Horkheimer, Max 7, 21, 117, 215, 225,
　　227–8
　'Studies in Prejudice' 224
　see also Frankfurt School
Horney, Karen 20
Hull, Cordell 169
'human condition' 87, 232, 244
human rights 168
Hussein, Saddam 229
Huxley, Aldous 88
Huxley, Julian 187, 207, 321 n.13

id, the 17
idealization 6, 116, 208
imperialism 9, 98, 268
India 14
'inferiority complex' 59, 142, 179
'ink-blot tests', *see* 'Rorschach' test
insanity 39, 50, 52, 67, 92, 105, 182–3
Institute for Social Research 7, 228
International Congress on Mental
　　Health 182–3, 190
International General Medical Society
　　for Psychotherapy 15
internationalism 97, 123
International Military Tribunal, *see*
　　Nuremberg Trial
International Military Tribunal for the
　　Far East 314 n.4
International Psychoanalytical
　　Association 12, 22
'interventionism' 195
Israel 244, 245, 332 n.79

Jackson, Robert 126, 166, 169–71
James, William 91
Janet, Pierre 158
Jeffery, Keith 101
jingoism 91
Jodl, Alfred 179
Johnston, M. K. 75
Jones, Ernest 17–18, 27, 189, 197, 233–4,
　　329 n.37
Jones, Ellis 76–8, 85
*Journal of Abnormal and Social
　　Psychology* 172
Journal of Modern History 330 n.50
Judgement at Nuremberg 206
Jung, Carl 14

Kaltenbrunner, Ernst 179
Kelley, Douglas 85, 158–60, 170, 174
Kendrick, Thomas 55
Kennedy, John F. 195
Kernberg, Otto 254
Kershaw, Ian 49, 140, 145,
　　236, 240
Keynes, John Maynard 92
　'communal hatred' 93
　The Economic Consequences of the Peace
　　(1919) 92–3
　*The General Theory of Employment,
　　Interest and Money* (1936) 93
Kirkpatrick, Ivone 53–4, 56
Klein, Melanie 18–20, 28, 83, 98, 130,
　　183–4, 186, 199, 255–6
　impact in the United States 21
　Narrative of a Child Analysis (1961) 20
　The Psycho-Analysis of Children
　　(1932), 20
　treatment of infants 20
Koeppler, Heinz 203–4
Krafft-Ebing, Richard von 142
Krasnushkin, Eugene 158
Kris, Ernst 20, 22, 112, 133–4
Krueger, Kurt 105–6, 141
　Inside Hitler 105–6, 141
Krupp von Bohlen, Gustav 155
Kubie, Lawrence 120

Lacan, Jacques 192, 256, 287 n.14
Lagache, Daniel 215
Langer, Leonard 112
Lang, Fritz 106–7
　Ministry of Fear (1944) 221
　The Testament of Dr Mabuse (1933) 106
Langer, Walter 4, 8, 28–32, 36, 84, 96, 99,
　　177, 308 n.35, 309 n.44, 335 n.12
　propaganda 108
　study of Hitler 111–52, 261–3
　see also Office of Strategic Services
　　(OSS): *The Mind of Adolf Hitler*
Langer, William 128, 231
Lasswell, Harold 95
　Psychopathology and Politics (1930) 96
Latin America 14
Lawrence, Geoffrey (Lord Justice) 154;
　　see also Nuremberg Trial
Lawson, John 'Jack' 51

League of Nations 97–8
Lebensraum 35
Le Bon, Gustave 91–2, 123
Leitgen, Alfred 50
Lemkin, Raphael 168
Lenin, Vladimir 103
Lerner, Daniel 230–1
Levi, Primo 234, 251, 332 n.96
Levi-Strauss, Claude 215
Levy, David 188, 201–2
Lewin, Bertrand 133–4
Lewin, Kurt 191–2, 248
Lewis, Nolan 158–9, 188
Lewis, Sinclair 124
   It Can't Happen Here (1935) 124
Ley, Robert 150, 160
Libeskind, Daniel 267–8
Lindbergh, Charles 55
Linebarger, Paul 13, 229
Lippitt, Ronald 191
Littell, Jonathan 242–3
   Les Bienveillants (2006) 242
Lloyd George, David 100, 280, 304 n.38
Lockhart, Robert Bruce 51, 57
Loewenberg, Peter 238–9
Loewenstein, Rudolph 20, 22
Lombroso, Cesare 82, 142
London School of Economics 91, 195
Lovejoy, Arthur O. 125
Lovell, Stanley 119–20
Ludecke, Kurt 38
Luftwaffe 45, 155

Macdonald, Ramsay 98
Macfie Campbell, Dr C. 29
'madness' 93, 97, 101,
   155, 236
Magnan, Valentin 142
Main, Tom 28
Maindiff Court 65, 76
Manhattan Project 109
Manchurian Candidate, The 120
Marcuse, Herbert 115–16
   'Private Morale' 116
   'The New German Mentality' 116
Marx Brothers Go West, The (1940) 53
Marxism 7, 103, 196
'mass psychology' 97
Massachusetts Institute of Technology 29

Maudsley, Henry 142
Maudsley Hospital 12, 255
Maxwell-Fyfe, David 162
McDougall, William 29
McGinty, Stephen 264
   Camp Z: The Secret Life of Rudolf Hess
    (2011) 264
McLean, David 46
McMoran Wilson, Charles 158
Mead, Margaret 28, 176, 183, 210, 212
Medical Institute of Moscow 158
Medical Research Council 63
Mein Kampf, see Hitler, Adolf
memory 162, 229, 266–7
Mennell, Stephen 322 n.27
Menninger, Karl 120
Menninger, William 120
Mental health 11–12, 27, 94, 189–90
   infant 212–13, 222
   mental hygiene 15, 94
   see also individual entries
Mental Hygiene School for Boys 29;
   see also Langer, Walter
Menthon, François de 170
mescaline 120
Mesmer, Franz-Anton 67
Messerschmitt, Willi 50
Métraux, Alfred 215
MI6 54, 100, 111, 228, 298 n.57; *see also*
   Sinclair, Hugh
Milgram, Stanley 247–8
Military Intelligence Division (MID) 26,
   109–10, 115
Millet, John 126, 188–9
Mill, John Stuart 167
Ministerial Council for the Defence of
   the Reich 37
Mitscherlich, Alexander/Margarete 252
   The Inability to Mourn (1967) 252
Money-Kyrle, Roger 187–8,
   196–9, 202
Morgenthau, Henry 125
Morrison, Herbert 56
Mosley, Oswald 100
motherhood 184, 186, 187, 208
Mueller, Rene 140
Munich Conference (1938) 98
Munich Putsch, *see* Beer Hall Putsch
Munich University 33

Murphy, James 37
Murray, Gilbert 203
Murray, Henry 3, 99, 113, 120–2, 131–43,
  151, 207, 215
Mussolini, Benito 18, 51, 88, 95, 102
Mytchett Place 55–6, 58, 65
  Hess at 64, 264

narcissism 6, 139
nationalism 9, 91–2, 94, 215
national character 28, 72, 86
National Socialism 96–7, 136; see also
  fascism; Hitler, Adolf; Nazism
Nazism 1, 7–8, 86, 103–4, 124–5,
  217, 226
  de-Nazification 9, 12, 28, 67, 76, 104,
    182, 197, 200, 202, 205–6, 228, 247
  eugenics 95
  fanaticism 59
  ideology 7, 184–6
  impact across Europe 30
  in cinema 220–2
  'mental disease' 97
  'Nazi mind' 3, 9
  psychopathology 6, 113, 143, 251
  studies of Nazism by Jewish
    intellectuals 227–8
  violence 36, 91
  see also individual entries
Neave, Airey 76, 157, 315 n.16
necrophilia 7
Needham, Joseph 215
neo-Nazis 265
Neumann, Franz 117, 215
neurasthenia 99
neurology 13
neuroses 6, 16, 98, 110–12
  'neurotic alibi' 59
New Left Review 3
New Yorker 177, 245
New York Psychoanalytic Society
  21, 188
'Night of the Long Knives' 39
Night Porter, The (1974) 243, 331 n.73
Northfield Hospital 198
Norway 26
'Nuremberg mind', see 'Nazi mind'
Nuremberg race laws 168
Nuremberg rally (1934) 38

Nuremberg Trial 59, 61, 68, 75, 78, 85,
  110, 117, 126, 144, 152–81, 206, 223,
  244, 278–82, **284**
  conspiracy charge 166–9
  crimes against humanity 179
  crimes of war 169
  judgments 180–1

Observer 47, 200, 234, 329 n.38
Oedipus complex 3, 19, 84, 139, 147, 233,
  261, 270
Oeser, Oscar 201
Office of Strategic Services (OSS) 3–4,
  37, 42, 58, 78, 108–27
  OSS Sourcebook 132–6
  plots against Hitler 118–19
  recruitment 117
  rivalry with the FBI 115
  The Mind of Adolf Hitler: The Secret
    Wartime Report 33–8, 128–52, 261–2
Ohlendorf, Otto 179
Old Bear Mountain Range School, see
  Mental Hygiene School for Boys
Olivier, Lawrence 264
Operation Barbarossa 46; see also Russia
Orwell, George 101–2, 149–50, 200, 220,
  305 n.42
  Nineteen Eighty-Four (1949) 222
Osborn, Alex Faickney 117
Overy, Richard 171, 175, 240
Oxford English Dictionary 97

Palestine 15
Pappen, Franz von 180
paranoia 58, 62, 76, 80, 99, 104, 105, 157,
  158, 164, 171, 199, 254, 257, 259, 260
Pareto, Vilfredo 92
Parsons, Talcott 28, 104, 125
Pasewalk military hospital 145
paternalism 72, 91, 202, 209, 257
'pathological organizations' 255
Pavlov, Ivan 13
Pearl Harbor 113
Peck, Martin 29
Persilschein 200
Phillips, Nathanial Richard 76–8
Piaget, Jean 210
Pintsch, Karl-Heinz 50
Poland 98, 124

Political Intelligence Department 203–4
Political Quarterly 95
Political Warfare Executive 203
Pope, Arthur 133
Popper, Karl 195, 322–3 n.37
  The Open Society and its Enemies
  (1945) 195
Prince, Morton 29
prisoners of war (POWs) 3, 9, 11, 50, 73,
  76, 84, 111, 120, 171–3, 179, 193,
  203–4, 208, 220, 223–4,
  223, 230–1
Pröhl, Ilse 36
propaganda 5, 45, 52, 84, 96, 112, 122–3,
  154–5, 218, 220, 230, 242, 310 n.53
  'black propaganda' 114, 116–17, 122,
  308 n.34
  Hess flight 57
Prussia 104
psychoanalysis 2, 10, 14–15, 30–1, 91
  see also individual entries
'Psychoanalytic Field Unit' 134
psychobiography 23, 99, 128, 131, 229
psychological discourse 2, 174, 179, 216
psychological profiling 151–2, 229
psychological warfare 229
'psychologism' 2–3, 217, 232
psychopathology 3, 6, 12, 24, 86, 111, 132,
  143, 177, 215, 223, 234, 240, 252–4

'Quisling' 233–4

race
  'racial regeneration' 39
  'racial health' 15
  'race relations' 211
  racial theory 9, 142, 185–7
  see also individual entries
radio 10, 51
Radó, Sándor 188
Raubal, Geli 105, 144, 148, 239–40,
  330 n.52
Rauschning, Hermann 98–9, 135
Realpolitik 93
reductionism 8, 104
Red Cross 167
'Red scare' 88
Reed, Carol 222
  The Third Man (1949) 222

Rees, John Rawlings 58–9, 64, 158, 160,
  183, **284**, 299 n.80
  The Case of Rudolf Hess (1947) 58,
  62, 73
Reichstag 44
Reich, Wilhelm 8, 89–90, 216
  The Mass Psychology of Fascism
  (1933) 8, 89
Reinisch, Jessica 200
Renan, Ernest 267–8
Ribbentrop, Joachim von 51, 154,
  163–4, 181
Richard, Graham 122
Rickman, John 12, 82, 121, 198, 211
Riddoch, George 158
Riefenstahl, Leni 38–9
  Triumph of the Will (1935) 38–40, 218
Rivers, W. H. R. 27
Riviere, Joan 98
Roberts, Andrew 240
Rockefeller Foundation 95, 248
Röhm, Ernest 39, 119
Rommel, Erwin 46
Roosevelt, Franklin D. 45, 98–9, 109,
  137, 166
  New Deal 114
'Rorschach' test 78, 161
Rohrscheidt, Gunther von 161–2
Rosenbaum, Ron 145
Rosenfeld, Herbert 255
Roth, Samuel, *see* Krueger, Kurt
Russell, Bertrand 97
Russia 14, 25, 49–50, 96, 115, 196
  German invasion of 71
  Kremlinology 229
  Russian Revolution 25, 110

Sachs, Hanns 30, 263
sadism 6, 17–19, 72, 141, 147–8, 156, 179,
  225, 243–51, 259
  sado-masochism 7, 214, 259–60,
  331 n.73
Salpêtrière Hospital 156, 158
Sartre, Jean-Paul 288 n.14, 328 n.15
Sauckel, Fritz 163
Sayre, Francis 168–9
Schacht, Hjalmar 180
Scharp, Vilhelm J. 210–11
Schiller, Friedrich 58

Schlesinger, Arthur 194–6
    The Vital Center: The Politics of Freedom
        (1949) 195
Schmidt, Paul 178
Schopenhauer, Arthur 58
Schroeder, Paul 174
Scotland 1, 20, 45, 163
Scull, Andrew 121
Segal, Hanna 254
Segerstedt, Torgny 210
Sepp, Eugene 158
Sereny, Gitta 171
sexuality 8, 16, 40, 61, 80, 90, 118–19, 131,
    139, 147, 179, 190, 208, 234, 240,
    241–2, 270, 240, 294 n.70
shame 34, 60, 74, 176, 243, 252,
    320 n.42
'shellshock' 2, 24, 268
Shils, Edward 28, 207
Shirer, William 39, 134–5, 156, 166,
    314 n.73
    Berlin Diary (1941) 135
Shoah, *see* Holocaust
Sidis, Boris 91
Simmel, Ernst 89
Simon, John Allsebrook 56
Simpson, Wallis 100
Sinclair, Hugh 100–1
Skinner, Quentin 329 n.43
Smith, Bradley 32
social Darwinism 9, 243
socialism 89, 94–5, 195
Solzhenitsyn, Alexander 103
Sonderweg theory 116
South Africa 185
Spandau prison 263–6
Speer, Albert 154, 171, 265
Spencer, Herbert 82
Spender, Stephen 210
Sperr, Ingeborg 160
SS (Schutzstaffel) 3, 111, 168, 220,
    246, 260
Stalin, Joseph 45, 58, 103
Steiner, George 242
    The Portage to San Cristobal of A. H.
        (1981) 242
Steiner, John 255
Stimson, Henry L. 125, 169
Stone, Norman 239

Strasser, Otto 132, 135–6, 144, 148,
    330 n.52
Streicher, Julius 68, 156, 179
Strong, Kenneth 20
Sudetenland 98
suicide 69, 149–50, 160, 173, 175–6
Sullivan, Henry Stack 215
superego 6, 17, 83, 105, 184, 202, 225,
    256–7, 289 n.34
Supreme Headquarters Allied
    Expeditionary Force 230
Switzerland 43
syphilis 60, 145

Tansley, Arthur 26
Tavistock Clinic 1, 12, 24–7, 59, 65, 111,
    194, 255
Tavistock Institute of Human
    Relations 248
Taylor, A. J. P. 203
Theresienstadt 31
The Times 103
Theweleit, Klaus 8, 243
    Male Fantasies (1987) 8
Third Reich 2, 5, 92, 124–5; *see also*
    individual entries
Thirring, Hans 214–15
Thomas, D. M. 242
    The White Hotel (1981) 242
Thompson, Dorothy 96, 103
    I Saw Hitler! (1932) 96
    The New Russia (1928) 96
Thule Society 35
Todt, Fritz 51
Toland, John 128, 133, 262
torture 159, 169, 172, 228–9, 247
totalitarianism 102–3, 182, 196,
    222, 268
Tracey, Spencer 206
Treblinka 31
Trevor-Roper, Hugh 45, 130, 263
Trist, Eric 28
Trotter, Wilfred 5
    Instincts of the Herd in Peace and War
        (1916) 5
Truman, Harry 126–7, 166, 189

unconscious envy 214
United Nations (UN) 168, 182, 185

United Nations Educational, Scientific and Cultural Organization (UNESCO) 182–3, 187, 190, 206–10, 214
'Tensions' project 207–9, 213–15
United States of America 21, 32, 87–8, 95, 109, 115, 121, 188; *see also* individual entries
US intelligence 4, 28, 86, 116; *see also* Office of Strategic Services (OSS)

Vansittart, Robert 98
Black Record (1941) 98
Vergès, Jacques 250
Versailles (Treaty of) 96, 125
Vienna 2, 14, 18, 21, 30–2, 145–6, 171, 222, 241
Völkischer Beobachter 279

Waite, Robert 106
The Psychopathic God (1977) 106
Wallas, Graham 91–2
Human Nature in Politics (1908) 91
Wallon, Henri 215
Weber, Max 92, 235
Wechsler-Bellevue test 161
Wehrmacht 77, 111
Weimar Republic 38, 106
Weindling, Paul 174, 319 n.30

Welles, Orson 222
Wells, H. G. 101–2
West, Rebecca 154–156, 165–6, 175–6, 180
White, Ralph K. 191
'wild analysis' 6
Wilson, 'Tommy' 28
Wilson, Woodrow 92, 95, 99
Wilton Park 203–4
Winnicott, Donald 186–7, 213
Woolf, Virginia 208
Three Guineas (1938) 208
'working towards the Führer', *see* Kershaw, Ian
World Federation for Mental Health 59, 190
World Health Organisation (WHO) 184, 190
World War One 2, 5, 24, 38
impact on social sciences 88–9
post-war settlement 92–4, 125
psychiatric casualties 27

xenophobia 213

Yale University 247
Yalta Conference (1945) 151

Zimbardo, Philip 248